Sustainability Certification Schemes in the Agricultural and Natural Resource Sectors

This book provides a balanced critique of a range of international sustainability certification schemes across nine agricultural and natural resource industries.

Certification schemes set standards through intramarket private and multistakeholder mechanisms, and while third-party verification is often compulsory, certification schemes are regulated voluntarily rather than legislatively. This volume examines the intricacies of certification schemes and the issues they seek to address and provides the context within which each scheme operates. While a distinction between sustainability certifications and extramarkets or intrabusiness codes of conducts is made, the book also demonstrates how both are often working towards similar sustainability objectives. Each chapter highlights a different sector, including animal welfare, biodiversity, biofuels, coffee, fisheries, flowers, forest management and mining, with the contributions offering interdisciplinary perspectives and utilising a wide range of methodologies. The realities, achievements and challenges faced by varying certification schemes are discussed, identifying common outcomes and findings and concluding with recommendations for future practice and research.

The book is aimed at advanced students, researchers and professionals in agribusiness, natural resource economics, sustainability assessment and corporate social responsibility.

Melissa Vogt has been involved with and considering outcomes associated with sustainability certifications since 2006. She completed doctoral studies early 2019. She has experience as a consultant to small and medium-sized business in developing countries; and as an evaluator for community-based projects and programmes, and for commercialised scientific projects. She has taught in higher education in Rwanda and Australia and is currently based at the University of New South Wales, Australia.

Earthscan Studies in Natural Resource Management

Forest Management Auditing
Certification of Forest Products and Services
Edited by Lucio Brotto and Davide Pettenella

Agricultural Land Use and Natural Gas Extraction Conflicts
A Global Socio-Legal Perspective
Madeline Taylor and Tina Hunter

Tropical Bioproductivity
Origins and Distribution in a Globalized World
David Hammond

The Commons in a Glocal World
Global Connections and Local Responses
Edited by Tobias Haller, Thomas Breu, Tine De Moor, Christian Rohr, and Heinzpeter Zonj

Natural Resource Conflicts and Sustainable Development
Edited by E. Gunilla Almered Olsson and Pernille Gooch

Sustainable Governance of Wildlife and Community Based Natural Resource Management
From Economic Principles to Practical Governance
Brian Child

Sustainability Certification Schemes in the Agricultural and Natural Resource Sectors
Outcomes for Society and the Environment
Edited by Melissa Vogt

For more information on books in the Earthscan Studies in Natural Resource Management series, please visit the series page on the Routledge website: www.routledge.com/books/series/ECNRM/

Sustainability Certification Schemes in the Agricultural and Natural Resource Sectors

Outcomes for Society and the Environment

Edited by Melissa Vogt

LONDON AND NEW YORK

from Routledge

First published 2019 by Routledge

2 Park Square, Milton Park, Abingdon, Oxon, OX14 4RN
605 Third Avenue, New York, NY 10017

Routledge is an imprint of the Taylor & Francis Group, an informa business

First issued in paperback 2020

British Library Cataloguing-in-Publication Data
A catalogue record for this book is available from the British Library

Library of Congress Cataloging-in-Publication Data
A catalog record has been requested for this book

ISBN: 978-1-138-57297-3 (hbk)
ISBN: 978-0-367-72964-6 (pbk)

Typeset in Bembo
by Wearset Ltd, Boldon, Tyne and Wear

Contents

Figures

Tables

Contributors

Editor

Melissa Vogt has considered outcomes associated with sustainability certifications since 2005. She commenced studies in 2007/2008 to consider the influence of certifications in producer countries, and before that time considered the influence of certifications on consumer education and approaches to national and international trade. She completed doctoral studies early 2019. She has worked as a consultant for small and medium sized business in developing countries and as an evaluator for community based projects and programmes for commercialised scientific projects. She has taught in higher education in Rwanda and Australia and is currently based at the University of New South Wales.

Contributors

Shannon Arnold has worked in marine conservation and small-scale fisheries research and advocacy since 2007. She leads the Marine Program at the Ecology Action Centre (EAC) with a focus on ensuring responsible, equity-based fisheries policy at the local, national and international level. She also is focused on opportunities for community empowerment in the sustainable use of marine resources. She and the EAC have a long history of engagement in eco-certifications in Canada and globally. Shannon has a background in community organising with small-scale fishery communities in Canada and internationally as well as ethnographic and political-ecological research.

Graeme Auld is an Associate Professor, Public Affairs Research Excellence Chair, and Director of Carleton University's School of Public Policy and Administration. He has broad interests in comparative environmental politics and global environmental governance, with a particular focus on the emergence, evolution and impacts of transnational private governance regimes. He is co-author (with Benjamin Cashore and Deanna Newsom) of *Governing through Markets: Forest Certification and the Emergence* of *Non-state Authority* (2004), and is the solo-author of *Constructing Private Governance: The Rise and Evolution of Forest, Coffee, and Fisheries Certification* (2014).

Megan Bailey, is an Assistant Professor and Canada Research Chair in the Marine Affairs Program at Dalhousie University, Canada. She studies the intersection of private and public governance as it relates to fisheries management and sustainable seafood consumption. Megan is co-editor with Jessica Duncan of the book *Food Secure Futures: Multidisciplinary Solutions* (Routledge). Megan is Associate Editor with the journals *Marine Policy* and *People and Nature*, and serves on the Scientific and Technical Advisory Committee for the International Pole and Line Foundation, and the Board of Directors for the Fishermen and Scientists Research Society.

Ana Catarina Bastos, Department of Biology (DBIO), Centre for Environmental and Marine Studies (CESAM), University of Aveiro, Portugal.

Harry J. Blokhuis worked, until 2007, for almost 30 years in the Netherlands where he carried out research projects and was managing research groups in the area of animal behaviour and welfare. Since 2007 he has been a professor in ethology at the Swedish Agricultural University in Uppsala. He has coordinated seven EU-funded international research programmes. These include the coordination of the Welfare Quality project which was the largest coordinated research effort in this area to date. Currently he coordinates collaborative work between former leading partners in Welfare Quality called the 'Welfare Quality Network' and is involved in several European initiatives. He has published about 275 publications as first author or co-author, of which about 110 appear in refereed journals.

Oskar Englund is an independent research consultant (https://geolab.bio) associated with Chalmers University of Technology, Gothenburg, and Adjunct Senior Lecturer at the Mid Sweden University in Ostersund, Sweden. He studies sustainability aspects of land use in the context of where humanity requires increasing resources from a planet with a limited surface. Primarily, he is interested in issues concerning the production and use of bioenergy, which interlinks the food, forest and energy sectors. He has had a large focus on governance but is also a GIS expert and a keen spatial modeller. Given the interdisciplinary nature of the research topics, he often combines methods from the natural and social sciences.

Keith Flett, Fishery Development Strategist. Growing up in the fishing industry, Keith developed firsthand knowledge of fishing methods, landings and sales/price discovery procedures of the fishing industry. Learning through two generation's worth of family experience, he developed in-depth knowledge of how fishery supply chains work (vessel harvest through landings and delivery to market). Working with family members and industry stakeholders who owned fishing vessels and the co-op, he started his entrepreneurial career by launching his first wholesale seafood company at the young age of 21. It was through this experience of direct sales he learned how the supply chain and power dynamics in the supply chain influence fisher behaviour in production, and birthed his life-long career in fishery finance and supply chain innovation.

Diana Franco Gil, Policy Manager, Forest Management Programme, FSC International, Bonn, Germany.

Jean-Pierre Imbrogiano, Centre for Social Responsibility in Mining, Sustainable Minerals Institute, the University of Queensland, Australia.

Simon Jeffery, Crop and Environment Sciences Department, Harper Adams University, UK.

Malin Jonell, is a post-doctoral researcher at the Stockholm Resilience Centre, Stockholm University, Sweden. Her research focuses on sustainable food production and in particular the role of markets, trade and the private sector in driving positive change in the growing seafood sector.

Bryan Jones is currently a consultant in animal behaviour and welfare. His research focused on internal and external factors regulating fear, distress, injurious behaviour, aggression and sociality in poultry, pigs and cattle. He has published more than 220 scientific papers in international refereed journals, 33 book chapters, two co-edited books and 110 abstracts, reviews, popular articles etc. His work has influenced the formulation of policy, research priorities and recommendations by organisations such as Defra, Farm Animal Welfare Council, RSPCA, European Community, Humane Society of the USA, Meat & Livestock Authority, Australia, etc.

Marion Karmann, At the time of writing: Monitoring and Evaluation Programme Manager, FSC International, Bonn, Germany. Currently: Senior Research Relations Manager, FSC International, Bonn, Germany.

Fritz Kleinschroth is a post-doc in the Department of Environmental Systems Science, ETH Zurich, Switzerland. He specialises in global landscape-planning issues, working on interdisciplinary nexus approaches for nature conservation and land-use planning. He graduated in landscape planning from TU Berlin, Germany, while volunteering in several projects in Asia and Latin America. He recently obtained a dual-PhD degree in Ecology and Biodiversity from AgroParisTech, France and in Forestry from Bangor University, UK, with his studies about logging roads in the Congo.

Scott McIlveen is a recent graduate of the Marine Management Program at Dalhousie. During his studies he focused on resource management, particularly in regard to shark fins in Canada. Under Dr Megan Bailey he designed a project which revealed a high proportion of threatened shark species in Toronto markets. Scott is excited to continue working in fisheries and resource management as a fisheries management intern in Vietnam.

Patricio Mena-Vásconez is a PhD candidate at Wageningen University, the Netherlands. He holds a Master's degree in Botany from City University of New York, and a Master's degree in Journalism from the University of Wales College of Cardiff. Initially interested in the ecology of Andean ecosystems in Ecuador, he founded the environmental NGO EcoCiencia and participated in several projects related to the biodiversity and participatory management of *páramos* in South America. His current research focuses on the socio-environmental conflicts related to irrigation water in the floricultural watershed of Pisque in the vicinity of Quito.

Mara Miele is a professor of human geography in the School of Geography and Planning at Cardiff University, UK. Her research addresses the geographies of ethical foods consumption and the role of animal welfare science and technology in challenging the role of farmed animals in current agricultural practices and policies. In recent years she has worked with a large interdisciplinary network of social and animal welfare scientists for developing innovative forms of critical public engagement with science that produced the EU animal welfare standard (Welfare Quality, www.welfarequality.net). She is currently working on a Leverhulme-funded project 'Shaping Inter-species Connectedness' (University of Warwick, Cardiff University and SRUC-Edinburgh, 2018–2020), exploring human animal relations and animal emotions in the context of animal (dog) training.

Renzo Mori Junior, Industry Research Fellow, Centre for Social Responsibility in Mining, Sustainable Minerals Institute, the University of Queensland, Australia, and Senior Advisor for Sustainable Development, RMIT.

Daniela Perbandt holds an agricultural PhD in field spectroscopy. From 2012 to 2017 Daniela was a tutor at the Fraunhofer Institute UMSICHT in Oberhausen and the FernUniversitat, Hagen, Germany, for the advanced Master's course in interdisciplinary environmental science. In 2017, she switched to the chair of Policy Analysis and Environmental Policy at FernUniversitat in Hagen, where she works as a post-doc researcher in the project 'BIO-ECOPOLI – Political Processes of the Bioeconomy between Economy and Ecology', analysing problem structures and the influence of indicators on political processes.

Patrik Rönnbäck, is a professor in sustainable development, with a focus on natural resources, in the Department of Earth Sciences, Natural Resources and Sustainable Development, Uppsala University, Sweden. His academic interests and expertise include evaluation of eco-certification programmes for food commodities, sustainability analyses of aquaculture and recreational fisheries, and ecosystem services trade-offs in temperate and tropical settings.

Hans-Peter Schmidt, Ithaka Institute for Carbon Strategies (Director), Germany and Switzerland. He co-developed the European Biochar Certificate (EBC) and is currently engaged to build the framework for pyrogenic carbon capture and storage (PyCCS) to mitigate climate change.

Riley Schnurr is an engaged young professional now working in the public service. He is a lifelong student and believes in acting local while thinking global. Riley studied at Dalhousie University, Canada where he focused on marine plastic pollution and the legislative interventions that aim to tackle the problem. In his spare time Riley is an active curler and enjoys getting lost in museums and art galleries.

Kathryn Sturman, Senior Research Fellow, Centre for Social Responsibility in Mining, Sustainable Minerals Institute, the University of Queensland, Australia.

Michael Tlusty, Associate Professor of Sustainability and Food Solutions, School for the Environment University of Massachusetts Boston, USA. Michael's work focuses on linking science, technology and innovation to transform the world's aquatic food systems by working to create more, waste less and do a better job producing what we already produce.

Max Troell, Associate Professor, Stockholm Resilience Centre, Stockholm University, Stockholm, Sweden, Beijer Institute of Ecological Economics, The Royal Swedish Academy of Sciences, Stockholm, Sweden. He is a system ecologist mainly working with environmental problems associated with aquaculture. This work focuses on inter-linkages between aquaculture and fisheries, on different spatial scales.

Franck Trolliet was the monitoring and evaluation officer at FSC International, Bonn, Germany, at the time of writing. He is currently the officer of data analytics, evaluation and learning. He is in charge of monitoring the scientific literature related to FSC certification and compiling findings about its various impacts. He recently obtained a PhD in Ecology at the Université de Liège, Belgium, and is interested in plant–animal interactions and conservation strategies aiming to maintain forest ecosystem functioning and to integrate human dimensions.

Pippi van Ommen is a Dutch Master's student of international land and water management at Wageningen University, the Netherlands. She conducted several months' field research in Ecuador on floriculture and its certifications. Currently she is the appointed focal point for Europe for the World Youth Parliament for Water and is focusing on the political ecology of water in her Master's thesis.

Isabelle Veissier (women, DVM, PhD) is a research director from INRA, the French National Institute for Research in Agriculture. She is the head of UMR1213 herbivores (Clermont-Ferrand, France), a joint research unit between INRA and VetAgro Sup (school for vets and agronomists) that comprises 130 permanent staff working on cattle and sheep and their associated farming systems. After her veterinary studies, she started to work at INRA (from 1983) with a focus on animal behaviour and welfare. She has published over 100 scientific articles in peered reviewed journals and supervised 13 PhD theses.

Frank G.A. Verheijen, Department of Environment and Planning (DAO), Centre for Environmental and Marine Studies (CESAM), University of Aveiro, Campus Santiago, 3810–193, Aveiro, Portugal.

Thomas Vogelpohl is a trained political scientist who graduated from the universities in Potsdam, Germany, and Bologna, Italy, in 2008. After a year as a junior researcher at the Institute of Forest, Environmental and Natural Resource Policy (InFER) at the University of Natural Resources and Life Science (BOKU) in Vienna, Austria, he worked at the Institute for Ecological Economy Research (IOW) in Berlin from 2009 on. In 2016, he received his doctorate from the Environmental Policy Research Centre (FFU) of the Free University of Berlin with a dissertation on German biofuels policy. Since 2017, he has been working at the FernUniversitat in Hagen, Germany, as the Chair for Policy Analysis and Environmental Policy as a post-doc researcher in the project 'BIO-ECOPOLI – Political Processes of the Bioeconomy between Economy and Ecology', in which he analyses the case group of biofuels.

Jeroen Vos is an assistant professor in the Department of Water Resources Management at Wageningen University, the Netherlands. As a water policy advisor he worked almost a decade in Peru and Bolivia with different international development organisations. His current research interests are the dynamics and discourses of water use by agribusinesses and local responses in Latin America. He has published several articles on the effects of virtual water trade and water stewardship certification.

Preface

Sustainability certifications in use, and as a topic for study is a work and pursuit of nearly 30 years. While another book on the topic might appear unnecessary, identified implications and possibilities for improvement and alternatives, and the significant detail in research and practice required to thoroughly consider and understand one or multiple sustainability certification efforts within one industry or across industries, and subsequent outcomes is substantial.

There is plenty more to explore and understand related to sustainability standards, the certification process and alternatives as contributory, complementary or as competition within a greater 'sustainability' intention perspective for use and/or trade of natural resources. Certainly an absolute endorsement of any sustainability certification requires more care, while recognising significant contributions already made by its efforts.

Presenting findings and considerations related to sustainability certifications in a book provides a useful resource to reflect on the current state of such efforts, and how they are understood by practitioners and academics of various disciplines.

It is hoped that readers of this collection of studies will develop a well-rounded comprehension that allows their own reflections on the sustainability certification effort, as a quite unique and somewhat ever-changing effort to improve sustainability within a trade context, to inform an improved understanding. The suggestions for future study and recommendations for enhancements will hopefully further propel understandings and practice toward improved and long-term outcomes which demonstrate adaptability for what are often considered dynamic circumstances.

Acknowledgements

Collaboration and cooperation from all contributing authors has made this book possible, resulting from two-and-half years of work, and an idea for a book which was originally proposed in 2013. Agreeing to be part of a book with a PhD candidate as lead editor was quite a 'strange' or different situation for many authors and so I very much appreciate their being willing to contribute despite this quite untraditional arrangement.

Thanks goes to Malin Jonell for being involved since the beginning of the process, and for having reviewed some chapters of the book; to Peter Luetchford for agreeing to provide the additional guidance which might have been necessary through the process, also from before the book proposal was accepted; and to Megan Bailey for agreeing to be involved toward the end of the process, providing additional reviewer comment.

The idea to allow authors to determine their own approach to their chapters was suggested by me and supported by all involved. Appreciation is expressed to Routledge for allowing the authors, and the volume of a possible series, this flexibility.

Thanks also goes to FSC representatives for being willing to present some professional reflections on evaluating associated outcomes from a certification point of view, thus providing a valuable opportunity to consider how certifications understand effectual evaluations.

All authors, as is standard, added the writing of chapters to their normal day-to-day obligations and appreciation is expressed to all for making time for this.

1 Sustainability certifications

Changes over time and their unique position of influence

Melissa Vogt

Introduction

'Sustainable' business practices have challenged a legacy of economic and production priority for three or so decades. Balancing industry requirements with social and environmental protection is intricate and interests within and between stakeholder groups can differ significantly. International and local trade dynamics over time and across geographic regions, stakeholders and industries complicate how sustainable trade and business practices can be achieved with various sustainability mechanisms and approaches used. Market mechanisms work internally, or provide direct external guidance and support to business. Extra-market efforts via policy and legislation, and non-governmental effort guide sustainable business practice. All or most mechanisms rely on a pivotal verification need which requires accurate and specific yet encompassing findings regarding compliance and associated outcomes. There is variable evidence of associated outcomes and understandings of benefit across industries, according to the mechanism for change used and whether coordinated complementarity between mechanisms is encouraged.

Sustainability in business practices can still therefore be understood as a newly progressing movement in terms of actual reach of improvement across stakeholders, across and within industries and according to the various sustainability mechanisms. It is possible that what 'doing this well' means is yet to be appropriately or comprehensively known by all stakeholders given the ranging dynamics to be addressed and managed. The legacy of economic and production priority might require more time to significantly shift all stakeholders, and availability of and interest in sustainably extracted, produced and sourced natural resources must also increase. Gradual advance and improvement in these efforts and in understanding outcomes is evident. With ongoing experience, improved research and increased ambition is expected.

Sustainability certifications have a unique role among the various mechanisms used. They work according to the premise that increased market demand for sustainable products leads to improvement in sustainable trade practices, and rely on and work with several stakeholders and actors directly involved in production, and in international sourcing and trade practices.

They deal with varying business types and sizes, along international and national sourcing chains, and have an informal interchange with policy and law due to their distinctive role of independent sustainability standard development, introduction and compulsory verification. Their position of influence is therefore unique and relevant across sectors and countries, with significant potential to encourage consistency across involved stakeholders, also referred to as a form of transnational governance (Gulbrandsen 2010). Yet, they also often rely on market demand for maintained momentum, presenting a label on products at point of sale to lead preferential purchases, with potential to set up forms of competition between the different labels within the same industry and possible implication of market-based preferences for producer and sourcing countries. Where consumers or a company believe an approach is positive for sustainability they may be more inclined to demand and purchase certified labelled products (Singh and Pandey 2012).

Inconsistent market demand, yet a need to have certified natural resources available, means that working toward sustainable sourcing and trade practice with sustainability certifications may not follow a linear process. There are some interesting dynamics to consider in seeking improvement and increased ambition. For example, (1) an increase in popularity and sales can contribute to improvement in outcomes instead of expecting such improvements before availability on the market. A significant grey area of stating associated outcomes, distinct from greenwashing, which may already be proven or simply intentionally misleading (Dahl 2010; Schmuck *et al.* 2018), emerges. (2) Producer or extraction practices might be certified prior to secured market access and demand. The benefit to the environment of certifying hectares or extracted natural resources prior to securing market access, influenced by the calibre of standards, approach to implementation and verification, and associated outcomes, can be recognised. The societal outcomes would, however, need to be substantiated.

While the flexibility allowed for consumer preference has arguably been a crucial element for increases in certified markets and sustainability practices, market-based preference provisions a more distanced, subjective and unpredictable possible influence on associated outcomes. Where consumer or business preference subsequently determines other stakeholder preferences for sustainability certifications or certified produce, verified versus subjectively preferred labels is a necessary consideration. Verification requires not only an effective monitoring of compliance. It must also consider associated outcomes from compliance, and, as associated to standard criteria, approaches to implementation and to verifying practices through a sourcing chain. Certification must also be according to the type or definition of sustainability sought, providing additional variance in how outcomes are considered, measured and explained. An outcome is any identifiable benefit or disadvantage associated with a sustainability certification. Identifiable refers not only to tangible observations but to an understanding of what was involved to achieve any outcome, and the associated outcomes of the involved process.

The chapters in this book seek to provide an example of the range of disciplinary, industry and certification-specific considerations that are relevant for determining societal and environmental outcomes resulting from sustainability certifications. Expectations for comprehensive studies and practices according to required specificity can be better set, and ideas for combining or coordinating the consideration of several specific disciplinary studies, as well as studies and efforts across certification and/or industry encouraged.

To introduce the book, this chapter provides background to the influence of trade on societal and environmental outcomes resulting from production and trade. Two examples are provided: the green revolution and general political economic dynamics by country. A foundational understanding of why intramarket and sustainability efforts exist, and how they attempt to resolve a somewhat negative legacy of production and trade influence on the environment and society is explained. Codes of conduct dependent on ideas of Corporate Social Responsibility and Accountability (CSR and CSA) are explained, relevant to corporations and smaller international and local business, and then sustainability certifications as a complementary mechanism. A history of sustainability certifications provides more specific foundational understanding of origins and subsequent development, and an idea of the range of labels and certifications that currently operate are listed. Further information is provided for the certifications, labels and industries discussed in this book and the chapters are summarised as an introduction to content.

Trade: social and environmental concern

Trade-related environmental concerns include deforestation and land degradation caused by agricultural, tree plantation or mining expansion and natural resource extraction (Ceddia *et al.* 2014) and processing (Kobayashi *et al.* 2014). Societal concerns can be associated with or isolated from environmental outcomes. Pollution and contamination resulting from farming, extraction, processing and manufacturing are significant land, air and water-based environmental concerns (Cottrell *et al.* 2018; Chen *et al.* 2018) with influence on and subsequent social concern for health and worker care at individual, community and national levels (Agardy 2000; Moss 2008; Downey *et al.* 2010; Hamilton *et al.* 2016; Cusack *et al.* 2017; Carvalho 2017; Schrecker *et al.* 2018; Zhang *et al.* 2018). Recognising the negative influence of production for trade purposes has taken time to develop, relying on improved understanding according to subsequent outcomes for society and environment. Not only is improved understanding required, the responsible parties must also be willing to listen and respond. In some cases new and more sustainable industries have developed over time. They can, however, result in similar environmental damage – biofuels is an example.

Developing detailed understanding of negative influence alongside effective and realistic compromises with trade needs is required. Two considerations will be addressed here: (1) the green revolution and fluctuations in supply and demand for other natural resources as influential to production and extraction approaches, and environment and society. These provide an example of how trade can promote or compromise positive environmental and societal outcomes and present an idea of the intricacy of comprehending a positive or negative outcome for these situations. (2) The political economy of each country as influential to systemised approaches and to how market-based influences can overwhelm government priorities.

Systemised and market-based approaches to intensive production and extraction: influence on environment and society

The green revolution, as a systemised approach to intensive production, substantially influenced not only agricultural practice but also economic and societal distributions and balance resulting from international trade from developing countries between the 1950s and 1970s (Wolf 1986). The advantages and disadvantages of the green revolution did eventually vary with contrary findings according to economic outcomes, and societal and environmental implications, including exacerbating existing inequalities. In particular cases hybrid crop varieties reduced need for synthetic inputs and resulted in economic benefits for farmers and households (Ali and Abdulai 2010; Hossain *et al.* 2013). For farmers, however, cost reductions and productivity were only beneficial where price paid allowed a significant margin (Evenson and Gollin 2003). While green revolution techniques are attributed to reduced forest or natural habitat conversion for agricultural production (Stevenson *et al.* 2013), the outcome was not uniform, with several regions and countries continuing to experience the significant conversion of forest to agricultural land use (Parayil and Tong 1998; Geist and Lambin 2002). High crop yield varieties also required intensive industrial agricultural techniques (Hoisington *et al.* 1999) and harmful chemical inputs (Pimentel 1996), with influence on the production system and surrounding environments (Horrigan *et al.* 2002; Bellamy 2010; Vogt 2011, 2017, 2018).

Green revolution agricultural systems did degrade the environment, over use natural resources and result in significant social implications (Pingali and Rosegrant 1994; Singh 2000; Horrigan *et al.* 2002; Gruere and Sengupta 2011; Shiva 2016) including exacerbated social inequalities (Freebairn 1995). Some macro-level studies suggest an increase in food supply in developing countries (Pingali 2012); however, access across region or across societal category is not specified and was actually variable. Non-food crops, coffee, sugar, cotton, spices, tea, for example, did dominate food crops in some regions (Paige 1997; Higman 2000; Parayil 2003; Adams and Ghaly 2007), leaving significant reliance on imported food. The question of heterogeneous food availability and nutritional content also requires additional qualification for findings that food supply increased. Intensive homogenous crop density for productivity requires a significant amount of discretion and care. Where negative outcomes result they can be significant and cannot be compensated by positive outcomes in other regions. A new wave of 'green revolution' has been observed more recently (Cartel *et al.* 2006; Pingali 2012). Kerr (2012) has argued that without addressing social inequality and environmental concerns, this new wave, despite integrating a consideration of environment and society, will, just like the previous, result in increased inequality, environmental degradation and malnutrition for the rural poor.

There was no such 'green revolution' for extractive industries such as logging, mining or fisheries. There has, however, been a significant lack of effective regulation and standards for conducting these activities in a sustainable way (Sierra 2001; Geist and Lambin 2002; Gaveau *et al.* 2014; van Solinge 2014; Davis and Manzano Mazzali 2018; Bebbington *et al.* 2018; Vivoda and Kemp 2018). Booms in supply and/or demand for these resources directly and positively associate with intensive extractive activities through particular decades and in many countries. These fluctuations are influenced by market demand for particular minerals or resources (Kurien and Achari 1990; Radomski 1999; Sissenwine *et al.* 2014; Ellem and Tonts 2017; Hancock *et al.* 2018) and can also be influenced by booms in other industries which rely on mined (Browne 2008; West 2017) or extracted natural resources (Goldburg and Naylor 2005; Naylor *et al.* 2009). The more intensive phases of these booms in demand or supply often indicate increased negative environmental outcome, and variable societal outcomes as ecosystems are thrown out of balance. These phases are also indicative of a dominance of extractive industries over other industries or land uses that may generate improved environmental and societal outcomes (Ocansey 2013; Doso Jnr *et al.* 2015), perhaps even improved economic outcomes in the longer term in extremely contextual situations (Chen and Randall 2013), or an opportunity to seek complementarity between extractive and agricultural land use (Cartier and Burge 2011; Mkodzongi and Spiegel 2018).

Political economy, trade agreements and sustainability

Political economy considers state and societal spheres and how they interact, with the idea that economy and politics act as institutions within society (Polanski 1957, 71), and law and government institutions within the state. A central consideration of political economy focuses on access and control over resources. Hegel (1802/03) searched for balance between the market, and social and political institutions, discussing the limitation of a self-regulating market and the need for ethical regulation through government intervention, distinguishing between private and public interests.

Within this understanding, the market serves private interest and the state serves public interest by the conventional nature of their role. This in turn affects the balance of the interactions and the impact on justice — justice including ideas of quality and equity, equal opportunity and regard, which complement ideas of poverty reduction (Anderson 2001) and sustainable development. In practice, the private sector is involved in and influential on public interest, it is therefore the state's role to ensure their involvement and influence is reasonable. Frey and Schneider explain that the government can be considered 'an endogenous' part of social systems (1978, 181–82) while holding significant influence and a responsibility to set expectations of care for the public, and to ensure that such expectations are met. As the government's role within the economy varies, dependent on the political and economic interchange and dynamic of each country, the private sector's contribution, influence on and/or involvement with public interest is recognised as variably significant dependent on these political and economic dynamics.

Where relying on national law to ensure environmental and societal protection, the varying contexts of legislated practice and effective implementation and regulation according to country can influence the situation. The government interest or need to prioritise economic interests for the country's development (Gilpin 2000) are additional factors and can be a factor in the speed at which economic development occurs and a subsequent influence on social conditions (Cole 2017). Where economic development overwhelmingly dominates over societal and environmental interest, and is prioritised for some above others, the idea and expectation of future stability (McKay and Vizard 2005) often relies on a 'trickle-down effect'. Within this understanding, social and environmental outcomes follow once sufficient economic development has occurred. The significant indirect costs resulting from these 'necessary' and 'short-term' sacrifices is not yet proven to evenly or adequately contribute to economic or national development (Deakin 2016; Akinci 2017). The green revolution is a case in point (Conway and Barbie 1988).

The need among developing and emerging economies for foreign investment, as well as competition with neighbouring countries and regions can, however, further encourage such an approach. A subsequent 'race to the bottom' can decrease incentive to follow laws that favour society and environment, and may increase the pace of economic development (Li *et al.* 2017; Ghauri 2017; Hollander and Thornthwaite 2018). This is particularly the case where foreign investors bargain and compare countries by cost and ease of investment, eventually leading to power dynamics heavily in favour of multinational[1] and transnational[2] corporations (MNCs and TNCs) ('corporations') and a need to satisfy their preferences. Where the presence or offerings of corporations dominate, national law may compromise foreign investment. Incentive to follow or enforce legal requirements may reduce alongside recourse for illegal corporate activity according to environmental and societal care.

Preferences of corporations and trade agreements can also complicate trade routes involving intermediaries and complicating efforts for transparency and responsible and sustainable conduct (Stoll *et al.* 2018; Gardner *et al.* 2018). The benefit of these more complicated trade routes are recognised for business (Vedel and Ellegard 2013) and can also accommodate, perhaps take advantage of intraregional disputes or conflicts (Meenu 2008). The consideration of trade routes is industry and region specific. Improved implementation of Free Trade Agreements (FTA) (Orbie *et al*. 2018) may be conducive to addressing these issues, particularly for developing countries within extremely specific conditions. There is, for example, the opportunity to strengthen intraregional, and perhaps interregional, industry cooperation and community involvement to reduce the need and benefit of segregated intermediary involvement (Meenu 2008; Chan 2010). Addressing or ensuring sustainability outcomes has not, however, been a consistent, substantial or significant inclusion or contribution of FTAs (Gaines 2002; Doumbia-Henry and Gravel 2008; Morin and Bialais 2018). In fact, international conventions and laws have developed to counter international trade agreements and unsustainable trends in international trade (Alston 2004; Gillespie 2018; Freestone 2018) with varying effect and incentive in terms of eventual national legal requirements (Bohmelt and Butkute 2018).

The effectiveness of relying on government to regulate markets for the interest of people and the environment is therefore country or region specific. A continuing ability of or interest from government to ensure care for community and environment, particularly within a context of agricultural and industrial revolution, relies in part on international effort and the government of the time. The green revolution and developing economies seeking to become emerging to developed economies contributes to the dynamic. The freedom allowed to the market to self-regulate can subsequently leave the well-being of a population reliant on the market more than a government (Monshipouri *et al*. 2009). It is a controversial model of interaction between the economy and state with additional dimensions and considerations for developing countries and economies.

Resolving the legacy of trade influence for the environment and society

In several cases the influence, contribution and responsibility of the private sector to the public can become comparable to roles and responsibilities traditionally understood as within government influence. There is then an opportunity for consistency or inconsistencies in protection of society and environment from within the market channel. Private sector and corporate responsibility to society should increase as their influence and as power dynamics shift. Among a quite complicated dynamic for improving sustainability of international and national trade activities, well developed intramarket approaches can therefore be favoured. They rely on corporations' cooperation as they follow guidance through voluntary codes of conduct and standards. Assigning market value to socially responsible activities can then further encourage social responsibility and move beyond a private interest prerogative. To summarise these developments, CSR and CSA are explained as foundational considerations of intramarket sustainability efforts.

Corporate Social Accountability

Discussion of CSR commenced in the 1960s as a self-regulating ethical principle of responsibility to control the effect of corporate behaviour on society and the environment. With this understanding, private interest may extend to public concern given its influential role. Corporations would therefore become more willing and aware of their responsibility to increase positive influence of their activities. Where associated with a market incentive, socially responsible behaviour can be incentivised. Brand reputation and consumer (individual, community or business) preference for ethically traded goods can facilitate an understanding of benefit in corporate and market language. As a relatively new area, subsequent and inevitable progress and transition was to come through the decades following the 1960s, and became most relevant in the 1990s and beyond. The World Business Council for Sustainable Development (1998) states:

> Corporate Social Responsibility is the continuing commitment by business to behave ethically and contribute to economic development, while improving the quality of life of the workforce and the families of the local community.

When bringing sustainability and CSR together, definitions can be complex and subjective, which is significant when looking at how CSR explains its value in the market. There are many working definitions of sustainability: the most common but not the first is 'development that meets the needs of the present without compromising the ability of future generations to meet their own needs' (Keeble 1988). The sustainable development goals seek to 'end poverty, protect the planet, ensure prosperity' (SDGs 2015). CSR extends the concerns of corporate or foreign business priorities to include and consider society and, where appropriate and recognised as linked to protecting society, the environment. The 1992 Rio Earth Summit focused effort toward environmental sustainable development and the influence and therefore responsibility of corporations to local governments and the people. An idea of equity among the three pillars of sustainability became relevant in this process.

Continuing dissatisfaction with the liberal approach to trade became evident through the Seattle protests of 1999 when many of the world's governments met at a WTO ministerial meeting to discuss international and free trade. The protests highlighted a strong dissatisfaction with deregulated and market-controlled approaches to trade and saw free speech cracked down on in the name of free trade (Shah 2002). Attention was refocused on labour and human rights violations alongside environmental exploitation encouraged by a deregulated market. The first collapse of the Doha Development Round in 2001 and the next four collapses were a strong indication of resistance to further deregulation of international markets. These concerns came from the countries whose interests they claimed to be meeting. Brazil, China and India refused to agree to the conditions offered (Gallagher 2008; Cho 2009). The idea that deregulated international markets is in everyone's interest was therefore a point of contention.

Social justice and ethical discourses (Monshipouri *et al.* 2009; Ssenyonjo 2011) led to methods that seem to ensure socially responsible practices can continue with or without regulated markets. Codes of conduct and foundational standards guide socially and environmentally responsible behaviour. This responsibility can be directly tied to corporate operations, or external and 'compensatory' to the effects of direct operations. In each case setting standards and codes of conduct is distinct. Internal codes of conduct are often developed by the business, in consultation with national and regional requirements. CSR and CSA codes of conduct ('codes of conduct') are internal and directly relevant to a business with indirect and variable effective influence on external activities. External standards or codes of conduct are often developed unilaterally and external to a corporation or business, or in consultation with stakeholders.

The voluntary nature of direct and external efforts each leave questions regarding enforceability and therefore effectiveness, and suggestions for Corporate Social Accountability (CSA), instead of Responsibility (Hamann and Kapelus 2004; Valor 2005). As a complement to responsibility, accountability is how to achieve and demonstrate fulfilment of the responsibility. Approaches such as triple bottom line accounting (TBL) (Fauzi *et al.* 2010) might be used to understand the full cost and benefit of sustainable business operations in financial, environmental and societal terms. To aptly carry out such accounting, and to ensure responsibility is fulfilled, compliance to sustainably or ethically aligned codes of conduct must be verified; the quality and included criteria of such codes are also relevant with newly developed indicators and concepts continually developing, such as ideas of need for Corporate Political Responsibility (CPR) (Lyon *et al.* 2018).

Several different regulatory mechanisms, including independent external actors or observers, exist. Understanding compliance status helps demonstrate validity, and a need to respond where compliance is not complete. Validity also relies on the approach taken to verify compliance, and the standards and code of conduct to adhere to. In most cases, verification and response to findings of noncompliance is dealt with though 'soft-penalty', unless standards and codes of conduct align with legal requirements. This is particularly the case for internal codes of conduct which do not require external compulsory verification; instead evidence of care and effort as aligned with CSR is sufficient. There is, however, an important influencing role for codes of conduct and standards for guiding positive change. Understanding different external standards as a uniform effort to improve CSR or CSA oversimplifies the heterogeneity within these efforts. Sustainability certifications as independent external actors to business and corporations develop and introduce 'external' standards, and represent a diverse range of standard criteria influenced by the industry and sustainability premise used.

Sustainability certifications

Sustainability certifications are voluntary intramarket, extra-business mechanisms which require compulsory verification of compliance. They seek to improve environmental and societal outcomes through production, and international sourcing and trade practices. The location they occupy within market but not within companies and corporations lends a significant power of influence on practices. This was not the case upon their creation and became more so the case as their role extended beyond simple intentions, to encompass what sustainability practices require. They have been most used for improving practices and approaches within existing industries rather than certifying or encouraging diversified or diversification to more sustainable commodities, crops and products. Extensive improvements are required within existing industries, and opportunity to develop only certified product markets within larger industries and markets is sufficient. Established industries and companies also provide opportunity for certifications to expand their market share within existing conventional markets. Between 2011 and 2015 the growth in the certified area within agriculture was most significant for cotton at 250 per cent, followed by bananas and oil palm. Soy bean also expanded by 61 per cent between 2008 and 2015. The agricultural areas with the largest proportion of certification in 2015 were coffee (24%) and cacao (16%) (Lernoud et al. 2018).

Sustainability certifications operate alongside CSR and complement and contribute to CSA through compulsory third-party verification of compliance with variably aligned sustainability standards and objectives. Practices are certified across a range of agricultural and natural resource products and industries, along the trade chain and across stakeholders directly. Standards are developed through private and multistakeholder mechanisms which are eventually introduced to the relevant stakeholders. The heterogeneity between codes of conduct and external sustainability certification standards even within the same industry results in a loosely defined sustainability with implication for intentions and outcomes. This range of variables provides significant opportunity to understand, evaluate and communicate sustainability in various ways, and significant variance and difficulty in adequately determining outcomes.

Before sustainability certifications became a matter for comment and critique, not only from a consumer, business, social justice or environmental action standpoint but also from institutional understanding (ITC 2017) and academia, some intentions were quite simple. The simplicity could be considered spurred by the complicated political context, or as a self-driven complementary movement developed through common observations of the influence of trade practice. The rationale appears to indicate that intramarket approaches were understood as a straightforward way to change and improve practices and conditions in source and producing countries. This was instead of relying on government via trade relations, domestic or international law and policy. Some were originally standards for agricultural practice only. Others were more focused on trade and social justice aspects.

Within agricultural industries, the International Federation of Organic Agriculture Movements (IFOAM), the first effort to move agricultural practices to organic, set up an international alliance with the intention of sharing scientific and experimental data in 1972. This was the beginning of sharing information internationally to improve understanding and eventually agricultural practice, with efforts developing within distinct countries. The first attempt at a market incentive through labelling produce for consumer awareness and brand association was an organic certification, developed by Oregon Tilth, established in 1982.

With origins in the non-labelled fair trade for handicrafts of the 1940s, the label Max Havelaar was launched in 1988, and has developed to be known as the Fairtrade label. The initiative sought to improve payment to small farmers in disadvantaged regions. It started with a community of coffee farmers in Oaxaca, Mexico by arranging direct export from producers to the international market where the coffee would be roasted and then sold, shortening the trade chain significantly. Intentions were distinct to organic or sustainable farming factors as it focused more on trade and worker condition imbalances. In fact, this was one of the first intramarket sustainability mechanisms to counter the advantage taken by business of complicated trade routes (Meenu 2008; Vedel and Ellegard 2013).

The official label Fairtrade, certified by the Fairtrade Labelling Organisation (FLO), has alongside fair trade developed their networks for certified and noncertified products across multiple industries. This has more recently included fisheries and farm animal well-being. Fairtrade certifies six main commodities and other products such as cosmetics, soccer balls and alcohol. Just over 50 per cent of Fairtrade certified crops are also organic certified. Simplified trade routes have been variably maintained, depending on industry and business consumer. Rainforest Alliance (RA) was established in 1987, and labelling developed in 1990 with the intention of reducing deforestation. The sustainable agricultural network (SAN) was established in the late 1990s and developed standards to certify commodities according to RA principles. RA now certifies over 100 crops.

Farm animal welfare has been a topic for consideration since the early 1900s with associations established all over the world. Labels have developed since the 1990s and the number of certified labels and number of unverified claims is quite extensive (AWIonline 2016; Lundmark *et al.* 2018). Developing unified standards and frameworks has met difficulty with evident differences in cultural approaches and philosophies of what animal welfare is (Main *et al.* 2014). The Animal Welfare Quality protocol developed in 2009 (Blokhuis *et al.* 2013) continues to improve. It has been used to inform several existing sustainability certifications that include related criteria or that are dedicated only to farm animal welfare.

Dolphin-safe or dolphin-friendly eco-labels emerged in the 1980s as the first seafood certification labels, used across tuna products. Since then, Friend of the Sea, Monterey Bay Aquarium's Seafood Watch, the Marine Steward-ship Council (MSC), Oceanwise, the Aquaculture Stewardship Council (ASC), Naturland and Fair Trade USA, among others, have developed. The council-based labels have followed a multistakeholder process toward estab-lishment. The MSC was established in 1997 on the back of a cod industry collapse in Canada in 1992, and a statement of intent signed by the WWF and representative of Unilever in 1996. The ASC was based on a multistake-holder roundtable in 2004 and established in 2010.

The Forest Stewardship Council (FSC), which grew from three years of dialogue between NGOs and industry leaders in the lead up to the Rio Earth Summit, was eventually founded in 1993 and incorporated in 1996. It was the first effort to define a global certification system for sustainable forest management. The only comparable system for forestry certification is the Pan European Forestry Certification (PEFC), which provides meta-standards to verify quality of national forestry certification schemes. There are also smaller forest certifications, some of which also developed through the 1990s – Natura is one example for forestry and mining. Mining and Metals for Sus-tainable Development (MMSD) commenced in the 1990s and since then several sustainability standards and certificates have emerged (Sturman *et al.* 2018) with more momentum evident since the early 2000s. Between 2006 and 2008 a multistakeholder process in Latin America developed a collective vision and principles for responsible artisanal and small-scale mining (ASM). This led to the world's pioneering standard for responsibly mined gold and associated silver and platinum. In 2009, based on Standard ergo, the first version of the Fairmined Standard was developed in partnership with Fair-trade. In 2014 version 2 of the Fairmined standard was released. The Responsible Jewellery Council (RJC), established in 2005 by a group of 14 organisations from a cross-section of the diamond and gold jewellery supply chain, expanded the number of minerals it considers and certifies.

In 2008, the Roundtable for Sustainable Biofuels released suggested stand-ards for sustainable biofuel, and Voluntary Certification Schemes (VCS) – sustainability certifications – were decided as the most effective approach for ensuring compliance. There are numerous labels used to complement imple-mentation of these standards and intentions for sustainable biofuel. The majority developed as a response to this Roundtable and the subsequent EU Roundtable, many are listed in the chapter on biofuels. Biochar certification is certainly one of the most recent 'items' or natural resources to be certified, with only two certifications currently operating. While scientific studies have preceded the certifications by decades (see Verheijen *et al.* in Chapter 5), the International Biochar Initiative (IBI) and the European Biochar Certificates (EBC) were established this decade.

The sustainability certification process has demonstrated a requirement for more layers of intricacy than many originally intended or included. As a result, certifying other industries and providing additional labels and certifica-tions for the same industry have partially resulted from multistakeholder initiatives. Within existing certifications and for the more recently developed certifications, emphasis on standard quality and certification process has increased. More recent developments have seen industry-specific certifications emerge, and existing certifications expand their reach across industries. The Ecolabel Index (2018) lists details for 464 eco-labels operating around the world in 199 countries and across 25 industry sectors. This evidences the fact that within the same industry there can be several certification efforts. This list is not inclusive of standard setters, regulators and service providers who are the 21 members of the International Social and Environmental Accreditation Labelling Alliance (ISEAL). These members include:

- Accreditation Services International
- Alliance for Water Stewardship
- Aquaculture Stewardship Council
- Better Cotton Initiative
- BONSUCRO
- Fairtrade
- FSC
- GEO Foundation
- Global Coffee Platform
- Good weave
- IOAS
- Linking Environment and Farming
- Marine Stewardship Council
- Rainforest Alliance
- Responsible Jewellery Council
- Roundtable on Sustainable Biomaterials
- Roundtable on Sustainable Palm Oil
- Social Accountability Accreditation Services
- Sustainable Agriculture Network (SAN)
- Union for Ethical Bio-trade
- UTZ

and two associated members

- Fair Trade USA
- Textile Exchange

Nor is it inclusive of all 14 of the sustainability standards for agriculture and forestry considered most significant by the ITC (2017):

- 4C‡
- Better Cotton Initiative★
- BONSUCRO★
- Cotton made in Africa†

- Fairtrade International★
- Forest Stewardship Council★
- GLOBAL G.A.P.†
- IFOAM – Organics International†
- Programme for the Endorsement of Forest Certification‡
- ProTerra Foundation†
- Rainforest Alliance/SAN★
- Roundtable on Sustainable Palm Oil★
- Round Table on Responsible Soy†, and
- UTZ★

  (★ ISEAL member; †; ISEAL subscriber; ‡ Not listed by ISEAL)

Of the numerous labels currently operating in the sustainable trade area, each represents varying standard criteria and approaches to implementation and verification. The same label might certify across different geographic regions, and different labels can work with distinct, similar or the same philosophical intentions related to the definition of sustainability used. The approach to addressing varying types of 'irresponsibility' with different solutions can also alter and become contextual. While different labels are distinct in several ways, the majority do introduce uniform standards exclusive to each label with slight variation to criteria and processes according to context. Another commonality is the location of the effort and the 'third-party' approach to certifying and auditing standard implementation within different countries and regions, and across or within industries. This could be understood as further confusing or better representing the intricacy of these certification efforts where considering their unique intramarket, extra-business location, their reach across multiple industries and how they align with bigger picture ideas for sustainability solutions within business practices.

Further research and practical measures can improve understanding of, and actual, outcomes and legitimacy of claims. Research might consider environmental, societal or economic outcomes as indicative of sustainability, and implications as associated exclusively with any one certification effort, pillar of sustainability or across certifications and pillars. Within even one pillar of sustainability a conceptualisation has been suggested as necessary to better encompass the range of topics to which outcomes are relevant (Janker and Mann 2018). Disciplinary studies also reveal different implications, where one discipline may reveal particular findings, recognising that other disciplinary findings for the same context and situation provide a more comprehensive understanding. Findings that influence popularity or preference for any one certification are more so the case. For example, the science of observing environmental change and how to resolve eco–systemic problems can overlook whether an international trade dynamic and context is conducive to resolution. In other cases trade, governance, economic or cultural studies and findings might overlook the importance of conservation science findings associated with standard criteria, and the associated outcomes of effective implementation. In either situation, greenwashing can easily be promoted and further, it could be understood as encouraged where findings exclusive to one discipline are understood as comprehensive proof of effectiveness (Bowen and Aragon-Correa 2014). This is an important example as the credibility of disciplinary claims can often stabilise a perceived market, sustainability and even trade benefit, and 'expert' opinion can easily be understood as a recommendation.

Sustainable trade 'solutions' might then be recommended or endorsed without adequately addressing or considering two areas: (1) the associated issues that must be managed to achieve intended outcomes through certification or other trade solution; (2) an association between scientifically proven required improvements and the calibre of the sustainable trade solution. Research findings that do not address these areas remain valuable and important. They cannot, however, be considered as providing comprehensive recommendations, solutions or considerations, rather contributing to advancing understanding within only one aspect. Considering and ensuring understanding of trade intricacies alongside the science of conservation is therefore important for sustainable international trade and sourcing solutions within agricultural and natural resource industries. As a corresponding inclusion, specific studies should recognise the limitation in findings given the omission of any one aspect such as a discipline or detail within a sustainability pillar. They may also clarify any explicit endorsement of a sustainability label or certification.

Overview

This book provides a balanced critique of several international sustainability certifications across nine agricultural and natural resource industries according to outcomes for society and environment.

An outcome is any identifiable benefit or disadvantage associated with a sustainability certification. Identifiable refers not only to tangible observations but to an understanding of what was involved to achieve any outcome, and the associated outcomes of the involved process. The intricacy of issues certifications seek to address and an understanding of context within which each operates is encouraged through the lens of several disciplines and informed by different methods and methodologies. Industries include:

- Farm animal well-being
- Farmed seafood
- Ocean fisheries
- Biochar
- Forests
- Coffee
- Roses
- Biofuel
- Gold

Certifications include:

- Fairtrade
- Rainforest Alliance
- FSC
- MSC
- Fairmined
- Responsible Jewellery Council
- A range of biofuel certifications endorsed by the EC
- Organic
- European Biochar Certification
- Welfare Quality Protocol – a standard open for use by any farm animal well-being standard or certification

The representation of standards and labels included are based on certified hectares; commodities, necessities and luxuries; newly certified natural resources; contributory elements for production systems; and terrestrial and aquatic production locations. The difference between certification efforts within the same industry or between different industries according to outcomes for society and environment is of interest. In addition, the difference between standards and certificates as contributory to sustainability certifications is significantly considered. Each chapter considers sustainability certifications from varying disciplines and perspectives, using distinct and mixed methods. The range of structured critiques, reviews and evaluations use scientific and quantitative, empirical and qualitative methods and are conducted by academics and practitioners from a range of disciplinary backgrounds. The methods, methodologies, conceptual advances and disciplines of authors are listed and further explained in the concluding chapter.

The chapters are ordered first to discuss more general topics of culture and biodiversity as associated with sustainability certifications, then to discuss the more detailed standards of biochar and farm animal welfare which can be integrated to existing certifications or become autonomous labels. Thereafter, industry-specific standards and certifications are considered, informed by specific certifications and labels and/or inclusive of several different certifications and labels. In this way, the chapters eventually consider more general considerations of culture and biodiversity, more recent developments in certification processes to improve existing certification efforts, and then decade-long situations that particular industries have experienced through involvement with certifications. Suggestions for improvement are provided either as the basis for chapter topics, or to conclude each chapter. Findings and outcomes from each chapter are collated in the concluding chapter, providing an overview of the role the different certifications considered in this book play within different industries and around the world despite a similar intention of sustainability. The concluding chapter also seeks to provide recommendations and ideas for future direction in research, evaluations and practice.

Included chapters

2 Cultural implications of sustainability certifications

An understanding and assessment of the cultural implications of sustainability certifications across stakeholders, and for individual consumers is encouraged. Participatory Guarantee Systems (PGS) are explained and facilitate a comparison between locally based and verified requirements, and third-party certification.

3 Biodiversity outcomes and sustainability certifications

Biodiversity intentions and outcomes associated with sustainability certifications are evaluated, and how they are understood as positive is considered. Intentions through standard criteria, and outcomes associated with implementation of standards provide two foundational categories.

4 FSC opinion on evaluation of biodiversity outcomes

Research approaches and findings on impacts of FSC certification for biodiversity conservation are summarised. We also present the potential for FSC to provide benefits for biodiversity conservation in Intact Forest Landscapes (IFL).

5 Biochar

The Optimum Biochar Dose (OBD) concept addresses the optimal ecosystem service's (ES) trade-off, by determining the biochar application rate at which various ESs respond in relation to their overall desired response. Several possible trade-offs are addressed in certification schemes, namely associated with biodiversity outcomes, directly or indirectly. Biochar can also have positive biodiversity outcomes, and thus, potentially contribute to sustainable management, preservation and/or function recovery in vulnerable or degraded ecosystems.

6 Farm animal well-being

Animal welfare research and welfare assessment are discussed, and the case of developing the Welfare Quality® protocols promoted by the European Union illustrated. Finally, current initiatives for improving the transparency of the market for animal-friendly produced products via labelling and technological developments for improving animal welfare are discussed.

7 Aquaculture

This chapter summarises the existing literature on aquaculture eco-certification and the knowledge on environmental and social short-term effects and long-term impacts.

8 MSC

The extent to which transparency is forthcoming in the Marine Stewardship Council (MSC), currently the gold standard for seafood certification, is examined and compared with the Forest Stewardship Council (FSC).

9 Biofuels and the EU

Using the EU system of sustainability certification of biofuel as a case example, this chapter seeks to provide a balanced critique of the regulatory strategy of sustainability certification of biofuel, and of the potentials and pitfalls regarding its democratic legitimacy and its environmental and social effectiveness.

10 Responsible Jewellery Council (RJC) and Alliance for Responsible Mining (ARM)

The interoperability of mineral certification schemes through a case study of collaboration by two initiatives – the Responsible Jewellery Council (RJC) and the Alliance for Responsible Mining (ARM) – is explored.

11 Certifying coffee in Costa Rica

This chapter discusses experience with sustainability certifications in Costa Rica over the period 2008–2018.

12 Certifying flower production in Ecuador

This study looks at power relations shaping different stakeholder practices in the case of certifying flower production and export in Ecuador.

List of terms

Outcome

An outcome is any identifiable benefit or disadvantage associated with a sustainability certification output. Identifiable refers not only to tangible observations but to an understanding of what was involved to achieve any outcome, and the associated outcomes of the involved process. Outcomes therefore include not only the subsequent environmental outcome from complying with a sustainability certification, they also consider the societal outcomes, a part of which includes the required changes in procedures and processes and the cultural changes resulting from using sustainability certifications.

Sustainability

Several definitions exist. Simple references are used in the introduction with each author determining the definition most appropriate for their chapter.

Sustainability pillars

There are two definitions and understandings of sustainability pillars: (1) environment, economy and society; and (2) people, planet and profits. The first definition is most used in this book; however, authors did not receive guidance or instruction to use this definition, and so variation through chapters can exist.

Sustainability certifications

Also referred to as voluntary sustainability schemes and third-party certifications. This book refers mostly to sustainability certifications to recognise inclusion of labels and therefore integrate the consumer or market-level influence or consideration. Voluntary sustainability schemes as a term seeks to emphasis the approach to regulation used, and varying market or extra-market locations for these efforts. Third-party certifications are a way of recognising the location or position of certifications as intramarket but external to the varying business types. Authors have had opportunity to use which ever term they prefer in their chapter and in some chapters the terms are used interchangeably to accommodate more specific discussion points.

Fairtrade

Fairtrade certification is, as an organisation, composed of several different departments or organisational entities. Their names and existence have changed over time. They include Fairtrade Labelling Organisation (FLO) also referred to as FairtradeInternational and FLOCERT among others. Reference to Fairtrade in the chapters interchange; however, where fairtrade is used, it is in reference to the entire certification process of standards, verification and labelling and allows for times when fairtrade was the only way to reference the process. Most studies are producer country based or related, making reference to FLOCERT and FLO appropriate.

Business

The position or location of sustainability certifications within the context of efforts toward sustainable practices are explained as intramarket and extra-business, or within market but external to business. The reference to business in this explanation refers to extractors, producers or producer groups who eventually sell to local or international markets, processors, intermediary businesses also including exporters and importers, for consumer country business types, that further prepare the natural resource for market, and also distributors toward point of sale. Business types are then considered in different ways; common distinctions between corporations and smaller or medium-sized businesses which are local or international are provided.

Farmers or producers can be distinct from this category depending on definitions of involvement in business–business transaction, likely through cooperatives or associations.

Extractors and producers are also distinct from labourers; labourers within a natural resource extraction or farming industry are not included in the reference to business.

Summary

The chapters in this book seek to contribute to an understanding of the current status for certification approaches after three or more decades of effort, by providing examples from particular industries and certifications. From these examples improvements to date can be considered and some preliminary guidance for future study, research and practice is available. Multidisciplinary perspectives and evaluations of several sustainability certifications are compiled, encouraging understanding of the sectors and disciplines such efforts encompass, and the intricacy of what appear simple market-based efforts. Clarifying the role such certifications play and the value they represent according to outcomes for society and the environment progresses understanding of their potential contribution in the future. Foundational, preliminary and more advanced findings provided through the chapters are relevant for future sustainability intentions, evaluations, research and practice for trade, production and consumption. There are opportunities for industry- and nonindustry-specific certification processes to learn and improve reciprocally from the examples provided.

Ensuring appropriateness, significance and relevance of extrapolated findings and experiences for other industries or certifications is important and may limit or condition how lessons will be used. There are some key certified commodities and industries, and various sustainability certifications across numerous countries. Lessons can be learned according to standard setting, implementation and certifying processes and how certifications contribute compared to other mechanisms and approaches. Governance structures and approaches to developing and introducing standards, legitimising their implementation and ensuring particular trade conditions and organisational processes are additional considerations. Relevance to other and between industries may condition the appropriateness of such extrapolation and comparison. The concluding chapter will provide ideas of comparison between the findings of each chapter as indicative of common ideas, findings, achievements and areas for improvement. Alongside, ideas questions and recommendations for future research and practice are presented.

Notes

1 A multinational corporation (MNC) operates across several countries with one headquarters, adapting products to local markets.
2 A transnational corporation (TNC) is a type of MNC which operates as separate entities within each country of operation.

References

Adams M., Ghaly A.E. (2007). Maximizing sustainability of Costa Rican coffee industry. Journal of Cleaner Production 15(17): 1716–29.

Agardy T. (2000). Effects of fisheries on marine ecosystems: a conservationist perspective. Journal of Marine Science 57: 761–65.

Akinci M. (2017). Inequality and economic growth: trickle-down effect revisited. Development Policy Review 36(s1): 01–024.

Ali A., Abdulai A. (2010). The adoption of genetically modified cotton and poverty reduction in Pakistan. Journal of Agricultural Economics 61(1): 175–92.

Alston P. (2004). 'Core labour standards' and the transformation of the international labour rights regimes. European Journal of International Law 15(3): 457–521.

Anderson J. (2001). Liberalism and communitarianism: studies in Hegel's philosophy of right. Proceedings of the Hegel Society of America 15: 185–205.

AWIonline (2016). A consumers guide to food labels and animal welfare. https://awionline.org/sites/default/files/products/FA-AWI-FoodLabelGuide-Web.pdf.

Bebbington A., Abdulai A., Bebbington D.H., Hinfelaar M., Sanborn C.A. (2018). Governing Extractive Industries: Politics, Histories, Ideas. Oxford University Press.

Bellamy A.S. (2010). Weed control practices in Costa Rican coffee farms: is herbicide use necessary for small-scale producers? Agriculture and Human Values 28(2): 167–77.

Blokhuis H.J., Jones R.B, Veissier I., Miele M. (Eds.) (2013). Improving Farm Animal Welfare. Science and Society Working Together: The Welfare Quality Approach. Wageningen Academic Publishers.

Bohmelt T., Butkute E. (2018). The self-selection of democracies into treaty design: insights from international environmental agreements. International Environmental Agreements: Politics, Law and Economics 18(3): 351–67.

Bowen F., Aragon-Correa A. (2014). Greenwashing in corporate environmentalism research and practice: the importance of what we say and do. Organisation and Environment 27(2): 107–12.

Browne R. (2008). 'Blood cell phones' worsen crisis in Congo. Le Journal des Alternatives 19 July.

Cartel M., Smale M., Zambrano P. (2006). Bales and balance: a review of the methods used to assess the economic impact of Bt cotton on farmers in developing economies. AgBioForum 9(3): 195–212.

Cartier L.E., Burge M. (2011). Agriculture and artisanal gold mining in Sierra Leone: alternatives or complements. Journal of International Development 23(8): 1080–99.

Carvalho F.P. (2017). Pesticides, environment, and food safety. Food and Energy Security 6(2): 48–60.

Ceddia M.G., Bardsley N.O., Paloma S.G., Sedlack S. (2014). Governance, agricultural intensification and land sparing in tropical South America. PNAS 111(20): 7242–47.

Chan A. (2010). Racing to the bottom: international trade without a social clause. Third Quarterly Review 24(6): 1011–28.

Chen B., Han M.Y., Peng K., Zhou S.L., Shao L., Wu X.F., Weig W.D., Liuh S.Y., Lia Z., Lid J.S., Chena G.Q. (2018). Global land–water nexus: agricultural land and freshwater use embodied in worldwide supply chains. Science of the Total Environment 613–14: 931–43.

Chen C., Randall A. (2013). The economic contest between coal seam gas mining and agriculture on prime farmland: it may be closer than we thought. Journal of Economic and Social Policy 15(3).

Cho S. (2009). A long and winding road: the Doha round negotiation in the world trade organisation. http://scholarship.kentlaw.iit.edu/fac_school/162.

Cole W.M. (2017). Too much of a good thing? Economic growth and human rights 1960–2010. Social Science Research 67: 72–90.

Conway G.R., Barbie E.B. (1988). After the Green Revolution: sustainable and equitable agricultural development. Futures 20(6): 651–70.

Cottrell R.S., Fleming A., Fulton E.A., Nash K.L., Watson R.A., Blanchard J.L. (2018). Considering land–sea interactions and trade-offs for food and biodiversity. Global Change Biology 24(2): 580–96.

Cusack L.K., Smit E., Kile M.L., Harding A.K. (2017). Regional and temporal trends in blood mercury concentrations and fish consumption in women of child bearing age in the United States using NHANES data from 1999–2010. Environmental Health 16: 10.

Dahl R. (2010). Green washing: do you know what you are buying? Environmental Health Perspectives 118(6): A246–52.

Davis G., Manzano Mazzali O. (2018). The extractive industries in Central America. The Extractive Industries and Society 5(3): 215–17.

Deakin S. (2016). The contribution of labour law to economic development and growth. Centre for Business Research. WP 478. www.cbr.cam.ac.uk/fileadmin/user_upload/centre-for-business-research/downloads/working-papers/wp478.pdf.

Doso Jnr S., Ayensu-Ntim A., Twumaski-Ankara B., Barimah T. (2015). Effects of loss of agricultural land due to large-scale gold mining on agriculture in Ghana: the case of the Western Region. British Journal of Research 2(6): 196–221.

Doumbia-Henry C., Gravel E. (2008). Free trade agreements and labour rights: Recent Developments. International Labour Review 145(3): 185–206.

Downey L., Bonds E., Clark K. (2010). Natural resource extraction, armed violence and environmental degradation. Organisation and Environment 23(4): 417–45.

Ecolabel Index (2018). All Ecolabels. www.ecolabelindex.com.

Ellem B., Tonts M. (2017). The global commodities boom and the reshaping of regional economies: the Australian experience. Australian Geographer 49(3).

Evenson R.E., Gollin D. (2003). Assessing the impact of the Green Revolution, 1960 to 2000. Science 300(5620): 758–62.

Fauzi H., Svensson G., Rahman A.A. (2010). 'Triple bottom line' as 'sustainable corporate performance': a proposition for the future. Sustainability 2(5): 1345–60.

Freebairn D.K. (1995). Did the Green Revolution concentrate incomes? A quantitative study of research reports. World Development 23(2): 265–79.

Freestone D. (2018). Review article: sustainable development and international environmental law. Elgar Research Reviews in Law. https://doi.org/10.4337/9781786431097.

Frey B., Schneider F. (1978). An empirical study of politico-economic interaction in the United States. The Review of Economics and Statistics 60(2): 174–83.

Gaines S. (2002). The masked ball of NAFTA Chapter 11: foreign investors, local environmentalists, government officials, and disguised motives. In J.J. Kirton, V.W.

Mclaren (Eds.). Linking Trade, Environment and Social Cohesion. Routledge, chapter 6.

Gallagher K.P. (2008). Understanding developing country resistance to the Doha round. Review of International Political Economy 15(1): 62–85.

Gardner T.A., Benziea M., Börner J., Dawkins E., Ficka S., Garrett R., Godara J., Grima-rdd A., Laked S., Larsena R.K., Maria N., McDermott C.L., Meyfroidt P., Osbeck M., Perssom M., Sembresi T., Suaveta C., Strasburg B., … Wolvekamp P. (2018). Transparency and sustainability in global commodity supply chains. World Development.

Gaveau D.L.A., Sloan S., Molidena E., Yaen H., Sheil D., Abram N.K., Ancrenaz M., … Meeijard E. (2014). Four decades of forest persistence, clearance and logging in Borneo. PloS ONE 9(7): e101654.

Geist H.J., Lambin E.F. (2002). Proximate causes and underlying driving forces of tropical deforestation: tropical forests are disappearing as the result of many pressures, both local and regional, acting in various combinations in different geographical locations. Bioscience 52(2): 143–50.

Ghauri P.N. (2017). Multinational enterprises and sustainable development in emerging markets. In J.-S. Bergé, S. Harnay, U. Mayrhofer, L. Obadia (Eds.). Global Phenomena and Social Sciences. Springer, 21–36.

Gillespie A. (2018). The Long Road to Sustainability: The Past, Present and Future of International Environmental Law and Policy. Oxford University Press.

Gilpin R. (2000). The Challenge of Global Capitalism: The World Economy in the 21st Century. Princeton University Press.

Goldburg R., Naylor R. (2005). Future seascapes, fishing, and fish farming. Frontiers in Ecology and the Environment 3(1): 21–28.

Gruere G., Sengupta D. (2011). Cotton and farmer suicides in India: an evidence-based assessment. The Journal of Development Studies 47(2): 316–37.

Gulbrandsen L.H. (2010). Transnational Environmental Governance: The Emergence and Effect of the Certification of Forests and Fisheries. Edward Elgar.

Hamann R., Kapelus P. (2004). Corporate Social Responsibility in mining in southern Africa: fair accountability or just greenwash? Development 47(3): 85–92.

Hamilton P.B., Cowx I.G., Oleksiak M.F., Griffith A.M., Grahn M., Stevens J.R., Carvahlo G.R., Nicol E., Tyler C.R. (2016). Population-level consequences for wild fish exposed to sublethal concentrations of chemicals: a critical review. Fish and Fisheries 17(3): 545–66.

Hancock L., Ralph N., Ali S.H. (2018). Bolivia's lithium frontier: can public private partnerships deliver a minerals boom for sustainable development. Journal of Cleaner Production 178: 551–60.

Hegel G.W.F. (1802/3). The System of Ethical Life. State University of New York, Albany. www.marxists.org/reference/archive/hegel/works/se/index.htm.

Higman B.W. (2000). The sugar revolution. The Economic History Review 53(2): 213–36.

Hoisington D., Khairallah M., Reeves T., Ribaut J., Skovmand B., Taba S., Warburton M. (1999). Plant genetic resources: what can they contribute toward increased crop productivity? PNAS 96(11): 5937–43. https://doi.org/10.1073/pnas.96.11.5937.

Hollander R., Thornthwaite L. (2018). Competitive federalism and workers' compensation: do states race to the bottom? Australian Journal of Political Science 53(3).

Horrigan L., Lawrence R.S., Walker P. (2002). How sustainable agriculture can address the environmental and human health harms of industrial agriculture. Environmental Health Perspectives 110(5): 445–56.

Hossain F., Pray C.E., Lu Y., Huang J., Fan C., Hu R. (2013). Genetically modified cotton and farmers' health in China. International Journal of Occupational and Environmental Health 10(3): 296–303. https://doi.org/10.1179/oeh.2004.10.3.296.

ITC (2017). The state of sustainable markets 2017: statistics and trends. ITC Report in collaboration with FiBL and ISSD. www.standardsimpacts.org/sites/default/files/State-of-Sustainable-Market-2017_web.pdf.

Janker J., Mann S. (2018). Understanding the social dimension of sustainability in agriculture: a critical review of sustainability assessment tools. Environment, Development and Sustainability. https://doi.org/10.1007/s10668-018-0282-0.

Keeble B.R. (1988). The Brundtland Report: our common future. Medicine and War 4(1): 17–25.

Kerr R.B. (2012). Lessons from the old Green Revolution for the new: social, environmental and nutritional issues for agricultural change in Africa. Progress in Development Studies. https://doi.org/10.1177/146499341101200308.

Kobayashi H., Watandoa H., Kakimotoa M. (2014). A global extent site-level analysis of land cover and protected area overlap with mining activities as an indicator of biodiversity pressure. Journal of Cleaner Production 84(1): 459–68.

Kurien J., Achari T.T.R. (1990). Overfishing along Kerala coast: causes and consequences. Economic and Political Weekly 25(35/36): 2011–18.

Lernoud J., Potts J., Sampson G., Schlatter B., Huppe G., Voora V., Willer H., Wozniak J., Dang D. (2018). The state of sustainable markets: statistics and emerging trends 2018. ITC, Geneva.

Li Y., Kanbur R., Lin C. (2017). Minimum wage competition between local governments in China. The Journal of Development Studies. https://doi.org/10.1080/00220388.2018.1536263.

Lundmark F., Berg C., Rocklinsberg H. (2018). Private animal welfare standards: opportunities and risks. Animals 8(1).

Lyon T.P., Delmas M.A., Maxwell J.W., Bansal P., Chiroleu-Assouline M., Crifi P., Durand R., Gond J., King A., Lenox M., Toffel M., Vogel D., Wijen F. (2018). CSR needs CPR: corporate sustainability and politics. California Management Review 60(4): 5–24.

Main D., Mullana S., Atkinson C., Cooper M., Wrathall J.H.M., Blokhuis H.J. (2014). Best practice framework for animal welfare certification schemes. Trends in Food Science and Technology 37(2): 127–36.

McKay A., Vizard P. (2005). Rights and economic growth: inevitable conflict or 'common ground'? ODI. www.odi.org/sites/odi.org.uk/files/odi-assets/publications-opinion-files/4353.pdf.

Meenu T. (2008). Depending intraregional trade and investment in South Asia: the case of textiles and clothing industry. ICRIER Working Paper.

Mkodzongi G., Spiegel S. (2018). Artisanal gold mining and farming: livelihood linkages and labour dynamics after land reforms in Zimbabwe. The Journal of Development Studies. http://doi.org/10.1080/00220388.2018.1516867.

Monshipouri M., Welch C.E., Kennedy E.T. (2009). Multinational corporations and the ethics of global responsibility: problems and possibilities. In D. Kinley (Ed.). Human Rights and Corporations. Taylor & Francis, chapter 5.

Morin J., Bialais C. (2018). Strengthening multilateral environmental governance through bilateral trade deals. CIGI Policy Brief 123.

Moss B. (2007). Water pollution by agriculture. Philosophical Transactions of the Royal Society of London. Series B, Biological Sciences 363(1491): 659–66.

Naylor R.L., Hardy R.W., Bureau D.P., Chou A., Elliott M., Farrell A.P., Forster I., Gatlin D.M., Goldburg R.J., Hua K., Nichols P.D. (2009). Feeding aquaculture in an era of finite resources. PNAS. https://doi.org/10.1073/pnas.0905235106.

Ocansey I.T. (2013). Mining impacts on agricultural lands and food security. Tuku University of Applied Sciences Thesis. www.theseus.fi/bitstream/handle/10024/53720/Ocansey_Ignitious.pdf?sequence.

Orbie J., van den Putte L., Martens D. (2018). Civil society meetings in EU Free Trade Agreements: the purposes unravelled. In H. Gotts (Ed.). Labour Standards in International Economics Law. Springer.

Paige J.M. (1997). Coffee and Power: Revolution and Rise of Democracy in Central America. Harvard University Press.

Parayil G. (2003). Mapping technological trajectories of the Green Revolution and the Gene Revolution from modernization to globalization. Research Policy 32(6): 971–90.

Parayil G., Tong F. (1998). Pasture-led to logging-led deforestation in the Brazilian Amazon: the dynamics of socio-environmental change. Global Environment Change 8(1): 63–79.

Pimentel D., Houser J., Preiss E., White O., Fang H., Mesnick L., Barsky T., Tariche S., Schreck J., Alpert A. (1996). Water resources: agriculture, the environment, and society. BioScience 47(2): 97–106.

Pingali P.L. (2012). Green Revolution: impacts, limits, and the path ahead. PNAS 109(31).

Pingali P.L., Rosegrant M.W. (1994). Confronting the environmental consequences of the Green Revolution in Asia. International Food Policy Research Institute (IFPRI). EPTD Discussion Papers 2.

Polanyi K. (1957 [1944]). The Great Transformation. Foreword by Robert M. MacIver. Beacon Press.

Radomski PJ. (1999). Commercial over fishing and property rights. Fisheries 24(6): 22–29.

Schmuck D., Matthes J., Naderer B. (2018). Misleading consumers with green advertising? An affect–reason–involvement account of greenwashing effects in environmental advertising. Journal of Advertising 47(2): 127–45.

Schrecker T., Birn E., Aguilera M. (2018). How extractive industries affect health: political economy underpinnings and pathways. Health and Place 52: 135–47.

SDGs (2015). Transforming Our World: 2030 Agenda for Sustainable Development Goals. https://sustainabledevelopment.un.org/post2015/transformingourworld.

Shah A. (2002). The mainstream media and free trade. Global Issues. www.globalissues.org/article/41/the-mainstream-media-and-free-trade.

Shiva V. (2016). The Violence of the Green Revolution: Third World Agriculture, Ecology and Politics. University Press of Kentucky.

Sierra R. (2001). The role of domestic timber markets in tropical deforestation and forest degradation in Ecuador: implications for conservation planning and policy. Ecological Economics 36(2): 327–40.

Singh P.B., Pandey K.K. (2012). Green marketing: policies and practices for sustainability development. Integral Review: A Journal of Management 5(1): 22–30.

Singh R.B. (2000). Environmental consequences of agricultural development: a case study from the Green Revolution state of Haryana, India. Agriculture, Ecosystems and Environment 82(1–3).

Sissenwine M.M., Mace P.M., Lassen H.J. (2014). Preventing overfishing: evolving approaches and emerging challenges. ICES Journal of Marine Science 71(2): 153–56.

Ssenyonjo M. (2011). The applicability of international human rights law to non-state actors: what relevance to economic, social and cultural rights. In M. Ssenyonjo (Ed.). Economic, Social and Cultural Rights. Taylor & Francis, chapter 2.

Stevenson J.R., Villoria N., Byerlee D., Kelley R., Maredia M (2013). Green Revolution research saved an estimated 18 to 27 million hectares from being brought into agricultural production. PNAS 110(21): 8363–68.

Stoll J.S., Crona B.I., Fabinyi M., Farr E.R. (2018). Seafood trade routes for lobster obscure teleconnected vulnerabilities. Frontiers Marine Science. https://doi.org/10.3389/fmars.2018.00239.

Sturman K. Rogers P., Imbrogiano J., Mori Junior R., Ezeigbo C. (2018). Monitoring impact of mineral sustainability standards to align with the Sustainable Development Goals. Centre for Social Responsibility in Mining (CSRM), the University of Queensland.

Valor C. (2005). Corporate Social Responsibility and corporate citizenship: towards corporate accountability. Business and Society Review 110(2): 191–212.

van Solinge T.B. (2014). Researching illegal logging and deforestation. International Journal for Crime, Justice and Social Democracy 3(2): 35–48.

Vedel M., Ellegard C. (2013). Supply risk management functions of sourcing intermediaries: an investigation of the clothing industry. Supply Chain Management: An International Journal 18(5): 509–22. https://doi.org/10.1108/SCM-09-2012.

Vivoda V., Kemp D. (2018). How do national mining industry associations compare on sustainable development. The Extractive Industries and Society 6(1): 22–28.

Vogt M. (2011). Tico time: the influence of coffee certifications on sustainable development and poverty reduction in Costa Rica: a discussion with coffee farmers and cooperative managers. PhD. Flinders University, Faculty of Social and Behavioural Sciences.

Vogt M. (2017). Toward functional pollinator abundance and diversity. Biological Conservation 215: 196–212.

Vogt M. (2018). Variance in Approach toward a 'Sustainable' Coffee Industry in Costa Rica: Perspectives from Within; Lessons and Insights. Ubiquity Press (UNDER REVIEW).

West K. (2017). Carmakers' electric dreams depend on supplies of rare minerals. The Guardian 30 July. www.theguardian.com/environment/2017/jul/29/electric-cars-battery-manufacturing-cobalt-mining.

Wolf E.C. (1986). Beyond the Green Revolution: new approaches for Third World agriculture. Worldwatch Paper 73.

World Business Council for Sustainable Development. (1998, September). WBCSD – Corporate Social Responsibility. Retrieved July 11, 2011, from World Business Council for Sustainable Development (WBCSD): www.wbcsd.org/DocRoot/hbdf19Txhmk3kDxBQDWW/CSRmeeting.pdf.

Zhang L., Yan C., Guo Q., Zhang J., Ruiz-Menjivar J. (2018). The impact of agricultural chemical inputs on environment: global evidence from informetrics analysis and visualization. International Journal of Low-Carbon Technologies 13(4): 338–52.

Part I

Cultural considerations associated with sustainability certifications

2 Cultural implications, flows and synergies of sustainability certifications

Melissa Vogt[1]

Introduction

Embedding sustainability in mind and practice for all stakeholders can influence efficacy of sustainability efforts and a cultural shift can make this possible. Cultural sensitivity in approaches that encourage change, particularly within international trade dynamics, is essential.

Change in human behaviour through individual, institution and society has been considered necessary for effective sustainability outcomes (Beddoe *et al.* 2009; Assadourian 2010; Kinzig *et al.* 2013). Introducing sustainability as the guiding philosophy for cultural change is expected to better align a cultural awareness through all stakeholders. Understanding distinct stakeholder sustainability can avoid any one stakeholder dominating ideas of sustainability for other stakeholders. Coordinating sustainability cultural shifts according to stakeholder can address ingrained international trade power dynamics and provide opportunity to recognise and address cultural inappropriateness. The heterogeneity within stakeholder groups is important to recognise within a consideration of cultural implication and coordination of cultural shifts.

The process and methods used to encourage cultural shifts are rarely linear and are highly contextual (Steward 1972). A conscious cultural change toward improved sustainability can effectively ensure direction and method used to guide such change. There are cultural implications of managing, producing, sourcing and trading natural and human resources (Packalen 2010; De Beukelaer and Duxbury 2014) at institutional, government, organisational and producer or extractor levels, and then the societal level. Trade is considered a 'tool' of influence in the development and culture of a producing country (Watts 2006) with additional influence on cultural conservation and sustainability of a culture (Soini and Dessein 2016).

Original definitions of culture were in agriculture and the practice of producing or doing something routinely. It has since been used to explain the process and outcomes of training or refinement of the mind (Jahoda 1993; Shore 1998; Heyes 2012), with connotations of an educated person. Associating with the social phenomena of thinking, feeling and reacting, informed by understanding of symbols and then the human character and values

(Goldstein 1957; Girard 2008), culture relates to all people, and no one is born with it (Brocchi 2008). A process of social phenomena results in culture and there are numerous ways to define it (Jahoda 2012).

For this chapter, culture is considered relevant to training and refinement of the mind influenced by all components of character, values, social phenomena and symbols as related to sustainability and the sustainable management and trade of natural and human resources. With this understanding the investment, financial or resource-based, and variance in pedagogical approaches required to encourage a cultural shift is predominant as a significant consideration. Understanding of, communicating and achieving sustainability as a cultural shift can vary significantly, influenced by the many definitions used. A simplified idea of balanced outcome between environment, economic and societal outcomes, including ideas of equity and responsibility to future generations, is used. Further definitions and complementary concepts of sustainability are included through this book.

Culture is implicit to sustainability as it is implicit to the existing rationale and actions of all stakeholders involved in international and local trade and development. As such culture change can be a goal (Packalen 2010; De Beukelaer and Duxbury 2014), perhaps even a requirement, within all sustainability outcomes sought. Sustainable trade is a philosophical, social and practical movement with relevance to the channels and mechanisms which influence, regulate or practice production, sourcing or trade locally and internationally.

Several chapters in the book, while not explicitly mentioning culture, consider how sustainability certifications require changes in practice and mind, and the influential, occasionally underlying dynamics within specific contexts. This chapter will explicitly consider the cultural implications of sustainability certifications with relevance to several of these points. First, mechanisms for sustainability in international and local trade are explained; then, the cultural considerations of sustainability certifications as organisations. The influence of and on the different stakeholders that become certified or trade in certified produce are considered within cultural implication terms. The influence of and on producer countries is considered within the stakeholder category. The example of participatory guarantee systems (PGS) as a parallel sustainability effort that has come to be integrated and included in some sustainability certification procedures explains the possibility to improve options for cultural appropriateness. Finally, the cultural implication of consumer preference allowed by the premise of sustainability certifications as reliant on market demand is discussed.

Mechanisms for sustainability in international and local trade

Sourcing locally and eating seasonally as a cultural practice encourages improved investment in local production systems conducive to sustainable development through trade (Feenstra 1997; Stagle 2002; Birch *et al.* 2018). While local sourcing can improve transparency and verification of practices (Lindley 2019), efficacy of verification relies on proficient understandings and an ability to recognise practices that are truly sustainable. Consumption and production habits, and value given to 'the exotic' of imported products and resources might not easily or ever change. Shifts in consumption and international trade patterns will be gradual and possibly never be completed in terms of being 100 per cent local. As such, reliance on and dependence between countries through trade, with positive and negative cultural implications is expected to remain a necessary point for attention. Encouraging sustainable international trade may also allow opportunity for extended sustainable outcomes in other countries, valuable for preliminary or even long-term sustainability intentions.

Mechanisms that facilitate or require sustainability in international and local trade can assist with types of synergies, consistency and organisation in sustainable trade effort. There are several that work directly with trade stakeholders to shift practices. They often rely on codes of conduct and standards to guide consistency in sustainable practice. Requiring compliance to a code of conduct or standard will implicitly result in a cultural shift through understanding and behaviour change. Encouraging legitimacy and regulating sustainable trade across stakeholders also has cultural implication.

Corporate Social Responsibility (CSR) and Corporate Social Accountability (CSA) facilitate a sustainability culture shift within corporations with indirect cultural implication for contracted business, producers and their communities in terms of sourcing and processing natural and human resources (Prahald in Watts 2006), perhaps also for distributors. Their influence is therefore expected to be isolated to a corporation or business with indirect cultural implication for contracted business and producer organisations and communities. The approach to verification and therefore accountability has additional implications. Sustainability certifications complement CSR and CSA efforts, providing external guidance and facilitating behaviour change aligned with principles of sustainable development in trade. This guidance is provided to multiple stakeholders, adjusted according to their involvement with the certification process. Certifications and contracted third-party verifiers are directly involved with producer groups and countries and have greater direct reach across stakeholders through the standard introduction and verification of compliance, including, for example, a producer or extractor, a cooperative or producer business, smaller international or local business, a corporation and the consumer.

Whether the direct reach of sustainability certifications across stakeholders' results in more significant cultural influence and implication is not clear. There will, however, be variance in the cultural implication by stakeholder primarily due to the different culture of each stakeholder despite a commonality of interest in trade, perhaps not, however, trade terms. The extent of influence and implications of sustainability certifications may also vary across stakeholders with the implication of specific standard criteria varying for each stakeholder.

Codes of conduct and certifications are often voluntary approaches with distinct associated cultural implications compared to policy and legislated requirements. The definition of sustainability used conditions shifts as contributory to sought outcomes, and provisions against the likelihood of difference between codes of conduct and certifications. These differences influence the encouraged culture of sustainable development in trade, and the cultural implications of standards and certifications. Codes of conduct will often work with sustainability definitions that allow business to continue as close as possible to usual with some exceptions where innovation in business practice is considered positive and beneficial. Sustainability certifications on the other hand introduce sustainability-based standards that can complement, guide and better substantiate sourcing practices and codes of conduct. Their primary intention is sustainability for producing communities. They can complement, even improve codes of conduct where used by a business or corporation to guide purchases of particular certified products.

Certifications are entities: cultural considerations

Certifications, while stakeholders in the cultural shift toward sustainable production and trade, are also, as organisations or entities, explicit influencers external to international production and trade stakeholders. Their approach to 'business' has led to an industry or product range of certifications and labels. The cultural implication of international trade dynamics, international relations, academia and NGOs to their operations is important to recognise. They are not only impelling cultural implication, they are also subject to these implications from several different sources.

Many certifications started with small certified producer numbers and crop types subsequently developing organisational structure. Or, they developed organisational structure first through multistakeholder initiatives normally for one industry. The ladder became more common from the mid-1990s and 2000s. Momentum as an increase in certified markets has maintained through interaction with businesses of varying size and culture, and through social promotion and movements to garner support and improve community and consumer education and awareness. While fair trade has been involved in social promotion and movements, the other certifications have for the most part worked directly with existing business and producers to stir change and increase certified hectares and market sales. Promotion is normally directed to business, and to individual consumers through business marketing.

Gradually, certifications have had to respond and adapt to requirements of ISEAL, NGOs, international institutions and other observers of the sustainability certification movement. Simply trading products that improve forms of sustainability by any means is no longer sufficient. Compliance and standard quality has become required but remains variably assured. The intramarket but external to business role or position of sustainability certifications is unique and pertains to a level of cultural isolation by role and interactions with market actors. As the number of labels increases, competition between labels can also emerge. Within regionally specific trade channels, producers are subject to the cultural implication of numerous labels influenced by compliance ability and perhaps relationship between the certification and producer groups. Certifications or labels might be preferred by corporations and business based on criteria of minimal consequence to sustainability. For example, price, a preferred person or trade terms might tip a corporation or business preference for a certification or certified producer or extractor.

There are therefore cultural implications associated with the business model of sustainability certifications and their occasional real or perceived position between producer groups and greater business interests. Within this facilitator role, power dynamics in international trade make negotiating terms not only likely but necessary, case by case. How involved certifications become in this process between a sourcing and producing business will depend on the organisation and philosophical approach. The cultural implications of a certification organisation's original intentions, to certified producer groups and indirectly to a sustainability consumer movement, are relevant. The culture of sustainability certification organisations and associations is recognised therefore as an interesting area for future reflection. This chapter will, however, maintain attention on the cultural implications vis-à-vis the range of stakeholders who become certified or trade in certified produce.

Cultural implications for and of stakeholders

Sustainability certification efforts through standard development, implementation, verification and certificate processes have a cultural context. The unique location of sustainability certifications offers an intersection of cultures according to the numerous stakeholders, industries and countries involved, and then according to the number of sustainability certifications in operation. Cultural flows, influence and implication may change slightly by situation. For example, Sommer (2017, 17) considers spheres of facilitator, constraints and drivers for implementing sustainability standards against several factors. A consideration of cultural flows and contexts allows mobility in how each sphere reflects the different factors, depending on situation and stakeholder responsibility, with the exception of negative indicators, inadequate transparency and inoperability of standards, which remain as constraints.

Understanding cultural implication can therefore encourage fluidity in understanding successful approaches based on situation or context. Cultural influence can be a facilitator, driver or a constraint; it can also move in different directions between stakeholders. Approaching conscious and intentional cultural change varies by stakeholder and situation. Involvement with sustainability certifications requires adjustment in routine production, administrative and trade practice leading to cultural shifts. The cultural implications for and of consumers, corporations, smaller international business, and source/producer countries are considered in Table 2.1. In addition the influence of and on public regulation are included to recognise their presence and role. These are simplified points with opportunity for improving detail of considerations in the future.

Table 2.1 Influence of and on sustainability certifications

	Influence on	*Influence of*
Consumer	Culture of sustainable consumption through increased awareness and availability.	Preferences for one certification above another influencing sales. Potentially influencing corporate and business preferences where group consumption patterns and preferences are obvious.
Corporation★	Complementary effort to embed organisational sustainability and create a sustainability culture. Guide sourcing practices directly or indirectly.	Opportunity to increase sale and demand for certified products. Potentially imbalanced according to certification need to secure sales. Negotiating contracts and trade terms.
Smaller international or local business	As above for corporation. Possibly more direct than certification standard criteria requirements.	Potentially through direct interactions with producers toward implementation.
Producers and producer community	Conditioned by: Certification requirements Producer context. Evident according to cultural indicators.	Minimal with varying opportunity dependent on certification. Variance relies on inclusion of representative producers within certification structures. Option to not be involved.
Public regulation	Possible initiator through standard criteria, and philosophy in international trade.	Support and complementary measures to promote sourcing and distribution of certified produce. Support in regulation by national mechanisms.

Note
★ International and larger businesses with significant operations across multiple nations directly and/or possibly through joint business arrangement. Larger business determined by annual revenue, employee numbers, gross assets, market share within any industry.

A cultural shift is necessary for all stakeholders including consumers. It may, however, be more significant or necessary for those with tangible control and involvement, and for those less convinced or practiced in sustainability. Awareness raising about certifications is now rarely directly targeted at the individual consumer, instead via an existing product and brand. Numerous cultural indicators and flows determine the influence of sustainable practice for the various stakeholders (Axelsson *et al.* 2013; Miska *et al.* 2018; Testa *et al.* 2018). A business-to-business-based sustainability serves consumer demand and remains 'stakeholder centric' (Sheth and Sinha 2015), for example. The inevitable increase in tangible control from the stakeholder approach compared to the individual consumer approach can be positive and directly address common barriers to sustainability performance (Long *et al.* 2018), conditioned by reliability and control over the sustainability claims of each stakeholder. Particular nonconformity and misleading performance claims can become more obvious (Maniora 2018; Albareda and Waddock 2018), and synergies across stakeholder sustainability practice encouraged. The obligatory verification of sustainability certifications can also assist stakeholder-centric sustainability. Public regulation can control or officially recognise a certification process, serving as a form of endorsement and improving ideas of and, where possible, verifying legitimacy. The verification will ultimately determine how such public regulation ensures accuracy of such endorsement.

To consider Table 2.1 in more detail, consumers are separated from 'stakeholders', as the involvement of individual consumers in the certification process is limited to selecting a product based on a label with subsequent influence. The following explains, first, the cultural influence of and on corporations and smaller international business; then, the cultural implication of required processes from international and third-party certification systems in producing countries including an explanation of PGS. Finally, the consumer and their influence on and the influence of cultural flows resulting from sustainability certifications are considered.

Corporations and business

The influence of and on corporations is highly contextual and associated with specific power dynamics between several stakeholders and then between certifications and corporations. To discuss the difference, the simpler aspects of what can be complicated and situational dynamics are presented.

Influence of corporations

Improving foreign business activities in developing countries through CSR or CSA (Lobel 2017) thrusts transnational and multinational corporations (TNCs and MNCs) into 'the complex territory between economy and culture' (Prahald *et al.* in Watts 2006). The cultural implication in producing countries was likely never irrelevant; the difference now is a responsibility to be culturally appropriate as part of a social responsibility. TNCs and MNCs demonstrate significant control and are occasionally influential to or exempt from national and international legislative requirements, becoming a power unto themselves (Bartley 2018; Seid 2018).

> An increasing number of transnational entities and networks are carrying out the kinds of governing functions which are normally carried out by states, [and as such] questions of [the] authority and legitimacy [of] the source of any obligation to obey [arise].
>
> (de Burca 2005, 10–11)

This substantial and perhaps disproportionate control in international trade positively associates with market share and sales in most cases. Where significant proportions are owned by a few corporations, preference for one or multiple sustainability certifications is a significant influencing factor, with cultural implications. Corporations select certified products and become compliant to required procedures where trading certified products. Ease in transaction between a corporation and certification, preferred standard criteria or sourcing region, or resonance with a label's appearance or slogan may cause a corporation to prefer one certification above another. Consumer demand, internal codes of conduct or public regulation may also influence preference. Selecting a certification based on the most sustainable outcome is not therefore often possible due to limited proof or demonstration of outcomes.

Preference for particular certifications can also be considered in terms of cultural implications. Their own subjectivity according to preferred terms of use can easily be disassociated from an interest in effective societal and environmental outcomes resulting from particular sustainability certifications.

Relying on corporations to increase certified markets may easily provide opportunity to negotiate contracts and trade outside standard criteria. The influence of, compared to on, corporations will determine how certifications are able to ensure compliance. The influence of corporations may adjust certification requirements to ensure or ease corporate use. The cultural implication of this dynamic may be best understood within a 'culture of trade' context (Burch and Lawrence 2005). The influence on corporations and subsequent compliance can determine a corporation's positive sustainability influence on producers and trade brokers.

Influence on corporations

For corporations, there is usually an interest and need for sustainability education, particularly as embedding sustainability into all company operations can result in difficulty (Bertels *et al.* 2010; Wirtenberg 2014; Bernal *et al.* 2018). Synergy between internal business goals and externally set societal goals support sustainability through CSR (Ismail 2009; Baric 2017). Internal corporate practices can also be defined as corporate sustainability, with a possible influence on CSR outcomes (Montiel 2008). As a power unto itself an internal corporate cultural shift is essential. Internal codes of conduct can more easily embed sustainability through a corporation depending on approach to implementation.

External mechanisms continue to adapt pressure, and manage, support and encourage this relatively new dynamic toward embedding sustainability. Some are significantly attributed to encouraging corporate cooperation toward socially responsible and sustainable sourcing behaviour (Thorlakson *et al.* 2018), while others provide additional guidance and support to achieve these intentions. Sustainability certifications are an example of such an external mechanism, providing support toward achieving improved sustainable sourcing and increasing social responsibility. They can complement, influence and possibly improve internal codes, subsequently improving corporate or business sustainability and social responsibility. They can also become subject to such 'concerned citizen groups'.

Where used appropriately, sustainability certifications can also guide, complement, contribute to and influence any ongoing cultural change promoted by codes of conduct, and therefore influence corporate culture. As a voluntary mechanism the strength of influence depends ultimately on the cooperation and will depend on leverage held by certifications. Corporate compliance to voluntary certification requirements and therefore the influence on corporations may be supported by clarified alignment with existing internal codes of conduct, negative incentives and complementary external mechanism support via policy (see Chapter 8) or legislative requirements (Bruckner 2018).

Smaller international business

The influence of and on smaller business of sustainability can be considered similar. Cultural shifts resulting from compliance with sustainability certification standards are, however, distinct for smaller business and in terms of expected influence on producers, and producer countries. For a smaller company, direct involvement with farmers, farmer groups and community stakeholders, and the possibility of direct verification of sustainable practices can be more feasible and frequent (Vogt 2011, 2019; Latta 2014). Verification will, however, be limited by understandings held by any business representative. The power dynamic between smaller business and certifications, and smaller business and producers compared to corporations is also distinct, with an expected cultural implication. A smaller financial and resource ability to compensate or support required changes in practices may also distinguish smaller business effort from corporations, with contextual variance.

Cultural implication of systems and processes required by international sustainability certifications within producing countries

The role of certifications at international and national levels is multi-dimensional. To access a particular market, producers meet specific criteria which aim to benefit the farmer, the community and the environment. The criteria for the certification process depend on the philosophy of development and sustainability used by the certification and this can evolve and change. Efficacy is not synonymous with market presence. The cultural implications of these two angles provide for an understanding of changing practices with variable evidence of effectiveness or cultural appropriateness. The involvement of stakeholders in the sustainability certification process within the producer country may influence this situation. Stakeholders can include producers, extractors or labourers, and the involvement of each can vary. Where producers are organised into a cooperative or supply a standard business model directly the cooperative or business will be the primary 'inter-actor', with the exception of certified farmers well ingrained in the cooperative or business structure.

Direct interaction with a certification versus indirect or distant compliance is influential to but may not limit cultural implications. Understanding this impli-cation will depend on the sensitivity of the assessment. Distanced compliance compared to direct interaction with the certifications can cause distinct cultural implication at an organisational level and particularly in terms of paperwork and coordinating information dissemination. At a more conceptual level and within standard compliance requirements expected of producers, two examples are considered while many exist. First, the practices required associated with the certified natural resources. Second, the workers and labourers. Each example, particularly where requiring compliance within varying cultural and contextual situations, supports ideas of ensuring contextual rapport between stakeholders.

Practices required

Farming as a progression from foraging (Bar-Yosef 1998) is a cultural practice adjusted over the centuries with productive intention (Lund and Olsson 2006). Extracting natural resources at a small scale has also been considered this way (Ballick and Cox 1996; Tscharkert 2009; Vidhan 2010). While certi-fying conventional industries is required and beneficial for transforming some of the more harmful practices, international standard criteria can encourage or have homogenising effects where used for new initiatives seeking to sell through certified sustainable markets. Converting one agricultural practice for another to sell through a certified market may not for example result in improved environmental or societal outcomes. The incentive for particular crops, animals, species or other natural resources may change as the range of certified products increases and such change could reduce such conversions.

Transforming clearly damaging conventional practices to more sustainable practices through homogenous standard criteria does not guarantee cultural relevance or appropriateness. For example criteria to improve chemical handling practices, restricting crops, animal, species or other natural resources farmed or extracted, controlled harvest quotas and water management practices.

The practices required through standard criteria can also have variable efficacy for positive outcomes (see Chapter 3, for example) with possible cultural implication. Where positive outcomes are demonstrated, contextual relevance and cultural appropriateness are essential considerations that might demonstrate otherwise. Locally adapted and developed standards can assist to ensure such appropriateness.

Labour standards

The intricacy of developing and implementing labour standards effectively in agriculture or other industries is recognised for sustainability standards and certifications (Vogt 2011; Tampe 2016; Bennett 2017). Labour standards do vary and can represent more complicated cultural implications according to national and international labour standards and laws (Faist 2000). Certifications' understanding of cultural implication is necessary as they become involved, by distance, and/or in the day-to-day of implementing labour standard requirements via certified producers, producer groups and businesses. In some circumstances the conditions for labourers is beyond the more subtle intricacies of cultural appropriateness, moving into considerations of human rights, particularly for migrant workers (Azapagic 2014; Servin *et al.* 2018). Cultural appropriateness does, however, remain a relevant and important consideration, particularly where migrant or indigenous populations represent significant proportions of labourers and perhaps the community population. Appropriateness can relate to physical conditions, treatment, allowed flexibility or other labour rights inclusions, including gendered considerations.

Voluntary standards provide the opportunity to facilitate the implementation of nationally required labour conditions as well as flexibility conducive to cultural appropriateness. For example, the need to document, report and legitimise illegal or informal migrant workers can conflict with culturally related practices such as travel as a survival pattern, and other requirements of these populations. The industry within which they work and the time work is available (Toksöz 2018) is also related. Reporting and legalising their presence and employment can increase an ability to protect them; however, legal requirements may not easily or adequately allow for short-term or seasonal employment needs (Vogt 2011, 2019).

Cultural implication also relates to child labour, versus the cultural practice of including children in harvest. Drawing attention to the communities, particularly farming communities that have included and relied on the family for harvest and farm maintenance and management, variance must be addressed to avoid the significant and obvious exploitation of children while allowing for the cultural relevance of children working on a farm (Personal communication 2014) without significant disruption to schooling.

The cultural implication of labour standards is not therefore only according to what the certification allows and effectively restricts according to national and international labour standards and laws. It also provides the opportunity to address cultural appropriateness and adjust within the bounds of national laws that protect labourers and business. Where labour standard criteria of a certification system are limited in scope, or ineffectively implemented or audited, their relevance reduces alongside their cultural implication and opportunity for improved conditions for labourers with positive or neutral cultural influence. International sustainability certifications must therefore encapsulate perceptions of 'developed world' and 'human rights' while dealing with the in-community cultural realities and international trade dynamics to ensure cultural appropriateness.

Organisations such as the International Organisation for Migration (IOM) and International Labour Organisation (ILO), where present in-country, can provide some additional guidance. The extended experience that most producing communities would have with migrant labour communities can also be considered valuable, depending on how they value these populations and the conditions they have come to provide. This will vary according to industry and community and the significant difference between agricultural and extractive labour, such as mining according to conditions and the potential for exploitation (Downing 2002; see also Chapter 3). Guidance through labour standards is therefore considered necessary to ensure forms of consistency in conditions and treatment provided. The cultural intricacies of introducing such standards must be appropriately managed.

Participatory guarantee systems and certifications

Sustainability certifications are often referred to as third-party certifications due to the external approach to standard development, introduction and regulation. The processes required to be certified, as administrative and according to farming and employment practices, can occur in parallel to in-community and local efforts to improve sustainable farming and trade practices. Where third-party international certifications accommodate food security for example, parallel efforts may promote sustainable farming practices for food sovereignty and community relations rather than market need (Plieninger *et al.* 2018). Or simply promote sustainable noncertified farming to be traded locally, regionally or internationally.

These parallel efforts, many of which are parallel by time, and loosely by intention, have been integrated into third-party certification processes, considered an indication of cultural shift within the certification effort. Whether third-party certification processes should or do shift the cultural processes of parallel efforts is not addressed in this chapter. Details within each can be complementary; however, given in–community roots of the parallel efforts, it would not be considered a positive outcome unless hybrid combinations prove beneficial to the producing community. One parallel in–community effort is participatory guarantee systems (PGS) (see Figure 2.1).

A third–party sustainability certification process can integrate PGS, as do organic certifications for example, or PGS may develop into a unique certification and label – for example, Forest Garden Products is a smaller PGS–led certification label. All approaches can contribute to CSR or CSA efforts that seek to adjust practices of dominant market players. For a third–party certification effort, PGS can contribute to societal outcomes as related to social processes as well as farm system outputs. For example, where PGS are used by third–party certification schemes for international and local trade they can contribute to food sovereignty by local subsistence and community level production systems, with or without certification.

The guiding philosophy of farming or production standards is open, introducing opportunity for optimising environmental outcomes. Agroecology and/or organic are often combined with PGS processes. Forest Garden Products use different types of environmental processes and principles. PGS can also contribute to noncertified international or national markets, external to sustainability certification, or to local produce for subsistence or barter (see Figure 2.1). In this last situation, PGS can become an example of an emerging producer and landscape sustainability solution, contributing to local sustainability questions of food sovereignty and farmer connection outside the international trade and certification discussion.

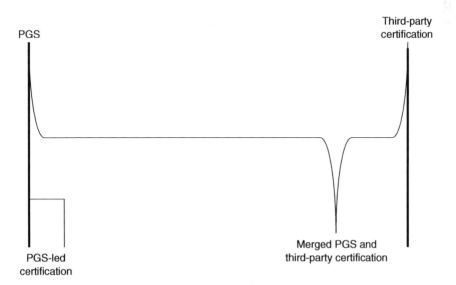

Figure 2.1 Third–party certification and PGS as parallel efforts: as they merge or maintain independence.

Two independent studies explain the definition and implications of PGS and demonstrate the contexts within which PGS may be used. They are recommended as complementary reading for this chapter. Study 2.1 considers how PGS can complement organic certification processes through participatory compliance assessment. Study 2.2 is a summary of an independent study of PGS in Spain. The two perspectives facilitate understanding of PGS and sustainability certification contributions as parallel efforts, and then how they might merge at particular points to encourage sustainable outcomes in productive landscapes.

The cultural implication of PGS is comparable to the cultural implication of 'third-party' or international sustainability certification processes for producer countries and landscapes. However, each represents distinct cultural implications for producers and producer landscapes. PGS are locally led yet rarely a natural cultural process in agricultural or productive landscapes and systems. A learning and information exchange process of accumulating and disseminating information, developing conditioned social relationships and then verification is involved. Peer verification of PGS compared to independent, as used by third-party certification, is a point for further consideration. PGS do offer an opportunity to provide locally driven ideas and promote cultural appropriateness distinct to international sustainability certifications.

Study 2.1 What PGS are and how they work

Excerpt from IFOAM EU 2015 publication 'Feeding the People: Agroecology for Nourishing the World and Transforming the Agri-Food System'. Authors: Robert Home and Erin Nelson.[2]

Participatory guarantee systems are locally focused quality assurance systems that certify producers based on active participation of stakeholders, and are built on a foundation of trust, social networks, knowledge building and exchange (IFOAM 2015). They are viable organic verification systems that offer an alternative and are complementary to third-party certification. With their relatively low associated costs and reduced paperwork burden, PGS are particularly appropriate for local markets and organized smallholder farmers (Nelson *et al.* 2010). PGS are also context-specific, with each one responding to the particular challenges and conditions faced by producers, consumers and stakeholders in the organic sector of a specific place. Although this means that every PGS initiative is locally adapted and, to some extent unique, all share a number of key elements and features, including: a shared vision; active participation of multiple stakeholders; transparency of process; trust as a foundational element; conceptualizing certification as a learning process; and horizontality, meaning that all members share equally in the rights and responsibilities related to how the system is established and maintained (IFOAM 2015).

A typical PGS initiative involves producers and other stakeholders such as consumers, staff from NGOs, universities and extension services, government representatives, and consultants (Nelson *et al.* 2010). Producers, and sometimes other stakeholders, are typically organized in local groups that are collectively responsible for ensuring that the participating producers adhere to PGS standards and processes. Generally, each farmer receives an annual site visit from this locally-based group. Results of the farm visit are summarized in a report, which serves as a basis for the group to make decisions regarding the extent to which a producer is in compliance (or not) with the agreed upon organic standards. Summaries of this documentation and certification decisions are usually then communicated to a higher level, for example a regional or national council representing PGS stakeholders. These higher-level councils or organizations are generally responsible for the overall oversight and administration of the PGS program and they often represent the PGS in communications with external stakeholders such as the government and IFOAM (Castro 2014). In some cases, they endorse certification decisions made by the local groups, while in other cases they grant general approval to local-level authorities for independent use of the PGS label.

PGS and social processes

Participatory guarantee systems are more than just a low-cost mechanism for organic certification. They are also a means of facilitating social processes that enable inclusion, farmer empowerment and mutual support among farmers and between farmers and consumers. Social processes include the networking involved in gaining PGS accreditation and a range of parallel processes that both support, and are supported by, the PGS. Among the most important and consistent findings of research on PGS has been the contribution of these parallel social processes – including collective use of knowledge and resources – to the maintenance and union of PGS groups. Participation in social processes has proven to help foster the mutual trust and strong personal relationships that are a key factor in the long-term success of PGS. In addition to contributing to the stability and success of the PGS, social processes also provide direct and indirect benefits to participating farmers.

The trust-based relationships play an important role in providing organic farmers a sense of community that might otherwise be lacking. Experience from PGS initiatives around the world has shown that participation in PGS provides opportunities, and creates favorable environments, for peer learning and sharing of knowledge and resources between farmers (Kirchner 2014), which enables farmers to build capacity that can help them improve the quality and quantity of their organic production over time. A manifestation of social processes frequently observed in combination with PGS is the organization of collective use of resources, sometimes known as self-help groups, which are important to the success of many PGS. Self-help groups have become an entry point into many PGS communities at a grassroots level and provide a platform for various intervention activities, such as:

- Collective buying, which reduces costs;
- Joint marketing, which is essential to the expansion of market opportunities;
- Establishing seedbanks, which gives farmers access to varieties suited to local conditions;

- Supporting collective logistics in transportation for farmers who are often geographically isolated; and
- Enabling farming households to access affordable credit for agricultural and other purposes (Home *et al.* 2017).

Participation in the collective actions of self-help groups, with their own social processes, reinforces the social inclusion, farmer empowerment and mutual support between producers and consumers that are inherent in PGS. Given that PGS are commonly composed of people living in close proximity and sharing the same ideals, support needs can be delivered in a way that is tailored to the individuals. For example, monitoring of credit usage and repayment is easier and the need for coercion is also reduced (Home *et al.* 2017).

PGS contributions to food security

By increasing market access and, specifically, making the organic label and associated price premiums more accessible to small-scale producers, PGS often lead to at least some measure of increased income for participating farmers. Because many farmers still rely heavily on purchased foods to meet their household needs, increased income directly contributes to improvements in food security.

Study 2.2 Some learnings from Spanish PGS initiatives

Mamen Cuellar Padilla[3]

Confidence building in the organic sector is based, after the European public regulation in 1991, on the third-party certification system. It is the only procedure officially recognised. However, many CSA and short food supply chains initiatives are building their own procedures, within the participatory guarantee systems (PGS) umbrella. PGS are not an officially recognised system, so farmers using such procedures will not be legally recognised as organic producers. They will therefore face major limitations as they seek to develop their businesses, whether in terms of marketing (they will be excluded from all officially organic certified supply chains, for instance); or in terms of public support (they will be excluded from public organic food procurement programmes, for instance). Despite these draw backs, PGS have experienced important growth in the last years. After fieldwork based on participatory observation and qualitative research of five cases of PGS in Spain, and the configuration of a national PGS network in the last four years, we can conclude that PGS are presenting many political issues relevant to the organic sector. After the outcomes of the research, we can affirm that these issues run in parallel to the discussion between organic and agroecological production, and food security and sovereignty.

The shape, shapes

Farmers participating in PGS generally express their rejection of the third-party certification. In the situation that both systems are combined, the reasons are related to the need of the official label to sell in certain channels or to access certain public subsidies, but never as a free option. In Table 2.2, we present the characteristics of the PGS studied and compare them with those of the official third-party certification system, allowing us to identify the key differences and possible reasons for this rejection.

Table 2.2 Main differences of PGS and official third-party certification systems identified

Basic parameters	Third party certification (based on the ER834/2007)	Participatory guarantee systems
Decision making	The decisions on what is evaluated and how are taken at an institutional level and by the certification entity or body. Producers and consumers are passive actors, no decisions from them are required.	All the decisions on what, how and when are taken at the social network level. Producers and consumers define what they want it to be and how.
Guarantee responsible/s	Certification bodies or entities (public administrations or private enterprises). Always nonlocal technical and institutional figures.	Local social networks of producers and consumers.
Bureaucracy required	Complex documents designed at technical bureaus. Public administration and private enterprises assume the task.	Flexible documents designed by the networks. Producers and consumers design how to translate into documents the principles to be evaluated and the procedures.
Costs	Expensive mechanism. Costs related to qualified technical staff (auditors and managers at the certification body); costs related to the maintenance of the certification body structure; costs related to the travel expenses of the technical inspectors to the farms.	Cheap procedure. The implication of the members allow substitution of monetary costs by time, which is not remunerated; costs related to travel expenses of the group visit to the farm.
Transparency	None. Confidentiality is guaranteed by law. None of the operators information can be published.	Complete. All the members of the networks know exactly the results of the proceedings.
Nonconformity consequences	The certification is denied. Loss of commercialisation opportunities.	The producer is dropped from the network. The person loses not only the guarantee, but confidence inside the network (social consequences). They lose commercialisation channels; support and mutual aid mechanisms.

Source: Cuéllar-Padilla and Ganuza-Fernández (2018, 1142).

There are parallels between PGS/third-party certification, and 'alternative food networks'/'neoliberal food systems'. PGS are part of what has also been commonly invoked as 'food citizenship', 'food democracy', and 'civic food networks' (Renting *et al.* 2012).

Indeed, PGS are consistent with the idea of re-localising and re-socialising the concept of the food system (Marsdem *et al.* 2000), as expressed by Schermer (2015) via the notion of 'food from somewhere'. PGS establish trust in local food systems and refer to goals of autonomy and empowerment, similar to ideas first developed in 1996 as a result of proposed food sovereignty policies (Cuéllar *et al.* 2013), driven by the Via Campesina international movement (cf. McMichael 2009; Desmarais 2007).

The regional groups that have built PGS in Spain are not following official regulations. Instead, they subscribe to an alternative system that is not officially recognised and assume the consequences. PGS do not correspond to either of the movement types defined by Friedmann and McNair (2008): (1) movements that adopt constructive, nonconfrontational strategies with regards to the powers that be (i.e. governmental institutions and for-profit corporations); and (2) movements that adopt radical, combative strategies. PGS do not seek to either inform or fight government regulations and/or official systems of governance. Their strategy is building autonomy, and they assume the resulting costs and disadvantages; the official recognition of PGS is not therefore assumed or considered an advantage (IFOAM 2014, 2–3).

Such verification invites us to affirm that the regulations a society establishes are not neutral. They are framed by a specific perspective on the role of public institutions, private stakeholders and civil society. When establishing regulations such as those governing the organic sector, policy choices have important implications. Society can choose an approach that strengthens the tendency toward globalisation and that bolsters international markets via the adoption of common technical rules, or an approach that favours local initiatives emerging from the needs and interests of local stakeholders. These decisions are not made based on economic/societal concerns or on in-depth analyses. Instead they arise from cognitive systems or systems of reference, which inform not only practices (cf. Stassart and Jamar 2009) but also government regulations. As such, regulations in the organic sector are the product of conventional cognitive systems; they have established mandatory mechanisms that significantly impact the sector's development. And this is the basis of the main reasons why producers getting engaged in PGS in Spain reject the official organic certification system.

The coexistence of the two types of approaches has therefore developed: (1) a production-based paradigm that promotes international trade and globalised agri-food systems and that thus adopts commonly shared international standards and procedures that are determined by government regulations and technical bodies; or (2) principles such as food sovereignty and food democracy (Cuéllar and Calle 2011) which have not been taken into account in any of the European organic regulations discussed and approved until now. The shift in certification-related responsibilities implies an alternative vision of food and farming, one in which food is a 'commons' rather than a politicised 'commodity' associated with differential rights (Vivero-Pol 2017). Such proposed changes fit within the idea of food citizenship (Lozano and Gómez 2017), whereby everyday citizens participate in the governance of food systems, whether by producing food, making food consumption choices, or both. And the affirmation that directly arises is: these preconditions are strongly contextual, by location and time.

PGS are not recipes, nor a global solution for alternative food systems

The main internal challenges for every community that aims to build a PGS are related to a radical governance change. As a result, PGS are not adapted to all contexts, nor are they universal solutions to the certification problem. In the context of the Spanish PGS network, participants' initiatives stressed that one of the main internal challenges faced is time requirements. Another important internal challenge identified is handling disagreements. Expressing a member's noncompliance to established standards can be difficult. As such, fear of creating open conflict can prevent PGS from functioning properly. A third element to be considered is the required consensus about specific principles for a PGS. This initial step requires a concerted collective effort to determine what PGS members want and why. This process, which involves negotiation and teamwork, requires openness and tolerance on the part of those involved. Finally, it can be challenging to carry out farm visits to check for compliance and generate spaces for learning and exchange. Members shared that they may feel insecure about their ability to look for and properly identify evidence of noncompliance.

The main difficulties encountered by PGS are therefore presented by the suite of tasks that are usually outsourced in third-party certification. In addition, PGS require a high degree of social mobility, and significant political involvement. While intentions for a horizontal structure may be pursued, when there are project leaders at certain points in time, they might assume important responsibilities. When the procedure is promoted by one or a few people that have the time or the resources to dedicate to the PGS, collective action as non-horizontal structure might be developed.

Consumers and influential cultural flows

Individual consumers are not certified, leaving them slightly external to the above stakeholder considerations. The influence of individual consumers according to purchase patterns, behaviours and preference is, however, significant. A low level of resistance to changes in price or procedure required by certifications, and a positive response from consumers often motivates corporations and business to integrate CSR through their activities and principles. Greig-Gran (2006) believed in the strength of a consumer movement while Leclair (2002) and Shaw and Black (2010) warned against overestimating the influence of certifications, consumer awareness and the action upon which they rely.

Positive association with a brand is one tactic used by many businesses to increase and maintain demand and sales (Bartels and Hoogendam 2011); sustainable labels complement this tactic. It is realistic to suppose that sustainability logos hold significant brand association value and contribute to brand salience further influencing business preference. Sustainability logos therefore reinforce or guide sustainable purchases by using a surface sustainability measure for consumers at the point of sale. The influence of logos and branding can be significant (Carpenter *et al.* 1994; Singh and Pandey 2012) and individual consumer preference, particularly at a population level, may influence business, and subsequently market supply and demand. Compared to the effort required to develop, introduce and implement standards, marketing messages and psychology can appear surface level. They do, however, contribute significantly toward promoting and facilitating a cultural shift in consumption practices. The certification system works from this idea to promote change through these softer measures.

Usually and particularly to begin with only standard commodities were certified, and 'normal' products labelled, easing the cultural implication and transition for consumers and increasing chances of success. There needed only to be a lack of opposition to a sustainable product in this case. An increase in a certified product range requires further refinement of the mind and cultural change for the consumer. This is more so the case where detailed consumer understanding of what the logo represents in sustainability terms is considered necessary.

Table 2.3 provides an example of slogans and basic online and point-of-sale information available for a selection of certifications. Bearing in mind the number of labels that currently operate as listed in Chapter 1, this is not representative. Where the consumer does pay attention and purchases accordingly, the difference between these messages can be relevant.

Sustainability is the most consistent principle from these examples, with limited specificity as to what sustainability is. Outcomes resulting from implemented and verified standards are most important (Ditlev-Simonsen and Midttun 2011) and from this information indeterminable. It is therefore up to a consumer cultural shift that includes more detailed understanding where consumer influence can ensure and encourage positive cultural flows.

Centralised and subtle cultural flows: consumer to producer

The consumer influence through compassion and preference has been necessary and arguably significant in encouraging sustainable trade practices. Labels have in part guided their involvement and influence, as entry and education points. Reliance on labels and possibly label preferences does introduce a level of subjectivity with potential cultural flow to producer countries. The subjectivity is only significant where subsequent outcomes are not substantiated or assured.

Accommodating consumer niche preferences for a label or having labels compete and adapt marketing to attract consumer preference makes sense in market terms. Cultural implications may not, however, be positive at the producer level. The distance between consumer and producer within international trade can limit the ability to ensure legitimacy and adequately connect consumer or business surface understanding and a producer, and producer countries', positive outcome. The cultural implication for producing countries can

Table 2.3 Examples of basic marketing information available to consumers

Examples of marketing messages
Slogans are not always displayed on the package. The length of time these certifications have been on the market usually indicates a reduced need for explanation or slogan next to the label. Familiarity is already established or was decided to be consequential but not primarily significant for purchase. This can also be influenced by marketing and communication approach, and the certification requirements. Slogans and marketing claims that can be found online, though official information sources are included in the table.

Certification	Slogan	Online information
Fairtrade	Fairtrade	Fairtrade International/FLOCERT Fairtrade International(FI) is a multistakeholder, nonprofit organisation focusing on the empowerment of producers and workers in developing countries through trade. Fairtrade International provides leadership, tools and services needed to connect producers and consumers, promote fairer trading conditions and work towards sustainable livelihoods. Fairtrade.com.au Fairtrade is about stable prices, decent working conditions and the empowerment of farmers and workers. Fairtrade.net Fairtrade is an alternative approach to conventional trade.
Rainforest Alliance	Rainforest Alliance We work with you to rebalance the planet	We are an international not for profit organisation. We stand for biodiversity conservation and sustainable livelihoods.
Utz Kapeh Merged with Rainforest Alliance in 2018	Utz Kapeh Better farming better future: endorse sustainable farming	A programme and label for sustainable farming. UTZ certification shows consumers that products have been sourced, from farm to shop shelf, in a sustainable manner. To become certified, all UTZ suppliers have to follow our Code of Conduct, which offers expert guidance on better farming methods, working conditions and care for nature. This leads to better production, a better environment and a better life for everyone.

continued

Table 2.3 Continued

Certification	Slogan	Online information
Organic Twenty-seven country and regional labels and variations within	Organic certified Some include biodynamic farming. Some specify soil organics.	Label or association based.
Veriflora	Veriflora sustainably grown	Certification for sustainable ornamental horticulture. Veriflora® Sustainably Grown certification provides cut flower and potted plant producers from all over the world with a detailed roadmap to satisfy the emerging market for sustainable products.
European Biochar Certificate	EBC foundation/ certificate	The European Biochar Certificate (EBC) has been developed by biochar scientists to become the voluntary European industrial standard. The EBC ensures a sustainable biochar production and low hazard use in agronomic systems. It is based on the latest scientific data, it is economically viable and close to technical and agricultural practice. Users of biochar and biochar-based products will benefit from a transparent and verifiable monitoring and independent quality control.
Fairmined	From Responsible Mining Communities	Fairmined transforms mining into an active force for good, providing everyone with a source of gold to be proud.
RSB	RSB	Our user-friendly certification scheme is the strongest and most trusted of its kind. RSB's certification ensures that any bio-based feedstock, biomass-derived material and any advanced fuel, and complete supply-chains and novel technologies are socially responsible, environmentally sustainable and credibly sourced – supporting the mitigation of business, environmental and social risk.
FSC	Forests for all, forever	When you choose FSC you help support principles and actions that protect our air, water and overall quality of life.
MSC	Supporting sustainable fishing	The Marine Stewardship Council is an international nonprofit organisation. We recognise and reward efforts to protect oceans and safeguard seafood supplies for the future.

also differ depending on how many certification standards are developed and implemented.

Certified producer organisations change organisational and production practices with cultural adjustment, as well as financial and time resource requirements. Understanding the benefit of certified hectares depends on perspective and the availability of studies. Increases in certified hectares and certification numbers (Lernoud *et al.* 2017) does not closely associate with changes in sales over time through certified markets (Potts *et al.* 2014). Sales are often required to support and compensate necessary efforts to certify hectares conditioned by financial or other incentives from certified markets. Given the required resources, cultural adjustments and the international trade context of developing and developed economies, compliance with minimal market incentive may be considered a negative cultural implication. Outcomes are also conditioned by overall benefit of compliance to the producer and producer community associated, benefit which can be influenced by the sustainability certification most requested. A market demand premise of sustainability certifications does therefore represent possible cultural flows from consumers to producers, distanced or direct. The significance of these flows will be determined by how influential individual consumer preference is, and how consistently effective associated environmental and societal outcomes are.

In most cases standards and certification procedures are developed and introduced in a centralised manner. A centralisation of cultural flows between consumer, individual or business and producers does then occur. Evans (2002, 59) considers 'centralisation of power over the cultural flows that shape preferences [as] a more subtle form of "unfreedom" than [the dimensions of development as freedom] that Sen highlights but no less powerful'. Within a power dynamic context, centralised requirements of sustainability certifications could be understood as necessary. In this circumstance, centralising cultural flows across developing and developed economy divides requires some care and discretion. Chapter 1 lists the many certificates and labels available, demonstrating how cultural flow may centralise across a range of certification efforts. Distanced yet somewhat direct and subjective flows from consumer to producer may, however, be difficult to define as appropriate.

Variable regulation of positive brand association approaches, occasionally called 'defensive CSR', does mean labels can support greenwashing. Accepting a level of inaccuracy in logo claims can be necessary to address the preliminary phase of many certifications and labels and a need to increase sales and demand for certified produce. Where potential to correct or improve efforts is assured and intended it could be considered acceptable, and extended centralised cultural flows could decline.

Alternatively, removing the 'blind' influence of consumers and improving the reliability of products available on the market (Dine and Shields 2008) can reduce the 'burden' to consumers and the opportunity for subjective cultural implications on producers and producing communities. Required procedures and standards across the range of labels and certificates available must therefore be of a quality and appropriateness to reduce the opportunity for subjective influence. Label preferences based on inaccurate claims require further and critical examination, as do misaligned outcomes to intentions. Thresholds for sustainability certification label claims might be introduced to manage and reduce misleading claims. Examples already exist, including stating the percentage of product content certified or including the stories of producer groups. However, they do not yet clarify the efficacy of aligned label intentions as associated environmental or societal outcomes.

Complementary efforts such as policy, law, in-country programmes and standards, and other independent expert efforts are likely to strengthen certification efforts. Improving evaluations and studies related to sustainability certifications is also expected to improve efforts. Recognising cultural differences between scholarly disciplines where seeking interdisciplinary studies, or drawing together disciplinary studies and findings related to associated outcomes can also contribute positively. Local policy, institutions, community organisation, codes of conduct and law (Singh and Pandey 2012) within producer or consumer countries, and locally developed and verified standards supported by certifications and labels could also assist. Such complementary efforts can support an increase in import, distribution, availability and market share of certified produce (CBI 2018), reducing reliance on consumer and corporate demand and standardising the sustainability of produce available.

Summary: limiting rifts in positive cultural flows

Correcting a historic legacy of economic and production priority is significant. Change requires strict and softer approaches to address the variety of stakeholders influential to and reliant on production and international trade. Sustainability is not often a natural progression and conscious effort for change is easily complemented by a cultural shift. Embedding sustainability within a corporate, business or producer association or organisation is expected to improve compliance and various pedagogical methods have developed to facilitate intracorporate cultural shifts (Schulz *et al.* 2018). The exercise of embedding sustainability can, however, be challenging (Bertels *et al.* 2010; Wirtenberg 2014; Bernal *et al.* 2018), conditioned by the type of sustainability required, intention across efforts and an aligned sustainability culture across stakeholder groups. Coordinating cultural shifts across stakeholders encourages more sustainable practice for three reasons. First, the number of cultures a product transfers through, by country or region and by stakeholder, before reaching a consumer provides significant opportunity for cultural difference and inappropriateness. Second, an ingrained power dynamic can substantially influence cultural flows and dominance conducive to cultural inappropriateness unless care is taken. Finally, a cultural shift for each stakeholder, rather than for only one, can encourage long-term change in practice and mind toward sustainability, and, where coordinated, dominance from one stakeholder and resulting inappropriateness can reduce.

A refinement of mind and social phenomena based on sustainability values across sector and stakeholder is expected to result from embedding sustainability. The required shift will differ according to stakeholder, influenced by the varying definitions of sustainability used. Intercultural compromise is likely necessary and inevitable within international trade contexts, and cultural inappropriateness and dominance should be kept to a minimum. Gradual improvement and an openness to recognising and reducing negative cultural implications where necessary and possible is required. There are several mechanisms used to facilitate such a shift with varying cultural implications including centralised cultural flows.

Sustainability certifications provide direct external guidance across stakeholders through somewhat centralised standard development, introduction and verification processes. Centralised guidance can cause a homogenisation effect with variable benefit to sustainability outcomes. Where occurring across stakeholders, countries and industries there is an increasingly significant opportunity for cultural inappropriateness and dominance influenced also by sustainability definitions used and subsequent guidance provided. Commonalities and apparent alignment in definitions of sustainability are likely at the macro level where cultural implications might also appear appropriate. Granular similarities or differences between codes of conduct and sustainability certifications can better indicate cultural appropriateness and implications according to the definitions of sustainability evidently used.

A sustainability culture and appropriateness of cultural implication relies on several flows between stakeholders, between stakeholders and sustainability certification organisations, and between consumers, stakeholders and sustainability certifications. The influence of sustainability certifications on resulting practices at more intricate levels are still to be well understood. In-community cultural realities represent a significant learning curve for sustainability certifications. Significant research and practical shifts are required to ensure consistency in cultural appropriateness. Developing contextual rapport, particularly where seeking compliance in culturally appropriate ways, can certainly ease potential intricacies and contribute well to cultural shifts. Unifying sustainability intentions and approaches while allowing for contextual variations may also assist to ensure a sustainability culture and appropriate cultural implications. Improvements in appropriateness across certifications are continually evident.

PGS provide an opportunity to recognise producer-based and -initiated processes using locally developed standards and verification processes. They can improve opportunity for cultural appropriateness within producing countries and reduce the centralisation of cultural flows. Hybrids of locally developed and international sustainability certification standards and verification processes are limited by contextual appropriateness according to the certification and the producing community and country, and adjustment phases might be required. Influence for consumers will be minimal and for producing countries and communities potentially significant. However, and to ensure cultural appropriateness and comprehensive consideration, producer preference toward international trade structures conducive to their autonomy within the community compared to local systems such as PGS is important to consider. The effectiveness of sustainability certifications and PGS, and sustainability cultural shifts may well rely on getting this balance right.

Increasingly more attention is given to business above individual consumer preference by certifications. Further cultural implication considerations might become more sophisticated and stakeholder inclusive.

Advanced individual sustainable consumption patterns rely on country of origin, seasonality, distributor or other indicator to guide purchase preferences. Environmental and local economy concerns can also shift consumption practices conducive to sustainable international and local production and trade, and consumption (Welch and Graham 1999; Cakmak 2002; Toledo and Burlingame 2006; Ebert 2014; Kumar and Smith 2017; Valley *et al.* 2017; Lachat *et al.* 2018). These additional consumer preferences may remove the relevance of or increase the preference for sustainable produce (Luchs *et al.* 2010; Torquati *et al.* 2018). A strengthened culture of sustainable consumption, and allowance for these additional preferences, can ensure that consumer preference and business incentive for sustainable produce are maintained. It may also prove useful in promoting improved ambition in sustainable trade practices. Increasingly more attention is given to business over individual consumer preference by certifications, which furthers market level support and demand for certified produce. Leveraging market demand to support a sustainable culture shift has proven useful; however, with numerous labels and standards available there is still a possibility that a consumer preference, particularly business and population-level preferences, lead demand for particular standards which are not verified as culturally appropriate or adequately sustainable. Cultural shifts often but not only rely on ideas of responsibility contributing to momentum and stability within a sustainability culture. Feelings of complacency driven by ideas of ineffectiveness or greenwashing should therefore be avoided, particularly where change and understanding are at a cultural level across stakeholders and consumers. As an additional point, cultural shifts can be conducive to limiting greenwashing (Testa *et al.* 2018) and here is an example of influential multidirectional cultural flows. Sustainability certifications are also only one of many mechanisms and points of influence for consumer preference.

Common cultural contexts provide opportunity for coordinated cultural shift, such as workplaces (Süßbauer and Schäfer 2018), education institutions (Christensen *et al.* 2018) and between generations (Powell and Wittman 2018), supported by accreditation processes including or without labels (Goldman *et al.* 2018). Recognising additional cultural differences among the various stakeholders involved in sustainable trade practice, or the evaluation and promotion of it such as the difference between scholarly disciplines, and the various formal and informal 'concerned citizen groups' of sustainable trade efforts, may also improve appropriateness of response, expectations and approach to promoting change and improvement.

Embedding sustainability through the culture of all involved stakeholders in an appropriate and meaningful way is expected to improve outcomes and possibly contribute to an improved balance in power dynamics within international national trade contexts. Sustainability certifications can contribute to such cultural embedding and will most likely be more effective where complemented by other mechanisms and an organisation that is already 'sustainable' by intention and operation.

Acknowledgements

Melissa Vogt wrote this chapter based on learnings and reflections after considering sustainability certifications for garments and coffee over an 11-year period. The reflections and considerations included here are intended as basic, and preliminary to support existing studies related to cultural implications of sustainable trade, and sustainability certifications, and to provoke some new areas for future considerations and research. She learnt about PGS while carrying out fieldwork in 2014 and was able to learn more about farmer to farmer networks and information sharing while conducting fieldwork in Cuba. The invited contributing authors' work is considered essential for the understanding encouraged in this chapter. The contribution of PGS within local and international supply contexts is an important distinction within PGS considerations, which provides rationale for the summaries included. Appreciation is expressed to the contributing authors for summarising their work or seeking permissions efficiently to allow for inclusion in this chapter.

The majority of the chapters in this book reinforce ideas touched on in this chapter. These chapters provide additional detail by specific certification or country contexts. They might not, however, explicitly mention cultural implications.

Notes

1 With an excerpt from Robert Home and Erin Nelson; and a study summary by Mamen Cuella Padella.
2 For further information about how PGS contribute to food security outside the scope of organic certification, and recommendations for how PGS can facilitate the potential for agroecology to feed the world, see the original publication and associated (Home and Nelson 2015).
3 This summary was developed systematising different field work moments developed between 2012 and 2017. Related publications are cited through the text. For further information see these publications and a more recent article by Cuéllar and Ganuza-Fernandez (2018).

References

Albareda L., Waddock S. (2018). Networked CSR governance: a whole network approach to meta-governance. Business and Society 57(4): 636–75.

Assadourian E. (2010). The rise and fall of consumer cultures. In Worldwatch Institute. State of the World 2010: Transforming Cultures. W.W. Norton and Co., 3–20.

Axelsson R., Angelstam P., Degerman E., Teitelbaum S., Andersson K., Elbakidze M., Drotz M.K. (2013). Social and cultural sustainability: criteria, indicators, verifier variables for measurement and maps for visualisation to support planning. Ambio 42(4): 215–28.

Azapagic A. (2014). Developing a framework for sustainable development indicators for the mining and minerals industry. Journal of Cleaner Production 12(6): 639–62.

Ballick M.J., Cox P.A. (1996). Plants, People and Culture: The Science of Ethnobotany. Scientific American Library.

Bar-Yosef O. (1998). The Natufian culture in the Levant, threshold to the origins of agriculture. Evolutionary Anthropology 6(5): 159–77.

Baric A. (2017). Corporate Social Responsibility and stakeholders: review of the last decade (2006–2015). Business Systems Research 8(1): 133–46.

Bartels J., Hoogendam K. (2011). The role of social identity and attitudes toward sustainability brands in buying behaviours for organic products. Journal of Brand Management 18(9): 697–708.

Bartley T. (2018). Transnational corporations and global governance. Annual Review of Sociology 44: 145–65.

Beddoe R., Costanza R., Farley J. et al. (2009). Overcoming systemic roadblocks to sustainability: the evolutionary redesign of worldviews, institutions, and technologies. Proceedings of the National Academy of Sciences 106: 2483–89. https://doi.org/10.1073/pnas.0812570106.

Bennett E. (2017). Voluntary sustainability standards: a squandered opportunity to improve workers' wages. Sustainable Development 26(1): 65–82.

Bernal E., Edgar D., Burnes B. (2018). Building sustainability on deep values through mindfulness nurturing. Ecological Economics 146: 645–47.

Bertels S., Papania L., Papania D. (2010). Embedding Sustainability in Organisational Culture: A Systematic Review of the Body of Knowledge. Network for Business Sustainability. https://api.van2.auro.io:8080/v1/AUTH_6bda5a38d0d7490e81ba33fbb4be21dd/sophia/blox/assets/data/000/000/058/original/Systematic-Review-Sustainability-and-Corporate-Culture.pdf?1492524392.

Birch D., Memery J., De Silva Kanakarantke M. (2018). The mindful consumer: balancing egoistic and altruistic motivations to purchase food. Journal of Retailing and Consumer Services 40: 221–28.

Brocchi D. (2008). The cultural dimension of sustainability. In S. Kagan, V. Kirchberg (Eds). Sustainability: A New Frontier for the Arts and Cultures. VAS, 26–58.

Bruckner K.D. (2018). Development in an era of capital control: embedding Corporate Social Responsibility within a transnational regulatory framework. Journal of Energy and Natural Resource Law 36(2): 255–58.

Burch D., Lawrence G. (2005). Supermarket own brands supply chains and the transformation of the agri-food system. International Journal of the Sociology of Agriculture and Food, 13: 1–28.

Cakmak I. (2002). Plant nutrition research: priorities to meet human needs for food in sustainable ways. Plant and Soil 247(1): 3–24.

Carpenter G.S., Glazer R., Nakamoto K. (1994). Meaningful brands from meaningless differentiation: the dependence on irrelevant attributes. Journal of Marketing Research 31(3): 339–50.

Castro F. (2014). Overview of participatory guarantee systems in 2013. In H. Willer, J. Lernoud (Eds.). The World of Organic Agriculture: Statistics and Emerging Trends 2014. IFOAM (Bonn) and FiBL (Frick).

CBI (2018). Exporting sustainable coffee to Europe. Ministry of Foreign Affairs. www.cbi.eu/node/2170/pdf/.

Christensen L.J., Peirce E., Hartman L.P., Hoffman W.M., Carrier J. (2018). Ethics, CSR, and sustainability education in the Financial Times Top 50 Global Business Schools: baseline data and future research directions. Journal of Business Ethics 73(4): 347–68.

Cuéllar-Padilla M., Calle A. (2011). Can we find solutions with people? Participatory action research with small organic producers in Andalusia. Journal of Rural Studies, 27: 372–83.

Cuéllar M.C., Ganuza-Fernandez E. (2018). We don't want to be officially certified! Reasons and implications of the participatory guarantee systems. Sustainability, MDPI, Open Access Journal 10(4): 1–15.

Cuéllar-Padilla M., Calle-Collado A., Gallar-Hernandez D. (2013). Procesos hacia la Soberanía Alimentaria. Icaria.

De Beukelaer C., and Duxbury N. (2014). Real sustainable development requires change through culture. The Conversation.

de Burca G. (2005). Democratising transnational governance: Lessons from the EU experience. Presentation at faculty lunch, Columbia Law, Fall. pp. 10–11.

Desmarais A. (2007). La Vía Campesina. La globalización y el poder del Campesinado. Editorial Popular.

Dine J., Shields K. (2008). Fair trade and reflexive democracy. European Business Organisation Law Review (EBOR) 9(2): 163–86.

Ditlev-Simsonsen C.D., Midttun A. (2011). What motivates managers to pursue corporate responsibility? A survey among key stakeholders. Corporate Social Responsibility and Environmental Management 18(1): 25–38.

Downing T.E. (2002). Avoiding new poverty: mining-induced displacement and resettlement. IIED. www.sdsg.org/wp-content/uploads/2010/02/AvodingNewPovMMSD.pdf.

Ebert A.W. (2014). Potential of under-utilised traditional vegetables and legume crops to contribute to food and nutritional security, income and more sustainable production systems. Sustainability 6(1): 319–35.

Evans G.R.J. (2002). Between the global and the local there are regions, culture areas, and states: a review article. Journal of Southeast Asian Studies 33(1):147–62.

Faist T. (2000). Transnationalisation in international migration: implications for the study of citizenship and culture. Ethnic and Racial Studies 23(2): 189–222.

Feenstra G.W. (1997). Local food systems and sustainable communities. American Journal of Alternative Agriculture 12(1): 28–36.

Friedmann H., McNair A. (2008). Whose rules rule? Contested projects to certify 'local production for distant consumers'. Journal of Agrarian Change 8(2–3): 408–34.

Girard R. (2008). Evolutions and Conversion: Dialogues of the Origin of Culture. Bloomsbury.

Goldman D., Ayalon O., Baum D., Weiss B. (2018). Influence of 'green school certification' on students' environmental literacy and adoption of sustainable practice by schools. Journal of Cleaner Production 183(10): 1300–13.

Goldstein L.J. (1957). On defining culture. The American Anthropologist 59(6): 1075–81.

Greig-Gran M. (2006). The cost of avoiding deforestation. Report prepared for Stern Review. London.

Heyes C. (2012). Grist and mills: on the cultural origins of learning culture. Philosophical Transactions of the Royal Society B: Biological Sciences 367(1599): 2181–91.

Home R., Nelson E. (2015). Feeding the People: Agroecology for Nourishing the World and Transforming the Agri-Food System. IFOAM. www.ifoam-eu.org/sites/default/files/ifoameu_policy_ffe_feedingthepeople.pdf.

Home R., Bouagnimbeck H., Ugas R., Arbenz M. (2017). Success factors in the implementation and maintenance of participatory guarantee systems. Agroecology and Sustainable Food Systems 41(5).

IFOAM (International Federation of Organic Agriculture Movements) (2014). The Global PGS Newsletter, November/December 2014. IFOAM. www.ifoam.bio/sites/default/files/pgs_newsletter_11_12_2014.pdf (accessed 2 February 2018).

IFOAM (International Federation of Organic Agriculture Movements) (2015). Policy Brief: How Governments Can Support Participatory Guarantee Systems (PGS). IFOAM. www.ifoam.bio/sites/default/files/page/files/policybrief-howgovernmentscan supportpgs_0.pdf.

Ismail M. (2009). Corporate Social Responsibility and its role in community development: an international perspective. The Journal of International Social Research 2(9).

Jahoda G. (1993). Crossroads between Culture and Mind: Continuities and Change in Theories in Human Nature. Harvard University Press.

Jahoda G. (2012). Critical reflections on some recent definitions of 'culture'. Culture and Psychology 18(3): 289–303.

Kinzig A., Ehrlich P.R., Alston L.J., Arrow K., Barrett S., Buchman T.G., Daily G.C., Levin B., Levin S., Oppenheimer M., Ostrom E., Saari D. (2013). Social norms and global environmental challenges: the complex interaction of behaviors, values, and policy. Bioscience 63: 164–75.

Kirchner C. 2014. Participatory guarantee systems (PGS): how PGS can intensify knowledge exchange between farmers. Paper presented at IFOAM Organic World Congress 2014, 'Building Organic Bridges', 13–15 October, Istanbul, Turkey.

Kumar A., Smith S. (2017). Understanding local food consumers: theory of planned behavior and segmentation approach. Journal of Food Products Marketing 24(2): 196–215.

Lachat C., Raneri J.E., Walker Smith K., Kolsteren P., Van Damme P., Verzelen K., Penafiel D., Vanhove W., Kennedy G., Hunter D., Oduor Odhiambo F., Ntandou-Bouzitou G., De Baets B., Ratnasekera D., Ky H.T., Remans R., Termote C. (2018). Dietary species richness as a measure of food biodiversity and nutritional quality of diets. Proceedings of the National Academy of Sciences 115(1): 127–32. DOI: 10.1073/pnas.1709194115.

Latta P. (2014). Direct trade: the new fair trade. Global Societies Journal 2: 1–8.

Leclair M.A. (2002). Fighting the tide: alternative trade organisations in the era of global free trade. World Development 30(6): 949–58.

Lernoud J., Potts J., Sampson G., Garibay S., Lynch M., Voora V., Willer H., Wozniak J. (2017). The State of Sustainability Markets: Statistics and Emerging Trends 2017. ITC Geneva.

Lindley J. (2019) Sustainably sourced seafood: a criminological approach to reduce demand for illegal seafood supply. In W. Leal Filho, A. Consorte McCrea (Eds.). Sustainability and the Humanities. Springer.

Lobel O. (2017). The paradox of extralegal activism: critical legal consciousness and transformative politics. Harvard Law Review 120(4): 937–88.

Long T.B., Looijen A., Blok V. (2018). Critical success factors for the transition to business models for sustainability in the food and beverage industry in the Netherlands. Journal of Cleaner Production 175: 82–95.

Lozano-Cabedo C., Gómez-Benito C. (2017). A theoretical model of food citizenship for the analysis of social praxis. Journal of Agricultural and Environmental Ethics 30: 1–22.

Luchs M.G., Naylor R.W., Irwin J.R., Raghunathan R. (2010). The sustainability liability: potential negative effects of ethicality on product preference. Journal of Marketing 74(5): 18–31.

Lund V., Olsson A.S. (2006). Animal agriculture: symbiosis, culture, or ethical conflict? Journal of Agricultural and Environmental Ethics 19(1): 47–56.

Maniora J. (2018). Mismanagement of sustainability: what business strategy makes the difference? Empirical evidence from the USA. Journal of Business Ethics 152(4): 931–47.

Marsden T., Banks J., Bristow G. (2000). Food supply chain approaches: exploring their role in rural development. Sociologia Ruralis 40(4): 424–38.

McMichael P. (2009). A food regime genealogy. Journal of Peasant Studies 36: 139–69.

Miska C., Szocs I., Schiffinger M. (2018). Culture's effects on corporate sustainability practices: a multi-domain and multi-level view. Journal of World Business 53(2): 263–79.

Montiel I. (2008). Corporate Social Responsibility and corporate sustainability: separate pasts, common futures. Organisation and Environment 21(3): 245–69.

Nelson E., Gómez Tovar L., Schwentesius Rindermann R., Gómez Cruz M. (2010). Participatory organic certification in Mexico: an alternative approach to maintaining the integrity of the organic label. Agriculture and Human Values 27(2): 227–37.

Packalen S. (2010). Culture and sustainability. Corporate Social Responsibility and Environmental Management 17(2): 118–21.

Plieninger T., Kohsaka R., Bieling C., Hashimoto S., Kamiyama C., Kizos T., Penker M., Kieninger P., Shaw B.J., Bruno G., Yuki S., Osamu Y. (2018). Fostering biocultural diversity in landscapes through place-based food networks: a 'solution scan' of European and Japanese models. Sustainability Science 13(1): 219–33.

Potts J., Lynch M., Wilkings A., Huppé G., Cunningham M., Voora V. (2014). The State of Sustainability Initiatives Review 2014: Standards and the Green Economy. SSI. www.iisd.org/pdf/2014/ssi_2014.pdf.

Powell L.J., Wittman H. (2018). Farm to school in British Colombia: mobilising food literacy for food sovereignty. Agriculture and Human Values 35(1): 193–206.

Renting H., Schermer M., Rossi A. (2012). Building food democracy: exploring civic food networks and newly emerging forms of food citizenship. International Journal of the Sociology of Agriculture and Food 19: 289–307.

Schermer M. (2105). From 'food from nowhere' to 'food from here': changing producer–consumer relations in Austria. Agricultural Human Values 32: 121–32.

Schulz K., Finstad-Milion K., Janczak S. (2018). Educating corporate sustainability: a multidisciplinary and practice-based approach to facilitate students' learning. Journal of Cleaner Production 198: 996–1006.

Seid S.H. (2018). Global Regulation of Foreign Direct Investment. Routledge.

Servin A., Roche-Jimenez T., Munoz R., Brouwer K. (2018). Labour exploitation and sexual violence in Latin America: the experience of Central American migrant women. European Journal of Public Health 28(1).

Shaw D., Black M. (2010). Market based political action: a path to sustainable development? Sustainable Development 18(6): 385–97.

Sheth J.N., Sinha M. (2015). B2B branding in emerging markets: a sustainability perspective. Industrial Marketing Management 51: 79–88.

Shore B. (1998). Culture in Mind: Cognition, Culture and the Problem of Meaning. Oxford University Press.

Singh P.B., Pandey K.K. (2012). Green marketing: policies and practices for sustainability development. Integral Review: A Journal of Management 5(1): 22–30.

Soini K., Dessein J. (2016). Culture-sustainability relation: towards a conceptual framework. Sustainability 8(2): 167.

Sommer C. (2017). Drivers and constraints for adopting sustainability standards in small and medium sized enterprises (SMEs). German Development Institute. Discussion Paper 21. www.die-gdi.de/uploads/media/DP_21.2017.pdf.

Stagle S. (2002). Local organic food markets: potential and limitations for contributing to sustainable development. Empirica 29(2): 145–62.

Stassart P., Jamar D. (2009). Agriculture biologique et verrouillage des systèmes de connaissances. Conventionalisation des filières agroalimentaire bio. Innovations Agronomiques 4: 313–28.

Steward J. (1972). Theory of Culture Change: The Methodology of Multilinear Evolution. University of Illinois Press.

Süßbauer E., Schäfer M. (2018). Greening the workplace: conceptualising workplaces as settings for enabling sustainable consumption. International Journal of Innovation and Sustainable Development 12(3): 327–49.

Tampe M. (2016). Leveraging the vertical: the contested dynamics of sustainability standards and labour in global production networks. An International Journal of Employment Relations 56(1): 43–74.

Testa F., Boiral O., Iraldo F. (2018). Internalization of environmental practices and institutional complexity: can stakeholders pressures encourage greenwashing? Journal of Business Ethics 147(2): 287–39.

Thorlakson T., de Zegher J.F., Lambin E.F. (2018). Companies' contribution to sustainability through global supply chains. Proceedings of the National Academy of Sciences 115(9): 2072–77. DOI: 10.1073/pnas.1716695115.

Toksöz G. (2018). Irregular migration and migrants' informal employment: a discussion theme in international migration governance. Globalisations 15(6): 779–794.

Toledo A., Burlingame B. (2006). Biodiversity and nutrition: a common path toward global food security and sustainable development. Journal of Food Composition and Analysis 19(6–7): 477–83.

Torquati B., Tempesta T., Vecchiato D., Venanzi S. (2018). Tasty or sustainable? The effect of product sensory experience on a sustainable new food product: an application of discrete choice experiments on Chianina tinned beef. Sustainability 10(8): 2795.

Tscharkert P. (2009). Recognising and nurturing artisanal mining as a viable livelihood. Resources Policy 34(1–2): 24–31.

Valley W., Wittman H., Jordan N., Ahmed S., Galt R. (2017). An emerging signature pedagogy for sustainable food systems education. Renewable Agriculture and Food Systems 33(5): 467–80.

Vidhan J. (2010). Culture and ethnobotany of Jaintia tribal community of Meghalaya, Northeast India: a mini review. Indian Journal of Traditional Knowledge 9(1): 38–44.

Vivero-Pol, J.L. (2017). Food as commons or commodity? Exploring the links between normative valuations and agency in food transition. Sustainability 9(3): 442.

Vogt M. (2011). Tico time: the influence of coffee certifications on sustainable development and poverty reduction in Costa Rica: a discussion with coffee farmers and cooperative managers. PhD. Flinders University, Faculty of Social and Behavioural Sciences.

Vogt M. (2019). Variance in Approach toward a 'Sustainable' Coffee Industry in Costa Rica: Perspectives from Within; Lessons and Insights. Ubiquity Press (UNDER REVIEW).

Watts M. (2006). Culture, development and global neo-liberalism. In S. Radcliff (Ed.). Culture and Development in a Globalising World: Geographies, Actors and Paradigms. Routledge.

Welch R.M., Graham R.D. (1999). A new paradigm for world agriculture: meeting human needs. Productive, sustainable, nutritious. Field Crops Research 60(1–2): 1–10.

Wirtenberg J. (2014). Building a Culture for Sustainability: People, Planet and Profits in a New Green Economy. Praeger, ABC-CLIO.

Part II

Evaluating biodiversity outcomes

3 Biodiversity outcomes associated with sustainability certifications

Contextualising understanding and expectations, and allowing for ambitious intentions

Melissa Vogt and Oskar Englund

Introduction

Certifying terrestrial and water-based production and extractive activities can protect and guide the sustainable management and use of natural resources. The definition of sustainability can vary, and comprehensive consideration of and compromise between society, economy and environment is necessary. Sustainability is sought within different contexts which influence an effective and equitable balance between these three areas. Biodiversity outcomes as associated with various sustainability certifications are of interest, and definitions of biodiversity will influence the understanding of intentions and outcomes. For this chapter, biodiversity is species, genetics, ecosystems and functional diversity, according to commonly used definitions. A conceptual frame suggests understanding, intending for and evaluating functional biodiversity outcomes, identifying why this is relevant for productive systems according to existing biodiversity outcome intentions and evaluations. Biodiversity is an environmental outcome, it is not, however, isolated in this alignment and can influence and be influenced by economic and social factors.

How certifications improve biodiversity outcomes is likely to differ between certifications, as evidenced through the chapters in this book and other literature. Standard criteria vary between certifications influential to how certifications differ. They provision the protection of, and guidance for managing and using natural resources, restricting activities with negative impacts, and encouraging activities with positive ones. Outcomes require the effective implementation of and ongoing compliance with a certification standard. Variance in approach to encouraging and regulating this compliance can also vary between certifications, with direct and indirect consequences for biodiversity outcomes. Understanding biodiversity outcomes attributable to sustainability certification efforts therefore relies on individual evaluations of standard criteria, outcomes resulting from standard implementation, and an ability to synthesise across evaluations.

This chapter provides an overview of some key considerations, positive examples and recommendations for ongoing and future evaluations of biodiversity outcomes associated with any sustainability standard and certification. Three key contexts which may influence or confound the evaluation of biodiversity outcomes associated with sustainability certifications are explained. An assessment summary of standard criteria for a select number of sustainability certifications for agriculture, forestry and bioenergy are compared against a biodiversity benchmark. The Fairmined standard for mining activities is discussed as a separate consideration. A selection of existing evaluations is discussed as related to Rainforest Alliance as examples. Finally, improving functional biodiversity intentions for productive landscapes through farm and landscape heterogeneity is suggested.

Method and study scope

This chapter evaluates biodiversity outcomes as associated with sustainability certifications using existing literature. A conceptual frame provides an additional layer and consideration for understanding and evaluating biodiversity outcomes. Included studies were organised according to methods used, and communication of findings. Evaluating versus implying biodiversity outcomes was a consideration, alongside macro-level, community- or country-specific and comparative studies, by certificate, or country/region. The number of country or region-specific studies is limited and as such some individual and context-specific evaluations are provided as examples, which are not representative of all existing studies. Criteria for inclusion were a clear attribution of biodiversity outcome to a certification standard alongside reliable counterfactual and accurate baseline considerations (Ferraro 2009; Baylis *et al.* 2015). The influence on biodiversity of subsequent trade practices in processing, transport and preparation for consumption are recognised but not considered in this chapter.

Conceptual frame

Balancing the productive intention of a system and landscape and ensuring biodiversity outcomes can be difficult and requires compromise. Functional biodiversity can complement such balance, ensuring system stability and self-regulation, and without degrading natural resources.

Functional biodiversity outcomes align with the ecological sensitivity within human realities (ESHR) concept. This concept considers ecological interactions and processes, across varying spatial scales, as basal to functional biodiversity. It also recognises the significant influence that human realities, both tangible (capability, access to resources) and intangible (opinions, perspectives, interests), can have on biodiversity outcomes in productive landscapes. The reciprocity between human realities and ecological conditions is the final aspect of the concept. An ESHR approach encourages and facilitates a consistent sensitivity to ecological conditions and human realities, and their reciprocity through human natural environment interactions and any assessment of associated biodiversity outcomes. Sensitivity reduces a need for adaptive capacity of productive systems as exerted negative pressures through external human influences would reduce. Natural external influences are not, however, within this type of human control, so the adaptive capacity and ecological robustness or resilience (Holling 1973; Gunderson 2000) of productive natural resource systems remain relevant and necessary.

Direct human natural environment interactions are most relevant for the concept; however, assessing significant indirect influencing factors on human–natural environment interactions is encouraged (Ostrom 1990). Also important is recognising heterogeneity within particular 'stakeholder' groups. Sustainability certifications are an indirect influencing factor and an influencing stakeholder group. Working within a trade and productive landscape context they seek to address a range of interests toward stated 'sustainability' outcomes, one of which is, could be, or should be a positive biodiversity outcome. These interests, as part of a human realities consideration, provide a reminder that the context of certified production can become a limiting or conducive factor to ambitious and positive outcomes. Within these considerations, any biodiversity outcome associated with a sustainability certification can be further contextualised and understood, and potential for improved ambition identified.

In this chapter, the ESHR provides an additional layer for understanding and framing biodiversity definitions, intentions and outcomes. The word biodiversity throughout the chapter reflects current use, and ESHR and functional biodiversity are mentioned where incidentally relevant to the discussion. Recommendations for future practice, studies and evaluations include aligning biodiversity definitions and considerations, and human–natural environment interactions with the ESHR toward functional biodiversity outcomes.

Contexts which may influence or confound the evaluation of biodiversity outcomes

Existing studies include context-specific influencing factors for biodiversity intentions and outcomes (Donald 2004; Azhar *et al.* 2015a, 2015b; Vogt, 2016, 2017; Milder *et al.* 2016; Toledo-Hernandez *et al.* 2017; Nesper *et al.* 2017; Waldron *et al.* 2012; Yankit *et al.* 2018). Consistency is not, however, evident. Three categories of contextual consideration – certified industry, bioregion, and country and landscape context – can improve consistency.

Certified industry

The impact on biodiversity of different agricultural production systems varies according to crop (Donald 2004). Landscape appropriateness for the crop, and additional understandings of system requirements to maintain yield will also influence outcomes. For example, growing coffee in its native landscape but within a monoculture system might have varying influence on outcomes for biodiversity compared to growing a crop in a landscape of inappropriate climate or conditions. Extractive industries such as mining, fisheries and harvesting products from forests present individual situations for biodiversity outcome considerations. Forest products versus forestry may provide a different category for forest certification, converting forest or other land use to monoculture plantations for harvest versus harvesting from a forest, for example. Considering context of extremity across all industries can condition industry-specific considerations of a 'positive biodiversity outcome'.

Terrestrial biodiversity outcomes have implications for, and reliance on fresh water systems and oceans (Moss 2008). Considering terrestrial and water-based production as interdependent increases the reach of biodiversity considerations, and understanding improves. For example, an aquatic sourced, instead of terrestrially sourced, product may be considered as having positive terrestrial biodiversity outcome. An improved biodiversity outcome for both environments cannot, however, be assured without adequately considering the influence of sourcing from an aquatic rather than terrestrial environment. Examples are provided in the chapter for micro algae used for biofuels. Variance in actual or expected biodiversity outcome according to bioregions (Richards 1990) is also discussed. As particular crops are grown only within their preferred climate, and therefore bioregions, the considerations of industry and bioregional context can be brought together. This may not, however, be consistent, and the two contexts require distinct recognition.

Examples

Mining practices

Artisan small-scale mining operations have predated large-scale operations and are often informal and unregulated (Ayree *et al.* 2003; Owusu-Nimo *et al.* 2018). Informal instead of illegal mining is a more appropriate term (Lebwaba and Nhlengetwa 2016), and reliance on the activity is significant around the world (Hilson 2009). Commonly discussed for gold mining, the influence of small-scale compared to large-scale operations on environmental and biodiversity outcomes is less. However, when the number of small-scale operations are significant within the same region influence increases. Attention to small-scale operations can reduce negative influence and outcomes (Tom-Dery *et al.* 2012; Bansah *et al.* 2016; Ebus 2018; Gomez 2018) and represent significantly different dynamics.

New small-scale mines can stem from frustration with larger mining company operations in developing countries (TV360 Nigeria 2013; Vice-News 2018; Vice on HBO 2018). Large-scale mining operations demonstrate limited societal benefit, and often damage surrounding communities in environmental and societal terms (Wilson 2015). While unpredictability is more likely in illegal or informal operations, regulating formal operations is difficult and the implication for biodiversity remains significant. This is particularly so where their operations can initiate new small-scale mines.

Drawing similarity between illegal logging and therefore challenges of legitimacy across forestry management, as an industry context consideration, is possible. The environmental and societal outcome of extractive mine operations is more extreme (Vyas 2018), with limited ability to present a newly mined product as sustainable. Certifications seeking to improve environmental outcomes for the mining industry with little evidence of legitimacy or effect are understood as allowing illegitimate operations with ideas of being sustainable. They can, however, be important as even with minimal effect there is opportunity to improve practice and complement other mechanisms. Maintaining relative biodiversity intention and outcome according to industry context is suggested. Particularly so where outcomes will be compared between industries. This relative consideration may reduce complacency in effort and better emphasise that certification effectiveness and contribution to biodiversity outcomes can differ between industries. The comparison can determine value of standard and certification influence.

Biodiversity versus yield

Yield quantity is often positively associated with the intensive spatial distribution of crops per land area, crop density. As such, farm level biodiversity increases are often associated with a decrease in crops and therefore yield quantity. The industry-specific context can influence the effective balance between biodiversity and yield. As an example, trade-offs between biodiversity according to bird presence, yields and revenue for smallholder oil palm plantations (Teuscher *et al.* 2015), and effects of habitat and landscape characteristics on biological conservation (Azhar *et al.* 2013, 2014a, 2014b, 2015a, 2015b; Freudmann *et al.* 2015) demonstrate the potential benefit of increasing biodiversity in existing palm oil plantations while centralising the yield versus biodiversity consideration.

Encouraging biodiversity within a yield priority ultimately depends on the crop, and how easily it can produce within a biodiverse system. Some crops perform better where grown in a diversified system. For example, coffee and cacao can support biological conservation through encouraged shade trees and diversified farm profiles (De Beenhouwer *et al.* 2013; Tscharntke *et al.* 2015). More biodiverse agricultural systems can also contribute to crop quality (Toledo-Hernandez *et al.* 2017; Nesper *et al.* 2017; Waldron *et al.* 2012; Wietzke *et al.* 2018; Yankit *et al.* 2018). Other crops rarely grow in a biodiverse system and as such expectation for biodiversity outcomes may differ particularly within a biodiversity versus yield consideration.

Farm and landscape heterogeneity, as explained later in the chapter, may encourage more conducive situations for this compromise. Different biodiversity outcomes are expected for other industries and crops, particularly for crops grown primarily for commercial purposes and outside appropriate climate and physical conditions. Floriculture is an example. Floriculture often encourages monoculture commercial flower farm systems, occasionally growing in an artificial environment such as a greenhouse. While a preference for growing flowers over other crops exists, using artificial environments accommodates inappropriate conditions and climate (see Chapter 12 for more details). Biofuel from crops or feedstock may also rely on monoculture systems for production priority, and standard criteria might improve biodiversity outcomes with varying effect, and depending on the crop and landscape context (see Chapter 8 for more details). Farm and landscape heterogeneity, as explained at the end of the chapter, and crop and plant selections encourage situations conducive to this compromise.

Bioregion of certificates

Alongside industry-specific considerations, a bioregion provides a consistent context for understanding and evaluating a biodiversity outcome associated with any sustainability certification effort. Boreal, tropical and temperate bioregions are all distinct according to requirements for biodiversity protection, conservation and optimal conditions (Miller 1996). Tropical rainforests constitute the most extensive areas of high-biomass forest, representing the most significant species richness of all forests (Pan *et al.* 2013). The world's densest and tallest forests are in temperate rainforests (Pan *et al.* 2013). Aquatic ecosystems are also distinct by bioregion (Schindler 1998; Pan *et al.* 2013).

Tropical landscapes receive much attention and effort in terms of number of certificates and studies. Certified products are often agricultural commodities from tropical bioregions, and agricultural expansion has been one of the most important proximate causes of tropical forest loss, accounting for 80 per cent of deforestation worldwide, with significant loss recorded during the 1980s and 1990s (Gibbs *et al.* 2007; Houghton *et al.* 2007). The rationale behind the attention can therefore be understood (Richards 1990; Gibbs *et al.* 2007; Houghton *et al.* 2007). On the other hand, Gauthier *et al.* (2015) suggest increased attention to boreal productive regions to ensure the continued management of threats against their health. In 2008, boreal regions represented some of the last large remaining expanses of intact and unmanaged natural ecosystems (43.8%), at similar levels of tropical and subtropical forests (45.3%) (Potapov *et al.* 2008). An understanding of 'need for sustainability' may therefore lead to a higher propensity for certification within particular bioregions.

With this understanding, it is likely that all bioregions require and can benefit from evaluation (Gauthier *et al.* 2015). Future research in this area could therefore consider the number and proportion of certificates specific to a label according to bioregion. It may also consider how existing studies and evaluations of associated biodiversity outcomes represent this proportion (see Chapter 4 for an example), and how the socioeconomic situation and a country's development stage influence where studies are conducted. Where evaluating or intending for biodiversity outcomes, bioregion can become a consistent category or criterion to ensure contextual detail.

Country and landscape contexts

Several studies recognise the importance of country and landscape contexts for increasing the rigour and detail of evaluations and assessments (Milder *et al.* 2016; Carlson *et al.* 2017; Tayleur *et al.* 2016, 2018). They clarify trends associated with sustainable certifications and ensure effective understanding.

Examples

Influence of certified land units on landscape biodiversity outcomes and vice versa

Certified land units can provide additional and valuable measures of biodiversity outcomes for a landscape according to their influence on neighbouring landscape patches (Milder *et al.* 2016; Takahashi and Todo 2017). The external influence relates to the landscape consideration of the ESHR concept, and can flow in either direction between certified land unit and neighbouring patches. Forest or native land conversion, and negative and positive spillover from land use activities (Toledo *et al.* 2018; Rodrigues and Chiarello 2018) are all possible alongside land degradation, leaching of chemical applications through soil or water ways, or via species movement, influencing ecological interactions and processes in neighbouring patches (Blitzer *et al.* 2012).

Compliance and facilitating standard implementation according to certification

Country- and landscape-specific studies provide opportunities to assess a number of certificates, approaches to encouraging implementation and implementation status according to certified land unit and certification. Land units of 100 per cent compliance are theoretically an example of optimal biodiversity outcome, conditioned by an adequate understanding of a potentially variable 'baseline' across certified land units; the original state of and intentions for the certified land unit; and standard criteria. An additional confounder could be the approach taken by different certification schemes to encourage and facilitate implementation, also influenced by the number of certificates held by one land unit.

Standard implementation requires behaviour change, financial and nonfinancial investment, and may require significant change in land unit composition and configuration. Sometimes, certifications allow and recognise incremental stages toward compliance through the certification process (RA 2017; NASAA 2018). Such an approach avoids the expectation of immediate absolute compliance, conditioned by evidence that noncompliance issues can be realistically addressed within a timeframe. Implementation may not therefore be immediate with certification, and an awareness of implementation status relies on effective audit processes.

Understanding implementation status therefore relies on legitimacy and transparency, effective facilitating procedures and processes for producers and land unit managers, and verification by effective audit. A country and landscape context, particularly in-field assessments, can facilitate the effective inclusion of implementation and compliance status in evaluations of biodiversity outcomes. This confounder may be further considered between certification schemes within a comparative context of complementary or competitive alternatives (Gulbrandsen 2005; Miller and Bush 2014; Chaudhary *et al.* 2016; Tysiachniouk and McDermott 2016).

Standard reach by bioregion: implying biodiversity outcomes

Quantification of certificate, producer or certified hectare by location can provide a valuable yet preliminary understanding of associated biodiversity outcomes. Clarifying implied versus evaluated biodiversity outcomes, need according to bioregion, and proportion of certificates versus studies within each bioregion – and then how accurately existing studies reflect implied biodiversity outcomes – can improve the interpretation of environmental or societal benefits of certifications according to bioregion (Gibbs *et al.* 2007; Houghton 2007).

The 78,544 commodity crop group certificates considered by Tayleur *et al.* (2018) were taken from 'major standards' for certifying commodity crops (Potts *et al.* 2014). They covered 1,042,734 farms, most located in tropical regions. The crops considered, and excluding organic certificates, can easily explain the bioregional location of the included certificates.

In 2015, 50.9 million hectares of farm land and 86.5 million hectares of 'organic land use' (Willer and Lernoud 2017, s25, s27) were certified organic. The Willer and Lernoud (2017) study indicates that most organic producers and perhaps therefore organic certificates are located in tropical bioregions. Most organic permanent crops are found in Europe, Latin America and then Africa, with coffee representing the highest number of certified hectares, followed by olives, nuts and then tropical fruits and grapes (Willer and Lernoud 2017, s27). The majority of organic certified permanent crops, such as coffee and tropical fruits, and therefore the majority of the 2.4 million producers of organic certified permanent crops are understood to be located in tropical bioregions of Latin America, Africa, Asia and some Oceania countries. Specifically, India, Ethiopia and Mexico represent the highest proportion of producers: approximately one million (Willer and Lernoud 2017, s16). Tropical bioregions may not, however, be the most certified area by hectares. Australia, Argentina, USA and Spain represent the largest area of organic production (Willer and Lernoud 2017, s26). Farmland, then wild collection and permanent grassland are the most certified land uses, followed by arable and permanent crop (Willer and Lernoud 2017, s27).

Between organic certified hectares, producers and organic certificates, the most correlated quantification between the Tayleur *et al.* (2018) and the Willer and Lernoud (2017) studies is certificate and producer number. A correlation is, however, difficult as 'producer' is not easily identifiable by individual or group. A group or an individual producer can hold an organic certificate. Unifying and clarifying quantification criteria for certificates and certifications can improve understanding of representation across bioregions. Quantification should include producer, farm and certificate numbers, and certified hectares. Smaller-scale certification standards and labels, as listed in Chapter 1, also require quantification. Confidentiality of producers and availability of information may, however, present challenges to comprehensive quantification. Improved macro-level quantifications are therefore necessary. Existing quantification still offers an implied biodiversity outcome and valuable preliminary understanding; however, existing evaluations and studies cannot complement the implied bioregional findings, and extrapolating findings to substantiate implied biodiversity outcomes may not adequately represent all certification schemes, contextual considerations or confounders.

Biodiversity outcomes attributable to certifying productive and extractive activities

Attributing biodiversity outcomes to certification efforts according to intention by standard criteria and outcome of effective implementation can contribute to the understanding of existing situations and also inform future evaluations.

Standard criteria

Biodiversity benchmark standard

Certification standard criteria can indicate intended and actual biodiversity outcomes, and as such they are a valuable information source for evaluation. A benchmark standard against which performance is measured can facilitate standard criteria assessment according to biodiversity intentions. It relies on clearly defined and detailed biodiversity criteria which adequately represent appropriate considerations for different industries, commodities and land uses. Englund and Berndes (2015) assessed 26 certification standards (11 forest management, nine agriculture and six biofuel-related) on their potential biodiversity performance using a benchmark standard. The standard includes seven categories and 26 criteria which demonstrate high ambitions for biodiversity conservation. The seven categories include: (i) endangered species,

(ii) habitat destruction and fragmentation, (iii) habitat degradation and modification, (iv) overexploitation, (v) invasive species and GMOs, (vi) energy use and GHG emissions, and (vii) research, awareness and education. Against this benchmark, each certification standard was assessed to indicate its potential for biodiversity conservation. Below, the outcome of this assessment is summarised and discussed, followed by reflections on the method and recommendations for potential improvements. For more information on the study, and visual representation for the summary of findings please see the original research article (Englund and Berndes 2015).

Assessment of sustainability standard performance against the biodiversity benchmark standard

In general, criteria well considered across all three standard categories include those related to (i) habitat destruction, (ii) water resources, (iii) soil erosion, (iv) soil quality, and (v) long-term sustainability. Overall poorly considered criteria include those related to (i) fossil energy and (ii) support for research. Forestry management standards complied with 60 per cent, agricultural standards with 61 per cent, and biofuel-related standards with 72 per cent of the benchmark criteria, respectively.

To further rate performance according to compliance, standards complying with many criteria were classified as 'Stringent', while standards complying with few criteria were classified as 'Unstringent'.[1]

Overall, Fairtrade and SAN/RA (agriculture), and RSPO and RTRS (biofuel) were the most stringent standards, while GGLS5 and PEOLG (forest), GLOBALGAP, EU Organic, NOP, and GGLS2 (agriculture), and ISCC (biofuel) were the least stringent.

The nine agricultural standards complied with seven to 23 of the 26 criteria. Compliance was most demonstrated for principles on (i) overexploitation, (ii) habitat destruction and fragmentation, and (iii) habitat degradation and modification. Four principles were poorly considered overall: (i) invasive species and GMOs, (ii) endangered species, (iii) energy use and GHG emissions, and (iv) research awareness and education. Fairtrade, SAN/RA, Naturland and KRAV were classified as 'Stringent', while Global Partnership for Good Agricultural Practices (GLOBAL/GAP), European Union Organic (EU Organic) and National Organic Programs (NOP and GGLS2) were classified as 'Unstringent'.

The nine forest management standards complied with eight to 19 of the 25 relevant criteria. Compliance was most demonstrated for principles on (i) endangered species, (ii) habitat destruction and fragmentation, and (iii) overexploitation. Four principles were poorly considered overall: (i) energy use and GHG emissions, (ii) habitat degradation and modification, (iii) invasive species and GMOs, and (iv) research awareness and education. Forest Stewardship Council (FSC), Sustainable Forestry Initiative (SFI), Malaysian Timber Certification System (MTCS), Naturland and International Tropical

Timber Organization and International Union for Conservation of Nature (ITTO/IUCN) were classified as 'Stringent', while GGLS5 and PEOLG were classified as 'Unstringent'.

The nine biofuel-related standards complied with 13 to 21 of the 25 relevant criteria. Compliance was most demonstrated for principles on (i) endangered species, (ii) habitat destruction and fragmentation, (iii) habitat degradation and modification, and (iv) overexploitation. Two principles were poorly considered overall: (i) invasive species and GMOs, and (ii) research awareness and education. Roundtable on Sustainable Palm Oil (RSPO), RTRS, Bonsucro and Greenergy were classified as 'Stringent', while ISCC was classified as 'Unstringent'.

An additional analysis on how the different standards restrict conversion of specific ecosystem types revealed that six of nine agricultural standards require that natural vegetation remain unmanaged. One relies solely on identifying high conservation value (HCV) land (FLO). All six biofuel standards include ecosystem conversion criteria, which are attributable to compliance with requirements in the EU Renewable Energy Directive (EU-RED), that prohibit the conversion of specific ecosystem types for the production of bioenergy feedstock. All 11 forestry standards address ecosystem conversion, regulated by identification and protection of HCV land. Naturland also restricts the conversion of forested land, and GGLS5 protects forested land from conversion to plantation. While three forestry standards (ATO/ITTO, ITTO/IUCN, PEOLG) and two biofuel standards (RSPO and RTRS) encourage the restoration of degraded land, one forest standard (Naturland) and three agriculture standards (GLOBALGAP, IFOAM and SAN/RA) effectively protect degraded land by prohibiting all ecosystem conversion.

Discussion, recommendations and implications

A biodiversity benchmark standard is a useful format for assessing criteria of different certification standards. The level of detail required to determine the biodiversity performance of specific standards may be difficult to include in such a generic benchmark standard. The benchmark standard presented here may thus be primarily useful for assessing and comparing many standards, as a meta-standard assessment. A biodiversity benchmark standard could also contribute to the harmonisation of standards based on meta-standards, which has been a topic of discussion since the early 2000s (Ponte 2004; Fischer *et al.* 2005). While standards of different certifications for the same crop or industry have been observed as becoming more similar by producers in some countries, the assessment against a biodiversity benchmark demonstrates significant differences in stringency, even between standards with a similar scope. For example, IFOAM, which sets the norms for organic agriculture, is significantly more stringent than either EU Organic or NOP. In addition, KRAV endorses EU Organic, even though KRAV classifies as 'Stringent' and EU Organic as 'Unstringent'. Further, the SFI standard, which is a forest industry initiative, shows similar stringency as the FSC standard, which is often regarded as more thorough in its coverage of ecological issues.

Measuring performance according to an expected positive biodiversity outcome relies on extensive benchmark categories and criteria. Adding new criteria or categories for additional biodiversity aspects to this existing benchmark standard could see the inclusion of specific production systems, crops or industries (Correa *et al*. 2017), or farm and landscape heterogeneity (Azhar *et al*. 2015a, 2015b; Vogt 2016) and system impacts on external landscape patches. Some benchmark criteria rely on terms which provide scope for interpretation of definitions, and intentions and outcomes. More clearly defined criteria can facilitate the accurate measurement of biodiversity performance. Promoting biochar application for soil fertility, and subsequent biodiversity impacts is an example. Where more detail is considered, biochar production and application approaches significantly influence biodiversity outcomes, as discussed by Verheijen *et al*. in Chapter 5.

Assessing against criteria reliant on variable definitions, specifically degraded lands and HCV areas (Edwards *et al*. 2011; Capmourteres and Anand 2016), is another example as it leaves interpretation open to the assessor. Other examples are 'long-term sustainability' with criteria of overexploitation, and practices which avoid over-harvesting and maintaining soil fertility. These criteria could arguably improve by detail, and encouraging optimised harvests might be appropriate, particularly for systems with diverse crops and plants, and a more complex and heterogeneous structure (Strevens and Bonsall 2011). In this situation, the timing of harvest will influence quota and therefore the definition of over-harvest. Another example related to optimal harvest for micro algae is provided later in the chapter.

Retaining the generic structure of the benchmark at a principle and criteria level, and then complementing with different variations of indicators for different production systems can facilitate contextual considerations, comparisons and detailed assessments. Where seeking to allow the benchmark to consider more detail, and therefore further improve opportunity for use, categories and criteria could increase, and detail of criteria definitions, including contextual definitions for different certification types, be included. This could require parallel benchmark standards relevant for different certification and production systems, as discussed above. Although a general harmonisation of standards is often recommended, they must maintain relevance for the intended production system. Improving detail of criteria and definitions in the benchmark standard could inform meta-standard harmonisation, and parallel contextual standards may be harmonised separately. The benchmark is therefore considered a foundational starting point for understanding the intended or actual biodiversity performance of different sustainability certification standards, and may contribute to a level of harmonisation between standard criteria.

Fairmined standard

Standards for environmental protection and biodiversity outcomes in the mining industry provide a different context to agriculture, forestry and fisheries. As addressed in the industry context discussion earlier in the chapter, risk of environmental damage is much higher if not certain during preparation for, and actual mining operations. Corruption within mining activities, particularly of, but not limited to, developing countries is common (Lahiri-Dutt 2006; Edwards *et al.* 2013; Chene 2014; Long 2016; McDonnell *et al.* 2017). Depending on benefit to government versus to the population of a country, promoting small-scale artisan mining operations may be more sustainable for social and environmental reasons, compared with large-scale mining operations. Regulating small-scale mining operations does, however, depend on knowledge of, and an ability to control operations as an essential piece for improving formality in these commonly informal operations.

Given these circumstances, private sector guidance and regulation can become useful, with softer yet more direct influence. The Fairmined standard includes 44 environmental protection criteria (Fairmined 2014), all with direct and indirect implications for biodiversity outcomes. Restoration planning post-mining is a separate category of criteria within these 44. It includes conditions under which mining within protected areas is acceptable. The standard provides a new intra-market mechanism for an industry that can be difficult to regulate, with the efficacy of legal or policy requirements highly dependent on government motivation. Certifying artisanal small-scale mining may also positively contribute to addressing issues sourced from large-scale mining industry operations. The limited benefit of regulating small-scale mining for individuals involved does, however, reduce incentive despite the significant gains to be obtained (Banchirigah 2006). Mori Junior *et al.* provide more information about these challenges and opportunities for improving certification processes for gold mining in Chapter 10. Increasing the legitimacy of the certification process will assist with effective implementation. This can often be easier said than done.

Evaluating implemented certification standards

Independent scholars conduct the majority of evaluations associated with sustainability certifications. Some evaluations and studies are 'endorsed' by and provided by standard-setting and regulating bodies, such as ISEAL and the certifying organisations themselves. Certifying organisations maintain independence from the evaluation activity, removing scope for bias. There is, however, opportunity to provide valuable input to these 'external' evaluations, to clarify findings and/or guide an improvement in methods. They may also assist with the synthesis and critical assessment of existing evaluations as recommended by Romero *et al.* (2013) for forest management certification. Chapter 4 provides an example of how this may be so from the FSC viewpoint.

Existing evaluations of biodiversity outcomes associated with certifications are not yet comprehensive (Romero *et al.* 2013; Tscharntke *et al.* 2015; Milder *et al.* 2016; Ting *et al.* 2016; Chaudhary *et al.* 2016; Tayleur *et al.* 2018; see Chapter 4). An integrated assessment of biodiversity outcomes attributable to the implementation of sustainable certification standards requires more literature and study (Blackman and Rivera 2010; DeFries *et al.* 2017). Confounding variables, limited demonstration of direct influence and causal relationships can reduce the attributability of outcomes to a certification. Insufficient temporal consideration may also limit the demonstration of enduring influence or associations (Damette and Delacote 2011; Sollman *et al.* 2017; Polisar *et al.* 2017). For example, Carlson *et al.* (2017) compared RSPO certified and noncertified oil palm forest as associated with deforestation rates in Indonesia. They used satellite-based estimates of tree cover loss indicating deforestation. Rates in certified land units were calculated as reduced by 33 per cent in high tree cover areas and primary forest compared with similar noncertified plantations. The findings were not, however, consistent across Kalimantan and Sumatra, suggesting the importance of landscape context, pre- versus post-certification land unit status, and baseline conditions where evaluating outcomes.

Additional confounders such as small versus large landholdings (Jones 2013) can influence standard criteria requirements even within the same certification systems. They must be addressed to understand attributable outcomes. Land units holding multiple certificates is an additional consideration. Existing and improved quantifications can further guide future evaluations to substantiate initial findings. The location of certificates by bioregion may be compared to the number of evaluations conducted for a specific certification scheme. Such understanding would indicate how representative existing evaluations and studies related to location of certificates are (see Chapter 4 for an example). They may also inform locations for future studies, particularly where bioregional context and 'need' are considered. Contextual and in-community understandings are recognised as an important contribution for improved rigour and detail of assessments (Milder *et al.* 2016), and are consistently suggested in existing macro-level studies (Carlson *et al.* 2017; Tayleur *et al.* 2018).

Three advanced evaluations of biodiversity outcomes for coffee farming landscapes attributable to the Sustainable Agriculture Network (SAN) used by Rainforest Alliance (RA) are provided. All rely on remotely sensed satellite images and data, with some variable in-field observation which may provision against the oversight of contextual considerations. The first study compares landscape structure and connectivity within certified farms, before and then nine years after certification processes were introduced to a landscape. Based on this information, reduced forest conversion was attributed to the RA certification for coffee farms (Hardt *et al.* 2015). This finding was recognised as limited by the baseline or starting condition of certified farms, found as distinct and in better condition to noncertified farms. The second study found that tree cover, and landscape forest density and connectivity in RA certified coffee farms increased compared to noncertified coffee farms in Colombia (Rueda *et al.* 2014), contributing to tree cover and connectivity in already forested coffee farming patches and landscapes. A final study from Ethiopia found that forest degradation on-farm and within a 100 m distance of an RA certified forest coffee boundary reduced, compared with noncertified coffee forest areas under similar environmental conditions. This was in part attributable to an observed increase in on-farm forest density for RA certified farms (Takahashi and Todo 2017).

Despite these more advanced contributions to understanding, existing evidence of biodiversity outcomes attributable to SAN and RA remains insufficient (Milder *et al.* 2016). Documenting conserved natural ecosystems; improved conservation value of production systems and landscapes; and reduced off-site environmental impacts as outcomes, are considered priorities for future evaluations of RA certified land units (Milder *et al.* 2016). Limitations and challenges for future evaluations include understanding: (1) the profile of certified coffee farms prior to certification; (2) the subtle differences between groups and across temporal changes which make attribution of gain or loss in on-farm biodiversity difficult; (3) associated landscape conditions such as contribution to landscape habitat connectivity compared to noncertified farms, also relevant to (2); and (4) that satellite images can restrict the indication of tree or forest cover integrity and functionality. For this final challenge, evaluation findings are considered more reliable where using combined methods (Bolanos 2006; Haurez *et al.* 2017). Any synthesis and critical assessment of biodiversity outcomes associated with sustainability certifications requires the consistent consideration of common confounders, and additional influential layers. These may provide criteria for segregating evaluation findings associated with the same certificate, and guide approaches to synthesis and critical assessment. They can influence (1) how existing studies are interpreted and synthesised as comparable to other evaluations; and (2) how outcomes are attributed to a certificate.

Common confounders might include standard implementation status and the approach to facilitating implementation, and certificate standard criteria according to land unit size, and intention for the land unit. Additional layers include, as already summarised, bioregion, industry/crop/commodity, and country and landscape contexts. Evaluations can also improve where consistently considering comparable noncertified land unit examples, counterfactual scenarios at land unit and landscape level, and temporal variances. Improved understanding of variance across land units holding the same or multiple certificates is then expected. Considering confounders and layers can assist with determining the appropriateness of extrapolating or comparing study findings.

Improving biodiversity outcomes through farm and landscape heterogeneity: including conservation of generationally diverse farms

Landscape heterogeneity often refers to composition, described as the richness, diversity and evenness of land cover categories (Holzschuh *et al.* 2009). Simplified categories of land cover include natural or intact, and modified productive land uses, and within these categories there are differences. Landscape configuration is described as size and arrangement, or geometry of landscape patches, influenced by habitat fragmentation (Tolessa *et al.* 2016), and relevant to farm and landscape-level heterogeneity. Trade-offs between land cover categories, as composition, and between geometry of landscape patches, as configuration, are influential to farm and landscape heterogeneity ('heterogeneity'). Configuration and heterogeneity are associated with crop and plant selections and spatial distributions. The ESHR draws attention to the compromise between functional biodiversity, heterogeneity and production within ecological considerations. Within this understanding crop and plant selections and spatial distributions can influence species diversity and abundance (Fahrig *et al.* 2010), including avian (Wilson *et al.* 2017; Lee and Martin 2017), pollinator (Hass *et al.* 2018; Monck-Whipp *et al.* 2018) and mammals (Pardo *et al.* 2018; Riojas-López *et al.* 2018; Salek *et al.* 2018). This consideration will often be limited to a system outcome according to production. The ESHR draws attention to the compromise and interdependence between a system, or land unit and neighbouring landscape patches.

Relevance is most considered for ecological interactions and processes, but is also relevant to human realities. For example, heterogeneity will influence bee community and coffee pollination at different spatial scales (Saturni *et al.* 2016), and agricultural restoration efforts are influenced by proximity to existing forest (Toledo *et al.* 2018). Crop and plant selections and subsequent distribution are important for system function, and ensure functional connectivity levels across land cover categories and may influence landscape composition (Boscolo *et al.* 2017) and configuration. Where effectively considered, heterogeneity can have significant influence on plant and animal species of conservation concern (Katayama *et al.* 2014; Santana *et al.* 2017), with promising long-term functional biodiversity outcomes.

The contextual human realities, including the productive intention of each system, and the market need or demand for particular crops, will be influential. Human realities do therefore provide an additional layer. Encouraging understanding of how heterogeneity can benefit human realities, rather than allowing human realities to determine and potentially limit functional biodiversity according to existing understandings, may assist. An increase in, or maintenance of human capability as a tangible human reality, to manage more complex heterogeneous farms, and landscapes (Vogt 2017), will also be necessary. Compositional heterogeneity should not provision excuse for converting natural habitat to productive biodiverse systems, and the importance of conserving natural habitats remains relevant. Converted biodiverse shaded or forested systems may reduce the need for landscape composition changes. They will not, however, be capable of replacing natural habitats in terms of their contribution to biodiversity outcomes.

Using standard criteria and certifying to encourage farm and landscape heterogeneity

Improvements in standard criteria can contribute to biodiversity intentions (Englund and Berndes 2015) and outcomes (Schneider *et al.* 2014). While certification standards might include criteria for crop rotation, they do not include (i) a farm, or landscape heterogeneity criteria for composition or configuration of crops and systems across a landscape (Azhar *et al.* 2015a, 2015b; Englund and Berndes 2015). Nor do they (ii) certify crops grown in generationally diverse farms as a unique category. And rarely if ever do they (iii) redirect crop preference to promote farm or landscape conservation or conversion to more sustainable crop and plant options.

Certifying landscape mosaics was suggested in 2009 (Ghazoul *et al.* 2009) to extend the consideration of forest certification to include activities within other landscape patches which contribute positively to biodiversity outcomes. The idea of certifying farm and landscape heterogeneity is distinct but seeks to encourage a similar idea of labels that recognise connectivity between landscape patches and across farms as contributory to positive biodiversity outcomes. The landscape consideration can also draw attention to the rationale behind the selection of and preference for particular crops. Certifying or including heterogeneity, and protecting generationally diverse farms and forest-grown crops in standard criteria may be feasible. Inclusion can contribute to heterogeneity through crop, plant and tree cover diversity, and then to conservation of native and natural ecosystems on-farm, land unit or within neighbouring landscape patches.

Several of the benchmark criteria could complement such a category including criteria on endangered species, habitat fragmentation, HCV areas, pesticide use, buffer zones and soil erosion. Opportunity for uptake may be more likely for homogenous monoculture systems and landscapes already open to improvement, such as those certified for biofuels and organic certification (Allen *et al.* 2006). Slight improvements in crop rotations, hedgerows and other biodiversity outcomes across mainstream monoculture conventional farming systems (Barbieri *et al.* 2017; Caradonna 2018), with associated positive outcomes, can be interpreted as an indicator of interest in heterogeneity. In addition, integration of perennial plants into intensively managed agricultural systems can provide biomass for the bioeconomy. There is substantial potential for beneficial land use change in Europe (Englund *et al.* 2019; Hansson *et al.* 2019), and certification may improve incentive.

Certifying heterogeneity, particularly where aligned with the ESHR to ensure functional biodiversity, may discourage growing crops in inappropriate climate or conditions. A biodiversity versus yield consideration can guide the selection of crops for landscapes, facilitating production in a biodiverse system. This would require a balance between discouraging crops that grow outside climate or conditions, and encourage crops appropriate for the landscape. There is also a need to balance the effort between monoculture farms, or land units of degraded conditions, and protecting generationally diverse farm systems. Standard implementation and certification can occur more for land units with existing biodiversity and integrity (Rueda *et al.* 2014; Hardt *et al.* 2015; Carlson *et al.* 2017) with concern regarding minimal positive contribution to degraded or monoculture farm systems.

Heterogeneity will not necessarily support the existing preference for already biodiverse systems. It can, however, ensure understanding of a biodiverse system as distinct from a generationally biodiverse system and the subsequent benefit of protecting one compared to the other. The difference is determined by presence and function of biodiversity, indicative of system integrity and stability according to temporal measures. Generationally biodiverse systems are distinct to indigenous techniques used over many centuries and the criteria is relevant to commercial and wild crops. The ESHR also makes this difference more obvious, as explained in the previous section, particularly relevant to human capability. Standard criteria to protect generationally biodiverse farm systems certify longstanding biodiversity and long-developing knowledge sets for managing more complex systems.

The certification FairWild, for example, provides standards to promote the use and fair trade of wild harvests, without threatening long-term in situ survival (FairWild 2018). It indirectly seeks to certify existing forested and diversified farm and landscape systems, specific to native and naturally present wild crops, rather than diversified farm systems based on conventional crops. It is therefore complementary to protecting and ensuring value recognition of generationally biodiverse systems and landscapes. The culturally led implication of FairWild standard criteria may influence and improve biodiversity outcomes, and may be integrated or included in a farm and landscape heterogeneity standard. Identifying or evaluating the conservation of generationally diverse or forested crop systems is an additional consideration. Similar to forest types and structure, configuration of a forest system can be difficult to identify through remote sensing, and the human element almost impossible to determine. Mixed methods are necessary and should include in-field observation and information as verification.

Industry heterogeneity as influential to and synchronised with farm and landscape heterogeneity

Industry heterogeneity sources diverse products and supports diversified market profiles, rather than, or in addition to, homogenous commodity crops. It can influence, support and incentivise functional farm or landscape heterogeneity ('heterogeneity') with two potential implications. First, heterogeneity is supported where market demand for diversified farm and landscape profile is already arranged, or opportunity for diversifying market demand is easily available. Second, and within a land scarcity debate, industry heterogeneity may encourage resourcing from nonterrestrial sources as a replacement for land use. For the first point, synchronising industry heterogeneity to ensure functional farm and landscape heterogeneity is important, with extensive opportunity for future consideration. Where trends in industry heterogeneity are already complementary, the significance of influence for biodiversity outcomes can increase (Gardiner *et al.* 2009; McDaniel *et al.* 2014; Assandri *et al.* 2016; Grab *et al.* 2018). The previous section explains the influential flows related to sustainability certifications. For the second point, micro algae for biofuels is provided as an example.

Micro algae can reduce pressures on terrestrial biodiversity caused by biofuels (Correa *et al.* 2017; Carneiro *et al.* 2017). Freshwater algae can grow well on waste water, cleaning it before harvested for biofuel or other purposes (Dalrymple *et al.* 2013). Optimal rather than over-harvest is relevant as harvest costs are higher for smaller quantities (Udom *et al.* 2013). Higher harvest quotas may also be risk averse, given concerns of promoting and creating dense micro algae quantities and blooms within a contained area. Concerns relate to risks of toxic spills and contamination of external areas dependent on algae species (Masó and Garcés 2006; Zhu and Ketola 2011; Slade and Bauen 2013).

Without clear understanding of the 'alternative' that will allow heterogeneity according to industry and landscape context, biodiversity implication could be misleading. Aquatic and terrestrial implication, rather than assuming a positive biodiversity outcome with reduced land use, can improve understanding of micro algae as a solution for biofuel sustainability; further information is available in Chapter 9. The example also maintains relevance for other land versus water-based alternatives within the same industry. Within rather than between land or water-based alternatives of the same industry is also relevant. Furthermore, where additional crops are food based or monocultures are diversified to include food crops, they can contribute to food sovereignty (Waha *et al.* 2018; Garibaldi *et al.* 2018), supplying for subsistence or local markets alongside provisioning biodiversity outcome and benefit. They may also be selected for nutritional value, adding a beneficial dimension to food sovereignty. Where certified food crops cannot sell all harvested yields there can be alternative benefits. This may be considered complementary to industry heterogeneity as reliant on local rather than international demand. The outcome in terms of certification benefit will likely require evaluation.

Policy, national standards and legislation as supportive to farm and landscape heterogeneity

Complementary policy, national standards and legislation can make heterogeneity a consistent and realistic future prospect by requirement, and societal concern and preferences for local sustainable and nutritious produce might incentivise this support. The influence and contribution of sustainability certifications are also relevant for local and internationally sourced produce. For international sustainability certifications absolute complementarity with local policy, national standards and law is difficult. Additionally, standards of local produce versus internationally sourced produce for certifications of the same intention possibly vary. For example the stringency of the EU Organic standard compared to the international organic standards of IFOAM is lower (Englund and Berndes 2015). Variance in ability to verify implementation and outcomes according to local and internationally sourced produce can influence supportive capacity.

In any case, whether industry heterogeneity, market or societal demand and/or policy, national standards and law support a standard for heterogeneity, criteria can encourage and support prioritisation and redirection of industry crop preference (Correa *et al.* 2017) and complement functional farm and landscape heterogeneity aligned with the ESHR. Supportive company sourcing practices at the macro level can encourage industry heterogeneity conducive to and incentivising farm and landscape heterogeneity. Supportive policy, national standards and legislation can lead to a requirement for heterogeneity, and assist in substantiating standards and certifications.

The existing, the essential, the future

How biodiversity outcomes are intended, evaluated and ultimately understood as positive varies. A limited number of evaluations demonstrate biodiversity outcomes attributable to any sustainability certification. A need for further research and understanding exists. Improvement in detail, consistency and contextual considerations can substantiate intention and evaluation of benefit of sustainability standards and certificates. Evaluations specific to biodiversity and that consider how biodiversity outcomes are influential to and influenced by social and environmental factors, are essential. Encouraging functional biodiversity as aligned with the ESHR concept is an additional layer for future consideration. Farm and landscape heterogeneity can contribute significantly to functional biodiversity outcomes, particularly when supported by industry preference for diversified crop and plant commercial production systems. In addition, the positive contribution of heterogeneity for functional biodiversity outcomes may warrant inclusion as standard criteria and as a certified sustainable practice.

Acknowledgements

Melissa Vogt compiled information, and wrote the majority of the chapter. She also developed the conceptual frame, ESHR. A complementary framework is in development.

Oskar Englund contributed to the summary of his published research (Englund and Berndes 2015) and contributed to the discussion around this research in the context of this chapter.

Renzo Mori Junior reviewed and approved the Fairmined standard paragraphs.

Note

1 Each standard was given a numerical value (0–2) for each principle, indicating how well the principle was considered, based on the number of criteria with which it complied. The sum of these values for all principles was then used to indicate the overall *stringency* of the standard. Standards reaching a sum of 10 or more were classified as 'Stringent', and standards reaching a sum of six or less were classified as 'Unstringent'.

References

Allen H.D., Randall R.E., Amable G.S., Devereux B.J. (2006). The impact of changing olive cultivation practices on the ground flora of olive groves in the Messara and Psiloritis regions, Crete, Greece. Land Degradation and Development 17: 248–73.

Assandri G., Bogliani G., Pedrini P., Brambilla M. (2016). Diversity in the monotony? Habitat traits and management practise shape avian communities in intensive vineyards. Agriculture, Ecosystems and Environment 223: 250–60.

Ayree B., Ntibery B.K., Atorkui E. (2003). Trends in the small-scale mining of precious minerals in Ghana: a perspective on its environmental impact. Journal of Cleaner Production 11: 131–40.

Azhar B., Lindenmayer D.B., Wood J., Fischer J., Manning A., Mcelhinny C., Zakaria M., Marsden S. (2013). The influence of agricultural system, stand structural complexity and landscape context on foraging birds on oil palm landscapes. Ibis 155(2): 297–312.

Azhar B., Puan C.L., Zakaria M., Hassan N., Arif M. (2014a). Effects of monoculture and polyculture practices in oil palm practices in oil palm smallholdings on tropical farmland birds. Basic and Applied Ecology 15(4): 336–46.

Azhar B., Lindenmayer D.B., Wood J., Fischer J., Zakaria M. (2014b). Ecological impacts of oil palm agriculture on forest mammals in plantation and estates and smallholdings. Biodiversity and Conservation 23(5): 1175–91.

Azhar B., Saadun N., Puan C.L., Kamarudin N., Aziz N., Nurhidayu S., Fischer J. (2015a). Promoting landscape heterogeneity to improve the biodiversity benefits of certified palm oil production: evidence from Peninsular Malaysia. Global Ecology and Conservation 3: 553–61.

Azhar B., Puan C.L., Aziz N., Sainuddin M., Adila N., Samsuddin S., Asmah S., Syafiq M., Razak S.A., Hafzuddin A., Hawa A., Jamian S. (2015b). Effects of in situ habitat quality and landscape characteristics in the oil palm agricultural matrix on tropical understory birds, fruit bats and butterflies. Biodiversity and Conservation 24(12): 3125–44.

Banchirigah S.M. (2006). How have reforms fuelled the expansion of artisanal mining? Evidence from sub-Saharan Africa. Resources Policy 31(3): 165–71.

Bansah K.J., Yalley A.B., Dupey-Dumakor N. (2016). The hazardous nature of small scale underground mining in Ghana. Journal of Sustainable Mining 15(1): 8–25.

Barbieri P., Pellerin S., Nesme T. (2017). Comparing crop rotations between organic and conventional farming. Nature Scientific Reports 7(13761).

Baylis K., Honey-Roses J., Börner J., Corbera E., Ezzine-de-Blas D., Ferraro P.J., Lapeyre R., Persson U.M., Pfaff A., Wunder S. (2015). Mainstreaming impact evaluation in nature conservation. Conservation Letters 9(1): 58–64.

Blackman A., Rivera J.E. (2010). The evidence base for environmental and socio-economic impacts of 'sustainable' certifications. https://ssrn.com/abstract=1579083.

Blitzer E.J., Dormann C.F., Holzschuh A., Klein A., Rand T.A. (2012). Spillover of functionally important organisms between managed and natural habitats. Agriculture, Ecosystems and Environment 146(1): 34–43.

Bolanos S. (2006). Integrating GIS and Remote Sensing for coffee mapping. Paper presented at XII SELPER symposium, Cartagena, Colombia.

Boscolo D., Tokumoto P.M., Ferreira P.A., Ribeiro J.W., dos Santos J.S. (2017). Positive responses of flower visiting bees to landscape heterogeneity depend on functional connectivity levels. Perspective in Ecology and Conservation 15(1): 18–24.

Capmourteres, V., Anand, M. (2016). 'Conservation value': a review of the concept and its quantification. Ecosphere 7(10): e01476. doi: 10.1002/ecs2.1476

Carlson K.M., Heilmayr R., Gibbs H.K., Noojipady P., Burns D.N., Morton D.C., Walker N.F., Paoli G.D., Kremen C. (2017). Effect of oil palm sustainability certification on deforestation and fire in Indonesia. PNAS 115(1): 121–26.

Caradonna J.L. (2018). Organic agriculture is going mainstream, but not the way you think it is. The Conversation.

Carneiro M.L.N.M., Pradelle F., Braga S.L., Gomes M.S.P., Martins A.R.F.A., Turkovics F., Pradelle R.N.C. (2017). Potential of biofuels from algae: comparison with fossil fuels, ethanol and biodiesel in Europe and Brazil through life cycle assessment (LCA). Renewable and Sustainable Energy Reviews 72: 632–53.

Chaudhary A., Burivalova Z., Koh L.P., Hellweg S. (2016). Impact of forest management on species richness: global meta-analysis and economic trade-offs. Nature Scientific Reports 6(23954).

Chene M. (2014). Overview of corruption and anti-corruption in the Democratic Republic of Congo (DRC). Transparency International. www.transparency.org/files/content/corruptionqas/Country_Profile_DRC_2014.pdf.

Correa D.F., Beyer H.L., Psingham H.P., Thomas-Hall S.R., Schenk P.M. (2017). Biodiversity impacts of bioenergy production: microalgal vs. first generation biofuels. Renewable and Sustainable Energy Reviews 74: 1131–46.

Dalrymple O.K., Halfhide T., Udom I., Gilles B., Wolan J., Zhang Q., Ergas S. (2013). Wastewater use in algae production for generation of renewable resources: a review of preliminary results. Aquatic Biosystems 9(2).

Damette O., Delacote P. (2011). Unsustainable timber harvest, deforestation and the role of certification. Ecological Economics 70(6): 1211–19.

De Beenhouwer M., Aerts R., Honnay O. (2013). A global meta-analysis of the biodiversity and ecosystem service benefits of coffee and cacao agroforestry. Agriculture, Ecosystems and Environment 175(1): 1–7.

DeFries R.S., Fanzo J., Mondal P., Remans R., Wood S.A. (2017). Is voluntary certification of tropical agricultural commodities achieving sustainability goals for small-scale producers? A review of the evidence. Environmental Research Letters 12(3).

Donald P.F. (2004). Biodiversity impacts of some agricultural commodity production systems. Conservation Biology 18(1): 17–38.

Ebus B. (2018). The battle over gold buried in a Colombian mountain. Vice Canada. https://news.vice.com/en_ca/article/a3qexj/the-battle-over-gold-buried-in-a-colombian-mountain?utm_source=vicetwitterca.

Edwards D.P., Fisher B., Wilcove D.S. (2011). High conservation value or high confusion value? Sustainable agriculture and biodiversity conservation in the tropics. Conservation Letters 5(1).

Edwards D.P., Sloan S., Weng L., Dirks P., Sayer J., Laurance W.F. (2013). Mining and the African environment. Conservation Letters 7(3): 302–11.

Englund O., Börjesson P., Berndes G., Scarlat N., Dallemand J.-F., Grizzetti B., Dimitriou I., Mola-Yudego B., Fahl F. (2019). Beneficial land use change: strategic expansion of new biomass plantations can reduce environmental impacts from EU agriculture. EarthArXiv. March 17. https://doi.org/10.31223/osf.io/4h9dg.

Englund O., Berndes G. (2015). How do sustainability standards consider biodiversity? WIREs Energy Environment 4(1): 26–50.

Fahrig L., Baudry J., Briton's L., Burke F.G., Crist T.O., Fuller R.J., Sirami C., Sistwardena G.M., Martin J. (2010). Functional landscape heterogeneity and animal biodiversity in agricultural landscapes. Ecology Letters 14(2): 101–12.

Fairmined (2014). Fairmined standard for gold from artisanal and small-scale mining including associated precious metals. Current Version 2.0 RC (release candidate)/ ARM. www.responsiblemines.org/wp-content/uploads/2017/06/FAIRMINED_V2.0-RC_EN.pdf.

FairWild (2018). The FairWild standard in practice: certification and more. FairWild Foundation Secretariat. www.fairwild.org.

Ferraro P. (2009). Counterfactual thinking and impact evaluating in environmental policy. New Directions for Evaluation. Special Issue: Environmental program and policy evaluation: addressing methodological challenges. 122: 75–84.

Fischer C., Aguilar F., Jawahar P., Sedjo R. (2005). Forest Certification: Toward Common Standards? Resources for the Future, Discussion Paper 05–10.

Freudmann A., Mollik P., Tschapka M., Schulze C. (2015). Impacts of oil palm agriculture on phyllostomid bat assemblages. Biodiversity and Conservation 24(14): 3583–99.

Gardiner M.M., Landis D.A., Gratton C., DiFonzo C.D., O'Neal M., Chacon J.M., Wayo M.T., Schmidt N.P., Mueller E.E., Heimpel G.E. (2009). Landscape diversity enhances biological control of an introduced crop pest in the north-central USA. Ecological Applications 19(1): 143–54.

Garibaldi L.A., Andersson G.K.S., Requier F., Fijen T.P.M., Hipolito J., Kleijn D., Perez-Mendez N., Rollin O. (2018). Complementarity and synergisms among ecosystem services supporting crop yield. Global Food Security 17: 38–47.

Gauthier S., Bernier P., Kuuluvainen T., Schvidenko A.Z., Schepaschenko D.G. (2015). Boreal forest health and global change. Science 349(6250).

Ghazoul J., Garcia C., Kushalappa C.G. (2009). Landscape labelling: a concept for next-generation payment for ecosystem service schemes. Forest Ecology and Management 258: 1889–95.

Gibbs H.K., Brown S., Niles J.O., Foley J.A. (2007). Monitoring and estimating tropical forest carbon stocks: making REDD a reality. Environmental Research Letters 213: 054023.

Gomez C. (2018). LACCCB2018 Strengthening conservation connections between the Caribbean and the Americas. IUCN Red list of ecosystems. https://iucnrle.org/blog/lacccb2018.

Grab H., Danforth B., Poveda K., Loeb G. (2018). Landscape simplification reduces classical biological control and crop yield. Ecological Applications 28(2): 348–55.

Gulbrandsen L.H. (2005). Sustainable forestry in Sweden: the effect of competition among private certification schemes. The Journal of Environment and Development 14(3): 338–55.

Gunderson L.H. (2000). Ecological resilience – in theory and application. Annual Review of Ecology and Systematics 31: 425–39.

Hansson J., Berndes G., Englund O., Freitas F.L.M., Sparovek G. (2019). How is biodiversity protection influencing the potential for bioenergy feedstock production on grasslands? Global Change Biology, Bioenergy 11(3): 517–38.

Hardt E., Borgomeo E., dos Santos R.F., Pinto L.F.G., Metzger J.P., Sparovek G. (2015). Does certification improve biodiversity conservation in Brazilian coffee farms? Forest Ecology and Management 357: 181–94.

Hass A.L., Kormann U.G., Tscharntke T., Clough Y., Baillod A.B., Sirami C., Fahrig L., Martin J., Baudry J., Bertrand C., Bosch J., Brotons L., Burel F., Goerges R., Gialt D., Marcos-Garcia M.A., Ricarte A., Siriwardena G., Batary P. (2018). Landscape configuration heterogeneity by small-scale agriculture, not crop diversity maintains pollinators and plant reproduction in western Europe. PNAS 285(1872): 20172242.

Haurez B., Dainou K., Vermeulen C., Kleinschroth F., Mortier F., Gourlet-Fleury S., Doucet J. (2017). A look at Intact Forest Landscapes (IFLs) and their relevance in Central American forest policy. Forest Policy and Economics 80: 192–99.

Hilson G. (2009). Small-scale mining, poverty and economic development in sub-Saharan Africa: an overview. Resources Policy 34(1–2): 1–5.

Holling C.S. (1973). Resilience and stability of ecological systems. Annual Review of Ecology and Systematics 4: 1–23.

Holzschuh A., Steffan Dewenter I., Tscharntke T. (2009). Grass strip corridors in agricultural landscapes enhance nest site colonization by solitary wasps. Ecological Applications 19: 123–32.

Houghton R.A. (2007). Balancing the global carbon budget. Annual Review of Earth and Planetary Sciences 35: 313–47.

Jones E.G. (2013). Personal communication. Ulaanbaatar, Mongolia.

Katayama T., Amano T., Naoe S., Yamakita T., Komatsu I., Takagawa S., Sato N., Ueta M., Miyashita T. (2014). Landscape heterogeneity–biodiversity relationship: effect of range size. PLoS ONE. https://doi.org/10.1371/journal.pone.0093359.

Lahiri-Dutt K. (2006). 'May God give us chaos, so that we can plunder': a critique of 'resource curse' and conflict theories. Development 49(3): 14–21.

Lebwaba P., Nhlengetwa K. (2016). When policy is not enough: prospects and challenges of artisanal and small-scale mining in South Africa. Journal of Sustainable Development and Law 25(7). https://doi.org/10.4314/jsdlp.v7il.2.

Lee M., Martin J.A. (2017). Avian species and functional diversity in agricultural landscapes: does landscape heterogeneity matter? PLoS ONE. https://doi.org/10.1371/journal.pone.0170540.

Long S. (2016). Adani companies facing multiple financial crime, corruption probes. ABC News.

Masó M., Garcés E. (2006). Harmful microalgae blooms (HAB): problematic and conditions that induce them. Marine Pollution Bulletin 53: 620–30.

McDaniel M.D., Tiemann L.K., Grandy A.S. (2014). Does agricultural crop diversity enhance soil microbial biomass and organic matter dynamics? A meta analysis. Ecological Applications 24(3): 560–70.

McDonnell J., Menzies J., Stagg C., Choudhary P. (2017). Transparency International report on corruption risks in the mining approval process. KWM. www.kwm.com/en/au/knowledge/insights/transparency-international-report-corruption-risks-mining-approvals-20171010.

Milder J.C., Newsom D., Lambin E., Rueda X. (2016). Measuring impacts of certification on biodiversity at multiple scales: experience from SAN/Rainforest Alliance system and priorities for the future. In C. Pavel, D.J. Leaman (Eds.). Policy Matters: Certification and Biodiversity. How Voluntary Certification Standards Impact Biodiversity and Human Livelihoods. IUCN/CEESP. https://doi.org/10.2305/IUCN.CH.2014.PolicyMatters-21.en.

Miller A.M.M., Bush S. (2014). Authority without credibility? Competition and conflict between eco labels in tuna fisheries. Journal of Cleaner Production 107: 137–45.

Miller K.R. (1996). Balancing the scales: guidelines for increasing biodiversity's chances through bioregional management. World Resources Institute, Washington, USA.

Monck-Whipp L., Martin A.E., Francis C.M., Fahrig L. (2018). Farmland heterogeneity benefits bats in agricultural landscapes. Agriculture, Ecosystems and Environment 253: 131–39.

Moss B. (2008). Water pollution by agriculture. Philosophical Translations of the Royal Society B: Biological Sciences 363(1491): 659–66.

NASAA (2018). Into organics: your entry into organic certification with NASAA certified organics. www.nasaa.com.au/documents/publications/into-organics/45-into-organics-2014/file.html (accessed August 2018).

Nesper M., Kueffer C., Krishnan S., Kushalappa C.G., Ghazoul J. (2017). Shade tree diversity enhances coffee production and quality in agroforestry systems in the Western Ghats. Agriculture, Ecosystems and Environment 247: 172–181.

Ostrom E. (1990). Governing the Commons: The Evolution of Institutions for Collective Action. Cambridge University Press.

Owusu-Nimo F., Mantey J., Nyarko K.B., AppiahEfffah E., Aubynn A. (2018). Spatial distribution patterns of illegal artisanal small-scale gold mining (Galamsey) operations in Ghana: a focus on the Western Region. Heliyon 4(2): e00534.

Pan Y., Birdsey R.A., Phillips O.L., Jackson R.B. (2013). The structure, distribution and biomass of the world's forests. Annual Review Ecology, Evolution and Systematics 44: 593–622.

Pardo L.E., Campbell M.J., Clements G.R., Laurance W.F. (2018). Terrestrial mammal responses to oil palm dominated landscapes in Colombia. PLoS ONE. https://doi.org/10.1371/journal.pone.0197539.

Polisar J., de Thoisy B., Ruiz D.I., Santos F.D., McNab R.B., Garcia-Anleu R., Ponce-Santiago G., Arispe R., Venegas C. (2017). Using certified timber extraction to benefit jaguar and ecosystem conservation. Ambio 1–16. https://doi.org/10.1007/s13280-016-0853-y.

Ponte S. (2004). Standards and sustainability in the coffee sector: a global value chain approach. UNCTD and IISD. www.iisd.org/pdf/2004/sci_coffee_standards.pdf.

Potapov P.A., Yaroshenko S., Turubanova S., Dubinin M., Laestadius L., Thies C., Aksenov D., Egorov A., Yesipova Y., Glushkov I., Karpachevskiy M., Kostikova A., Manisha A., Tsybikanova E., Zhuravleva I. (2008). Mapping the world's intact forest landscapes by remote sensing. Ecology and Society 13(2).

Potts J., Lynch M., Wilkings A., Huppe G., Cunningham M., Voora V. (2014). The State of Sustainability Initiatives Review. International Institute for Sustainable Development. www.iisd.org/PDF/2014/ssi_2014.pdf.

Rainforest Alliance (RA) (2017). Sustainable Agriculture Standards Version 1.2: For Farms and Producer Groups Involved in Crop and Cattle Production. Sustainable Agriculture Network. www.rainforest-alliance.org/business/sas/wp-content/uploads/2017/11/03_rainforest-alliance-sustainable-agriculture-standard_en.pdf.

Richards J.F. (1990). Land transformation. In B.L. Turner, W.C. Clarke, R.W. Kates et al. (Eds.). The Land as Transformed by Human Action. New York, Cambridge University Press, 163–78.

Riojas-López M.E., Melink E., Luevano J. (2018). A semiarid fruit agroecosystem as a conservation-friendly option for small mammals in an anthropocised landscape in Mexico. Ecological Applications 28(2): 495–507.

Rodrigues T.F., Chiarello A.G. (2018). Native forests within and outside protected areas are key for nine-bandedarmadillo (Dasypus novemcinctus) occupancy in agricultural landscapes. Agriculture, Ecosystems and Environment 266: 133–41.

Romero C., Putz F.E., Guariguata M.R., Sills E.O., Cerutti P.O., Lescuyer G. (2013). An overview about current knowledge about the impacts of forest management certification: a proposed framework for its evaluation. Centre for International Forestry Research (CIFOR). Occasional Paper 91.

Rueda X., Thomas N.E., Lambin E.F. (2014). Eco-certification and coffee cultivation enhance tree cover and forest connectivity in the Colombian coffee landscapes. Regional Environmental Change 15(1): 25–33.

Salek M., Hula V., Kipson M., Dankova R., Niedobova J., Gamero A. (2018). Bringing diversity back to agriculture: smaller fields and non-crop elements enhance biodiversity in intensively managed arable farmlands. Ecological Indicators 90: 65–73.

Santana J., Reino L., Stoate C., Moteira F., Ribeiro P.F., Santos J.L., Rotenberry J.T., Beja P. (2017). Combined effects of landscape composition and heterogeneity on farmland avian diversity. Ecology and Evolution 7(4): 121–23.

Saturni F.T., Jaffe R., Metzger J.P. (2016). Landscape structure influences bee community and coffee pollination at different spatial scales. Agriculture, Ecosystems and Environment 235: 1–12.

Schindler D.W. (1998). Sustaining aquatic ecosystems in Boreal regions. Conservation Ecology 2: 18.

Schneider M.K., Luscher G., Jeanneret P., … Herzog F. (2014). Gains in species diversity in organically farmed fields are not propagated at the farm level. Nature Communications 5(4151).

Slade R., Bauen A. (2013). Microalgae cultivation for biofuels: cost, energy balance, environmental impacts and future prospects. Biomass and Bioenergy 53: 29–38.

Sollman R., Mohamed A., Niedballa J., Bender J., Ambushes L., Lagan P., Mannan S., Ong R.C., Langner A., Gardner B., Wilting A. (2017). Quantifying mammal biodiversity co-benefits in certified tropical forests. Diversity and Distributions 23: 317–28. https://doi.org/10.1111/ddi.12530.

Strevens C.M.J., Bonsall M.B. (2011). The impact of alternative harvesting strategies in a resource-consumer metapopulation. Journal of Applied Ecology 48: 102–11.

Takahashi R., Todo Y. (2017). Coffee certification and forest quality: evidence from a wild coffee forest in Ethiopia. World Development 92: 158–66.

Tayleur C., Balmford A., Buchanan G.M., Butchart S.H.M., … Phalan B. (2016). Global coverage of agricultural sustainability standards, and their role in conserving biodiversity. Conservation Letters 10(5).

Tayleur C., Balmford A., Buchanan G.M., Butchart S.H.M., Walker C.C., Ducharme H., Green R.E., Milder J.C., Sanderson F.J., Thomas D.H.J., Tracewski L., Vickery J., Phalan B. (2018). Where are commodity crop certified, and what does it mean for conservation and poverty alleviation? Biological Conservation 27: 36–46.

Teuscher M., Vorlaufer M., Wollni M., Brose U., Mulyani Y., Clough Y. (2015). Trade-offs between bird diversity and abundance, yields and revenue in smallholder in palm plantations in Sumatra, Indonesia. Biological Conservation 186(306).

Ting J.K.Y., Shogo K., Jerzebski M.P. (2016). The efficacy of voluntary certification standards for biodiversity conservation. In C. Pavel, D.J. Leaman (Eds.). Policy Matters: Certification and Biodiversity. How Voluntary Certification Standards Impact Biodiversity and Human Livelihoods. IUCN/CEESP. https://doi. org/10.2305/IUCN.CH.2014.PolicyMatters-21.en.

Toledo R.M., Santos R.F., Baeten L., Perring M.P., Verheyen K. (2018). Soil properties and neighbouring forest cover affect above-ground biomass and functional composition during tropical forest restoration. Applied Vegetation Science 21(2): 179–89.

Toledo-Hernandez M., Wanger T.C., Tscharntk T. (2017). Neglected pollinators: can enhanced pollination services improve cocoa yields? A review. Agriculture, Ecosystems and Environment 247: 137–48.

Tolessa T., Senbeta F., Kidane M. (2016). Landscape composition and configuration in the central highlands of Ethiopia. Ecology and Evolution 6(20): 7409–21.

Tom-Dery D., Dagben Z.J., Cobbina S.J. (2012). Effect of illegal small-scale mining operations on vegetation cover of arid northern Ghana. Research Journal of Environmental and Earth Sciences 4(6): 674–79.

Tscharntke T., Milder J.C., Schroth G., … Ghazoul J. (2015). Conserving biodiversity through certification of tropical agroforestry crops and local and landscape scales. Conservation Letters 8(1): 14–23.

TV360 Nigeria (2013). Battling oil theft in the Niger Delta. www.youtube.com/ watch?v=wEcp2gjp1LI.

Tysiachniouk M., McDermott C.L. (2016). Certification with Russian characteristics: implications for social and environmental equity. Forest Policy and Economics 62(C): 43–53.

Udom I., Zaribaf B.H., Halfhide T., Gillie B., Dalrymple O., Zhang Q., Ergas S.J. (2013). Harvesting microalgae grown on wastewater. Bioresource Technology 139: 101–6. doi: 10.1016/j.biortech.2013.04.002.

ViceNews (2018). The battle raging in Nigeria over control of oil. https://news.vice. com/en_us/article/j5aq98/the-battle-raging-in-nigeria-over-control-of-oil.

Vice on HBO (2018). The battle raging in Nigeria over control of oil. www.youtube. com/watch?v=vAgw_Zyznx0.

Vogt M. (2016). Within commercial constraints: functional biodiversity and agribiodiversity in coffee farming landscapes of Cuba and Costa Rica. Presented at the 4th Oceania Congress for Conservation Biology, Brisbane, Australia.

Vogt M.A.B. (2017). Toward functional pollinator abundance and diversity: comparing policy response for neonicotinoid use to demonstrate a need for cautious and well-planned policy. Biological Conservation 215: 196–212.

Vyas K. (2018). Desperate Venezuelans dig up paradise in search for gold. The Wall Street Journal 20 November.

Waha K., van Wijk M.T., Fritz S., See L., Thornton P.K., Wichern J., Herrero M. (2018). Agricultural diversification as an important strategy for achieving food security in Africa. Global Change Biology 24(8): 3390–400.

Waldron A., Justicia R., Smith L., Sanchez M. (2012). Conservation through chocolate: a win–win for biodiversity and farmers in Ecuador's lowland tropics. Conservation Letters 5(3): 213–21.

Wietzke A., Westphal C., Gras P., Krat M., Pfohl K., Kalrovsky P., Pawelzik E., Tscharntke T., Smit I. (2018). Insect pollination as a key factor for strawberry physiology and marketable fruit quality. Agriculture, Ecosystems and Environment 258: 197–204.

Willer H., Lernoud J. (2017). Organic Agriculture Worldwide 2017: Current Statistics. BIOFACH. http://orgprints.org/31197/1/willer-lernoud-2017-global-data-biofach.pdf.

Wilson S.A. (2015). Corporate Social Responsibility and power relations: impediments to community development in post-war Sierra Leone diamond and rutile mining areas. The Extractive Industries and Society (2)4: 704–13.

Wilson S., Mitchell G.W., Pasher J., McGovern M., Hudson M.R., Fahrig L. (2017). Influence of crop type, heterogeneity and woody structure on avian biodiversity in agricultural landscapes. Ecological Indicators 83: 218–26.

Yankit P., Rana K., Sharma H.K., Thakur M., Thakur R.K. (2018). Effect of bumble bee pollination on quality and yield of tomato (solanum lycopersicum mill.) grown under protected conditions. International Journal of Microbiology and Applied Sciences 7(1): 257–63.

Zhu L., Ketola T. (2011). Microalgae production as a biofuel feedstock: risks and challenges. International Journal of Sustainable Development and World Ecology 19(3): 268–74.

4 How does FSC certification of forest management benefit conservation of biodiversity?

Franck Trolliet,[1] *Melissa Vogt and Fritz Kleinschroth*

Introduction

Forest management certification has been developed to tackle pressing problems in the forestry sector such as conversion of forests into plantations or other land uses, illegal activities, biodiversity loss and social inequality. Certification by the Forest Stewardship Council (FSC) developed in the 1990s to promote socially beneficial, environmentally appropriate and economically viable forest management. As a voluntary, market-based and multistakeholder initiative relying on third-party verification for certification, FSC represents a unique strategy to ensure good, responsible and transparent forest management (Bernstein and Cashore, 2004). Understanding impacts resulting from FSC certification is increasingly important for both internal organisational learning and to inform consumers, donors, industries and a range of stakeholders involved.[2]

A growing number of scientific studies attempt to evaluate outcomes and impacts of FSC certification on a range of social, economic, ecological and political aspects (Burivalova *et al.*, 2017). The demonstration of environmental impacts such as benefits for biodiversity conservation given the current rates of deforestation and biodiversity loss across the globe (Dirzo *et al.*, 2014; Hansen *et al.*, 2013) is of particular interest. A literature review has recently assessed the impacts of forest certification and found considerable environmental benefits (Burivalova *et al.*, 2017). Yet, this work considers studies that evaluate effects of FSC certification and studies that evaluate effects of reduced-impact logging (RIL). While FSC certification typically requires the implementation of RIL guidelines, looking solely at those guidelines is not sufficient to comprehensively perceive the added value of FSC for conservation of biodiversity.

In this chapter, we provide an overview of studies that evaluate FSC certification and associated benefits for forest biodiversity conservation. We include studies with response variables that are known to be directly (animal and plant diversity) or indirectly (deforestation, forest degradation) related to forest biodiversity conservation. The chapter is divided into three parts: (1) an overview of published literature based on (a) operational-level outcomes as part of FSC standards compliance and certification processes and (b) on–the-ground, field-measured outcomes; (2) a discussion of some general gaps in impact evaluation and areas where our understanding could be improved; (3) a discussion of some of the benefits of certifying forest management in Intact Forest Landscapes.

Methods and study scope

Our literature selection was not limited to impact evaluation *sensu stricto*, but includes impact-related studies that present data about FSC certification and associated outcomes. We also included field studies providing on–the-ground data such as descriptions of biodiversity-related variables within FSC-certified forests, and studies such as standards content evaluations and analysis of Corrective Action Requests (CARs). CARs are issued by certification bodies when forest operations are not in compliance with specific indicators required by FSC standards. The operating company then has to change noncompliant behaviours or practices according to the indicator. The number of CARs, their category (minor or major) and the specific criteria they relate to are compiled in publicly available certification reports (https://info.fsc.org/). Certification reports and CARs indicate areas where operations have been improved to become certified. These improvements indicate outcomes associated with FSC certification. Thus, CARs do not truly inform about 'impacts', as actual *in situ* outcomes are not explicitly reported by certification bodies or by foresters. Certification reports and CARs do, however, remain a useful proxy for the change in behaviour of forest management practice, which must be or has been made. CARs provide information about operational-level changes, social, ecological, economic; and the specific criteria of the FSC standards. CAR analysis therefore allows clear identification of how certification directly influences forestry activities and sheds light on what baseline outcomes can be expected. Only impact evaluations can disentangle the true added value of certified logging as compared to conventional logging practices. We do, however, believe that all impact-related studies provide valuable insights to understand how FSC can be associated with biodiversity conservation.

We assessed the quality of each study according to research design and methods used to evaluate the level of evidence and attributability of the studied variables to FSC certification. We isolated those studies that provided the strongest evidence that an outcome was attributable to FSC certification. Studies with strong research designs typically compare FSC-certified forest management units with conventionally managed forest management units, perform assessment over time (pre- versus post-logging) and use multiple replicates per treatment (i.e. more than one certified and one uncertified operation). Moreover, robust studies will consider the effect of confounding variables and/or a robust choice of control replicates minimising the potential effects of such confounding factors. More detail on strong research designs necessary to investigate certification impacts is provided by Romero *et al.* (2017).

Standard compliance, operational-level outcomes: the baseline of impacts

A first category of research on FSC certification relates to operational-level and theoretical outcomes. Here, the typical research question is what has been changed in the forest management practices to comply with certification requirements? Answering this question allows clarification of what can be expected as a direct consequence of certification. A series of papers analysed FSC national standard content and the potential added value as compared to the respective national requirements (Lehtonen and von Stedingk, 2017a, 2017b, 2016).

A different research approach considers CARs from certification reports. For instance, some research reports that CARs issued for operations in boreal forests of Russia, Latvia and Estonia show that approximately half of all CARs raised ecological concerns. In these cases, FSC certification required the identification and protection of High Conservation Value (HCV) forests and woodland key habitats, increased the amount of biotope trees and dead wood, and enforced the monitoring of threatened species (Hirschberger, 2005a, 2005b, 2005c). Similarly, CARs raised in 32 European countries found that most nonconformities concerned environmental problems. Overall, the biggest effect of certification was an increase in the size of protected areas, newly conducted inventories of HCV forests and more dead wood and biodiversity trees left on site (Hain and Ahas, 2011).

In another study, Newsom and Hewitt (2005) analysed all CARs given by auditors in 129 forest management operations in tropical and temperate forests distributed across 21 countries around the world. They found that for 63 per cent of operations certification required an improved treatment for threatened and endangered species, riparian habitats and HCV forests.

Impacts in FSC-certified operations: on-the-ground evidence

The quality of sampling designs and analysis of studies that reported new findings using field data in FSC-certified operations varied greatly between studies. Overall, there were few studies that provided strong evidence of outcomes attributable to FSC certification, as a demonstration of causality (van der Ven and Cashore, 2018). The most common shortcoming in impact studies is the lack of spatiotemporal control treatments, replicates or consideration of the effects of confounding variables (Burivalova *et al.*, 2017; Romero *et al.*, 2017; van der Ven and Cashore, 2018). Indeed, several studies aiming at understanding the impacts of FSC certification compared FSC-certified forest management units with forests under other types of management such as protected areas or multiple-use zones (Hughell and Butterfield,

2008; Stokes *et al.*, 2010). Other studies solely described characteristics of certified concessions without comparing them with a counterfactual situation such as a conventionally managed operation (Polisar *et al.*, 2017; Tobler *et al.*, 2018). Such designs fail to address the added value of certification as compared to conventional logging practices. Also, limited control for confounding factors on response variables, and the lack of replicates, considering more than one certified and uncertified forest, prevent isolating the specific effect of certification from other factors that possibly influence the same biodiversity indicator – for example hunting level, forest connectivity and neighbouring activities (Bahaa-el-din *et al.*, 2016; Imai *et al.*, 2009; Sollmann *et al.*, 2017).

Existing research does therefore provide valuable and important information about how FSC certification possibly limits negative impacts of forestry activity and its subsequent role for biodiversity conservation. The designs and methods used can, however, limit our ability to draw any substantial conclusions. We identified 34 studies that explored how FSC certification could impact biodiversity conservation. Out of those 34, we retained only five that used a strong sampling and analysis design to investigate the problematic (Blackman *et al.*, 2018; Heilmayr and Lambin, 2016; Kleinschroth *et al.*, 2017; Panlasigui *et al.*, 2015; Rico *et al.*, 2017). These studies allow adequate testing of the effect of FSC certification on biodiversity conservation, i.e. to attribute potential impacts to FSC. Among the 34 selected studies, the represented forest biomes, tropical, temperate and boreal were found to be disproportionate. Indeed, most impact research is conducted in the tropics (Table 4.1). This imbalance is especially cogent since among approximately 200 million ha of FSC-certified forest as at the end of 2016, *c.*10 per cent were tropical, 40 per cent temperate and 50 per cent boreal forest (FSC M&E report, 2016). This equals approximately one scientific paper produced for *c.*0.7 Mha of tropical forest against one for *c.*26.7 Mha of temperate and one for *c.*33.3 Mha of boreal forest. Discussions about biodiversity outcomes in boreal and temperate forests are therefore limited by availability of studies as compared to tropical forests.

The analysed studies covered a variety of subjects, but a majority investigated if FSC certification curbed forest degradation and deforestation or provided relative benefits for plant and animal biodiversity. The five studies that we identified as using the strongest research designs all investigated the problem of forest cover change. Overall, findings related to forest degradation, fragmentation or deforestation varied from one study to another. Some studies reported that FSC certification led to a reduction in tree cover loss (Damette and Delacote, 2011; Heilmayr and Lambin, 2016; Hodgdon *et al.*, 2015; Hughell and Butterfield, 2008; Miteva *et al.*, 2015) or forest degradation (Feldpausch *et al.*, 2005; Medjibe *et al.*, 2013; Tritsch *et al.*, 2016). Such positive outcomes are not, however, consistent across all studies, with some being unable to find any effect of FSC on deforestation (Blackman *et al.*, 2018; Villalobos *et al.*, 2018), others finding both positive and negative effects depending on the country or region considered (Panlasigui *et al.*, 2015; Rana

Table 4.1 Studies providing evidence of benefits associated with FSC certification of forest management

Biodiversity outcomes	Bioregion		
	Boreal	Temperate	Tropical
Stream condition		Dias et al., 2015	
Forest disturbance, forest fragmentation; deforestation	Elbakidze et al., 2016, 2011; Villalobos et al., 2018	Heilmayr and Lambin, 2016	Blackman et al., 2018; Damette and Delacote, 2011; Feldpausch et al., 2005; Griscom et al., 2018; Hodgdon et al., 2015; Hughell and Butterfield, 2008; Kleinschroth et al., 2017; Medjibe et al., 2013; Miteva et al., 2015; Panlasigui et al., 2015; Rana and Sills, 2018; Rico et al., 2017; Tritsch et al., 2016
Animal community diversity			Azevedo-Ramos et al., 2006; Bahaa-el-din et al., 2016; Griscom et al., 2018; Haurez et al., 2016; Imai et al., 2009; Morgan et al., 2017; Polisar et al., 2017; Roopsind et al., 2017; Sollmann et al., 2017; Stokes et al., 2010; Strindberg et al., 2018; Tobler et al., 2018
Plant community diversity		Dias et al., 2016	Griscom et al., 2018; Kalonga et al., 2016; Kukkonen and Hohnwald, 2009; Medjibe et al., 2013; Sillanpää et al., 2017
FSC's Principles & Criteria related variables			Barbosa de Lima et al., 2009

and Sills, 2018; Rico *et al.*, 2017). For the Congo Basin, Kleinschroth *et al.* (2017) reported that the loss of roadless space in Intact Forest Landscapes (IFL) increased after FSC certification due to faster expansion of logging road networks compared to noncertified concessions. Studies with the strongest design reflect such varying outcomes with some studies reporting that FSC certification helps curb deforestation and forest degradation (Heilmayr and Lambin, 2016; Panlasigui *et al.*, 2015; Rico *et al.*, 2017) and others with no significant effect (Blackman *et al.*, 2018; Panlasigui *et al.*, 2015; Rico *et al.*, 2017).

Solid evidence for the outcomes of FSC certification on biodiversity based on field-based inventories is therefore lacking. While several studies explored the direct benefits for biodiversity conservation such as animal and plant diversity, none of them provided strong evidence for a direct effect of FSC certification. Some positive findings from case studies are worth highlighting. Several studies investigating animal diversity in tropical forests provide arguments for the positive benefits of FSC certification on populations of medium or large vertebrates in Latin America (Azevedo-Ramos *et al.*, 2006; Polisar *et al.*, 2017; Roopsind *et al.*, 2017; Tobler *et al.*, 2018), South-East Asia (Imai *et al.*, 2009; Sollmann *et al.*, 2017) or Africa (Bahaa-el-din *et al.*, 2016; Haurez *et al.*, 2016; Morgan *et al.*, 2017; Stokes *et al.*, 2010; Strindberg *et al.*, 2018). Most studies do not systematically compare the effect of FSC certification with noncertified forestry activity as a control. Some authors did, however, find animal species in FSC-certified forests to show similar abundances as in protected areas (Roopsind *et al.*, 2017; Tobler *et al.*, 2018). A commonly highlighted added value of certification is the required control of hunting within the forest management unit. A number of studies also investigated the response of plant diversity to certification. While some reported positive impacts (Kalonga *et al.*, 2016; Sillanpää *et al.*, 2017), others were less conclusive. For instance, Kukkonen and Hohnwald (2009) found that certified forests had higher abundance of light-demanding species relative to conventional logging and that the latter had a more similar floristic composition to protected than to certified forests. It is, however, important to recognise that several unaccounted factors most probably confound attributability to forest management practice. Similarly, Medjibe *et al.* (2013) did not find differences in tree species composition between certified and conventional logging. They concluded that this lack of differences was due to logging intensities being particularly low under both management regimes.

A few other studies addressed conservation outcomes in a more general way. Dias *et al.* (2015) found a positive effect of FSC certification on the ecological conditions of streams in Mediterranean cork oak woodlands compared to noncertified areas.

Griscom *et al.* (2018) modelled biodiversity and deforestation in response to different scenarios of land tenure security, harvest intensity and certification in tropical forests. They concluded that certified reduced-impact logging practices provided the highest benefits for conservation.

Figure 4.1 A stream crossing an FSC–certified temperate forest.
Source: © FSC GD/Milan Reška.

Figure 4.2 An FSC-certified concession in Central Africa demonstrates how certified
timber harvest conserves forest.

Source: © Jean-Louis Doucet.

Finally, using interviews and field observations in FSC-certified and
uncertified forests, Barbosa de Lima *et al.* (2009) reported that FSC certification positively impacted all environmental aspects evaluated.

Understanding the studied system and defining the norm

The lack of general consensus from research findings – see studies of Kukkonen and Hohnwald (2009) and Medjibe *et al.* (2013) above – remind us that
FSC certification is not a systematic guarantee of a given level of improvement of forest management. Sustainable forest management also clearly exists
without certification. In contrast, as a market-based instrument, FSC certification guarantees that a forest management operation is in compliance with a
standard that results from a multistakeholder engagement process. FSC allows
consumers to know that certified products come from responsibly managed
forests. Yet, CARs suggest that compliance with FSC standards very often
requires improvement in forestry operations as compared to business-as-usual.
The level of improvement, and therefore the outcome that can be expected
from certification, depends on the baseline of conventional forestry practices.
These practices are themselves influenced by the social, economic, ecological

and political context of the studied system, varying across scales (Lehtonen and von Stedingk, 2016; Sundstrom and Henry, 2017).

Socio-ecological systems, conventional logging practices and FSC requirements show wide differences across regions and countries (McDermott *et al.*, 2012, 2008). Hence, outcomes of FSC certification cannot be expected to be of the same type or magnitude everywhere. The counterfactual situations used in impact studies directly determine levels of impacts that can be detected. Therefore, we believe that the context of the studied system needs to be properly described to allow a complete and transparent interpretation of effects. For example, Villalobos *et al.* (2018) reported that certification of smallholders did not provide additional environmental value. However, what the authors failed to mention is that *c.*65 per cent of the study countries' productive forests has been certified by FSC and/or PEFC for *c.*20 years. That means, certification has become the norm and may have influenced practices in uncertified forests as well. Hence, the level of benefits that can be expected compared with uncertified forests is lower than in countries where conventional logging practices are far from what is required to comply with FSC standards. An important gap in the available literature is a clear description of conventional forestry practices and how FSC-certified practices differ from them. This would give an indication of expected, specific outcomes from certification. It is therefore important to ask, what is the norm, and what assumptions can we make with regard to outcomes of FSC certification in light of a specific social, economic and ecological context? Another challenge when evaluating the specific effect of certification intervention is the time since certification and the time since logging activity.

The spillover and unintended effects of FSC certification, such as its influence on national forest governance, has gained increased attention (Cashore *et al.*, 2007; Gulbrandsen, 2004; Heilmayr and Lambin, 2016; Sundstrom and Henry, 2017). Such findings are also important to consider in an evaluation of the dynamics of conventional forestry and when predicting levels of achievable certification impacts (Villalobos *et al.*, 2018). For instance, spillover effects can have longlasting positive effects on forest management and hence potential benefits for biodiversity conservation (Sundstrom and Henry, 2017).

While outcomes of FSC certification are usually assessed in a given field of social, economic or environmental outcomes, we highlight that national FSC standards are the result of negotiations between the three chambers. This process in itself has been described by governance scholars as one of the main values of FSC (Tysiachniouk and McDermott, 2016; Visseren-Hamakers and Glasbergen, 2007). Biodiversity conservation is not an isolated goal of FSC forest management certification. The findings reported in this chapter, as interpreted and discussed, could greatly benefit from an understanding of the outcomes related to other categories to facilitate a more comprehensive understanding of how certification influences forest management. An example is socioeconomic needs to ensure viability of forestry activity. Ensuring such consideration and understanding for system assessment, and providing complementary perspectives from other fields could help researchers' understanding of possible trade-offs between stakeholders' interests and consequential outcomes in a given chamber. This can allow a more tolerant understanding and expectation of outcomes for any given certificate. Having recognised the importance of a more comprehensive understanding of potential trade-offs between the chambers of sustainability, and how it may influence outcomes, a consistent and legitimate approach to assessing each, and biodiversity outcomes as relevant for this chapter remains necessary.

Certifying forest management in Intact Forest Landscapes

Forest management standards are subject to regular editions and developments due to the constant stakeholder engagement in the decision-making processes. An intended leap forward for improved biodiversity protection in the FSC system was the decision in 2014 to protect Intact Forest Landscapes (IFLs) as HCV areas. IFLs are defined as large forest areas that do not show any remotely detected sign of human activity (Potapov *et al.*, 2008). Intact forest ecosystems have been shown to retain crucial refuges for biodiversity, store large amounts of carbon and provide important ecosystem services (Watson *et al.*, 2018) – as such they are often considered as HCV. The optimal strategy to conserve intactness is their full, permanent and strict protection. Concentrating forest operations by harvesting in smaller areas may in theory spare intact forests from exploitation (Kleinschroth *et al.*, 2016).

Sparing large areas from human use requires protected areas, commonly put in place and enforced by governments, not by certification schemes. Yet, such spared forests will only remain intact if their effective protection is maintained over a long term, requiring stable governance, control of corruption and sufficient funding, which can be challenging in many countries. The integration of development rights and local stakeholders representing socioeconomic interests (e.g. through certification strategies) can improve the effectiveness of protected areas at achieving biological conservation objectives (Oldekop *et al.*, 2016). This line of research is supported by recent studies showing that many protected areas in the world experience high human pressures (Jones *et al.*, 2018; Schulze *et al.*, 2018).

FSC certification can be a useful tool to overcome some limitations in national environmental governance (Carey, 2008). While it is compelling to use the successful strategy of certification also for the protection of the last remaining intact forests, we emphasise that most forestry practices are in contradiction with the current definition of IFL. Selective logging, for example, which is common practice in many forests, requires roads to transport trees and machines. According to the current definition of IFL, the presence of any road immediately removes the IFL status from a forest, even if these roads are only used temporarily. The dilemma is that FSC, as a voluntary certification scheme, requires companies to voluntarily agree to be bound by its standards. If new IFL requirements include full protection of IFLs as HCV forests, this would prevent companies from using the forest in any way (Kleinschroth *et al.*, 2018). Under such a constraint it is not likely that a company whose operations overlap with an IFL would have an interest to be certified because the new rule would impede the economic viability of its operations.

In addition, given that the current definition of IFL is based on a globally remotely sensed map, it is unknown how intact IFLs actually are in terms of full forest functionality, despite apparently intact vegetation (Haurez *et al.*, 2017). For instance, tropical forests are subject to intense hunting pressure and being emptied of animals with important ecological functions (Fa *et al.*, 2002; Haurez *et al.*, 2017; Wright, 2003). Here, FSC controlled forest management could be a better strategy to limit bushmeat hunting and other illegal activities than protected areas without sufficient enforcement. Embedding the conservation of IFLs into certification could be achieved based on a local, context-specific definition of intactness that considers forest recovery processes after planned forestry operations. At the same time, further efforts are needed to reduce logging impacts resulting from the presence of roads (Kleinschroth and Healey, 2017).

Figure 4.3 Logging road in a concession in southeast Cameroon, built in a way that avoids large trees to reduce impact.

Source: © Fritz Kleinschroth.

As shown earlier in this chapter, FSC certification can help to maintain biodiversity values in managed forests. By fostering responsible forest operations, forest certification can maintain ecological and socioeconomic values, leading to long-term commitment of local stakeholders, such as companies and communities. FSC certification ensures multistakeholder dialogue with emphasis on the rights of indigenous peoples, while maintaining IFLs at relatively low disturbance levels and avoiding expanding uses of forestland, such as conversion to agriculture.

Conclusion

Our review shows that the vast majority of research on impacts has been conducted in tropical forests, despite the fact that tropical forests represent only 10 per cent of the total area of certified forests globally. This disproportionate interest in tropical forests may be the result of greater rates of tree cover and biodiversity loss in the tropics as compared to temperate and boreal regions. Yet, how FSC influences biodiversity conservation in temperate and boreal forests remains, to date, largely unknown given the dearth of research in these regions. Findings on the benefits of FSC to limit deforestation and forest degradation vary across countries and regions and do not facilitate a consensus or complete understanding. The disparity of results was expected, given the contrasting socio-ecological systems that can be found surrounding FSC-certified operations and the associated levels of threats to forests. The different ways of measuring deforestation contributes to this disparity.

For example, researchers regularly use the global dataset on forest cover change derived from satellite imagery by Hansen *et al.* (2013) to address the question of deforestation (Blackman *et al.*, 2018; Panlasigui *et al.*, 2015; Rana and Sills, 2018; Rico *et al.*, 2017). This dataset relates to gross tree cover loss without providing continuous data on forest gain. Subsequently, impact studies inevitably report on deforestation regardless of whether forest cover is maintained in the long term due to natural or aided regeneration. Other researchers define deforestation as natural forest conversion to other land uses such as agricultural activities or plantations (Curtis *et al.*, 2018; Heilmayr and Lambin, 2016). These discrepancies in what impact evaluators refer to when they test for effects of FSC certification on deforestation does therefore make inaccurate generalisation of impacts particularly likely. Impact evaluators need to understand improvements relative to a defined baseline and potential contextual confounders. Assumptions of expected on-the-ground impacts generated by FSC should be clearly defined before designing a study, as well as the mechanistic link between certified forestry operations and associated impacts to make sure expectations are realistic.

FSC certification has the potential to help maintain ecological values by overcoming gaps in national forest governance. This also applies to intact forests. Yet, the size of most IFLs largely exceeds the area of influence of FSC, which is limited to the area of certified concessions. Effective protection of intact forests therefore also requires landscape-wide approaches and the consideration of other disturbances than those associated with the forestry sector. FSC has an important political role in framing a progressive agenda for forestry standards. Putting such new standards into practice and showing their viability can then create potential spillover effects, leading to long-term changes towards a more biodiversity-friendly society.

Disclaimer

FSC staff conducting monitoring and evaluation activities contributed to the present chapter as part of their literature monitoring activity. Despite the inherent conflict of interest, the authors have used their best efforts in the time available to provide a transparent expertise on the published literature. The opinions expressed in this chapter are exclusively those of the authors and do not reflect the opinions of FSC.

Notes

1 Including contributions from Marion Karmann and Diana Franco Gil.
2 FSC is not a research organisation and usually does not commission or conduct its own research to avoid conflicts of interest. As part of monitoring and evaluation activities, the FSC welcomes interactions with scientists to discuss research topics, designs and findings, and supports them to identify relevant information for their work. The Data, Analytics, Monitoring and Evaluation Programme continuously analyses research papers to identify intended and unintended effects of certification interventions, to bring these topics to the attention of the research community and to FSC stakeholders.

References

Azevedo-Ramos, C., de Carvalho, O., do Amaral, B.D., 2006. Short-term effects of reduced-impact logging on eastern Amazon fauna. For. Ecol. Manage. 232, 26–35. https://doi.org/10.1016/j.foreco.2006.05.025.
Bahaa-el-din, L., Sollmann, R., Hunter, L.T.B., Slotow, R., Macdonald, D.W., Henschel, P., 2016. Effects of human land-use on Africa's only forest-dependent felid: the African golden cat *Caracal aurata*. Biol. Conserv. 199, 1–9. https://doi.org/10.1016/j.biocon.2016.04.013.
Barbosa de Lima, A.C., Novaes Keppe, A.L., Maule, F.E., Sparovek, G., Correa Alves, M., Maule, R.F., 2009. Does certification make a difference? Impact assessment study on FSC/SAN certification in Brazil. Imaflora report.
Bernstein, S., Cashore, B., 2004. Nonstate global governance : is forest certification a legitimate alternative to a global forest convention? In J.J. Kirton, M.J. Trebilcock (Eds.). Hard Choices, Soft Law: Voluntary Standards in Global Trade, Environment and Social Governance. Routledge. pp. 33–64.
Blackman, A., Goff, L., Rivera Planter, M., 2018. Does eco-certification stem tropical deforestation? Forest Stewardship Council certification in Mexico. J. Environ. Econ. Manage. 89, 306–333. https://doi.org/10.1016/j.jeem.2018.04.005.
Burivalova, Z., Hua, F., Koh, L.P., Garcia, C., Putz, F.E., 2017. A critical comparison of conventional, certified, and community management of tropical forests for

timber in terms of environmental, economic, and social variables. Conserv. Lett. 10, 4–14. https://doi.org/10.1111/conl.12244.

Carey, C., 2008. Governmental use of voluntary standards. Case study 2: Bolivia and Forest Stewardship Council Standard. ISEAL Alliance.

Cashore, B., Auld, G., Bernstein, S., McDermott, C.L., 2007. Can non-state governance ratchet up global environmental standards? Lessons from the forest sector. Rev. Eur. Community Int. Environ. Law 16, 158.

Curtis, P.G., Slay, C.M., Harris, N.L., Tyukavina, A., Hansen, M.C., 2018. Classifying drivers of global forest loss. Science (80-). 361, 1108–1111. https://doi.org/10.1126/science.aau3445.

Damette, O., Delacote, P., 2011. Unsustainable timber harvesting, deforestation and the role of certification. Ecol. Econ. 70, 1211–1219. https://doi.org/10.1016/J.ECOLECON.2011.01.025.

Dias, F.S., Bugalho, M.N., Rodriguez-Gonzalez, P.M., Albuquerque, A., Cerdeira, J.O., 2015. Effects of forest certification on the ecological condition of Mediterranean streams. J. Appl. Ecol. 52, 190–198. https://doi.org/10.1111/1365-2664.12358.

Dias, F.S., Miller, D.L., Marques, T.A., Marcelino, J., Caldeira, M.C., Orestes Cerdeira, J., Bugalho, M.N., 2016. Conservation zones promote oak regeneration and shrub diversity in certified Mediterranean oak woodlands. Biol. Conserv. 195, 226–234. https://doi.org/10.1016/j.biocon.2016.01.009.

Dirzo, R., Young, H.S., Galetti, M., Ceballos, G., Isaac, N.J.B., Collen, B., 2014. Defaunation in the Anthropocene. Science (80-) 345, 401–406. https://doi.org/10.1126/science.1251817.

Elbakidze, M., Angelstam, P., Andersson, K., Nordberg, M., Pautov, Y., 2011. How does forest certification contribute to boreal biodiversity conservation? Standards and outcomes in Sweden and NW Russia. For. Ecol. Manage. 262, 1983–1995. https://doi.org/10.1016/j.foreco.2011.08.040.

Elbakidze, M., Ražauskaitė, R., Manton, M., Angelstam, P., Mozgeris, G., Brūmelis, G., Brazaitis, G., Vogt, P., 2016. The role of forest certification for biodiversity conservation: Lithuania as a case study. Eur. J. For. Res. 135, 361–376. https://doi.org/10.1007/s10342-016-0940-4.

Fa, J.E., Peres, C.A., Meeuwig, J., 2002. Bushmeat exploitation in tropical forests: an intercontinental comparison. Conserv. Biol. 16, 232–237. https://doi.org/10.1046/j.1523-1739.2002.00275.x.

Feldpausch, T.R., Jirka, S., Passos, C.A.M., Jasper, F., Riha, S.J., 2005. When big trees fall: damage and carbon export by reduced impact logging in southern Amazonia. For. Ecol. Manage. 219, 199–215. https://doi.org/10.1016/j.foreco.2005.09.003.

FSC M&E report, 2016. Demonstrating the impact of FSC certification: measuring how FSC certification affects forests, people, and business practices. https://ic.fsc.org/en/what-is-fsc/what-we-do/demonstrating-impact.

Griscom, B.W., Goodman, R.C., Burivalova, Z., Putz, F.E., 2018. Carbon and biodiversity impacts of intensive versus extensive tropical forestry. Conserv. Lett. 11, 1–9. https://doi.org/10.1111/conl.12362.

Gulbrandsen, L.H., 2004. Overlapping public and private governance: can forest certification fill the gaps in the global forest regime? Glob. Environ. Polit. 4, 75–99. https://doi.org/10.1162/152638004323074200.

Hain, H., Ahas, R., 2011. Impacts of sustainable forestry certification in European forest management operations. Ravag. Planet III 148, 207–218. https://doi.org/10.2495/RAV110201.

Hansen, M.C.C., Potapov, P.V, Moore, R., Hancher, M., Turubanova, S., Tyukavina, A., Thau, D., Stehman, S.V., Goetz, S.J., Loveland, T.R., Kommareddy, A., Egorov, A., Chini, L., Justice, C.O., Townshend, J.R.G., 2013. High-resolution global maps of 21st-century forest cover change. Science (80-). 342, 850–854. https://doi.org/10.1126/science.1244693.

Haurez, B., Tagg, N., Petre, C.A., Vermeulen, C., Doucet, J.-L., 2016. Short term impact of selective logging on a western lowland gorilla population. For. Ecol. Manage. 364, 46–51. https://doi.org/10.1016/j.foreco.2015.12.030.

Haurez, B., Daïnou, K., Vermeulen, C., Kleinschroth, F., Mortier, F., Gourlet-Fleury, S., Doucet, J.-L., 2017. A look at Intact Forest Landscapes (IFLs) and their relevance in Central African forest policy. For. Policy Econ. 80, 192–199. https://doi.org/10.1016/j.forpol.2017.03.021.

Heilmayr, R., Lambin, E.F., 2016. Impacts of nonstate, market-driven governance on Chilean forests. Proc. Natl. Acad. Sci. 113, 2910–2915. https://doi.org/10.1073/pnas.1600394113.

Hirschberger, P., 2005a. The effects of FSC-certification in Russia. An analysis of Corrective Action Requests. WWF European Forest Programme report.

Hirschberger, P., 2005b. The effects of FSC-certification in Estonia. An analysis of Corrective Action Requests. WWF European Forest Programme report.

Hirschberger, P., 2005c. The effects of FSC-certification in Latvia. An analysis of Corrective Action Requests. WWF European Forest Programme report.

Hodgdon, B.D., Hughell, D., Ramos, V.H., Balas-McNab, R., 2015. Deforestation trends in the Maya Biosphere Reserve, Guatemala. New York, NY: Rainforest Alliance, CONAP, Wildlife Conservation Society.

Hughell, D., Butterfield, R.P., 2008. Impact of FSC certification on deforestation and the incidence of wildfires in the Maya Biosphere Reserve. Rainforest Alliance report.

Imai, N., Samejima, H., Langner, A., Ong, R.C., Kita, S., Titin, J., Chung, A.Y.C., Lagan, P., Lee, Y., Kitayama, K., 2009. Co-benefits of sustainable forest management in biodiversity conservation and carbon sequestration. PLoS One 4. https://doi.org/10.1371/journal.pone.0008267.

Jones, K.R., Venter, O., Fuller, R.A., Allan, J.R., Maxwell, S.L., Negret, P.J., Watson, J.E.M., 2018. One-third of global protected land is under intense human pressure. Science (80-). 360, 788–791. https://doi.org/10.1126/science.aap9565.

Kalonga, S.K., Midtgaard, F., Klanderud, K., 2016. Forest certification as a policy option in conserving biodiversity: an empirical study of forest management in Tanzania. For. Ecol. Manage. 361, 1–12. https://doi.org/10.1016/j.foreco.2015.10.034.

Kleinschroth, F., Healey, J.R., 2017. Impacts of logging roads on tropical forests. Biotropica 49, 620–635. https://doi.org/10.1111/btp.12462.

Kleinschroth, F., Healey, J.R., Gourlet-Fleury, S., 2016. Sparing forests in Central Africa: re-use old logging roads to avoid creating new ones. Front. Ecol. Environ. 14, 9–10. https://doi.org/10.1002/FEEKleinschroth.

Kleinschroth, F., Healey, J.R., Gourlet-Fleury, S., Mortier, F., Stoica, R.S., 2017. Effects of logging on roadless space in intact forest landscapes of the Congo Basin. Conserv. Biol. 31, 469–480. https://doi.org/10.1111/cobi.12815.

Kleinschroth, F., Garcia, C., Ghazoul, J., 2018. Reconciling certification and intact forest landscape conservation. Ambio. https://doi.org/10.1007/s13280-018-1063-6.

Kukkonen, M., Hohnwald, S., 2009. Comparing floristic composition in treefall gaps of certified, conventionally managed and natural forests of northern Honduras. Ann. For. Sci. 66, 809–809. https://doi.org/10.1051/forest/2009070.

Lehtonen, E., von Stedingk, H., 2016. The contribution of FSC certification to biodiversity in Estonian forests. FSC Sweden Report 2016.

Lehtonen, E., von Stedingk, H., 2017a. The contribution of FSC certification to biodiversity in Latvian forests. FSC Sweden Report 2017.

Lehtonen, E., von Stedingk, H., 2017b. The contribution of FSC certification to biodiversity in Finnish forests. FSC Sweden Report 2017.

McDermott, C.L., Noah, E., Cashore, B., 2008. Differences that 'matter'? A framework for comparing environmental certification standards and government policies. J. Environ. Policy Plan. 10, 47–70. https://doi.org/10.1080/15239080701652607.

McDermott, C.L., Cashore, B., Kanowski, P., 2012. Global Environmental Forest Policies: An International Comparison. Routledge.

Medjibe, V.P., Putz, F.E., Romero, C., 2013. Certified and uncertified logging concessions compared in Gabon: changes in stand structure, tree species, and biomass. Environ. Manage. 51, 524–540. https://doi.org/10.1007/s00267-012-0006-4.

Miteva, D.A., Loucks, C.J., Pattanayak, S.K., 2015. Social and environmental impacts of forest management certification in Indonesia. PLoS One 10, 1–18. https://doi.org/10.1371/journal.pone.0129675.

Morgan, D.B., Mundry, R., Sanz, C.M., Ayina, C.E., Strindberg, S., Lonsdorf, E., Kühl, H.S., 2017. African apes coexisting with logging: comparing chimpanzee (*Pan troglodytes troglodytes*) and gorilla (*Gorilla gorilla gorilla*) resource needs and responses to forestry activities. Biol. Conserv. 0–1. https://doi.org/10.1016/j.biocon.2017.10.026.

Newsom, D., Hewitt, D., 2005. The global impacts of smartwood certification. Rainforest Alliance report.

Oldekop, J.A., Holmes, G., Harris, W.E., Evans, K.L., 2016. A global assessment of the social and conservation outcomes of protected areas. Conserv. Biol. 30, 133–141. https://doi.org/10.1111/cobi.12568.

Panlasigui, S., Rico-Straffon, J., Swenson, J., Loucks, C.J., Pfaff, A., 2015. Early days in the certification of logging concessions: estimating FSC's deforestation impact in Peru and Cameroon. Duke Environ. Ener. Econ. Working Paper Series. EE 15–05.

Polisar, J., de Thoisy, B., Rumiz, D.I., Santos, F.D., McNab, R.B., Garcia-Anleu, R., Ponce-Santizo, G., Arispe, R., Venegas, C., 2017. Using certified timber extraction to benefit jaguar and ecosystem conservation. Ambio 1–16. https://doi.org/10.1007/s13280-016-0853-y.

Potapov, P., Yaroshenko, A., Turubanova, S., Dubinin, M., Laestadius, L., Thies, C., Aksenov, D., Egorov, A., Yesipova, Y., Glushkov, I., Karpachevskiy, M., Kostikova, A., Manisha, A., Tsybikova, E., Zhuravleva, I., 2008. Mapping the world's Intact Forest Landscapes by remote sensing. Ecol. Soc. 13, 16. https://doi.org/51.

Rana, P., Sills, E.O., 2018. Does certification change the trajectory of tree cover in working forests in the tropics? An application of the synthetic control method of impact evaluation. Forests 9. https://doi.org/10.3390/f9030098.

Rico, J., Panlasigui, S., Loucks, C.J., Swenson, J., Pfaff, A., 2017. Logging concessions, certification and protected areas in the Peruvian Amazon: forest impacts from combinations of development rights and land-use restrictions.

Romero, C., Guariguata, M.R., Sills, E.O., Cerutti, P.O., Lescuyer, G., Putz, F.E., 2017. Evaluation of the impacts of Forest Stewardship Council (FSC) certification of natural forest management in the tropics: a rigorous approach to assessment of a complex conservation intervention. Int. For. Rev. 19, 1–14. https://doi.org/10.17528/cifor/004347.

Roopsind, A., Caughlin, T.T., Sambhu, H., Fragoso, J.M.V., Putz, F.E., 2017. Logging and indigenous hunting impacts on persistence of large Neotropical animals. Biotropica 49, 565–575. https://doi.org/10.1111/btp.12446.

Schulze, K., Knights, K., Coad, L., Geldmann, J., Leverington, F., Eassom, A., Marr, M., Butchart, S.H.M., Hockings, M., Burgess, N.D., 2018. An assessment of threats to terrestrial protected areas. Conserv. Lett. 1–10. https://doi.org/10.1111/conl.12435.

Sillanpää, M., Vantellingen, J., Friess, D.A., 2017. Vegetation regeneration in a sustainably harvested mangrove forest in West Papua, Indonesia. For. Ecol. Manage. 390, 137–146. https://doi.org/10.1016/j.foreco.2017.01.022.

Sollmann, R., Mohamed, A., Niedballa, J., Bender, J., Ambu, L., Lagan, P., Mannan, S., Ong, R.C., Langner, A., Gardner, B., Wilting, A., 2017. Quantifying mammal biodiversity co-benefits in certified tropical forests. Divers. Distrib. 23, 317–328. https://doi.org/10.1111/ddi.12530.

Stokes, E.J., Strindberg, S., Bakabana, P.C., Elkan, P.W., Iyenguet, F.C., Madzoké, B., Malanda, G.-A.F., Mowawa, B.S., Moukoumbou, C., Ouakabadio, F.K., Rainey, H.J., 2010. Monitoring great Ape and elephant abundance at large spatial scales: measuring effectiveness of a conservation landscape. PLoS One 5. https://doi.org/10.1371/journal.pone.0010294.

Strindberg, S., Maisels, F., Williamson, E.A., Blake, S., Stokes, E.J., Aba'a, R., Abitsi, G., Agbor, A., Ambahe, R.D., Bakabana, P.C., Bechem, M., Berlemont, A., Bokoto de Semboli, B., Boundja, P.R., Bout, N., Breuer, T., Campbell, G., De Wachter, P., Ella Akou, M., Esono Mba, F., Feistner, A.T.C., Fosso, B., Fotso, R., Greer, D., Inkamba-Nkulu, C., Iyenguet, C.F., Jeffery, K.J., Kokangoye, M., Kühl, H.S., Latour, S., Madzoké, B., Makoumbou, C., Malanda, G.-A.F., Malonga, R., Mbolo, V., Morgan, D.B., Motsaba, P., Moukala, G., Mowawa, B.S., Murai, M., Ndzai, C., Nishihara, T., Nzooh, Z., Pintea, L., Pokempner, A., Rainey, H.J., Rayden, T., Ruffler, H., Sanz, C.M., Todd, A., Vanleeuwe, H., Vosper, A., Warren, Y., Wilkie, D.S., 2018. Guns, germs, and trees determine density and distribution of gorillas and chimpanzees in Western Equatorial Africa. Sci. Adv. 4, eaar2964. https://doi.org/10.1126/sciadv.aar2964.

Sundstrom, L., Henry, L., 2017. Private forest governance, public policy impacts: the Forest Stewardship Council in Russia and Brazil. Forests 8, 445. https://doi.org/10.3390/f8110445.

Tobler, M.W., Garcia Anleu, R., Carrillo-Percastegui, S.E., Ponce-Santizo, G., Polisar, J., Zuñiga Hartley, A., Goldstein, I., 2018. Do responsibly managed logging concessions adequately protect jaguars and other large and medium-sized mammals? Two case studies from Guatemala and Peru. Biol. Conserv. 220, 245–253. https://doi.org/10.1016/j.biocon.2018.02.015.

Tritsch, I., Sist, P., Narvaes, I. da S., Mazzei, L., Blanc, L., Bourgoin, C., Cornu, G., Gond, V., 2016. Multiple patterns of forest disturbance and logging shape forest landscapes in Paragominas, Brazil. Forests 7, 1–15. https://doi.org/10.3390/f7120315.

Tysiachniouk, M., McDermott, C.L., 2016. Certification with Russian characteristics: implications for social and environmental equity. For. Policy Econ. 62, 43–53. https://doi.org/10.1016/j.forpol.2015.07.002.

van der Ven, H., Cashore, B., 2018. Forest certification: the challenge of measuring impacts. Curr. Opin. Environ. Sustain. 32, 104–111. https://doi.org/10.1016/j.cosust.2018.06.001.

Villalobos, L., Coria, J., Nordén, A., 2018. Has forest certification reduced forest degradation in Sweden? Land Econ. 94, 220–238. https://doi.org/10.3368/le.94.2.220.

Visseren-Hamakers, I.J., Glasbergen, P., 2007. Partnerships in forest governance. Glob. Environ. Chang. 17, 408–419. https://doi.org/10.1016/j.gloenvcha.2006.11.003.

Watson, J.E.M., Evans, T., Venter, O., Williams, B., Tulloch, A., Stewart, C., Thompson, I., Ray, J.C., Murray, K., Salazar, A., McAlpine, C., Potapov, P., Walston, J., Robinson, J.G., Painter, M., Wilkie, D., Filardi, C., Laurance, W.F., Houghton, R.A., Maxwell, S., Grantham, H., Samper, C., Wang, S., Laestadius, L., Runting, R.K., Silva-Chávez, G.A., Ervin, J., Lindenmayer, D., 2018. The exceptional value of intact forest ecosystems. Nat. Ecol. Evol. 2, 599–610. https://doi.org/10.1038/s41559-018-0490-x.

Wright, S.J., 2003. The myriad consequences of hunting for vertebrates and plants in tropical forests. Perspect. Plant Ecol. Evol. Syst. 6.

Part III

Standard development and verification-based examples and considerations

5 Biochar and certification[1]

*Frank G.A. Verheijen, Ana Catarina Bastos,
Hans-Peter Schmidt and Simon Jeffery*

Introduction

Soil organic carbon (SOC) stores an estimated 1500 to 1600 Gt of carbon (C) (Mondal *et al.*, 2017). The decomposition of SOC leads to CO_2 emissions from soil. The organic C flux from soil is estimated to have resulted in a loss of 320 Gt since agricultural practice began causing deforestation and land use conversion, with more than half lost since 1750 (Houghton *et al.*, 2012; IPCC, 2014).

SOC sequestration or storage has been considered as a negative emissions technology (NET) to mitigate climate change for more than a decade (Smith, 2016; Minasny *et al.*, 2017; Rockström *et al.*, 2017). Theoretically, the world's cropland soils could sequester as much as $62 \, t \, ha^{-1}$ over the next 50 to 75 years (0.8 to $1.2 \, t \, ha^{-1} \, y^{-1}$) with a total C-sink capacity of ~88 Gt (Lal, 2016). There is now a consensus that SOC sequestration has the potential to play a significant role in climate change mitigation. Initiatives such as the 4/1000 initiative have sprung up with ambitious goals (Chabbi *et al.*, 2017), which are currently under discussion by the scientific community (Lal, 2016; Minasny *et al.*, 2017; Poulton *et al.*, 2018). The 4‰ initiative aspires to increase global SOC stocks by 0.4 per cent per year, as a compensation for the global emissions of greenhouse gases by anthropogenic sources. Studies across the globe suggest that an annual rate of 0.2 to 0.5 tonnes organic C per hectare is possible (Minasny *et al.*, 2017; Minasny and McBratney, 2018; Rumpel *et al.*, 2018) despite obvious limitations (e.g. Poulton *et al.*, 2018).

Biochar is charred (pyrolysed) biomass that is engineered to have specific physicochemical properties that make it both recalcitrant to decomposition and weathering, as well as potentially beneficial to soil functioning (e.g. Verheijen *et al.*, 2010, 2015), as long as specific sustainability criteria are met (Verheijen *et al.*, 2012). Biochar is often praised for addressing multiple agronomic and environmental challenges simultaneously. For instance, it has shown to increase soil carbon storage, fertility and water holding capacity (Woolf *et al.*, 2010; Jeffery *et al.*, 2011; Liu *et al.*, 2013; Gurwick *et al.*, 2013; Abel *et al.*, 2013), as well as reduce soil greenhouse gas emissions (e.g. Kammann *et al.*, 2012), nitrate leaching (e.g. Cayuela *et al.*, 2014; Hagemann *et al.*, 2017) and contaminant bioavailability (e.g. Fellet *et al.*, 2014; Rees *et al.*, 2014; Hilber *et al.*, 2017). These effects are often described as consistent and universal (Lorenz and Lal, 2014; Biederman and Harpole, 2013). There is, however, recent evidence to the contrary. Under specific biochar characteristics and soil–biochar–climate combinations, biochar can have little to no benefit for soil functioning. In fact, it can suppress plant growth (Crane-Droesch *et al.*, 2013; Jeffery *et al.*, 2017), reduce nutrient availability (Ghezzehei *et al.*, 2014) and pose potential risk to edaphic and aquatic organisms (Smith *et al.*, 2013; Bastos *et al.*, 2014; Domene *et al.*, 2014, 2015a, 2015b). Further, it seems unlikely that all benefits may be achieved simultaneously – trade-offs between them are inevitable (Jeffery *et al.*, 2015). While some management actions are reversible (Vaughan and Lenton, 2011), biochar application to soil is not, which urges caution (Jeffery *et al.*, 2014) until the main knowledge gaps concerning its long-term impact, mobility and fate remain to be addressed (Tammeorg *et al.*, 2017). A workable sustainable biochar certification system is essential to avoid potential negative side-effects, both for the environment and for the nascent biochar production industry. Further concerns would need to be addressed in a biochar sustainability scheme given that it is for application to soils, thus the range of biotic and abiotic interactions across large spatial and temporal scales in the soil ecosystem would also need to be considered. In fact, biochar persistence in soils when compared to traditional soil amendments such as manures or crop residues, increases the need for understanding how biochar will behave (interact, change) and be subject to transport in soil and into aquatic systems over a number of human generations.

What is biochar sustainability?

We can define biochar sustainability policy as 'a framework comprising a set of concepts, commitments and action plans towards optimizing environmental, societal and economic aspects of biochar production and application, as agreed between all interested parties (society, industry and government)'. Biochar sustainability needs to be addressed in an interdisciplinary and multi-dimensional framework due to the crosscutting nature of biochar, perhaps comparable to that of biofuels. Therefore, in essence, a biochar sustainability framework that is adaptive and knowledge-generated represents:

1   A commitment to protect soil-based ecosystem services, global environmental quality and human well-being;
2   An obligation to meet the relevant voluntary or regulatory product standard specifications, as well as environmental certification;
3   A dedication to communicate the relevant information and policy in an effective and transparent way;
4   A responsibility to continue improving and updating the sustainability system in relation to both, production and application components.

The benefits of developing a biochar sustainability policy are thus manifold and reflect environmental, social and economic gains, perhaps first at the local development scale and progressively extending to global scale. For instance, a biochar sustainability policy could potentially lead to increasing local economic development (particularly in rural areas), including enhanced and cost-effective local food production and supply. This can result in generating employment and new businesses, facilitating effective waste reduction and recycling strategies. Biochar research has grown exponentially in the last decade, along with a strong public and industrial interest and activity. We are moving fast towards the need for a rigorous sustainability policy to help us prevent environmental degradation, as well as to manage and optimize the impacts of biochar on all three environmental, economic and societal components.

Biochar sustainability criteria and indicators

Defining a set of sustainability criteria and indicators was required for implementing an objective, effective and transparent biofuel sustainability policy, supply chain and use policy. Repeating this process for biochar will require addressing further challenges, as extending biofuel sustainability criteria to biochar will need to also 'encompass the effects on soil, any substitution of soil amendments, as well as the sequestration value of the biochar' (Cowie *et al.*, 2012). Currently, sustainability criteria for biochar have not been developed in the literature. Buchholz *et al.* (2009) defined 35 sustainability criteria for bioenergy systems from a literature review, using a survey with 137 experts to rank the 35 identified sustainability criteria according to relevance, practicality, reliability and importance. Table 5.1 lists the top third of the criteria ranked by importance, and provides examples of how these criteria may be extended for biochar sustainability. In this chapter we focus on the environment domains only.

While such criteria themselves are not a direct measure of sustainability performance but rather are an area of focus, 'sustainability indicators' may also be outlined to feed objective information about the status of the selected criteria. Such indicators should meet specific scientific, functional and feasibility requirements in order to be effective, including:

1 Measurability and objectiveness: reflecting the extent and direction ('good' or 'bad') of the process under assessment, represented in standard units;
2 Robustness and reproducibility: whose measure is methodologically sound and repeatable;
3 Sensitivity, representation and specificity: they should be sensitive and respond quickly to changes in the system under assessment, while overall integrating systems variability;
4 Manageability and feasibility: easy and cost-effective to handle and measure;
5 Acceptability and comparability: should be recognized and accepted by the relevant scientific and policy communities.

Table 5.1 Sustainability criteria for bioenergy systems and proposed main adaptations for sustainable biochar production and use

Domain	Criterion	Explanation	Biochar extension
Economy	Microeconomic sustainability*	Cost-efficiency incl. start-up costs, internal rate of return, net present value, payback period	Economic trade-off between *bioenergy and biochar*
Environment	Climate change mitigation	GHG balance of system covering CO_2, CH_4, O_3, N_2O, H_2O	Sequestered C, N_2O and CH_4 emissions, black carbon aerosols, water holding capacity, land surface albedo change
	Natural resource efficiency*	Efficient use of resources at all stages of the system	Trade-offs between *resources*
	Ecosystem protection†	Safeguarding protected, threatened, representative, or other valuable ecosystems (e.g. forests), protecting internal energy fluxes/metabolism	Preservation and/or promotion of *functional biodiversity and biota-mediated ecosystem services*
	Waste management*	Disposal of ashes, sewage, hazardous/contaminated solid and liquid material	Use of *waste materials as feedstocks*; disposal of tar and bio-oil
Environment and society	Energy balance	Conversion efficiencies, energy return on investment, energy return per unit area	Production, storage, transport, handling and application
	Soil protection†	Impacts on soil fertility e.g. changes in nutrient cycling, rooting depth, organic matter, water holding capacity, erosion	Include effects of range of biochar types on range of soil types for soil functions and/or threat indicators: e.g. *soil biodiversity*, compaction, salinization, sealing, contamination (Optimum Biochar Dose concept)
	Water management†	Surface and groundwater impacts, riparian buffers, irrigation and cooling cycles and waste water management	Include environmental risk assessment based on analytical and *biological criteria* relevant to surface run off and groundwater; reduced pesticide and nutrient leaching
Society	Participation	Inclusion of stakeholders in decision making; facilitation of self-determination of stakeholders	Include agronomists, landowners, waste treatment and recycling companies (across spatial scales)
	Compliance with laws	Complying with applicable laws, internal regulations, certification principles, countering bribery, etc.	
	Monitoring of criteria performance	Monitoring systems in place for all criteria (e.g. leakage or additionality in GHG accounting)	Harmonized methods for monitoring biochar in soils; audit scheme
	Food security	Enough land locally available for food production including agricultural set aside land, preference of marginal sites for energy crops	Effect on crop yield within current agricultural area

Source: adapted from Buchholz *et al.* (2009).

Notes
† = criterion relevant to biodiversity outcomes;
★ = criterion relevant to natural resource management.

What is certification?

Certifying a biochar as being produced sustainably, and/or by stipulating on the label how it can be sustainably applied to soils, requires transparent procedures and processes. Certification can be one of the pathways towards achieving this, while being a useful strategy in the implementation of a sustainability policy. Depending on how the certification scheme is organized, it can be an approach, or a subsystem that employs approaches, such as life cycle assessment, zero waste or contamination control. Many types of certification exist, ranging from voluntary to compulsory, from self-determined to externally audited, and from focused on a single subject to integrating a range of subjects. Each type has advantages and disadvantages relevant to certifying biochar, some of which are discussed in the next section.

Sustainable biochar certification

As previously suggested, sustainable biochar systems depend on both 'sustainable production' and 'sustainable application' – this is not an 'either/or proposal'. These are two necessary halves of the sustainability equation, meaning that a sustainable biochar policy is only possible when both are adequately established. Since in this book, biochar is defined functionally as 'intended for use as a soil application or broader for environmental management', 'sustainable application' then can be interpreted as to include environmental management. Therefore, in addition to sustainable product standardization or certification, a sustainability label also needs to include the concept of 'sustainable application'. Alongside biochar's heterogeneity, soils have been shown to exhibit substantial variation in properties at spatial and temporal scales relevant to biochar application. This implies that sustainable biochar application to soil would need to explicitly consider spatial heterogeneity through categorization from field to regional scales, while accounting for the relevant socioeconomic context, including aspects of feedstock availability, competition for resources, land use, agricultural practices and GHG emissions.

Certification is normally communicated to the consumer by means of a stamp or an (eco) label, which is awarded upon verification that the product meets the relevant criteria. This would probably be enough for the product certification component but would not add information on the environmental certification, since it discards any spatial and temporal environmental variability. To overcome this, Verheijen *et al.* (2012) argued for biochar labelling to

> extend beyond a technical description and labelling of the biomass feedstock and biochar material to also include the environmental and socioeconomic context relevant to the site where biochar would be applied to soils, as well as to where the feedstock was grown.

Ideally, such a comprehensive labelling system would provide measured environmental data on pre-established parameters, or combination thereof, through life cycle assessment, set and verified by an impartial third party, such as a non-governmental organization (NGO), Environment Agency etc. As a first approach in this context, the authors suggested the inclusion of the following information:

> biochar with properties A, B, C (including concentrations of contaminants), which makes it appropriate for ecotopes with properties D, E, F to grow crop types G and H, but not crop type I, at biochar application rates of J (Mgha^{-1} per year) every K years, to L (Mgha^{-1} per year) every M years, up to a maximum biochar loading capacity of N (gkg^{-1}).

One perceived drawback associated with such a labelling system is that, whereas the product certification component is easily verifiable, the environmental certification component is likely more difficult to verify. This discussion deserves full attention and communication between all interested parties and suggests that accompanying the implementation of an effective biochar certification system is the awareness and adequate training of the various biochar players.

Biochar production certification: a work in progress

Two nascent biochar certification programmes and standards exist today: (i) standardized product definition and product testing guidelines for biochar that is used in soil (aka IBI Standards), which provided grounds for the IBI Biochar Certification Program; IBI 2013); and (ii) 'European Biochar Certificate' (EBC, 2012) (aka EBC Standards). Common aims between these schemes (Table 5.2) include: (i) providing an indicator of quality and safety with respect to basic product specifications for use as a soil amendment, being based on the latest relevant research and practice; (ii) driving expansion of this industry and product commercialization through providing the necessary quality assurances for both users and producers; (iii) providing state-of-the-art information as a sound basis for future legislative or regulatory approaches, while requiring that the existing relevant regional or national environmental quality criteria are met during production.

Biochar production technology is currently developing fast, with more than 500 research projects worldwide looking into biochar properties. Alongside it, there is an increasing awareness of the way these properties determine biochar environmental behaviour, mobility and fate, including interactions with soil mineral, organic and biological components. Every year, new manufacturers of pyrolysis equipment enter the market and the areas in which biochar and biochar products are used are steadily and rapidly growing. Usage ranges from application to soils individually, to combined soil applications in the form of compost additives, carrier for fertilizers, manure treatment, silage

Table 5.2 Comparison of existing biochar production standards/certification schemes.

	IBI★	EBC
Sustainable procuration of feedstock	Not controlled	Feedstock positive list, controlled use of energy crops, limited distance for transportation to the production site
Feedstock composition	Self-declaration, change of composition results in new lot of biochar, content of contaminants <2%, upon manufacturer's responsibility	Controlled declaration, change of composition results in new lot of biochar
Emissions during biochar production	Pyrogas combustion has to comply with local and/or regional and/or national emission thresholds	Pyrogas produced during the pyrolysis has to be trapped. Syngas combustion has to comply with national emission thresholds
Energy and GHG balance for production	Not controlled	Biomass pyrolysis must take place in an energy-autonomous process. No fossil fuels are permitted for reactor heating
Control of dust emission and ignition hazard.	Not controlled	Humidity of stored biochar must be >30%
Product definition (C, H/C, nutrient content, ash, EC, pH, particle size distribution, specific surface, VOCs, available nutrients)	$H/C_{org} < 0.7$; $C_{org} \geq 60\%/30\%/10\%$; other values to be declared, some only in category 2 resp. 3	$H/C_{org} < 0.7$; $C_{org} \geq 50\%$; other values to be declared, some only in premium quality
Control of heavy metal content	✓ (required in category 2)	✓
Control of organic content (PAHs, PCBs, Furans, Dioxins)	✓ (required in category 2)	✓
Independent lab analysis, control of analytical methods and standard laboratories	✓ (self-declaration of labs)	✓ (only accredited labs)
Record of production reference and complete traceability of product	✓	✓
Independent on-site production control	None	✓
Transparent product declaration for buyers	On package	On delivery slip or annexed to invoice
Handling advice and health and safety warning	Annexed delivery document for appropriate shipping, handling and storage procedures	Annexed delivery document for appropriate shipping, handling, and storage procedures

Note
★ The IBI Biochar Standards relate to the physicochemical properties of biochar only, and do not prescribe production methods or specific feedstocks, nor do they provide limits or terms for defining the sustainability and/or GHG mitigation potential of a biochar material.

additives or feed-additives. Considering that both biochar properties and its overall environmental footprint are interdependent on processing conditions and feedstock type, a framework that secures basic material quality control can positively impact on increasing sustainability with regard to production technology.

Following multidisciplinary research and field trials, the understanding of the biological and physicochemical processes involved in the production and use of biochar has improved. However, it should be acknowledged that most studies have investigated the effects of deliberate biochar application to soil only in the short term (except for charcoal or fire-derived char that may occur in soils of former charcoal producing sites or wildfire-affected areas), with a large number of studies investigating at the subannual scale, and the longest studies only running for up to 15 years.

Users of biochar and biochar-based products should benefit from a fully transparent and verifiable monitoring and policing of compliance to the reference specifications, for biochar production. While the EBC product certification scheme has stepped forward from essentially self-reporting to include an independent monitoring/policing of compliance component, it appears timely to discuss the prospects of more comprehensive frameworks that match an expanding industry and market.

Biochar production standardization/certification schemes promote optimizing the production and commercialization sector, by highlighting the need for developing a product that holds a minimum set of characteristics to ensure agronomic and environmental performance, including guidelines against misuse. It is certainly a prerequisite that biochars have to fulfil a set of basic quality specifications (e.g. C content, porosity, pH, contents of metals and polycyclic hydrocarbons contents) so that application to soil sustains the desirable effects, while minimizes negative effects. As biochar can remain in soils for decades to millennia, alongside the practical irreversibility of large-scale implementation to soil and sediments, such standardization and certification schemes are useful approaches towards sustainable biochar systems. For the user, the result is an increased level of confidence on the material performance, although cases where negative effects may outweigh positive may still occur, if adequate matching between biochar and soil properties is not achieved.

Ultimately, there is also potential for such schemes to provide sound basis for policy development. Biochar is a class of material for which an adequate legal framework is only now being sought. While in Europe, a possible integration under the REACH framework (i.e. European Regulation on Registration, Evaluation, Authorisation and Restriction of Chemicals) is still being disputed, governmental administrations can benefit from a sophisticated product standard to help define if/where biochar fits existing (non-mutually exclusive) legal ordinances, which may include aspects of that of fertilizers and organic amendments, as currently taking shape in the U.S. Moreover, those feedstocks for biochar production that are considered waste materials may not be allowed to be recycled for agronomic uses. It has thus to be shown, through production and quality standards, that biochar is not a waste product but a manufactured quality product, contributing to a zero-waste society.

Is it then possible to enhance such schemes (or develop new ones) in order to maximize their potential contribution to developing truly sustainable biochar systems? One obvious limitation of the current biochar standards/ certificates is that they rely on generalization and underestimate the influence of biochar–soil–crop/biota interactions in determining such sustainability. One explanation for this may be the very recent divergence between biochar research and the production sector. Clearly, it is vital that any certification programme that is implemented is built on sound objective science in order to maximize confidence in such certification schemes. While the current scientific level of understanding of the full range of environmental implications, both spatially and temporally, is slowly expanding, it is also important that such programmes are adaptive in order to accommodate newly generated knowledge and development. This would perhaps require regular revisions and guideline updates, as well as adjustment of specification thresholds and elimination or reintroduction of test methods, as necessary. The specific mechanisms of how the latest scientific evidence should be interpreted for updating and fully documented standards and certification schemes would need careful consideration, to ensure the most comprehensive, unbiased and transparent outcome.

A sustainable biochar system, consisting of sustainable production as well as sustainable application, and regulated by a sustainability policy, also requires verifiable monitoring and policing of compliance to the reference specifications (rather than a basic self-reporting procedure). In the case of a compulsory framework, certification would then be upgraded from a 'strategy' to a 'system' level at the top of the sustainability pyramid. As a sustainable system comprising a set of interdependent and interrelated strategies, such certification schemes would require a new level of organization and coherency, as well as a change in thinking patterns for enhanced environmental protection and human welfare. Compliance to standard specifications alongside on- and off-site control by an independent and accredited third party, such as those contemplated by the EBC, is one step forward in this direction.

Sustainable biochar application certification: the concept of Optimum Biochar Dose (OBD)

Many studies have investigated the effects of biochar application to soil on various ecosystem processes and services. Such experiments have used a range of soil and biochar characteristics, as well as application rates from $1\,t\,ha^{-1}$ to in excess of $150\,t\,ha^{-1}$. To make sense of the many studies published from across the world, which have often reported disparate results, a quantitative meta-analysis of crop productivity response to biochar application rates was performed (supplementary information in Jeffery *et al.*, 2017). It suggests that increased biochar doses (up to $50\,t\,ha^{-1}$) generally lead to increased crop productivity responses in tropical regions, but with largely no significant yield effects in temperate regions. Above $50\,t\,ha^{-1}$ of biochar application, yield responses increase more strongly when applied to tropical soils and decrease more strongly when applied to temperate soils, which are generally already yielding near their yield maximums. In this respect, the existence of such a dose–response pattern for biochar is not that dissimilar to those for any traditional soil amendment and management practices, including fertilizers, compost, lime etc. For example, Mia *et al.* (2014) found that grass, clover and plantain all increased in productivity with biochar applied at $1\,t\,ha^{-1}$ and increased further at $10\,t\,ha^{-1}$. However, there was no statistical significance in productivity levels between biochar and the control (i.e. no biochar application) treatments at $50\,t\,ha^{-1}$, suggesting that the negative balanced out the positive effects that were evident at lower application rates. Further, a negative crop productivity response was observed in all three crop types investigated at biochar concentrations in soil of $120\,t\,ha^{-1}$. This strongly suggests that in the studied system, there would be a specific biochar application rate that would correspond to optimal crop productivity levels and that can be referred as specific biochar dose-effect of that system. Importantly, such a pattern is likely to be a function of any given biochar–soil–crop–climate combination and highlights the need for a priori assessment of such system characteristics before biochar application should be considered. Such dependency as an inherent property of the system is not found in the traditional fertilizer literature. Furthermore, Graber *et al.* (2012) found biochars with high specific surface areas to decrease herbicide efficacy and suggested that weed control needs may be best served by low specific surface area biochars. The OBD should therefore be further extended to comprise biochar characteristics (quality), rather than solely application rate (quantity), as both aspects are interdependent. In addition, repeat applications of smaller amounts are likely to require different biochar qualities than a single large application.

The concept of OBD, as suggested here, is one that progressed from a universal and constant property of a given biochar system, to one that is specific to all dimensions of the biochar–soil–crop–climate setting. It has further utility as it can be applied in different ways depending on the desired goals. For example, referring back to the experiment of Mia *et al.* (2014), for maximizing grass, clover and plantain yield, the target biochar dose is apparently somewhere between 10 and $50\,t\,ha^{-1}$ for the studied crop–soil–biochar–climate combination. However, if carbon (C) sequestration is the goal, then the experiment demonstrated that it is possible to add biochar at $50\,t\,ha^{-1}$ and so maximize the amount of C input into the soil without experiencing negative effects in terms of the selected plants' productivity. Regarding suppression of soil-borne plant diseases, Graber *et al.* (2014) found 'hump-shaped' relationships with biochar concentration (soil-based ecosystem service (ES) B in Figure 5.1) with significant effects often only at intermediate biochar

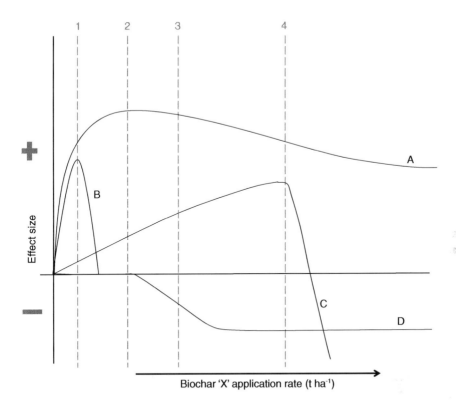

Figure 5.1 Conceptual representation of the Optimum Biochar Dose for any specific biochar–soil–crop–climate combination. Blue lines are response curves for individual soil-based ecosystem services (ESs) (A–D). The dashed lines are potential optimal OBDs (1–4), which may have to include value judgments. For example: is a 50% decrease in soil-based ES D offset by a 30% and a 50% increase in soil-based ESs B and C? Dose-effect curves for soil-based ESs may look significantly different for biochar 'Y' or 'Z', etc.

concentrations. In reality, it is likely that biochar application will be expected to have multiple goals. The OBD will then be a trade-off between the quantity and quality of the individual goals' target biochar doses (see Jeffery *et al.*, 2015, for a discussion of biochar trade-offs).

The conceptual diagram in Figure 5.1 highlights different biochar dose-effect scenarios in relation to soil-based ES (A–D) and is one way of representing the concept of OBD for any specific biochar–crop–soil–climate combination. For example, the OBD for Scenario 1 corresponds to an optimal soil-based ES A, as well as to benefits to soil-based ESs B and C, but it is the furthest that one can go without compromising soil-based ES D. However, should one consider the loss of soil-based ES D up to a certain extent acceptable, one may opt for OBD Scenario 2, reflecting in further enhanced B and C soil-based ESs, with only marginal impact on A, and so on.

The OBD concept can be integrated into an ES modelling framework for land management and policy (e.g. de Groot *et al.*, 2010). However, the factor 'time' must necessarily be adapted for biochar as well. Biochar's residence time in soil is generally orders of magnitudes longer than for traditional organic soil amendments. For situations at the higher end of this range, the residence time of biochar in soil is considerably longer than the average human life span. Any ES that may still be influenced beyond this time period – such as the C-sequestration service – is known as the 'bequest value', i.e. a value for future generations. This is a recognized challenge in ecosystem service modelling (de Groot *et al.*, 2010) and the same limitations apply to biochar. For many ESs, a time factor of one year is considered in ES modelling frameworks (e.g. Guerra *et al.*, 2014). Our current understanding of biochar effects and processes in soil is particularly limited for time scale >1 year. However, it is likely that many ESs will be affected for considerably longer time periods owing to the extended residence time of biochar in soils. It is also likely that these periods will vary substantially between ESs, as well as between soil types, biochar types and climatic and other environmental variables. The implication of this is that each ES in Figure 5.1 may have a different optimal application frequency and dose, e.g. for ES A it may be 1 t ha^{-1} every two years while for ES B it is 5 t ha^{-1} every ten years, and for ES C it is 10 t ha^{-1} every five years. This is an area where further research is urgent in order to maximize the potential beneficial interactions with ESs while minimizing negative effects and trade-offs.

As a concept, the OBD of a specific soil–biochar–crop–climate combination highlights the importance of allowing effective development of biochar application certification as introduced in this chapter. Considering the high level of inherent heterogeneity, both at the level of physico-chemical properties of the selected biochar and application site, but also of the organomineral as well as biological interactions that are likely to occur, the OBD is likely to be also influenced by soil type, climate and land use, as proposed by Verheijen *et al.* (2012). It is reasonable, therefore, to expect that sustainable biochar application for any given biochar–soil–crop–climate combination, communicated to the user through labelling, should be informative of the maximum rate at which that specific biochar may be applied to specified categorization of soil–crop–climate combinations. Whereas the current level of scientific understanding might still be low regarding the exact nature and extent of such environmental interactions, we are slowly but steadily moving towards filling such knowledge gaps (Tammeorg *et al.*, 2017). This also implies that biochar manufacturers would be encouraged to both take responsibility for their product quality standards, and work closely with academia for independent research on the environmental effects and mechanisms when applied to soils. Greater synergism at this level can be a path for environmental sustainability certification, where responsible manufacturers seeking to meet standard product specifications are offered adequate practical support, scientific guidance and training throughout the production and commercialization chains.

Academia–industry partnership

One could argue for the individualization of both production and application certification components, in order to overcome potential drawbacks of joined certification systems. For instance, Pacini *et al.* (2013) identified a possible bottleneck where producers and users in developing countries may be challenged in their capacity to cope with requirements of sustainability certification. Pacini *et al.* (2013) argued that smallholders and small producers in developing countries should receive adequate support, which may include technical and financial aid to meet sustainability certification. Issues such as this are fairly raised and allude to the aspect of the utility of any implemented certification system, underlining the necessity to include all relevant environmental, economic and sociocultural parameters in developing a practical and effective biochar certification framework. One could also argue that industry has an inherent interest in funding independent research on environmental effects, and side-effects, of biochar in soils and their associated mechanisms, and for the environmental certification to be an integral part of any biochar label. If biochar starts to be applied indiscriminately, cases of 'no effect', or even negative effects, on specific soil-based ecosystem services are likely, which would have the potential for damaging perceptions and reduced interest from consumers. Edwards (2016) laid out a further reason for the need of industry to team up with academia. He stated that to build the knowledge base required for a sustainable biochar management system, mostly reproducibility research is needed. Where innovative research – science funded – has determined the OBD for a specific biochar type in a specific location (soil, crop, climate), follow-up reproducibility research – industry funded – is required to find OBDs for that biochar type in other locations (soil, climate) and/or crops, and thereby build a comprehensive knowledge base.

Zhang *et al.* (2016) reviewed biochar for sustainable agriculture and concluded along the same lines that 'an international alliance/networking for promoting the biochar testing and industrial development needs to be developed'. Since competitive research funding strongly favours innovative research, this can only be achieved with additional industry funding for reproducibility research. Such a partnership between science and industry has been successful in the past, for example in the Structural Genomics Consortium, a research charity funded by business, government and other charities (Edwards, 2016). Among the eight essential principles that such a partnership would need to work on, are: objectives that cannot be achieved with current technology (aka 'stretch goals'); clear public quality criteria; mandated data sharing; public ownership of all research outputs; active governing body (Edwards, 2016).

Resource management?

Table 5.1 shows that resource management criteria can be found in the domains of the economy, and of the environment. The economic criteria are (i) microeconomic sustainability and (ii) natural resource efficiency. The main environmental criterion associated with biochar production and application is waste management. There is a move towards revaluing waste materials, particularly agri-wastes, such as manures, slurries and residue by redirecting them to alternative streams such as the generation of bioenergy, within the context of the move to the 'Circular Economy'. Biochar can be produced for a wide range of organic feedstocks, including agri-waste materials. As such, pyrolysis, the process by which biochar is produced, represents a means of adding value to waste materials as the pyrolysis process leads to the production of biofuels (i.e. pyrolysis gas and oils that are a potential source of biodiesel). As these compounds are driven off in the pyrolysis process, combined with the condensation of the solid fraction of the initial feedstock, biochar is generally less bulky and lighter than the initial feedstock from which it was produced. This has advantages in terms of transport and storage, reducing the associated costs due to the material being less bulky, and so this alone can help moderate the growing issues around waste management.

However, it should be noted that there are competing streams for such agri-waste materials. Government incentives in the form of financial support have led to a large growth of anaerobic digestion (AD) facilities in many countries. This represents a competing stream for the use of agri-waste materials. Whether pyrolysis or AD are the most efficient means of managing a particular waste, in terms of costs, offset costs in terms of fertilizers, and the payback from biofuels generated by the process are likely to vary between different soil–climate–waste combinations, and will be affected by the financial incentives offered for the support of such technologies by individual governments.

Other trade-offs linked to resource management that can occur are, for example, the criterion 'sustainable procuration of feedstock', which is intended to avoid negative impacts on biodiversity such as deforestation, monoculture biomass cropping and land use change that may reduce biodiversity. The criterion 'Emissions during biochar production', and many others, is intended to avoid impacts on biodiversity through both direct and indirect means. For example, the input of particulates in the form of soot particles or plant stress caused by dry and/or wet deposition of contaminants.

There are various key aspects that are often overlooked in the context of soil–biochar–organisms interactions. One is biochar's recalcitrance in soils – it is not mineralized to a great extent, as opposed to the more labile organic amendments such as compost. This must be acknowledged in any robust certification to ensure sustainability goals are achieved – a 'one size fits all' criterion in terms of soil carbon is unlikely to be sufficiently robust to ensure risks of negative impacts on biodiversity. Specific locational context and the soil/biochar types must necessarily be taken into account to ensure that bio-diversity outcomes are not diminished at the expense of trying to maximize other facets, such as crop yield increases.

Biodiversity outcomes?

Table 5.1 shows that biodiversity criteria can be found in the domains of 'environment', and of 'environment and society'. The environment criterion is ecosystem protection, and the 'environment and society' criteria are (i) soil protection and (ii) water management. Considering that environment and human and animal health and safety are virtually indissociable, both criteria are addressed together in this section.

As previously discussed, the largest challenge associated with widescale biochar application to soils is achieving the compromise between the intended benefit and the preservation of other soil-based ecosystem services – trade-offs are inevitable. The latter include organic matter decomposition, nutrient cycling, soil structure genesis and maintenance, erosion control, provision of habitat and raw materials, water quality regulation and supply, and pest management (Kibblewhite *et al.*, 2008). In addition, a number of key ecosystem processes can also be impacted by biochar amendment to soil. These include soil nitrogen availability (Hagemann *et al.*, 2017; Nguyen *et al.*, 2017), priming of organic matter (i.e. accelerated or reduced decomposition rates; Weng *et al.*, 2015; Wang *et al.*, 2016), and soil nitrous oxide and methane emissions (Cayuela *et al.*, 2013; Jeffery *et al.*, 2016). A highly diverse community of soil organisms, interacting among themselves and their surrounding abiotic environment, mediates each and all of these processes (Orgiazzi *et al.*, 2016). As such, biodiversity outcomes must necessarily be considered, and requirements and limits identified, before a successful certification scheme can be constructed that effectively maximizes the sustainable use potential of biochar as a soil amendment or an environmental management tool.

By aiming to minimize potential trade-offs between soil-based ecosystem services in biochar-enriched soils against the intended benefit, the OBD concept already addresses biochar's sustainability potential in relation to bio-diversity interactions.

Biochar's ecotoxicological potential is perhaps the most obvious example of trade-offs associated with soil–biochar–organism interactions. There is much evidence that biochar application to soils can impact, positively or negatively, microbial community abundance, composition and activity (Nielsen *et al.*, 2014; Lu *et al.*, 2015; Nguyen *et al.*, 2018), tree growth and species diversity (Thomas and Gale, 2015; Drake *et al.*, 2015), grassland plant diversity (van de Voorde *et al.*, 2014), plant germination (Busch *et al.*, 2012, 2013; Oleszczuk *et al.*, 2012; Oleszczuk and Kołtowski *et al.*, 2018) and root traits (Xiang *et al.*, 2017). Direct and indirect biochar effects on earthworm communities have also been widely reviewed (Lehmann *et al.*, 2011; Weyers and Spokas, 2011; Ameloot *et al.*, 2013). Only a handful of short-term studies addressed interactions with other soil invertebrate groups (Bielská *et al.*, 2018; Marks *et al.*, 2014; Castracani *et al.*, 2015; Domene *et al.*, 2015b; Madžarić *et al.*, 2018; Cook and Neto, 2018). Overall, both positive and negative effects were reported that are variable, often contradictory and deeply influenced by co-occurring and confounding factors, particularly soil characteristics and environmental combinations, biochar properties and ageing, application rates, and the indicator species, structural or functional parameter being measured.

It is likely that some of the reported negative effects on soil organisms are associated with specific biochar contaminants, but such a relationship is yet to be clearly demonstrated (Hilber *et al.*, 2017). Setting threshold contents of trace elements and organic compounds within biochars in current certification schemes may be a potential means of reducing biochar's ecotoxicity potential and so the risk of soil contamination (Hilber *et al.*, 2012; Bielská *et al.*, 2018). Consequences may extend to freshwater and marine ecosystems via runoff or leachates from amended soils (Jaffé *et al.*, 2013; Smith *et al.*, 2013; Bastos *et al.*, 2014; Oleszczuk *et al.*, 2012). Yet, what can be considered a potential toxicant in biochar may not always be easily identifiable, in the context of the whole heterogeneous matrix and the wide range of feedstocks and production techniques used. This highlights the need to explicitly address bioavailable or water-extractable contaminant fractions in biochar quality criteria, namely through effect-based approaches (Hilber *et al.*, 2017). Integrating bioassays in current certification schemes would address such limitations concomitantly and complement biochar quality characterization as established, for instance, for soils and soil materials (ISO/DIS 15799, 2001). However, it remains unclear which combinations of bioassays, soil properties, experimental designs, test organisms, endpoints and thresholds would provide the best compromise of biochar quality and safety. So far, effect-based approaches are excluded from biochar certification schemes, with the exception of a plant germination assay in the IBI Standards (IBI, 2015).

There is another side to this coin. Compelling evidence demonstrates that biochar can also have positive biodiversity outcomes, and thus, potentially contribute to sustainability management, preservation and/or function recovery in vulnerable or degraded ecosystems. Under the combined increasing challenges posed by climatic and anthropogenic pressures, biochar could be envisaged as a potential 'multipurpose' environmental and ecological management tool. Its remarkable sorption capacity for metals and organic compounds may provide a viable option for contaminant immobilization in soils and sediments, significantly reducing their bioavailability and uptake by biota (Kołtowski *et al.*, 2016, 2017; Bielská *et al.*, 2018). Combined with other functional properties, such as soil conditioning and carbon sequestration, biochar could play a crucial role in land reclamation and restoration. By promoting microbial habitat and performance (Atkinson *et al.*, 2010) as well as vegetation cover and tree establishment (Thomas and Gale, 2015), biochar can also support livestock (Calvosa *et al.*, 2010). Biochar may bring exciting prospects in reforestation (Thomas and Gale, 2015) or ecosystem function recovery in degraded rangelands (Stavi, 2012), such as landfill (Oziegbe *et al.* 2018; Reddy *et al.*, 2015) and mine tailings (Fellet *et al.*, 2011). Similarly, it may also represent a more sustainable course of action in plant pest management and disease suppression, both in field and greenhouse (Elad *et al.*, 2010; Graber *et al.*, 2014; Hou *et al.*, 2015; Kumar *et al.*, 2018), among other prospect uses particularly owing to its potential for production from waste materials.

As suggested by Chen *et al.* (2016), biochar-amended soil could be envisaged as a new soil type. As such, the range of environmental management benefits that biochar could entail, as well as the potential for negative impacts, are deeply rooted in the ability to fulfil rigorous quality and environmental safety standards, achieved only through comprehensive certification schemes based on robust empirical evidence. Considering that our knowledge is still limited on many aspects of biochar environmental behaviour, mobility and fate (Tammeorg *et al.*, 2017), particularly on the long-term, a comprehensive certification programme is paramount for protection of biota-mediated ecosystem services in biochar-amended soils. Further, it may also be a valuable aid in identification of the most suitable soil–biochar combination, and where necessary compromises must be made between application rate and strategy for any specific application and target ecosystem. As discussed in this section, quantification of bioavailable contaminant fractions and effect-based approaches may be key for achieving positive, or avoiding negative environmental and ecological implications. Nonetheless, for a comprehensive consideration of biodiversity outcomes, current criteria should be extended to also include dose-responses for the relevant soil-based ecosystem services, suitable matching between biochar and site-specific environmental and ecological properties and account for sustainable feedstock procurement.

Conclusions and outlook

A sustainable biochar system requires sustainable biochar production as well as sustainable biochar application, possibly certified individually but brought together in a label, to support the development of an effective sustainability policy. While biochar production certification is in progress, biochar application certification is a concept in its infancy with developmental challenges due to (i) trade-offs between soil functions, (ii) a much longer time horizon than traditional soil amendments and (iii) limited mechanistic understanding regarding the nature and extent of effects relevant to specific biochars and soil–crop–climate combinations. Integrative strategies are the most promising way forward, such as the OBD for any specific application, biochar contaminant bioavailability criteria and effect-based approaches, alongside synergistic programmes where responsible manufacturers and users are offered adequate support, scientific guidance and training throughout the production, commercialization and consumption chains. It is clear that a considerable effort is required to achieve such a comprehensive and practical certification system, but sustainable biochar production and sustainable environmental biochar application are two sides of the same coin (sustainable system). One cannot succeed without the other.

Acknowledgements

We acknowledge the Portuguese Science Foundation (FCT) for the post-doctoral fellowships of Frank G.A. Verheijen (SFRH/BPD/107913/2015) and Ana Catarina Bastos (SFRH/BPD/98231/2013). Thanks are due for the financial support to CESAM (UID/AMB/50017/2019), to FCT/MCTES through national funds, and the co-funding by the FEDER, within the PT2020 Partnership Agreement and Compete 2020. This work is funded by national funds (OE), through FCT – Fundação para a Ciência e a Tecnologia, I.P., in the scope of the framework contract foreseen in the numbers 4, 5 and 6 of the article 23, of the Decree-Law 57/2016, of August 29, changed by Law 57/2017, of July 19.

Note

1 This chapter is a partial update of the chapter 'Biochar Sustainability Certification', by Frank G.A. Verheijen, Ana Catarina Bastos, Hans-Peter Schmidt, Miguel Brandão and Simon Jeffery (2015), in Johannes Lehmann and Stephen Joseph (Eds.), *Biochar for Environmental Management, Science, Technology and Implementation*, 2nd Edition.

References

Abel, S., Peters, A., Trinks, S., Schonsky, H., Facklam, M., Wessolek, G. (2013). Impact of biochar and hydrochar addition on water retention and water repellency of sandy soil. Geoderma 202, 183–191.

Ameloot, N., Graber, E.R., Verheijen, F.G.A., De Neve, S. (2013). Interactions between biochar stability and soil organisms: review and research needs. European Journal of Soil Science 64(4), 379–390.

Atkinson, C.J., Fitzgerald, J.D., Hipps, N.A. (2010) Potential mechanisms for achieving agricultural benefits from biochar application to temperate soils: a review. Plant and Soil 337(1), 1–18.

Bastos, A.C., Prodana, M., Abrantes, N., Keizer, J.J., Soares, A.M.V.M., Loureiro, S. (2014). Potential risk of biochar-amended soil to aquatic systems: an evaluation based on aquatic bioassays. Ecotoxicology 23, 1784–1793.

Biederman, L.A., Harpole, W.S. (2013). Biochar and its effects on plant productivity and nutrient cycling: a meta-analysis. GCB Bioenergy 5(2), 202–214.

Bielská, L., Škulcová, L., Neuwirthová, N., Cornelissen, G., Hale, S.E. (2018). Sorption, bioavailability and ecotoxic effects of hydrophobic organic compounds in biochar amended soils. Science of the Total Environment 624, 78–86.

Buchholz, T., Luzadis, V.A., Volk, T.A. (2009). Sustainability criteria for bioenergy systems: results from an expert survey. Journal of Cleaner Production 17, S86–S98.

Busch, D., Kammann, C., Grünhage, L., Müller, C. (2012). Simple biotoxicity tests for evaluation of carbonaceous soil additives: establishment and reproducibility of four test procedures. Journal of Environmental Quality 41(4), 1023–1032.

Busch, D., Stark, A., Kammann, C.I., Glaser, B. (2013). Genotoxic and phytotoxic risk assessment of fresh and treated hydrochar from hydrothermal carbonization compared to biochar from pyrolysis. Ecotoxicology and Environmental Safety 97, 59–66.

Calvosa, C., Chuluunbaatar, D., Fara, K. (2010). Livestock and climate change. In IFAD (Ed.). Livestock Thematic Papers: Tools for Project Design. IFAD, 1–20.

Castracani, C., Maienza, A., Grasso, D.A., Genesio, L., Malcevschi, A., Miglietta, F., Vaccari, F.P., Mori, A. (2015). Biochar-macrofauna interplay: searching for new bioindicators. Science of the Total Environment 536, 449–456.

Cayuela, M.L., Sánchez-Monedero, M.A., Roig, A., Hanley, K., Enders, A., Lehmann, J. (2013). Biochar and denitrification in soils: when, how much and why does biochar reduce N_2O emissions? Scientific Reports 3, 1732.

Cayuela, M.L., van Zwieten, L., Singh, B.P., Jeffery, S., Roig, A., Sánchez-Monedero, M.A. (2014). Biochar's role in mitigating soil nitrous oxide emissions: a review and meta-analysis. Agriculture, Ecosystems and Environment 191, 5–16.

Chabbi, A., Lehmann, J., Ciais, P., Loescher, H.W., Cotrufo, M.F., Don, A., Sanclements, M., Schipper, L., Six, J., Smith, P., Rumpel, C. (2017) Aligning agriculture and climate policy. Nature Climate Change 7(5), 307–309.

Chen, X.-W., Wong, J.T.-F., Ng, C.W.-W., Wong, M.-H. (2016). Feasibility of biochar application on a landfill final cover: a review on balancing ecology and shallow slope stability. Environmental Science and Pollution Research 23(8), 7111–7125.

Cook, S.P., Neto, V.R.D.A. (2018). Laboratory evaluation of the direct impact of biochar on adult survival of four forest insect species. Northwest Science 92(1), 1–8.

Cowie, A.L., Downie, A.E., George, B.H., Singh, B.P., Van Zwieten, L., O'Connell, D. (2012). Is sustainability certification for biochar the answer to environmental risks? Pesquisa Agropecuaria Brasileira 47(5), 637–648.

Crane-Droesch, A., Abiven, S., Jeffery, S., Torn, M.S. (2013). Heterogeneous global crop yield response to biochar: a meta-regression analysis. Environmental Research Letters 8(4), 044049.

de Groot, R.S., Alkemade, R., Braat, L., Hein, L., Willemen, L. (2010). Challenges in integrating the concept of ecosystem services and values in landscape planning, management and decision making. Ecological Complexity 7(3), 260–272.

Domene, X., Mattana, S., Hanley, K., Enders, A., Lehmann, J. (2014). Medium-term effects of corn biochar addition on soil biota activities and functions in a temperate soil cropped to corn. Soil Biology and Biochemistry 72, 152–162.

Domene, X., Enders, A., Hanley, K., Lehmann, J. (2015a). Ecotoxicological characterization of biochars: role of feedstock and pyrolysis temperature. Science of the Total Environment 512–513, 552–561.

Domene, X., Hanley, K., Enders, A., Lehmann, J. (2015b). Shortterm mesofauna responses to soil additions of corn stover biochar and the role of microbial biomass. Applied Soil Ecology 89, 10–17. https://doi.org/10.1016/j.apsoil.2014.12.005.

Drake, J.A., Carrucan, A., Jackson, W.R., Cavagnaro, T.R., Patti, A.F. (2015). Biochar application during reforestation alters species present and soil chemistry. Science of the Total Environment 514, 359–365.

EBC (2012) European Biochar Certificate: Guidelines for a Sustainable Production of Biochar. www.european-biochar.org/en.

Edwards, A. (2016). Team up with industry: combining commercial and academic incentives and resources can improve science. Nature 531(7594), 299–302.

Elad, Y., David, D.R., Harel, Y.M., Borenshtein, M., Kalifa, H.B., Silber, A., Graber, E.R. (2010) Induction of systemic resistance in plants by biochar, a soil-applied carbon sequestering agent. Phytopathology 100, 913–921.

Fellet, G., Marchiol, L., Delle Vedove, G., Peressotti, A. (2011). Application of biochar on mine tailings: effects and perspectives for land reclamation. Chemosphere 83, 1262–1297.

Fellet, G., Marmiroli, M., Marchiol, L. (2014). Elements uptake by metal accumulator species grown on mine tailings amended with three types of biochar. Science of the Total Environment 468, 598–608.

Ghezzehei, T.A., Sarkhot, D.V., Berhe, A.A. (2014). Biochar can be used to capture essential nutrients from dairy wastewater and improve soil physico-chemical properties. Solid Earth 5(2), 953–962.

Graber, E.R., Tsechanski, L., Gerstl, Z., Lew, B. (2012). High surface area biochar negatively impacts herbicide efficacy. Plant and Soil 353(1–2), 95–106.

Graber, E.R., Frenkel, O., Jaiswal, A.K., Elad, Y. (2014). How may biochar influence severity of diseases caused by soilborne pathogens? Carbon Management 5(2), 169–183.

Guerra, C.A., Pinto-Correia, T., Metzger, M.J. (2014). Mapping soil erosion prevention using an ecosystem service modeling framework for integrated land management and policy. Ecosystems 17(5), 878–889.

Gurwick, N.P., Moore, L.A., Kelly, C., Elias, P. (2013). A systematic review of biochar research, with a focus on its stability in situ and its promise as a climate mitigation strategy. PloS One 8(9), e75932.

Hagemann, N., Kammann, C.I., Schmidt, H., Kappler, A., Behrens, S. (2017). Nitrate capture and slow release in biochar amended compost and soil. Plos ONE 12(2), e0171214. https://doi.org/10.1371/journal.pone.0171214.

Hilber, I., Blum, F., Leifeld, J., Schmidt, H.-P., Bucheli, T.D. (2012). Quantitative determination of PAHs in biochar: a prerequisite to ensure its quality and safe application. Journal of Agricultural Food Chemistry 60, 3042–3050.

Hilber, I., Bastos, A.C., Loureiro, S., Soja, G., Cornelissen, G., Bucheli, T. (2017). The different faces of biochar: contamination risk versus remediation tool. Journal of Environmental Engineering and Landscape Management 25(2), 86–104.

Hou, X., Meng, L., Li, L., Pan, G., Li, B. (2015). Biochar amendment to soils impairs developmental and reproductive performances of a major rice pest Nilaparvata lugens (Homopera: Delphacidae). Journal of Applied Entomology 139(10), 727–733.

Houghton, R.A., House, J.I., Pongratz, J., Van Der Werf, G.R., DeFries, R.S., Hansen, M.C., … Ramankutty, N. (2012). Carbon emissions from land use and land-cover change. Biogeosciences 9(12), 5125–5142.

IBI (2013). Standardized product definition and product testing guidelines for biochar that is used in soil (i.e. IBI Biochar Standards). www.biochar-international.org/characterizationstandard.

Intergovernmental Panel on Climate Change (IPCC) (2014). Climate Change 2014. Impacts, Adaptation and Vulnerability: Regional Aspects. Cambridge University Press.

International Biochar Initiative (IBI) (2015). Standardized Product Definition and Product Testing Guidelines for Biochar That Is Used in Soil. www.biochar-international.org/sites/default/files/IBI_Biochar_Standards_V2.1_Final.pdf.

ISO/DIS 15799 (2001). Soil quality: guidance on the ecotoxicological characterization of soil and soil materials.

Jaffé, R., Ding, Y., Niggemann, J., Vahatalo, A.V., Stubbins, A., Spencer, R.G.M., Campbell, J., Dittmar, T. (2013). Global charcoal mobilization from soils via dissolution and riverine transport to the oceans. Science 340, 345–347.

Jeffery, S., Verheijen, F.G., van der Velde, M., Bastos, A.C. (2011). A quantitative review of the effects of biochar application to soils on crop productivity using meta-analysis. Agriculture, Ecosystems and Environment 144(1), 175–187.

Jeffery, S., Verheijen, F.G., Bastos, A.C., Velde, M. (2014). A comment on 'Biochar and its effects on plant productivity and nutrient cycling: a meta analysis': on the importance of accurate reporting in supporting a fast moving research field with policy implications. GCB Bioenergy 6(3), 176–179.

Jeffery, S., Bezemer, T.M., Cornelissen, G., Kuyper, T.W., Lehmann, J., Mommer, L., Sohi, S.P., Voorde, T.F., Wardle, D.A. and Groenigen, J.W. (2015). The way forward in biochar research: targeting trade-offs between the potential wins. GCB Bioenergy 7(1), 1–13.

Jeffery, S., Verheijen, F.G., Kammann, C., Abalos, D. (2016). Biochar effects on methane emissions from soils: a meta-analysis. Soil Biology and Biochemistry 101, 251–258.

Jeffery, S., Abalos, D., Prodana, M., Bastos, A.C., Van Groenigen, J.W., Hungate, B.A., Verheijen, F. (2017). Biochar boosts tropical but not temperate crop yields. Environmental Research Letters 12(5), 053001.

Kammann, C., Ratering, S., Eckhard, C., Müller, C. (2012). Biochar and hydrochar effects on greenhouse gas (carbon dioxide, nitrous oxide, and methane) fluxes from soils. Journal of Environmental Quality 41(4), 1052–1066.

Kibblewhite, M.G., Ritz, K., Swift, M.J. (2008). Soil health in agricultural systems. Philosophical Transactions of the Royal Society B: Biological Sciences 363(1492), 685–701.

Kołtowski, M., Hilber, I., Bucheli, T.D., Oleszczuk, P. (2016). Effect of steam activated biochar application to industrially contaminated soils on bioavailability of polycyclic aromatic hydrocarbons and ecotoxicity of soils. Science of the Total Environment 566–567, 1023–1031.

Kołtowski, M., Hilber, I., Bucheli, T.D., Charmas, B., Skubiszewska-Zi ba, J., Oleszczuk, P. (2017). Activated biochars reduce the exposure of polycyclic aromatic hydrocarbons in industrially contaminated soils. Chemical Engineering Journal 310, 33–40.

Kumar, A., Elad, Y., Tsechansky, L., Abrol, V., Lew, B., Offenbach, R., Graber, E.R. (2018). Biochar potential in intensive cultivation of Capsicum annuum L. (sweet pepper): crop yield and plant protection. Journal of the Science of Food and Agriculture 98(2), 495–503.

Lal, R. (2016). Beyond COP 21: potential and challenges of the '4 per Thousand' initiative. Journal of Soil and Water Conservation 71(1), 20A–25A.

Lehmann, J., Rillig, M.C., Thies, J., Masiello, C.A., Hockaday, W.C., Crowley, D. (2011). Biochar effects on soil biota: a review. Soil Biology and Biochemistry 43, 1812–1836.

Liu, X., Zhang, A., Ji, C., Joseph, S., Bian, R., Li, L., … Paz-Ferreiro, J. (2013). Biochar's effect on crop productivity and the dependence on experimental conditions: a meta-analysis of literature data. Plant and Soil 373(1–2), 583–594.

Lorenz, K., Lal, R. (2014). Biochar application to soil for climate change mitigation by soil organic carbon sequestration. Journal of Plant Nutrition and Soil Science 177(5), 651–670.

Lu, H., Lashari, M.S., Liu, X., Ji, H., Li, L., Zheng, J., Kibue, G.W., Joseph, S., Pan, G. (2015). Changes in soil microbial community structure and enzyme activity with amendment of biochar-manure compost and pyroligneous solution in a saline soil from Central China. European Journal of Soil Biology 70, 67–76.

Madžarić, S., Kos, M., Drobne, D., Hočevar, M., Jemec Kokalj, A. (2018). Integration of behavioral tests and biochemical biomarkers of terrestrial isopod Porcellio scaber (Isopoda, Crustacea) is a promising methodology for testing environmental safety of chars. Environmental Pollution 234, 804–811.

Marks, E.A.N., Mattana, S., Alcañiz, J.M., Domene, X. (2014). Biochars provoke diverse soil mesofauna reproductive responses in laboratory bioassays. European Journal of Soil Biology 60, 104–111.

Mia, S., van Groenigen, J.W., van de Voorde, T.F.J., Oram, N.J., Bezemer, T.M., Mommer, L., Jeffery, S. (2014). Biochar application rate affects biological nitrogen fixation in red clover conditional on potassium availability. Agriculture, Ecosystems and Environment 191, 83–91.

Minasny, B., McBratney, A.B. (2018). Limited effect of organic matter on soil available water capacity. European Journal of Soil Science 69(1), 39–47.

Minasny, B., Malone, B.P., McBratney, A.B., Angers, D.A., Arrouays, D., Chambers, A., Chaplot, V., Chen, Z.-S., Cheng, K., Dash, B.S., Field, D.J., Gimona, A., Hedley, C.B., Hong, S.Y., Mandal, B., Marchant, B.P., Martin, M., McConkey, B.G., … Winowiecki, L. (2017). Soil carbon 4 per mille. Geoderma 292, 59–86.

Mondal, A., Khare, D., Kundu, S., Mondal, S., Mukherjee, S., Mukhopadhyay, A. (2017). Spatial soil organic carbon (SOC) prediction by regression kriging using remote sensing data. The Egyptian Journal of Remote Sensing and Space Science 20(1), 61–70. https://doi.org/10.1016/j.ejrs.2016.06.004.

Nguyen, T.T.N., Wallace, H.M., Xu, C.-Y., Xu, Z., Farrar, M.B., Joseph, S., Van Zwieten, L., Bai, S.H. (2017). Short-term effects of organo-mineral biochar and organic fertilisers on nitrogen cycling, plant photosynthesis, and nitrogen use efficiency. Journal of Soils and Sediments 17(12), 2763–2774.

Nguyen, T.T.N., Wallace, H.M., Xu, C.-Y., Van Zwieten, L., Weng, Z.H., Xu, Z., Che, R., Tahmasbian, I., Hu, H.W., Bai, S.H. (2018). The effects of short term, long term and reapplication of biochar on soil bacteria. Science of the Total Environment 636, 142–151.

Nielsen, S., Minchin, T., Kimber, S., van Zwieten, L., Gilbert, J., Munroe, P., Joseph, S., Thomas, T. (2014). Comparative analysis of the microbial communities in agricultural soil amended with enhanced biochars or traditional fertilisers. Agriculture, Ecosystems and Environment, 191, 73–82.

Oleszczuk, P., Kołtowski, M. (2018). Changes of total and freely dissolved polycyclic aromatic hydrocarbons and toxicity of biochars treated with various aging processes. Environmental Pollution 237, 65–73.

Oleszczuk, P., Rycaj, M., Lehmann, J., Cornelissen, G. (2012). Influence of activated carbon and biochar on phytotoxicity of air-dried sewage sludges to Lepidium sativum. Ecotoxicology and Environmental Safety 80, 321–326.

Orgiazzi, A., Bardgett, R.D., Barrios, E., Behan-Pelletier, V., Briones, M.J.I., Chotte, J.-L., De Deyn, G.B., Eggleton, P., Fierer, N., Fraser, T., Hedlund, K., Jeffery, S., Johnson, N.C., Jones, A., Kandeler, E., Kaneko, N., Lavelle, P., Lemanceau, P., Miko, L., Montanarella, L., Moreira, F.M.S., Ramirez, K.S., Scheu, S., Singh, B.K., Six, J., van der Putten, W.H., Wall, D.H. (Eds.) (2016). Global Soil Biodiversity Atlas. Publications Office of the European Union, 176. doi:10.2788/2613.

Oziegbe, O., Aladesanmi, O.T., Awotoye, O.O. (2018). Effect of biochar on the nutrient contents and metal recovery efficiency in sorghum planted on landfill soils. International Journal of Environmental Science and Technology (in press).

Pacini, H., Assunção, L., Van Dam, J., Toneto Jr, R. (2013). The price for biofuels sustainability. Energy Policy 59, 898–903.

Poulton, P., Johnston, J., MacDonald, A., White, R., Powlson, D. (2018) Major limitations to achieving '4 per 1000' increases in soil organic carbon stock in temperate regions: evidence from long-term experiments at Rothamsted Research, UK. Global Change Biology.

Reddy, K.R., Yaghoubi, P., Yukselen-Aksoy, Y. (2015). Effects of biochar amendment on geotechnical properties of landfill cover soil. Waste Management and Research 33(6), 524–532.

Rees, F., Simonnot, M.O., Morel, J.L. (2014). Short-term effects of biochar on soil heavy metal mobility are controlled by intra-particle diffusion and soil pH increase. European Journal of Soil Science 65, 149–161. https://doi.org/10.1111/ejss.12107.

Rockström, J., Williams, J., Daily, G., Noble, A., Matthews, N., Gordon, L., Wetterstrand, H., DeClerck, F., Shah, M., Steduto, P., de Fraiture, C., Hatibu, N., Unver, O., Bird, J., Sibanda, L., Smith, J. (2017). Sustainable intensification of agriculture for human prosperity and global sustainability. Ambio 46, 4–17.

Rumpel, C., Lehmann, J., Chabbi, A. (2018). '4 per 1,000' initiative will boost soil carbon for climate and food security. Nature 553(7686), 27–27.

Smith, C.R., Buzan, E.M., Lee, J.W. (2013). Potential impact of biochar water-extractable substances on environmental sustainability. ACS Sustainable Chemistry and Engineering 1, 118–126.

Smith, P. (2016). Soil carbon sequestration and biochar as negative emission technologies. Global Change Biology 22, 1315–1324.

Stavi, I. (2012). The potential use of biochar in reclaiming degraded rangelands. Journal of Environmental Planning and Management 55(5), 657–665.

Tammeorg, P., Bastos, A. C., Jeffery, S., Rees, F., Kern, J., Graber, E.R., Ventura, M., Kibblewhite, M., Amaro, A., Budai, A., Cordovil, C.M.S., Domene, X., Gardi, C., Gasco, G., Horak, J., Kammann, C., Kondrlova, E., Laird, D., Loureiro, S., Martins, M.A.S., Panzacchi, P., Prasad, M., Prodana, M., Puga, A.P., Ruysschaert, G., Sas-Paszt, L., Silva, F.C., Teixeira, W.G., Tonon, G., delle Vedove, G., Zavalloni, C., Glaser, B., Verheijen, F.G.A. (2017). Biochars in soils: towards the required level of scientific understanding. Journal of Environmental Engineering and Landscape Management 25(2), 192–207.

Thomas, S.C., Gale, N. (2015). Biochar and forest restoration: a review and meta-analysis of tree growth responses. New Forests 46, 931–946.

van de Voorde, T.F., Bezemer, T.M., Van Groenigen, J.W., Jeffery, S., Mommer, L. (2014). Soil biochar amendment in a nature restoration area: effects on plant productivity and community composition. Ecological Applications 24(5), 1167–1177.

Vaughan, N.E., Lenton, T.M. (2011). A review of climate geoengineering proposals. Climatic Change 109(3–4), 745–790.

Verheijen, F., Jeffery, S., Bastos, A.C., van der Velde, M., Diafas, I. (2010). Biochar application to soils: a critical scientific review of effects on soil properties, processes and functions. Office for the Official Publ. of the European Communities, Luxembourg.

Verheijen, F.G., Montanarella, L., Bastos, A.C. (2012). Sustainability, certification, and regulation of biochar. Pesquisa Agropecuária Brasileira 47(5), 649–653.

Verheijen, F., Bastos, A.C., Schmidt, H.P., Brandão, M., Jeffery, S. (2015). Biochar sustainability and certification. In J. Lehmann and S. Joseph (Eds.) Biochar for Environmental Management: Science, Technology and Implementation. Routledge.

Wang, J., Xiong, Z., Yan, X., Kuzyakov, Y. (2016) Carbon budget by priming in a biochar-amended soil. European Journal of Soil Biology 76, 26–34.

Weng, Z. (Han), Van Zwieten, L., Singh, B.P., Kimber, S., Morris, S., Cowie, A., Macdonald, L.M. (2015). Plant-biochar interactions drive the negative priming of soil organic carbon in an annual ryegrass field system. Soil Biology and Biochemistry 90, 111–121.

Weyers, S.L., Spokas, K.A. (2011). Impact of biochar on earthworm populations: a review. Applied and Environmental Soil Science 2011, 1–12.

Woolf, D., Amonette, J.E., Street-Perrott, F.A., Lehmann, J., Joseph, S. (2010). Sustainable biochar to mitigate global climate change. Nature Communications 1, 56.

Xiang, Y., Deng, Q., Duan, H., Guo, Y. (2017). Effects of biochar application on root traits: a meta-analysis. GCB Bioenergy 9, 1563–1572.

Zhang, D., Yan, M., Niu, Y., Liu, X., van Zwieten, L., Chen, D., Bian, R., Cheng, K., Li, L., Joseph, S., Zheng, J., Zhang, X., Zheng, J., Crowley, D., Filley, T.R., Pan, G. (2016). Is current biochar research addressing global soil constraints for sustainable agriculture? Agriculture, Ecosystems and Environment 226, 25–32.

6 Safeguarding farm animal welfare

Harry J. Blokhuis, Isabelle Veissier, Mara Miele and Bryan Jones

Introduction

Quality of life for the animals that become our food is an important concern in European societies and elsewhere. Activities of pressure groups and consumers' purchasing choices reflect these concerns and affect, through legislation as well as company policy, the way farm animals are currently housed and cared for. Animal welfare is now an important aspect of the acceptability and thus sustainability of animal production systems. Indeed, a system that results in poor welfare is unsustainable (Broom, 2010). Yet, this component of food sustainability has not received the amount of attention given to other sustainability initiatives in literature, or practice.

In this chapter we will first describe some developments in animal production and the related societal discussion on animal welfare with focus on the European Union. Then we will discuss animal welfare research and welfare assessment before finally looking at current developments in product labelling as well as welfare improvements via technological developments.

Animal production and important changes in the last 50 years

The livestock sector contributes substantially to the European economy, €130 billion annually, it amounts to 48 per cent of the total agricultural activity and it creates employment for almost 30 million people (Animal Task Force, 2016). The per capita total animal protein consumption in the EU remained relatively stable from 2000 to 2013. It increased modestly up to 2007 then fell slightly. This trend masks a diverging trend in consumption of protein from different types of animal products: cheese and poultry increased by about 15 per cent while bovine meat decreased by nearly 14 per cent (EEA AIRS_ PO2.10, 2017).

This trend is not necessarily observed throughout the world. Livestock production worldwide has grown enormously in recent decades. This is mainly due to increasing demand for animal-source foods in developing countries with growing populations and where people are adopting Western diets and styles of consumption (Delgado *et al.*, 1999; Hendrickson and Miele, 2009). Global meat production tripled over the last four decades, increasing 20 per cent in just the last ten years (www.worldwatch.org/global-meat-production-and-consumption-continue-rise).

Major changes took place in the Western European animal production sector during the latter part of the twentieth century (Ruttan, 1998). Farming intensified enormously, the overall number of farms decreased substantially while there was a significant rise in the number of animals per farm (Porcher, 2001; Blokhuis *et al.*, 2003, 2013). Due to sophisticated genetic selection programmes there was also an enormous increase in the production per animal. For example, between 1960 and 1995 the milk produced per cow in the Netherlands increased by almost 60 per cent and, in broiler chickens, the time required to reach a live weight of 1.8 kg decreased from 91 days in 1954 to 37 days in 1996 and to only about 31 days currently (authors' estimation). The changes in the structure of the sector were facilitated by increased mechanisation and other technological developments. These also changed dramatically the conditions in which the animals were kept as well as management practices. Housing conditions, especially for pigs and poultry, changed profoundly where low-density systems, often outdoor were replaced by housing systems, often indoor characterised by high animal density with minimal living space for the individual and a very barren environment (Blokhuis, 1999). Systems like battery cages for laying hens and stalls for dry sows were introduced and the workforce employed in EU (12 Member States) agriculture decreased enormously, falling from 13.5 per cent to 5.5 per cent between 1970 and 1994 (Grant, 1997). Currently the percentage employed in agriculture in these countries is 3.8 per cent (World Bank, Databank, retrieved 20 February 2018).

While these changes contributed to increased food security in Europe, the barren housing conditions, high production levels and profound mechanisation caused growing concern and fierce societal debate regarding the welfare of the animals (Blokhuis *et al.*, 1998; Fraser, 2008; Miele and Bock, 2007). It became increasingly recognised that poor welfare can result in poor animal health and productivity, and that product quality and profitability are often reduced if the animals' welfare is compromised (Jones, 1997, 1998). The concerns for the quality of life of a rapidly growing number of animals used in food production, first voiced by some animal advocates and pioneer scientists, quickly grew into a new social movement. This paralleled the development of a specific area of research that eventually integrated expertise from several disciplines, including veterinary science, biology, physiology, neuroscience, ethology, genetics and ethics, and gave birth to what is now known as 'animal welfare science' (Veissier and Miele, 2014).

Ongoing welfare discussion, concerns and drivers

Different groups, citizens, consumers, farmers, welfare organisations, policy makers and scientists, each with their own perspectives, concerns and drivers are all involved in the debate about the welfare of animals in the animal production sector. Pirscher (2016), among others, argued that in recent times consumers play a bigger role in social decision-making. With the establishment of a market for animal-friendly products via labelling, consumers should be able to act in accordance with their ethical value systems and consume '*for the sake*' of the farm animals. However, the role of consumers is very much affected by retailer initiatives (Miele and Lever, 2013). Particularly important are the different strategies with which animal welfare issues are used in the promotion of product quality to consumers. Within these new markets of animal-friendly products, the 'naturalness' of food products associated to labels such as 'free range' and 'organic', has often been presented as having mutually beneficial outcomes for retailers and NGOs (Miele and Lever, 2014).

Animal welfare standards have been developed and promoted by supermarkets and corporate retailers as part of their Corporate Social Responsibility (CSR) commitment. Their broad aim has been to enhance the perception of ethical commitments of brands by ensuring the integrity of their products, as well as to diversify their product range, and communicate the ethical status of products to consumers. The quality of life of farm animals is often communicated either on the packaging of food products or with specific labels. This is most evident in countries such as the UK and the Netherlands but far less in the Southern or Eastern European countries (Miele *et al.*, 2015). In Scandinavian countries, the role of public institutions in regulating animal welfare is more important than private initiatives.

The proliferation of these different strategies poses questions about the nature and validity of the welfare claims made and the transparency of the market on this matter (see Blokhuis *et al.*, 2003, 2013; Miele, 2011). Even with all the differences and variability across Europe, the commercialisation of animal welfare is becoming an important driver of innovation in animal farming (EU Animal Welfare Strategy 2012–2015, Compassion in World Farming[1]) and plays an important role in promoting initiatives for improving farm animal welfare: it signals the 'relevance' that producers and market operators attribute to improving animal welfare to differentiate their products (see Freidberg, 2004; Miele *et al.*, 2005; Miele and Lever, 2014). In the UK and the Netherlands supermarkets have often worked in partnership with NGOs campaigning for reform of the food system and some recent initiatives such as the British Benchmark of Animal Welfare promoted by CIWF, World Animal Protection and Coller Capital,[2] a leading investor in private equity secondary markets, have involved many food producers and retailers.

These strategies are not, however, easily transferrable to different contexts and/or countries. For example, certain conditions enable the segmentation of food markets according to the animals' welfare status (Miele and Lever, 2014). These include increased availability of consumer information about animal production systems and related welfare problems, lower relative food prices and a sufficient share of the population with enough disposable income to act upon political or ethical values and preferences (Koos, 2012; Evans and Miele, 2017).

Animal welfare science

The scientific study of animal welfare developed over the last four or five decades and is thereby a relatively young research area (Blokhuis *et al.*, 2008). Good animal welfare can mean different things to different people and scientific studies generally focus accordingly. Before it can be widely accepted and implemented, any sort of farm animal welfare definition needs to include criteria that reflect the range of scientific and societal views (Miele *et al.*, 2011). For some, the possibility for the animal to show natural behaviour is an absolute prerequisite for good animal welfare. For other people, animal welfare is mainly defined in terms of physical health, while yet others emphasise the importance of the mental or emotional state of the animal (Fraser, 2008). These three dimensions are also reflected in the definition of the World Health Organisation for animals (the OIE):

> Animal welfare means how an animal is coping with the conditions in which it lives. An animal is in a good state of welfare if (as indicated by scientific evidence) it is healthy, comfortable, well nourished, safe, able to express innate behaviour, and if it is not suffering from unpleasant states such as pain, fear, and distress.
>
> (OIE, 2017)

Animal welfare science aims to assess the state of the animal regarding these three dimensions. Veterinary medicine, animal behaviour, animal physiology and genetics are the main disciplines in these studies. The work often involves investigation of animal responses to exposure to acute and chronic stressors. Cognition refers to the mental abilities of animals, their perception, reasoning and development of expectations. Consequently, cognitive ability and processing are major determinants of animals' reactions to different situations, not least the extent to which they can experience suffering. The emerging areas of cognition and animal emotions are therefore increasingly important in animal welfare science (Forkman *et al.*, 2007; Boissy *et al.*, 2007; Jones and Boissy, 2011).

Of course, there are many other approaches where the animal and its responses are the focus of attention. In often more applied studies, behavioural and physiological responses are used to measure the way in which an animal perceives the nature and intensity of selected housing and husbandry features. Based on such studies, research aims to define optimal conditions, considering important consequences for productivity, product quality and profitability. Early studies concentrated on comparing the effects on welfare of keeping animals in different housing systems under controlled conditions. To identify risks for animal welfare, the effects of housing and husbandry conditions are also frequently addressed using an epidemiological approach that involves examination of animal physiology, behaviour, health and production under commercial conditions (Gunnarsson, 1999; Moinard *et al.*, 2003). In yet another type of study, knowledge about the basic needs of animals is applied to design alternative, animal-friendly, husbandry systems.

On-farm assessment of animal welfare for reasons of labelling, certification or quality assurance is a specific line of research that has received considerable attention in the last two decades. The first approaches aimed to assess the availability of welfare promoting conditions and to identify risk factors for poor welfare. Consequently, rather than focusing on aspects of the animals themselves, as animal welfare, these approaches concentrated on specific features of animal housing, for example the type of system and equipment, and their management such as feeding routines and diets, and handling. Obviously, these 'resource' and 'management' factors often referred to as the 'input' variables are crucially important for determining the quality of the environment as experienced by the animal, whereas animal welfare is the 'output'. Identifying and providing specific housing and management conditions can be most appropriately referred to as animal protection.

Welfare Quality®

About 15 years ago the first aims and approaches of what became the largest piece of integrated research work yet carried out on animal welfare in Europe were formulated and became the backbone of the Welfare Quality® research project when it was financed under the European 6th Framework Programme for Research and Technological Development. The full title of the project was 'Integration of Animal Welfare in the Food Quality Chain: From Public Concern to Improved Welfare and Transparent Quality'. The Welfare Quality® project addressed many of the issues outlined above and its main aims were:

* to develop a standardised system for the assessment of animal welfare;
* to develop a standardised way to convey measures into animal welfare information (and to disseminate such information);
* to develop practical strategies to improve animal welfare;
* to integrate and interrelate the most appropriate specialist expertise in the multidisciplinary field of animal welfare in Europe.

The project began in 2004 and comprised a partnership of 40 institutions in Europe and, since 2006, four in Latin America. The partners were leading research groups based in 13 European countries as well as in Uruguay, Brazil, Chile and Mexico, and they provided the multidisciplinary expertise in animal and social sciences as well as the geographic spread required to effectively address the project's and the EU's requirements. Furthermore, many different stakeholders, including general public, consumers, lobby groups, government, retailers, breeders, producers, processors, certification bodies, ethical organisations etc. were involved. For example, an advisory committee consisting of representatives from relevant and interested stakeholder groups, as above, was established to work closely with, and to advise the project's steering committee on: the progress made, the relevance and timeliness of the work and incoming proposals, the inclusion of specific issues and strategies, and future plans.

A scientific board (six international experts whose collective expertise covered all aspects of the project) was also formed to assess the scientific and technical quality of the work. Thus, the project clearly addressed the European Research Area concept of integration to achieve important societal and policy objectives. As expected, the original ideas (Blokhuis *et al.*, 2003) evolved and the priorities were modified accordingly during the project's lifetime. The main drivers underlying the vision, the general aims and the research did, however, remain the same.

Budgetary constraints meant that not all farm animal species could be covered so effort was primarily focused on pigs, chickens and cattle.

As well as developing reliable, science-based on-farm welfare assessment systems and a standardised way of conveying welfare measures into clear and understandable product information, Welfare Quality® also included research designed to identify practical strategies to solve some of the main welfare problems in animal production. So, studies were conducted in important areas such as handling stress, food and feeding regimes, lameness, temperament, neonatal mortality, injurious behaviours etc. Because the diversity in climatic, industrial and social-cultural conditions were considered the above instruments were believed likely to drive further developments both within and outside the European Union.

Over the years Welfare Quality® not only stimulated a widespread integration of research teams in Europe and beyond but it also generated a wide range of important outcomes and deliverables and these were disseminated in several ways:

- Numerous papers were published in international scientific journals as well as many popular articles and book chapters. Several talks were also given by Welfare Quality® partners at scientific and other meetings.
- A freely available interactive web platform was established to further promote science–society dialogue.
- Extensive protocol documents for welfare assessment in each of the various product groups were delivered (Welfare Quality® Consortium, 2009a, 2009b, 2009c).
- The welfare improvement strategies developed in the project (Jones and Manteca, 2009) and the associated Technical Information Resource, which describes possible risk factors and remedial measures, were placed on the Welfare Quality® website.

- Three large stakeholder conferences were held in Brussels, Berlin and Uppsala in 2005, 2007 and 2009, respectively and were very well attended by representatives of farmer associations, breeders, certification bodies, retailers, NGOs, scientists, members of the EU Parliament and Commission, the media etc.
- Symposia and training sessions mainly regarding the assessment systems were held for smaller groups in several countries.
- Multimedia programmes for stockpersons were made available and used for training purposes.
- Twelve illustrated fact sheets each covering different aspects of the project (e.g. lameness in cattle, sequential feeding regimes for broilers, social stress in cattle, human–animal interactions, aggression and neonatal mortality in pigs etc.) were produced in five languages. These were made available on the website, advertised in the Welfare Quality® Newsletters, and mailed to stakeholders and journalists.
- The Welfare Quality® Series comprising reports covering selected sectors/features of the project were widely distributed and are available on the Welfare Quality Network website (www.welfarequalitynetwork.net).
- The Welfare Quality® book, summarising the approach and outcomes of the project, was published by Wageningen Academic Publishers (Blokhuis *et al.*, 2013).

Collectively, the above achievements contributed significantly to the advisory component of the cyclical process of farm assessment – feedback and advice – welfare improvement – reassessment etc. They also provided guidance to policy makers and other stakeholders on research priorities as well as the potential implementation and use of the project's final deliverables, particularly the welfare assessment and product information systems, and the practical welfare improvement strategies.

Further stakeholder participation and involvement was secured by the formation of the European Animal Welfare Platform (EAWP). This unique and innovative platform originated from the Welfare Quality® project and comprised key industry players in the food chain, welfare organisations and welfare science. Working together in an atmosphere of openness and trust the EAWP identified the most pressing welfare problems in cattle, pigs, laying hens, broilers and salmon. The EAWP then described the consequences of such problems, ways of measuring them, existing best practices, and identified short- and long-term goals for welfare and economic improvement, and R&D priorities. These outcomes were gathered in a set of Strategic Approach Documents for each of the product groups. More recently, the Welfare Quality Network (WQN), comprising previous members of the Welfare Quality® project, works to maintain and update the assessment protocols and to foster relevant research (www.welfarequality network.net).

Animal welfare assessment

In contrast to defining optimal input variables, the Welfare Quality[®] project set out to propose a set of animal-based measures that could be used to describe the overall level of animal welfare on a given farm or absence of suffering in a slaughter plant. The project considered all dimensions of welfare and defined four principles and 12 welfare criteria for good welfare, that expanded the five freedoms of the Farm Animal Welfare Council (1992) (Table 6.1). Thus, these principles and criteria were constructed as a general framework that could be applied for different species and ensuring that all dimensions of welfare were covered in all species. It was never the intention to relate principles or criteria to specific certifications or labels. For each criterion animal indicators were then defined to measure if the criterion requirements were met or not. For instance:

- When animals are not fed correctly they may suffer hunger which can be measured by checking their body condition: animal too thin.
- If the resting area is not comfortable, cows may lie outside this area, collide with box partitions when lying down or suffer blisters and other external lesions due to friction with the floor.
- If pigs are kept in a barren and stressful environment, tail biting can develop and cause pain.
- If animals are in poor health then several clinical signs or injuries can be detected: lameness, mastitis in dairy cows, respiratory diseases etc.
- When housing conditions are varied: ample space, presence of litter or other objects to investigate and manipulate, access pasture etc., and the animals are in cohesive social groups they will express several natural behaviours such as exploration, play, positive interactions and reduced aggression.

A comprehensive list of possible animal measures/indicators was drawn up and evaluated: to be suitable these indicators must be specific, in that they measure what they are supposed to, sensitive, repeatable and feasible in commercial conditions. For some of the listed welfare criteria, the measures at our disposal did not fulfil these requirements. For example, thirst is hardly detectable with simple measures unless the animal is very dehydrated, and a pinch skin test can be used: in case of dehydration, when the skin is pinched it does not immediately resume its initial shape. Similarly, the pain induced by dehorning cannot be measured at the time of a farm visit because dehorning may have occurred a long time ago. In such cases where animal-based measures were not available, Welfare Quality[®] relied on resource- or management-based indicators. Thus, Welfare Quality[®] assessment systems use a mixture of output-based and input-based measures to evaluate the welfare of animals on farms (see Table 6.1).

As stated above, output- or animal-based measures refer to the quality of the environment as experienced by the animal and are essential to highlight

Table 6.1 Welfare Quality® principles and criteria for good welfare. The measures taken on farms or at slaughter are essentially input-based (measured at the animal) except when no such measure was available. Then output-based measures are used (measures of resources or management) (see 'Animal Welfare Science' section).

Principles	Welfare criteria		Input- vs. output-based measures[1]
Good feeding	1.	Absence of prolonged hunger	Output-based measure
	2.	Absence of prolonged thirst	Input-based measure
Good housing	3.	Comfort around resting	Output-based measure
	4.	Thermal comfort	Output-based measure
	5.	Ease of movement	Input-based measure
Good health	6.	Absence of injuries	Output-based measure
	7.	Absence of disease	Output-based measure
	8	Absence of pain induced by management procedures	Input-based measure
Appropriate behaviour	9.	Expression of social behaviours	Output-based measure
	10.	Expression of other behaviours	Output- or input-based measure
	11.	Good human–animal relationship	Output-based measure
	12.	Positive emotional state	Output-based measure

Note
1 Most frequent case across animal types (dairy cows, fattening cattle, calves, fattening pigs, sows and piglets, broilers, laying hens) and period in life (farm or slaughter).

welfare problems. Nevertheless, the registration and evaluation of 'resource' and 'management' factors, the input-based measures are also crucially important to identify the causes of welfare problems as well as possible risks for welfare. Indeed, farmers are more willing to adopt welfare-friendly changes on their farm if provided with the results of both animal-based measures and input-measures (Dereclenne, 2018). Similarly, laypeople acknowledge the importance of animal emotions but they seem to rely more on environmental features than animal behaviour or physiology when judging the animals' welfare (Robbins *et al.*, 2018).

In Welfare Quality® we proposed a scoring system to help the interpretation of data collected on farms or at slaughter and to integrate them into an overall evaluation. Farms could be categorised into either 'excellent', 'enhanced' or 'accepted' or be 'not classified' depending on the level of expected welfare of the animals on each farm. The scoring integrated the views of experts, animal scientists, social scientists and stakeholders, and reflected their ethical reasoning thanks to specific mathematical tools: spline functions, Choquet integrals, outranking methods etc. (Botreau *et al.*, 2009). A webtool is dedicated to the calculation of scores (available at www1. clermont.inra.fr/wq/).

Developments

Labelling

Food labels have become important tools by which consumers can evaluate and appreciate food qualities. In contemporary Western supermarkets foods are frequently presented with information on origin, nutritional value, potential health benefits or risks: allergies, cooking etc. More recently a significant increase in so-called 'ethic-political' food labels has addressed a wide range of concerns including animal welfare. These labels are conceived to grab consumers' attention, to address their ethical concerns and to influence purchasing decisions. Most information is simplified, and images/logos communicate the qualities of the products. For example, 'Cruelty Free' and 'Freedom Food' are dedicated logos that indicate 'better animal welfare', while organic logos for animal products indicate that these systems of production are both more environmentally friendly and more animal friendly.

Ethical food labels are numerous in the UK, Europe and USA and increasingly so in the Asia–Pacific region (see Agriculture and Agri-Food Canada, 2011). UK sales of ethically labelled food and drink, including organic, fairtrade, free range and freedom foods reached £8.4 billion in 2013 (about 8.5 per cent of household food sales) (DEFRA, 2015). Germany also has a large market for organic food and beverages in Europe (about US$9 billion in 2009) (Agriculture and Agri-Food Canada, 2011). The market for organic products also grew in China: from 1995 to 2006, export value rose from $300,000 to $350 million, with annual growth of 30 per cent,[3] while the internal market grew by 27.1 per cent from 2004 to 2009 (Agriculture and Agri-Food Canada, 2011).

It has been argued that, for consumers in these countries, they have become a way to '*care at a distance*' (Barnett *et al.*, 2005). Thus, labels can be viewed as tools that offer a relatively easy way of communicating the sustainability qualities and characteristics of food. Ethical food labels therefore work best when used for packaged products, especially in large supermarkets offering a wide range of similar products. Indeed, ethical food labels have achieved significant market success in several countries.

Advocates of ethical food labelling argue that it empowers consumer choice by increasing knowledge of food production, reconnecting consumers with distant producers, improving food market transparency and addressing consumer concerns. Ultimately it could lead to improvements across the entire agro–food system (EU Animal Welfare Strategy, 2012–2015; European Commission, 2012).

While ethical food labels are an important segment of contemporary global food markets they are still a small niche when compared with conventional products. Much research indicates a clear 'value-action-gap' when it comes to purchasing behaviour; for example, the number of people who declare concern about animal-friendly foods is much higher than that of people prepared to purchase ethical products (Kjærnes, 2012). Indeed, a major limitation is the 'premium price' attached to ethically labelled products. As Koos (2012) showed, consumers' *willingness-to-pay* for a given product is constrained by *ability-to-pay*, and the geographies of ethical labelled product purchasing indicate higher sales in those countries where household incomes are greater and where there is less inequality. Moreover, the reputations of the brand or of retailing companies are very important where credibility of claims made on product labels is concerned. A further complication that limits the market development of 'animal-friendly products' is the diversity of criteria that underpin the 'welfare claims' on products.

At present, most labels for animal welfare-friendly products do not comply with a common standard and, in Europe, the animal welfare claims on products are not regulated. For example, free range and organic production stress the importance of providing animals with more space and promoting natural behaviour, Freedom Food refers more explicitly to the 'Five Freedoms' but do not specify the need for access to outdoor. The 'animal welfare' improvements of different systems are difficult to compare because they are not based on the same criteria (i.e. organic systems offer better opportunities for animals to express natural behaviours, but they might lead to problems in terms of animal health; Freedom Food systems might offer opportunities for better animal health, but they do not guarantee access to outdoor … and so forth). Since the Welfare Quality® protocols were published in 2009 a growing number of certifying bodies have shown a great interest in adopting them and many included some measures developed for the Welfare Quality® protocols (i.e. Soil Association in the UK), however the full monitoring system is still considered too expensive and time consuming and only a small number of companies in Europe have adopted the full 'Welfare Quality[®]' monitoring system (see for example, ATO Natura in Spain[4]).

The science-based information gathered from the Welfare Quality[®] assessment and product information systems are constantly refined, and significant improvements have been made in the last ten years based on the first implementations. If more broadly adopted it could help the development of labelling systems by providing a standardised method for the assessment and monitoring of animal welfare and it could increase the reliability of the existing labelling systems as well as transparency of the market for animal-friendly produced products.

Precision livestock farming (PLF)

Precision livestock farming (PLF) entails the automated continuous monitoring of livestock to enable farmers to optimise production, and the health and welfare status of their animals. For instance, detecting oestrus allows timely insemination. Similarly, detecting lameness or imbalance in the nutritional status at an early stage can help the farmers to take rapid remedial actions quickly. PLF has also received criticism, for example, it is sometimes seen as a further industrialisation of animal production, legitimising current intensive systems and leaving little room for sentient animals to interact with their environment, including the farmer.

Data generated by PLF sensors can, however, provide crucial information to support animal welfare when used appropriately. For example, PLF systems are likely to support the detection of health disorders. Apart from their profound economic impacts (Steensels et al., 2016) health disorders are also a major issue for animal welfare. PLF devices often directly or indirectly measure changes in animal behaviour and are therefore particularly suited to the detection of behavioural changes reflecting illness-induced malaise (Aubert, 1999). For example, through the precise and continuous registration of the location of individual animals, their time budgets – time spent feeding, ruminating, resting, walking etc. – can be estimated. Subtle changes in time budgets or activity patterns over the day can be indicative of a health problem. Indeed, stressed animals may become hyperactive or conversely, apathetic. Sick animals generally spend less time eating, and eat less than healthy ones. They may also withdraw from the group and seek isolation. Changes in the daily rhythm of activity may also indicate illness (Veissier et al., 2017). Similarly, play behaviour and grooming are affected by pain or fever (Mintline et al., 2013; Mandel et al., 2017).

Early detection of disorders such as mastitis and ketosis in dairy cows or respiratory problems in pigs via PLF could help the farmer to treat the animals at an earlier stage and thereby prevent worsening of the condition or its spread to other individuals. PLF systems could also be used to monitor other behaviours with relevance for animal welfare. For instance, some promising

PLF techniques can provide information on the functioning of social groups. Farm animals belong to gregarious species, they live in social groups. The interactions between animals are regulated by dominant–subordinate relations and individual preferences. In unstable groups, where the dominance hierarchy is not yet clear, there is often an increased frequency of aggression. Such aggressive behaviours can be detected with PLF systems. For instance, head–to–head knocking and chasing in pigs can be detected using image analysis (Lee *et al.*, 2016). Preferential relationships result in particular animals staying close to each other and synchronising their activities (Veissier *et al.*, 1990).

The balance between aggressive vs non–aggressive interactions as well as the proximity and synchronisation of activities all provide information on the cohesiveness of the animal group. At present, this is not considered in farming because of difficulties of assessment. PLF systems that continuously record the animals' interactions, positions and activity provide opportunities to assess the functioning of the social group and then integrate this information into farm management. For example, by separating animals that suffer from fights or taking more care when forming the animals' groups. Furthermore, emotions can be detected by facial expression in humans and it was also thought that this could be the case in animals (Veissier *et al.*, 2009). Encouragingly, recently developed algorithms enabling the detection of pain via facial expressions in sheep indicate another avenue to manage pain and perhaps other negative emotions in farming (Lu *et al.*, 2017).

We therefore argue that PLF techniques offer a wide range of possibilities to use behavioural signs to address animal welfare in modern livestock farming, be the welfare related to health status, social relations, human–animal relationship or more general effects of a stressful environment. The main advantages of PLF techniques are that they allow continuous monitoring rather than short snap observations, they can provide information on individual animals and not just groups, especially important for large animals like cattle or pigs, and they record automatically, thus requiring less of the farmer's or inspector's time. The farmers would pay specific attention to warnings and indicators received on a mobile phone or a computer.

PLF should, however, only complement and not replace direct observation of the animals since it is likely that sensors will not 'see everything'. Currently, the possibilities offered by PLF to assess and improve animal welfare have been little explored. To our knowledge, PLF is not used at present to certify farms or slaughter plants regarding animal welfare. What PLF could provide to manage and guarantee animal welfare clearly merits further in-depth research. This can be the development of new sensors (e.g. to detect loss of consciousness after stunning at slaughter) and new algorithms to extract welfare information from the data produced by PLF solutions already available (e.g. from accelerometers, real time locating systems, videos thanks to image analysis …). In addition, PLF-generated data could be combined with that obtained from other sources: veterinary or other inspection to improve management and housing systems as well as the provision of information to all actors in the animal production chains, for example processors, retailers, consumers, governments; through labelling or other means of communication.

In conclusion, we believe that developments in the application of PLF technology can provide information that can be used for management and assurance of animal welfare (Blokhuis, 2018). Specifically, PLF can promote the reliability of existing labelling systems and the transparency of the market for animal-friendly produced products.

Notes

1 www.compassioninfoodbusiness.com/our-work/what-we-offer/business-benchmark-on-farm-animal-welfare/.
2 See www.bbfaw.com/.
3 https://gain.fas.usda.gov/Recent%20GAIN%20Publications/Organics%20Annual_Beijing_China%20-%20Peoples%20Republic%20of_10-14-2010.pdf.
4 www.ato.cat/en/uht-milk-in-brik/.

References

Agriculture and Agri-Food Canada (2011). Global trends. Sustainable food and beverages market analysis report (AAFC Publication No. 11428E). Agriculture and Agri-food Canada, Ottawa.

Animal Task Force (2016). A strategic research and innovation agenda for a sustainable livestock sector in Europe. ATF, Brussels.

Aubert, A. (1999). Sickness and behaviour in animals: a motivational perspective. Neuroscience and Biobehavioral Reviews 23, 1029–1036.

Barnett, C., Cloke, P., Clarke, N., and Malpass, A. (2005). Consuming ethics: articulating the subjects and spaces of ethical consumption. Antipode 37(1), 23–45.

Blokhuis, H.J. (1999). Integration of animal welfare in intensive animal production. In Th. Wensing (Ed.). Production Diseases in Farm Animals. Wageningen Academic Publishers, Wageningen, the Netherlands, 222–229.

Blokhuis, H.J. (2018). Animal welfare information in a changing world. In A. Butterworth (Ed.). Animal Welfare Challenges: Dilemmas in a Changing World. CABI, Wallingford, UK, 208–216.

Blokhuis, H.J., Hopster, H., Geverink, N.A., Korte, S.M. and Van Reenen, C.G. (1998). Studies of stress in farm animals. Comparative Haematology International 8, 94–101.

Blokhuis, H.J., Jones, R.B., Geers, R., Miele, M. and Veissier, I. (2003). Measuring and monitoring animal welfare: transparency in the food product quality chain. Animal Welfare 12, 445–455.

Blokhuis, H.J., Keeling, L.J., Gavinelli, A. and Serratosa, J. (2008). Animal welfare's impact on the food chain. Trends in Food Science and Technology 19, 75–83.

Blokhuis, H.J., Jones, R.B, Veissier, I. and Miele, M. (Eds.) (2013). Improving farm Animal Welfare: Science and Society Working Together: The Welfare Quality Approach. Wageningen Academic Publishers, Wageningen, the Netherlands.

Boissy, A., Arnould, C., Chaillou, E., Désiré, L., Duvaux-Ponter, C., Greiveldinger, L., Leterrier, C., Richard, S., Roussel, S., Saint-Dizier, H., Meunier-Salaün, M.C.,

Valance, D. and Veissier, I. (2007). Emotions and cognition: a new approach to animal welfare. Animal Welfare 16: 37–43.

Botreau, R., Veissier, I. and Perny, P. (2009). Overall assessment of animal welfare: strategy adopted in Welfare Quality®. Animal Welfare 18(4), 363–370.

Broom, D. (2010). Animal welfare: an aspect of care, sustainability, and food quality required by the public. Journal of Veterinary Medical Education 37(1), 83–88.

DEFRA (2015). Food statistics pocketbook 2015 in year update. Department for Environment Food and Rural Affairs, London.

Delgado, C., Rosegrant, M., Steinfeld, H., Ehui, S. and Courbois, C. (1999). Livestock to 2020 the next food revolution. IFPRI Food, Agriculture, and the Environment Discussion Paper 28. IFPRI, Washington, DC.

Dereclenne, A.-C. (2018). Clés de réussite de plans d'amélioration du bien-être animal: exemple des vaches laitières (Thèse de doctorat, Université Clermont Auvergne (UCA), FRA).

EEA AIRS_PO2.10 (2017). Food consumption: animal based protein. European Environment Agency. www.eea.europa.eu/airs/2017/resource-efficiency-and-low-carbon-economy/food-consumption-animal-based.

European Commission (2012). Communication from the Commission to the European Parliament, the Council and the European Economic and Social Committee on the European Union Strategy for the Protection and Welfare of Animals 2012–2015, Brussels, 15.2.2012, COM(2012) 6 final/2.

Evans, A. and Miele, M. (2017). Food labelling as a response to political consumption: effects and contradictions. In M. Keller, B. Halkier, T.-A. Wilska, M. Truninger (Eds.). The Routledge Handbook in Consumption. Routledge, London and New York, 191–204.

Farm Animal Welfare Council (1992). FAWC updates the five freedoms. Veterinary Record 17, 357.

Forkman, B., Boissy, A., Meunier-Salaün, M.-C., Canali, E. and Jones, R.B. (2007). A critical review of fear tests used on cattle, pigs, sheep, poultry and horses. Physiology and Behavior 92(3), 340–374.

Fraser, D. (2008). Understanding Animal Welfare: The Science in Its Cultural Context. Wiley-Blackwell, Oxford.

Freidberg, S. (2004). The ethical complex of corporate food power. Environment and Planning D: Society and Space 22(4), 513–531.

Grant, W. (1997). The Common Agricultural Policy. Macmillan, London.

Gunnarsson, S. (1999). Effect of rearing factors on the prevalence of floor eggs, cloacal cannibalism and feather pecking in commercial flocks of loose housed laying hens. British Poultry Science 40(1), 12–18.

Hendrickson, M. and Miele, M. (2009). Changes in agriculture and food production in NAE since 1945. In D. Beverly, R. McIntyre, H.R. Herren, J. Wakhungu and R.T. Watson (Eds.), Agriculture at a Crossroad. IAASTD North America and Europe. World Bank, Island Press, Washington, DC, 20–79.

Jones, B. and Manteca, X. (2009). Developing practical welfare improvement strategies. In L.J. Keeling (Ed.). An Overview of the Development of the Welfare Quality® Project Assessment Systems. Welfare Quality Reports No 12. Cardiff University, Cardiff, 57–65.

Jones, R.B. (1997). Fear and distress. In M.C. Appleby and B.O. Hughes (Eds.). Animal Welfare. CABI, Wallingford, UK, 75–87.

Jones, R.B. (1998). Alleviating fear in poultry. In G. Greenberg and M. Haraway (Eds.). Comparative Psychology: A Handbook. Garland Press, New York, 339–347.

Jones, R.B. and Boissy, A. (2011). Fear and other negative emotions. In M.C. Appleby, J.A. Mench, I.A.S. Olsson and B.O. Hughes (Eds.). Animal Welfare. CABI, Oxon, UK, 78–97.

Kjærnes, U. (2012). Ethics and action: a relational perspective on consumer choice in the European politics of food. Journal of Agricultural and Environmental Ethics 25(2), 145–162.

Koos, S. (2012). What drives political consumption in Europe? A multi-level analysis on individual characteristics, opportunity structures and globalization. Acta Sociologica 55(1), 37–57.

Lee, J., Jin, L. Park, D. and Chung, Y. (2016). Automatic recognition of aggressive behavior in pigs using a kinect depth sensor. Sensors 16, 631.

Lu, Y., Mahmoud, M. and Robinson, P. (2017). Estimating sheep pain level using facial action unit detection. In IEEE International Conference on Automatic Face and Gesture Recognition, 30 May–3 June, 2017, Washington, DC.

Mandel, R., Nicol, C.J., Whay, H.R. and Klement, E. (2017). Detection and monitoring of metritis in dairy cows using an automated grooming device. Journal of Dairy Science 100(7), 5724–5728.

Miele, M. (2011). The taste of happiness: free range chicken. Environment and Planning A 43(9) 2070–2090.

Miele, M. and Bock, B.B. (2007). Competing discourses of farm animal welfare and agri-food restructuring: editorial. International Journal of Sociology of Agriculture and Food 15(3), 1–7.

Miele, M. and Lever, J. (2013). Civilizing the market for welfare friendly products in Europe? The techno-ethics of the Welfare Quality® assessment. Geoforum 48, 63–72.

Miele, M. and Lever, J. (2014). Improving animal welfare in Europe: cases of comparative bio-sustainabilities. In T. Marsden and A. Morely (Eds.). Sustainable Food Systems: Building a New Paradigm. Earthscan, London, 143–165.

Miele, M., Murdoch, J. and Roe, E. (2005). Animals and ambivalence: governing farm animal welfare in the European food sector. In V. Higgins and G. Lawrence (Eds.). Agricultural Governance. Routledge, London, 169–185.

Miele, M., Veissier, I., Evans, A. and Botreau, R. (2011). Animal welfare: establishing a dialogue between science and society. Animal Welfare 20: 103–117.

Miele, M., Bock, B. and Horling, L. (2015). Animal welfare: the challenges of implementing a common legislation in Europe. In A. Bonanno and L. Busch (Eds.). The Handbook of International Political Economy of Agriculture and Food. Edward Elgar, New York and Cheltenham, Glos., 295–321.

Mintline, E.M., Stewart, M., Rogers, A.R., Cox, N.R., Verkerk, G.A., Stookey, J.M., Webster, J.R. and Tucker, C.B. (2013). Play behavior as an indicator of animal welfare: disbudding in dairy calves. Applied Animal Behaviour Science 144(1), 22–30.

Moinard, C., Mendl, M., Nicol, C.J. and Green, L.E. (2003). A case control study of on-farm risk factors for tail biting in pigs. Applied Animal Behaviour Science 81(4), 333–355.

OIE (2017). Terrestrial Animal Health Code. OIE, Paris.

Pirscher, F. (2016). Consuming for the sake of others: whose interests count on a market for animal-friendly products? Journal of Agricultural and Environmental Ethics 29(1), 67–80.

Porcher, J. (2001). Le travail dans l'élevage industriel des porcs. Souffrance des animaux, souffrance des hommes. In F. Burgat and R. Dantzer (Eds.). Un point sur … Les animaux d'élevage ont-ils droit au bienêtre? INRA Editions, Paris, 23–64.

Robbins, J., Franks, B. and von Keyserlingk, M.A.G. (2018). 'More than a feeling': an empirical investigation of hedonistic accounts of animal welfare. Plos One 13(3), e0193864.

Ruttan, V.W. (1998). The new growth theory and development economics: a survey. Journal of Development Studies 3(5), 1–26.

Steensels, M., Antler, A., Bahr, C., Berckmans, D., Maltz, E. and Halachmi, I. (2016). A decision-tree model to detect post-calving diseases based on rumination, activity, milk yield, BW and voluntary visits to the milking robot. Animal 10(9), 1493–1500.

Veissier, I. and Miele, M. (2014). Animal welfare: towards transdisciplinarity – the European experience. Animal Production Science 54(9), 1119–1129.

Veissier, I., Lamy, D. and Le Neindre, P. (1990). Social behaviour in domestic beef cattle when yearling calves are left with the cows for the next calving. Applied Animal Behaviour Science 27, 193–200.

Veissier, I., Botreau, R. and Perny, P. (2009). Scoring animal welfare: difficulties and Welfare Quality® solutions. In K.J. Keeling (Ed.). An Overview of the Development of the Welfare Quality® Project Assessment Systems. Welfare Quality® Reports Series no. 12. Cardiff University, Cardiff, 15–32.

Veissier, I., Mialon, M.-M. and Sloth, K.H. (2017). Short communication: early modification of the circadian organization of cow activity in relation to disease or estrus. Journal of Dairy Science 100(5), 3969–3974.

Welfare Quality® (2009a). Welfare Quality assessment protocol for cattle (fattening cattle, dairy cows, veal calves). Welfare Quality® Consortium, Lelystad, the Netherlands.

Welfare Quality® (2009b). Welfare Quality assessment protocol for pigs cattle (sows and piglets, growing and finishing pigs). Welfare Quality® Consortium, Lelystad, the Netherlands.

Welfare Quality® (2009c). Welfare Quality assessment protocol for poultry (broilers, laying hens). Welfare Quality® Consortium, Lelystad, the Netherlands.

Part IV

Industry or certification specific reviews, evaluation and recommendations

7 Certifying farmed seafood

A drop in the ocean or a 'stepping-stone' towards increased sustainability?

Malin Jonell, Michael Tlusty, Max Troell and Patrik Rönnbäck

Introduction

Seafood[1] is an important component of the world's food basket and provides 3.1 billion people with about 20 per cent of their daily intake of animal protein (FAO 2016). It is particularly important for the world's poor where fish eaten whole constitute a crucial source of essential micronutrients (Beveridge *et al.* 2013; Béné *et al.* 2015; Thilsted *et al.* 2016). With 90 per cent of global wild fish stocks being either overfished or maximally utilized, seafood extraction from the wild has reached a ceiling (FAO 2016) and even if fisheries are fully rebuilt (Sumaila *et al.* 2012; Costello *et al.* 2016), the continued expansion necessary to meet expected future demand of seafood must come primarily from aquaculture. This increasing need, as well as its potential positive contribution to the overall food portfolio (Troell *et al.* 2014), has led to aquaculture being the fastest growing food production sector in the world. Despite signs of slowed growth its contribution to the future seafood supply is expected to double within 30 years (Waite *et al.* 2014).

Such rapid development can, however, also come at a price, with negative environmental and social impacts including direct and indirect habitat destruction, biodiversity loss and wasteful resource usage through detrimental fishing for feed ingredients and also social displacement (Naylor *et al.* 2000; Cao *et al.* 2015). Brackish water aquaculture on terrestrial land suitable for agriculture can lead to soil salinization (Paprocki and Cons 2014) and conversion of coastal wetlands, e.g. mangrove forest (Hamilton and Lovette 2015), to loss of key ecosystem services, for instance fisheries production, carbon sequestration, water purification and protection from storms (Barbier 2007; Walters *et al.* 2008; Mcleod *et al.* 2011). A steady supply of environmentally sustainable feed from terrestrial and marine origin is also a key challenge for a continued growth of the aquaculture sector (Gephart *et al.* 2017; Troell *et al.* 2017). Additional negative environmental challenges include leakage of nutrients and chemicals (Islam 2005; Burridge *et al.* 2010), spread of invasive species (Beveridge *et al.* 1994), diseases (Krkošek *et al.* 2007) and emissions of greenhouse gases, for instance related to energy consumption (Pelletier *et al.* 2011).

While aquaculture can be touted as an overall low-impact animal protein, particularly in comparison to red meat (Tyedmers 2004; Tilman and Clark 2014), simple operational errors including but not limited to overstocking and improper siting, have continued to promulgate the image of aquaculture being an environmentally harmful food production system. In addition, different species and systems also vary in performance from an environmental and resource management perspective (Troell *et al.* 2014). Although the hope is that animal food production systems continually improve over time, one of the more recently highlighted challenges related to farmed animals, besides its dependency on feed resources, is over reliance on antimicrobials that may lead to antimicrobial resistance (Jorgensen *et al.* 2016). This is also true for farmed aquatic species (Henriksson *et al.* 2017). Therefore, a future expansion of future aquaculture production must strive for ever increasing sustainable production methods and a focus on less environmentally demanding species.

The sustainable seafood movement (Konefal 2013; Silver and Hawkins 2014) was born partly from a perceived failure of public policy instruments to address the increasingly evident environmental challenges related to fisheries and aquaculture. This was particularly evident in the developed world's impression of regulatory oversight of production in the developing world. Market-based tools such as eco-certification have been one of the main sustainability mechanisms used in the sustainable seafood movement. Implementation of aquaculture certification was gradual with organic farmed seafood (IFOAM) (Bergleiter 2008) and the Global Aquaculture Alliance's (GAA) Best Aquaculture Practices (BAP) standard (Lee 2008) being the first established schemes on the market (1996 and 2004, respectively). The latter was originally solely focusing on eliminating the worst performing shrimp farms (Steering Committee of the State-of-Knowledge Assessment of Standards and Certification 2012) (Table 7.1). GlobalGAP, primarily a business to business scheme, label products as GGN and in collaboration with the Friend of the Sea (FoS) by allowing use of their logo on packages, started certifying farmed seafood in 2004 and today accounts for the largest portion of eco-certified farmed seafood available on the market (Potts *et al.* 2016). In 2010, the Aquaculture Stewardship Council (ASC) was born through a collaborative effort between the Dutch Sustainability Trade Initiative (IDH) and the World Wildlife Fund, WWF. As of January 2018, 569 farms with a total annual production of 1.28 million metric tonnes were certified against the ASC standard (ASC 2018a). In contrast to the evolution of certification schemes in other sectors, most aquaculture and fisheries schemes, e.g. the MSC, GAA/BAP and ASC, were established on a global level rather than starting off with local activities (Auld 2014). Volumes of certified farmed fish and shellfish constitute about 8 per cent of global aquaculture production (76.7 million tons, 2015).

Alongside the spread of private, global eco-certification schemes, state-initiated national certification programmes for aquaculture have developed. Examples of standards for shrimp farming include the Good Aquaculture

Table 7.1 Major aquaculture certification schemes

Scheme	Year of establishment	Volume certified (million tons)	Species certified
ASC	2010	1.28	abalone, bivalve, pangasius, salmon, shrimp, tilapia, trout
GAA BAP	2004	1.80	(key groups) catfish, pangasius, salmon, shrimp, tilapia, trout
FOS	2008	0.70	(key groups) cod, clams, oysters, pangasius, salmon, sea bream, shrimp/prawn, trout, other
GLOBALG.A.P	2004	2.10	(key groups) pangasius, salmon, shrimp, tilapia, trout, sea bream, sea bass, meagre
IFOAM Organic	1996	0.19	(key groups) carp, mussels, oysters, pangasius, rainbow trout, salmon, seabass, shrimp/prawn, trout

Source: data on volume certified from ASC (2017a), BAP (2018) and the remaining schemes from Potts *et al.* (2016). Production volume data from 2017 (ASC, GAA/BAP), 2015 (GlobalG.A.P), 2014 (FOS) and 2013 (IFOAM).

Practice (GAP), Code of Conduct (CoC) and the GAP-7401 (TAS-7401) in Thailand (Samerwong *et al.* 2018), the National Standard on Good Aquaculture Practices in Vietnam (VietGAP) and IndoGAP (CBIB) in Indonesia (Tlusty *et al.* 2016). Contrary to most international programmes focusing on the best performing farms within a certain sector, these schemes generally target a large portion, if not the majority, of producers in a given country and have been perceived as less stringent in terms of scientific rigour than most international schemes (Samerwong *et al.* 2018). While fewer requirements can imply that a larger portion of producers are attracted to join, sector-wide progress towards sustainability requires that standards are continually improved. In order to increase the understanding of how national and international shrimp schemes compare, Tlusty *et al.* (2016) used statistical tools to assess six schemes (three state-initiated and three international) with respect to the number of factors covered (breadth) and the compliance mechanism applied (depth). Expectedly, results showed that the international schemes (ASC, GAA and GlobalGAP) had both greater breadth and depth than the national schemes (VietGAP, TAS-7401 and CBIB). Additionally, there was a substantial overlap between the international schemes, mainly due to similarities in factors covered in the standards. To strive towards greater horizontal diversification among the more rigorous global schemes, i.e. differences in requirements for compliance between standards, could be an important mechanism for including a larger set of producers without compromising scientific rigour and credibility of the standards.

Aquaculture is an important source of nutrition in the developing world (Béné *et al.* 2016; Belton *et al.* 2017) and has even been described as being a 'pro-poor' engine (Toufique and Belton 2014). The seafood sustainability movement began targeting environmental impacts (Haugen *et al.* 2017), largely without a lens on the social sustainability dimension (Bush *et al.* 2013a). Yet recently, the social dimension of seafood sustainability has gained increased attention, in both fisheries (Hilborn *et al.* 2015) and aquaculture (Krause *et al.* 2015). The FAO technical guidelines on aquaculture certification (FAO 2011) as well as the Ecosystem Approach to Aquaculture (EAA) have social factors embedded within (Soto *et al.* 2008; Tlusty *et al.* 2016) but a preponderance of literature suggests that additional work needs to occur in order to fully integrate the social into the ecological sustainability assessment (Krause *et al.* 2015). While there is much work to do, it is encouraging that one aquaculture certification, GAA BAP, was recently found to be compliant to the Global Social Compliance Programme criteria (BAP 2017). Despite the increased focus on the social, the focus in this chapter is on environmental sustainability and no thorough review on earlier work on social effects has been conducted.

Positive environmental effects of aquaculture certification: what is the evidence?

The general purpose of any certification is to ensure production occurs to a specific standard. For eco-labels, the environmental metrics should be set so that on average the certified producers have fewer impacts than those that are uncertified. Until now, only a few studies on the effectiveness of aquaculture eco-certification (shrimp and pangasius (Striped catfish)) in improving production practices have been published. Given that seafood certification programmes have been around since early 2000, and little effort was made two decades ago to assess the baseline condition, surprisingly few studies on the effectiveness of these programmes in reducing negative environmental and social impacts have been conducted.

Tlusty and Tausig (2014) investigated the effectiveness of the GAA Best Aquaculture Practices (BAP) programme in improving the performance of shrimp farms. In total, 323 audits between the years 2005–2012 from 192 shrimp farms located in 11 countries was used as the basis for evaluation. This study found that approximately 25 per cent of nonconformities (standard criteria that needed to be improved prior to obtaining certification) included environmental metrics. However, this was distributed over seven metrics, and therefore it was difficult to calculate the overall change in, for instance, nutrient discharge as a result of certification. In addition, this study showed that 10 per cent of farms exited the certification programme without becoming certified. It is not clear why these farms exited, yet this points to the fact that farms participating in certification schemes are self-selected. Undertaking an audit process is a business venture by the farms, and as such, it behoves the

farm to not fail. The corollary to this is that the rigour of a certification programme cannot be determined by the percentage of farms that fail, as the
process by nature self-selects for successful applicants. Similarly, the authors
point out that one of the main challenges of measuring impacts from aquaculture eco-certification is that changes and improvements in production
practices likely occurred prior to the first audit, thus at the early stage where
an operation chose to enter the certification process. Lack of a systematic
approach to gather these baseline data thus limits the extent to which we can
understand the role of eco-certification in improving the environmental performance of aquaculture (Tlusty and Tausig 2014) as well as other sectors,
e.g. forestry (van der Ven and Cashore 2018).

Jonell and Henriksson (2015) used a different approach by investigating
whether mangrove-integrated shrimp farms certified as organic performed
better from a Life Cycle Assessment (LCA) perspective than noncertified
farms. Results indicated slightly better performance by the certified farms
across all environmental impact categories investigated (climate change,
eutrophication potential and acidification). The differences in performance
could, however, not be attributed with high certainty to certification. Instead
certified farms were assumed to have been better performing already before
certification was implemented (Jonell and Henriksson 2015). Similarly, some
of the uncertified farms performed equivalently to the certified operations.
Nhu *et al.* (2016) also applied LCA to assess differences between ASC certified and noncertified pangasius farms. Water, land and total resources (including feed inputs) were evaluated together with global warming potential,
acidification, freshwater and marine eutrophication. Results indicated lower
environmental impacts for ASC certified farms, particularly for global
warming, acidification and eutrophication potential. It should be noted that
none of the studies cited above, however, applied any of the techniques to
assure that a credible counterfactual was used (types C–F in Table 7.2, Box
7.1). Difference in performance and potential environmental impacts were
found between certified and noncertified farms for both studies, however
attribution to certification is inconclusive given existing performance and
environmental impact of farms prior to certification.

Box 7.1 How to measure effects?

Three circumstantial and methodological challenges related to measuring
impacts of aquaculture certification appear. First, as certification standards for
farmed seafood have existed for a relatively short time period, some of their
effects may not yet have been realized. Second, as many schemes are practice-
based rather than results-oriented, using audit data as the basis for evaluation
limits the extent to which long-term environmental outcomes can be assessed.
Here an additional step of evaluating whether a certain practice has effects on
the environment and surrounding ecosystems is necessary, but seldom prioritized
by certification programmes (Steering Committee of the State-of-Knowledge

Assessment of Standards and Certification 2012). Third, the general challenge of ensuring credible counterfactuals, i.e. when determining whether implementation of certification has had an effect on environmental performance, what would the outcome be of a certain operation given that it would not have been certified (Blackman and Rivera 2010, 2011). A summary of credible and non-credible counterfactuals for evaluating effects of certification standards is presented in Table 7.2.

Ideally, certification will improve conditions of a baseline. However, there have been no studies that, together with an evaluation of the performance of certified farms have randomly assessed how farms operate in the complete absence of certification. From an experimental perspective, the ideal method to analyse the impact of certification would be the Before-After-Control-Impact (BACI) design (Table 7.2, Blackman and Rivera 2010). This would be a base case where a group of very similar farms would be assessed (the before). Half the farms would be randomly allocated to a control group (would not be trained/educated to be certified) while the other half would be trained/educated

Table 7.2 Summary of non-credible and credible counterfactuals that can be used to assess effects of certification. A counterfactual outcome can be defined as an estimate of the performance of an operation given that eco-certification would not have been developed

Counterfactuals for assessment of impacts from certification			*References*
Non-credible	A	Differences in performance of an operation over time. Environmental impact (t = 0) − Environmental impact (t = T) = effect certification	
	B	Comparison certified and noncertified operations. Impact (noncertified farm/fishery) − Impact (certified farm/fishery) = effect certification	
Credible	C	Approach using 'matching'. Impact (noncertified farm, incl. matching) − Impact (certified farm, incl. matching) = effect certification	Ruben and Fort (2011); Blackman and Naranjo (2012)
	D	'Instrumental variables' Use factors that co-vary with the likelihood that a unit of assessment is certified, but not with environmental outcomes. Otherwise like B.	Bolwig *et al.* (2009)
	E	'Difference in differences' or Before-After-Control-Impact (BACI) design	Bertrand *et al.* (2004); Blackman (2012)
	F	Experimental approach requiring that producers are randomly selected for certification. Otherwise like B.	

Source: Table adapted from Chaplin-Kramer *et al.* (2015), Supporting Information.

to be certified (the impact group). After the impact farms were certified, they would be assessed again, and certification would be demonstrated if the impact: after metric was significantly different than the other metrics (impact: before, and all control values). One complicating factor will be controlling uptake, adoption of better practices by uncertified farms over the study period. Where this isn't possible, shifting baselines will have to be allowed for within study models.

The potential of aquaculture certification to transform the seafood sector: a discussion on potentials and limitations

In addition to the aforementioned studies on the effectiveness of aquaculture certification to reduce negative environmental impacts, a separate body of literature has explored the potential of aquaculture certification to have effects on the global scale and on the fish farming sector as a whole (Bush *et al.* 2013a; Jonell *et al.* 2013). If the former section of this chapter focused on the evidence for certification to improve individual operations, the current elaborates primarily on its role in pushing the overall aquaculture industry towards sustainability. Important to note here is that the authors recognize that certification is only one of many existing governance mechanisms to improve the performance of the aquaculture sector and that other more conventional approaches such as state-led regulation may be more effective in reducing negative impact. The aim here is thus not to evaluate certification in relation to other instruments, but to outline how the effectiveness of this specific tool could be improved.

A number of barriers for seafood certification to significantly improve the aquaculture sector have been highlighted. For instance, limited coverage of species and markets targeted, exclusion of small-scale and poor performers and a too narrow focus on only a few sustainability dimensions. Furthermore, the limitation of certified units not being incentivized to improve beyond the required performance level has also been suggested to be a key limitation (Bush *et al.* 2013b; Tlusty and Thorsen 2016). In this section of the chapter, the earlier identified barriers are turned around and defined as prerequisites (I–V) for aquaculture certification to have long-term, substantial effects on global aquaculture production and growth. In other words, what are key prerequisites for certification to deliver major impacts? While this section uses aquaculture as a case, it should be noted that most barriers and opportunities could be applied to other commodity standards aiming for an improved environmental performance of production practices at sector level. The five prerequisites outlined in this section are summarized in Figure 7.2.

I Global coverage: production and consumption

Aquaculture is a tale of two worlds. The global north (here including Europe, North America, Australia and New Zealand) has for a long time preferred high value farmed species for instance salmonids and shrimp while farmed seafood consumption in the global south (primarily Asia, but also Africa and Latin America) has been centred on freshwater species such as carp, pangasius and tilapia (Belton *et al.* 2017). While the demand for high value species such as salmon is predicted to increase also in Asia, for instance by a staggeringly 25 per cent per year in China (The Fish Site 2017), the bulk of farmed seafood consumption in the region still consists of lower trophic freshwater species. Global aquaculture production is, by volume produced, dominated by the freshwater fish carp (29 million metric tonnes in 2015, 38 per cent of global aquaculture production, seaweeds excluded), followed by marine bivalves (15 million metric tonnes, 20 per cent) and miscellaneous freshwater fishes (nine million metric tonnes, 12 per cent) (FAO 2018).

Although the lion's share of global aquaculture production consists of low trophic species, current eco-certification programmes for aquaculture primarily target species groups preferred and sought after in markets in North America, Europe, Australia and New Zealand (Table 7.3, Jonell *et al.* 2013). This despite that the appetite for seafood is high in Asia with the per capita fish consumption (average 2013–2015) being 58.4 kg per person per year in the Republic of Korea, 50.2 kg in Japan, 39.5 kg in China, 35.4 kg in Vietnam and 35.0 kg in Indonesia, compared to the global average of 20.2 kg per person and year (FAO 2016).

Table 7.3 Rankings of top seafood species in the US (based on volume consumed), the EU (based on volume sold), and global production (million metric tonnes produced)

US 2015 – volume consumed[a]	EU 2015 – volume sold[b]	World 2014 – production (mmt)[c,d]
Shrimp	Tuna	Grass carp (5.5)
Salmon	Cod	Silver carp (5.0)
Canned tuna	Salmon	European carp (4.2)
Tilapia	Alaska pollock	Manilla clam (4.0)
Alaska pollock	Herring	Nile tilapia (3.6)
Pangasius	Mussel	Whiteleg shrimp (3.6)
Cod	Mackerel	Alaska Pollock (3.2)
Catfish	Hake	Anchoveta (3.1)
Crab	Squid	Skipjack tuna (3.1)
Clams	Tropical shrimp	Chub mackerel (1.8)
		Atlantic herring (1.6)

Notes
a www.aboutseafood.com/about/top-ten-list-for-seafood-consumption/.
b www.eumofa.eu/the-eu-fish-market.
c www.statista.com/statistics/240231/principal-fish-species-for-global-fishery/.
d www.statista.com/statistics/240268/top-global-aquaculture-producing-countries-2010/.

An emerging body of literature has been investigating the demand for eco-certified seafood in Asia (e.g. Xu *et al.* 2012; Uchida *et al.* 2013; Fabinyi 2016). In China, most efforts towards sustainable seafood have been in the form of campaigns against certain traditional eating habits, e.g. consumption of shark fin soup, and less on promotion of eco-labelled options (Fabinyi 2016). However, seafood eco-labels have also gained increased interest, particularly those focusing on food safety issues and signalling organic production practices (Fabinyi 2016), indicating that food safety is the prominent driver in the region. Despite the fact that eco-labelled seafood has slowly started to enter Asian markets, several hurdles for increased uptake have been identified. First, the region has no or little tradition of 'green consumerism', implying altruistic consumer action towards a greater good rather than being able to rely on ideas of benefit for the individual consumer (Liu *et al.* 2017). Second, in some nations, for instance China, a general perception appears to be that the government rather than the individual consumer should be responsible for environmentally sound production practices (Fabinyi 2016). While the view that consumers are less obliged to engage in seafood sustainability than other key actors, such as the state or the private sector, appears to be evident also in high income countries (Jonell *et al.* 2016), the superior role of the state in for instance China and Vietnam likely makes consumers even less susceptible to the message of the individual's role as a change agent (so-called consumer effectiveness, Vermeir and Verbeke 2006). The strive towards an 'eco-civilization', laid out in the Chinese 13th Five Year Plan, can potentially change the Chinese consumers perception with respect to environmental sustainability (Central Compilation & Translation Press 2016).

While most certification programmes nowadays can be applied to a large set of species groups, the drive by 'Western' or developed-world markets to engage in certification is limiting its overall effectiveness. The currently certified portion still consists mostly of species preferred primarily in these markets, and missing out on e.g. carps, the most cultured finfish by volume globally (Table 7.3). The consequence is that many species and systems that could be improved are not (e.g. carps) and that species with a potentially small environmental footprint (e.g. many freshwater species) are not targeted for certification (see also Prerequisite V). If certification is to have any substantial effects at scale, schemes need to engage Asian markets and consumers to a higher extent. The limited consumer interest for eco-labelled seafood products in Asia certainly implies certain challenges, but engaging large retailers and wholesalers active in the region to source more eco-labelled seafood may be a feasible way forward. Moreover, given the important role of the state in many nations in the region, engagement with governments will also likely be of pivotal importance.

II Inclusion of a critical set of producers

The exclusion of worst performing farmers (Tlusty 2012) and small-scale producers (Belton *et al.* 2010) risks limiting positive effects of aquaculture certification on the global scale. At the time of writing, few theoretical models on how eco-certification could improve the environmental performance of individual aquaculture farms and the sector as a whole have been suggested. One exception is the pull-threshold model by Tlusty (2012), proposing that only producers performing just below the certification threshold for a certain environmental variable can be expected to change their practices. Put differently, a key limitation with current schemes is that it remains only the producers performing relatively well and where the requirements for certification are plausible to reach that will improve their practices as an outcome of entering a certification programme. The worst performing producers, on the other side, will not attempt certification if the requirements are too demanding. Instead, a multi-threshold approach, i.e. horizontal differentiation between schemes (Tlusty 2012) or vertical differentiation within a certain scheme (Bush and Oosterveer 2015) (Figure 7.1), are suggested as potential mechanisms to increase the pull and thereby improve a standard's effectiveness in reducing negative environmental impacts. Similarly, Bush *et al.* (2013b) stress the challenge of seafood certification schemes to balance the three assets of credibility, accessibility and a continuous improvement of standards (see also Prerequisite III below), together conceptualized as a 'devil's triangle'. Echoing the conclusions drawn by Tlusty (2012), the authors argue that schemes should strive for a multitier mechanism to ensure that both worse producing performers currently not able to enter certification are included and producers willing to go beyond set requirements are incentivized to improve further (Bush *et al.* 2013b).

Challenges to reach small-scale producers in certification programmes are not unique to aquaculture. Instead, examples of exclusion of small-scale producers not able to pay for certification audits, technical improvements or general updates in production practices can be found from a number of sectors. Aquaculture Improvement Projects (AIP) and the counterpart for capture fisheries (FIP) facilitate for sequential improvement with the ultimate aim to get certified. These programmes are generally not tied to a specific certification scheme, but can rather be defined as an alliance of value chain actors, including e.g. producers, processors and retailers, striving to improve practices. AIPs constitute recent transformability interventions that have been suggested to be a viable means to attract small producers and those not yet compliant with eco-certification. Little research has, however, been conducted on the effectiveness of AIPs, and lack of transparency and independent third-party assessment has been suggested to limit the potential for these tools (Sampson *et al.* 2015). Certification schemes are developing improver programmes (e.g. the iBAP programme of GAA, Towers 2016), but these are too recent for results to be evaluated.

The certified portion of global aquaculture production amounts to around 8 per cent of the total production (Table 7.1). While it remains uncertain

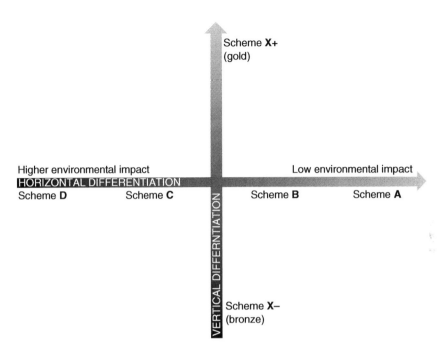

Figure 7.1 Vertical (scheme X– and X+) and horizontal (schemes D–A) differentiation within and between schemes could be a mechanism to increase
accessibility of certification for less well performing farms (Higher environmental impacts) and create incentives for better performing producers
(Low environmental impact) to improve further.

what extent of an increase by volume and producers would be needed to
create substantive 'pull' on a sectoral level, it can be assumed that if an insig-
nificant share of the global aquaculture industry is certified, effects will be
limited. If aquaculture certification is to ramp up and account for a more
significant portion, schemes need to better include both small-scale producers
(both better and worse performers) and worse performing farmers who are
currently far from the certification threshold. Horizontal differentiation and
multitier approaches within one certification programme implies certain challenges, e.g. potential confusion around what constitutes sustainable production or best choice, but may be the most promising approach to increase the
global portion of certified farmed seafood.

III Mechanisms in place for a continuous improvement of standards

As important as it is to assess the state of aquaculture pre-certification, it is
equally important to routinely address standards against audit data, and to
incorporate improvements to performance into new versions of the standard.

ISEAL's impacts code indicates in section 9.2, 'Improving Monitoring and Evaluation Effectiveness', that scheme owners should create a system to ensure 'results from performance monitoring, outcome and impact evaluations and the learning from these activities are used to inform a periodic review and refinement of the intended change and of the M&E strategy' (ISEAL 2014a). This is a key step in creating a system of continuous improvement necessary to reduce the negative impacts of aquaculture products (Tlusty 2012).

A prerequisite for certification standards to have effect on a sectoral level is for them to continually improve and adapt as science develops or when new technologies becomes available. Continual improvement has been suggested to theoretically take place at two levels, (i) producer level where operations show improved environmental performance over time after compliance with certification standards, and (ii) strategic/systemic or standards level where an increased ambition is expressed as stricter or more difficult criteria for compliance with certification standards (Bush *et al.* 2013b). The latter level is affected by external influences such as technical development and also internal processes related to the standard's strategies for improved credibility. Ideally, standards should be revised based on M&E data on actual farm improvement over time (Tlusty and Tausig 2014). Important to note, however, is that a continual improvement could imply a particular challenge for small producers struggling to afford technical investments potentially needed to comply with the updated standards. Continual improvement will also be challenging from a business standpoint as increasing metric rigour may result in the loss of farms that are no longer in compliance. One way to address this could be vertical differentiation within a scheme where less well performing farms could stay certified at a less demanding level of compliance.

A brief review of material available on standards' websites indicates that standards generally are continuously updated but with little transparency on revisions made or how often updates are needed to take place. The BAP standard for shrimp for instance remained the same for almost a decade before being harmonized with the finfish standard (Tlusty and Tausig 2014). Recently, the GAA process for updating standards has been formalized and occurs every three years (BAP 2017). Sustainability standards being members of ISEAL (ASC for aquaculture) are obliged to review a standard every fifth year to ensure that it is relevant and that standards have effects on the water (ISEAL 2014b). This includes an evaluation of audit data, and the incorporation of the learning from these data into the improved standard. Currently, data management systems for aquaculture standards are only first being developed if at all, and thus a database approach to standards revision has not yet been implemented. ASC have decided to review standards even more regularly on a three-year cycle (ASC 2018b). A formal revision process needs to take place and schemes ought to highlight the improvements incorporated into the standards. Even though some schemes, e.g. the ASC, are more transparent in terms of policies for when revisions are to be made and the content of such standard revision (ASC 2015), it still remains unclear how schemes make sure that all relevant new scientific knowledge is considered when reviewing and revising standards. In 2015, ASC commenced the process of updating its pangasius, tilapia and salmon standards due to feedback from producers and ASI (Accreditation Services International) (ASC 2015). A number of potential risks were identified prior to revision, for instance resistance from producers. Interestingly, the strategy for dealing with this concern was to 'make sure that the standards or changes are applicable and accessible'. To what extent such an approach stands in conflict with increasing standard credibility through raising the bar for sustainable production remains unclear. Note that the main focus on ASC above reflects more transparency in terms of publicly available documentation rather than a need for specific scrutiny.

IV Additionality to conventional state-led regulation

A key precondition for aquaculture certification to have positive environmental effects is for standards to go beyond what is required, and enforced, by national regulations. The term 'additionality' has been defined as 'outcomes beyond business as usual' (Garrett *et al.* 2016) and is conditional on eco-certification standard goals and local circumstances. A precipitating factor in the advent of aquaculture certification was the overall distrust that developing world national regulations were sufficient to limit environmental impacts of a growing food production platform. This is still present today as voluntary standards tend to be of greater breadth and depth than national standards (Tlusty *et al.* 2016). Any national standard will definitionally be less robust given that nation-states need to ensure for the economic well-being of their constituents. A nation that enacts aspirational regulations with regard to sustainability will likely, at least initially, be limited in production that will concomitantly limit the number of citizens that can participate and benefit in the industry. Thus, standards that are nationally focused will most likely be less aspirational than voluntary standards that can operate across multiple countries. This can be exemplified by the shrimp sector where voluntary certification programmes were of greater breadth and depth than national certifications (Tlusty *et al.* 2016).

V Ability to support 'truly sustainable' seafood production systems

One of the greatest challenges facing humanity today is how to feed a growing and more wealthy world population without increasing the pressure on the world's ecosystems (Garnett 2016). A large and growing body of literature is stressing that we need to considerably change what we eat and how food is produced in order for humanity to stay within planetary boundaries (Campbell *et al.* 2017; Gordon *et al.* 2017). The need for a biosphere-based sustainability science has become evident under the Anthropocene, the age of mankind, by recognizing that biosphere capacity serves as the foundation for human well-being (Folke *et al.* 2016). How increased aquaculture production can add resilience to the world's food portfolio has specifically been discussed (Troell *et al.* 2014). One question of relevance for aquaculture and sustainability standards communities is therefore how aquaculture certification systems can contribute to this major, and much needed, transformation.

Marine aquaculture production offers opportunity for opening up new regions for food production that are not directly dependent on land use (Troell *et al.* 2017). However, while expanding aquaculture, it will be important to consider a full suite of impacts as it compares to other proteins. Defining sustainable seafood production and products and clarifying its potential role in the future global food basket is a first step in the process of identifying the role of certification and other market-based tools. A potential criterion to explore further is whether the product or production system adds a net input to human food/protein/key nutrient provisioning, i.e. implies no net loss through excess use of fish meal and oil or terrestrial ingredients. Other examples include nutrient budgets in balance to avoid food systems to push the planetary boundaries relating to leakage of nitrogen and phosphorous and use of renewable energy sources.

Unfortunately, the bar for truly sustainable seafood (from systems characterized by strong sustainability) will vary based on the nature of the discussant. Tlusty and Thorsen (2016) argue that there is a risk associated with labelling seafood products to be 'sustainable enough' as this may prevent further improvements in production practices. The seafood industry needs to acknowledge that not all species are the same and have the same suite of impacts. In creating a more sustainable and food secure future, some species perform better and some worse than terrestrial proteins. What is the message being sent by a global market that sanctions the eco-labelling of fed aquaculture products, while many of the unfed products (filter feeders and plants) do not have a relevant label? As consumers concerned about ocean health generally look for eco-labelled alternatives, this may lead to the best alternatives being set aside. For instance, recent work showed that consumers perceive eco-labelled salmon to be a better environmental choice than non-eco-labelled farmed blue mussels, this despite the smaller footprint of the latter (Jonell 2016). In this context, eco-labelling is all about supporting, approving and marketing production practices with acceptable environmental and social impacts. The ambition to reduce a variety of impacts is positive, but caution and scrutiny is needed to avoid the mistake of automatically putting this on a par with most sustainable practices.

The discussion about what production systems and species are suitable for certification boils down to how the 'theory of change' of market-based instruments is described. All eco-certification programmes need to balance the two somewhat contradictory objectives of being inclusive and thereby attracting a large enough portion of a certain sector to stimulate substantive change, and having stringent enough standards to ensure that production practices comply with crucial sustainability criteria (Jonell *et al.* 2013). The former perspective is illustrated by Jason Clay (Senior Vice President, Food & Markets, WWF) who states in his TED-talk on using market mechanisms to improve food production globally 'We can't just focus on identifying the best; we've got to move the rest' (Clay 2010). Certification programmes that openly state that they aim to initially be within reach for a certain portion of the market (e.g. ASC aiming to set standards that around 15 per cent of best performing producers can reach at the time of launching a standard (ASC 2017b)), also is well in line with the more inclusive approach. Setting standards that can be reached by a large portion of the industry may lead to substantial net reductions of total negative environmental impacts, but at the expense of certifying individual farming systems that are very distant from sustainable practices. This 'legitimization of the unsustainable' may lead to consumer mistrust and discredit of market-based instruments such as eco-certification. If standards become too weak and inclusive, it could also be questioned whether this is the role and mandate of eco-certification schemes to address rather than relying on governance, institutional regulation and legal frameworks to be responsible for setting and enforcing baseline standards.

Functionally, this is a discussion of whether aquaculture standards should be absolute or relative. An absolute aquaculture certification would select a

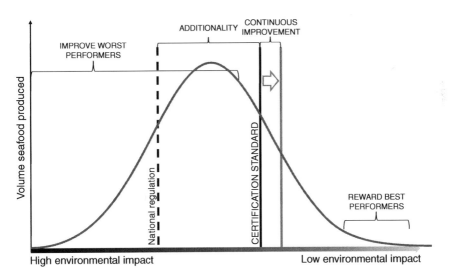

Figure 7.2 Conceptual figure demonstrating the environmental performance of the aquaculture sector (x-axis) and the volume of seafood produced (y-axis) together with prerequisite II–V. For simplicity, the curve is normally distributed and presents no multi-dimensionality with respect to environmental impacts. In order for certification to have substantial effect, it needs to stimulate improved performance of both worst performers (prerequisite II) and reward and incentivize improved practices among best performers (V). Moreover, certification standards need to continuously improve (III) and be more rigorous than national regulation (IV).

suite of common metrics (e.g. focused on planetary boundaries such as energy, GHG, P and N effluents, impacts on biodiversity and resource appropriation), and would set the standard at some level. This level would likely include all of some species, while other species would not be able to achieve the bar. For example, if N and P effluents were the selected metrics, then all seaweed and shellfish would be above the cut off (given they are primary producers and filter feeders respectively), whereas species with very high feed conversion ratios (e.g. Bluefin tuna) or production systems emitting substantial amounts of excess nutrients, would not be included. Current developed country market-based initiatives can, however, be defined as relative given that any species can be certified, also those from production systems highly criticized for unsustainable practices, e.g. tropical shrimp farming. In other words, certification currently helps consumers identify the best option in each species category but provides no assistance in distinguishing the seafood, or food, option with the smallest environmental footprint.

Future research needs

More work is needed to fill the knowledge gap on effects of aquaculture certification. Creating a metrics and evaluation framework that will encourage elucidation of the environmental and social gains made through certification will be paramount to raise certification beyond being a barrier to accessing specific markets. The trade-offs between two tentatively contradictory objectives of eco-certification (i.e. lowering impacts vs promoting sustainable practices) also need to be unravelled and better communicated. This is of relevance from the perspective of a range of value chain actors such as retailers and consumers, but also environmental NGOs aiming to advise consumers and others on the better environmental seafood choice. Moreover, insights for when certification leads to reduced environmental impacts is crucial for revising and updating certification standards (Tlusty and Tausig 2014) and is therefore also highly important for standard-holding organizations. Furthermore, broader systemic insights with respect to potential negative effects and impacts from certification are needed. For instance, whether certification may increase consumer demand for inherently more environmentally impactful products, incentivize producers to shift from a low-impact species or system not targeted by certification to more demanding species groups where certification can be achieved and thereby access to attractive export markets. These are important questions as they put emphasis on potential unwarranted effects from certification that can result in critical negative trade-offs. Thus, besides the pressing need to better understand when and how aquaculture certification has effects, there is also a need to go beyond measuring direct impacts and instead consider indirect spillover effects on noncertified units (Gutierrez et al. 2016).

 There is also a need for increased knowledge on general institutional and social conditions that influence whether a scheme is successfully implemented and drives long-term improvements of practices. Recent work by Thorlakson *et al.* (2018) investigating the effectiveness of a retailer-led certification standard in improving agricultural practices for instance suggested certain characteristic uncommon in conventional certification programmes to have been crucial for effectiveness on the ground. For instance, a lack of strict certification criteria together with a unique focus on capacity building rather than traditional auditing processes was suggested to be a key success factor. A close relationship between producers and the retailer chain responsible for the scheme was also highlighted to be of high importance (Thorlakson *et al.* 2018). Findings from this study are well in line with earlier work (e.g. Poynton 2015), stressing that there is a need to think beyond conventional certification and strict controlling systems and instead push for collaboration, transparency and stepwise learning. This emerging body of literature also calls for broader research on the role of the private sector in driving substantive change (Österblom *et al.* 2017), the role of market-based governance mechanisms beyond traditional eco-certification, e.g. effects of AIPs, and the linkages between corporate-led sustainability initiatives and state-led governance (Bailey *et al.* 2018)

Note

1 Here used as a broad term for fish, crustaceans and other aquatic species from both marine and freshwater production systems.

References

ASC (2015) ASC Standard Setting Procedure_v.1.0_Nov.2014_TOR for Operational review_2015. 1–15.
ASC (2017a) Certification Update: December 2017. In: http://mailchi.mp/asc-aqua/xr162vrjvq-2052705?e=[UNIQID].
ASC (2017b) ASC Monitoring & Evaluation System.
ASC (2018a) Certification Update: January 2018. In: https://mailchi.mp/asc-aqua/xr162vrjvq-2080661?e=[UNIQID].
ASC (2018b) 15 Facts about the ASC. In: www.asc-aqua.org/about-us/15-facts-about-the-asc/.
Auld G (2014) Constructing Private Governance: The Rise and Evolution of Forest, Coffee and Fisheries Certification. Yale University Press, New Haven, CT and London.
Bailey M, Packer H, Schiller L, *et al.* (2018) The role of Corporate Social Responsibility in creating a Seussian world of seafood sustainability. Fish Fish 1–9. doi: 10.1111/faf.12289.
BAP (2017) Best Aquaculture Practices Completes GSCP Equivalence Process. In: https://bapcertification.org/blog/tag/global-social-compliance-programme/.
BAP (2018) BAP-Certified Aquaculture Facilities. In: https://bapcertification.org/CertifiedFacilities.
Barbier EB (2007) Valuing ecosystem services as productive inputs. Econ Policy 22:177–229.

Belton B, Murray F, Young J, et al. (2010) Passing the Panda Standard: A TAD off the mark? Ambio 39:2–13. doi: 10.1007/s13280-009-0009-4.

Belton B, Bush SR, Little DC (2017) Not just for the wealthy: rethinking farmed fish consumption in the Global South. Glob Food Sec. doi: 10.1016/j.gfs.2017.10.005.

Béné C, Barange M, Subasinghe R, et al. (2015) Feeding 9 billion by 2050: putting fish back on the menu. Food Secur 7:261–274. doi: 10.1007/s12571-015-0427-z.

Béné C, Arthur R, Norbury H, et al. (2016) Contribution of fisheries and aquaculture to food security and poverty reduction: assessing the current evidence. World Dev 79:177–196. doi: 10.1016/j.worlddev.2015.11.007.

Bergleiter S (2008) Organic aquaculture. In: Willer H, Yussefi-Menzler M, Sorensen N (eds) The World of Organic Agriculture: Statistics and Emerging Trends 2008. International Federation of Organic Agriculture Movements (IFOAM) Bonn, Germany and Research Institute of Organic Agriculture (FiBL), Frick, Switzerland, 83–88.

Bertrand M, Duflo E, Mullainathan S (2004) How much should we trust differences-in-differences estimates? Q J Econ 119:249–275. doi: 10.1162/003355304772839588.

Beveridge MC, Ross LG, Kelly LA (1994) Aquaculture and biodiversity. Ambio 23:497–502.

Beveridge MCM, Thilsted SH, Phillips MJ, et al. (2013) Meeting the food and nutrition needs of the poor: the role of fish and the opportunities and challenges emerging from the rise of aquaculture. J Fish Biol 83:1067–84. doi: 10.1111/jfb.12187.

Blackman A (2012) Does Eco-Certification Boost Regulatory Compliance in Developing Countries? ISO 14001 in Mexico. J Regul Econ 42:242–263. doi: 10.1007/s11149-012-9199-y.

Blackman A, Naranjo MA (2012) Does eco-certification have environmental benefits? Organic coffee in Costa Rica. Ecol Econ 83:58–66. doi: 10.1016/j.ecolecon.2012.08.001.

Blackman A, Rivera J (2010) The evidence base for environmental and socio-economic impacts of 'sustainable' certification. Resources for the Future, Washington, DC. Discussion Paper 10.

Blackman A, Rivera J (2011) Producer-level benefits of sustainability certification. Conserv Biol 25:1176–1185. doi: 10.1111/j.1523-1739.2011.01774.x.

Bolwig S, Gibbon P, Jones S (2009) The economics of smallholder organic contract farming in tropical Africa. World Dev 37:1094–1104. doi: 10.1016/j.worlddev.2008.09.012.

Burridge L, Weis JS, Cabello F, et al. (2010) Chemical use in salmon aquaculture: a review of current practices and possible environmental effects. Aquaculture 306:7–23. doi: 10.1016/j.aquaculture.2010.05.020.

Bush S, Oosterveer P (2015) Vertically differentiating environmental standards: the case of the Marine Stewardship Council. Sustainability 7:1861–1883. doi: 10.3390/su7021861.

Bush S, Belton B, Hall D, et al. (2013a) Certify sustainable aquaculture? Science (80-) 341:1067–1068.

Bush SR, Toonen H, Oosterveer P, Mol APJ (2013b) The 'devils triangle' of MSC certification: balancing credibility, accessibility and continuous improvement. Mar Policy 37:288–293. doi: 10.1016/j.marpol.2012.05.011.

Campbell BM, Beare DJ, Bennett EM, et al. (2017) Agriculture production as a major driver of the Earth system exceeding planetary boundaries. Ecol Soc 22:art8. doi: 10.5751/ES-09595-220408.

Cao L, Naylor R, Henriksson P, *et al.* (2015) China's aquaculture and the world's wild fisheries: curbing demand for wild fish in aquafeed is critical. Science (80-) 347:133–135.

Central Compilation & Translation Press (2016) The 13th Five-Year Plan for Economic and Social Development of the People's Republic of China 2016–2020. Cent Compil Transl Press 219. Central Committee of the Communist Party of China.

Chaplin-Kramer R, Jonell M, Guerry A, *et al.* (2015) Ecosystem service information to benefit sustainability standards for commodity supply chains. Ann N Y Acad Sci 1355:77–97. doi: 10.1111/nyas.12961.

Clay J (2010) How big brands can help save biodiversity. Available from http://blog.ted.com/2010/08/16/how-.

Costello C, Ovando D, Clavelle T, *et al.* (2016) Global fishery prospects under contrasting management regimes. Proc Natl Acad Sci 1–5. doi: 10.1073/pnas.1520420113.

Fabinyi M (2016) Sustainable seafood consumption in China. Mar Policy 74:85–87. doi: 10.1016/j.marpol.2016.09.020.

FAO (2011) Technical Guidelines on Aquaculture Certification.

FAO (2016) The State of World Fisheries and Aquaculture 2016: Contributing to Food Security and Nutrition for All. Rome.

FAO (2018) FAO Fishstat J.

Folke C, Biggs R, Norström AV, *et al.* (2016) Social-ecological resilience and biosphere-based sustainability science. Ecol Soc 21:art41. doi: 10.5751/ES-08748-210341.

Garnett T (2016) Plating up solutions. Science (80-) 353:1202 LP-1204.

Garrett RD, Carlson KM, Rueda X, Noojipady P (2016) Assessing the potential additionality of certification by the Roundtable on Responsible Soybeans and the Roundtable on Sustainable Palm Oil. Environ Res Lett 11:045003. doi: 10.1088/1748-9326/11/4/045003.

Gephart JA, Troell M, Henriksson PJG, *et al.* (2017) The 'seafood gap' in the food-water nexus literature: issues surrounding freshwater use in seafood production chains. Adv Water Resour 110:505–514. doi: 10.1016/j.advwatres.2017.03.025.

Gordon LJ, Bignet V, Crona B, *et al.* (2017) Rewiring food systems to enhance human health and biosphere stewardship. Environ Res Lett 12:100201. doi: 10.1088/1748-9326/aa81dc.

Gutierrez NL, Defeo O, Bush SR, *et al.* (2016) The current situation and prospects of fisheries certification and ecolabelling. Fish Res. doi: 10.1016/j.fishres.2016.05.004.

Hamilton SE, Lovette J (2015) Ecuador's mangrove forest carbon stocks: a spatiotemporal analysis of living carbon holdings and their depletion since the advent of commercial aquaculture. PLoS One 10:e0118880. doi: 10.1371/journal.pone.0118880.

Haugen AS, Bremer S, Kaiser M (2017) Weaknesses in the ethical framework of aquaculture related standards. Mar Policy 75:11–18. doi: 10.1016/j.marpol.2016.10.011.

Henriksson PJG, Rico A, Troell M, *et al.* (2017) Unpacking factors influencing antimicrobial use in global aquaculture and their implication for management: a review from a systems perspective. Sustain Sci. doi: 10.1007/s11625-017-0511-8.

Hilborn R, Fulton EA, Green BS, *et al.* (2015) When is a fishery sustainable? Can J Fish Aquat Sci 72:1433–1441.

ISEAL (2014a) ISEAL impacts code. In: www.isealalliance.org/sites/default/files/resource/2017-11/ISEAL_Impacts_Code_v2_Dec_2014.pdf.

ISEAL (2014b) Setting Social and Environmental Standards – ISEAL Code of Good Practice. Version 60, December 2014, 1–23.

Islam MS (2005) Nitrogen and phosphorus budget in coastal and marine cage aquaculture and impacts of effluent loading on ecosystem: review and analysis towards model development. Mar Pollut Bull 50:48–61. doi: 10.1016/j.marpolbul.2004.08.008.

Jonell M (2016) Kind of turquoise: effects of seafood eco-certification and sustainable consumption. Stockholm University.

Jonell M, Henriksson PJG (2015) Mangrove-shrimp farms in Vietnam: comparing organic and conventional systems using life cycle assessment. Aquaculture 447:66–75.

Jonell M, Phillips M, Rönnbäck P, Troell M (2013) Eco-certification of farmed seafood: will it make a difference? Ambio 42:659–74. doi: 10.1007/s13280-013-0409-3.

Jonell M, Crona B, Brown K, et al. (2016) Eco-labeled seafood : determinants for (blue) green consumption. Sustainability. doi: 10.3390/su8090884.

Jorgensen PS, Wernli D, Carroll SP, et al. (2016) Use antimicrobials wisely. Nature 537:159–161. doi: 10.1038/537159a.

Konefal J (2013) Environmental movements, market-based approaches, and neoliberalization: a case study of the sustainable seafood movement. Organ Environ 26:336–352. doi: 10.1177/1086026612467982.

Krause G, Brugere C, Diedrich A, et al. (2015) A revolution without people? Closing the people-policy gap in aquaculture development. Aquaculture 447:44–55. doi: 10.1016/j.aquaculture.2015.02.009.

Krkošek M, Ford J, Morton A, et al. (2007) Declining wild salmon populations in relation to parasites from farm salmon. Science (80-) 318:1772–1775.

Lee D (2008) Aquaculture certification. In: Ward T, Phillips B (eds) Seafood Ecolabelling: Principles and Practice. Wiley-Blackwell, Singapore, 106–133.

Liu Q, Yan Z, Zhou J (2017) Consumer choices and motives for eco-labeled products in China: an empirical analysis based on the choice experiment. Sustain. doi: 10.3390/su9030331.

Mcleod E, Chmura GL, Bouillon S, et al. (2011) A blueprint for blue carbon: toward an improved understanding of the role of vegetated coastal habitats in sequestering CO_2. Front Ecol Environ 9:552–560. doi: 10.1890/110004.

Naylor RL, Goldburg RJ, Primavera JH, et al. (2000) Effect of aquaculture on world fish supplies. Nature 405:1017–1024. doi: 10.1038/35016500.

Nhu TT, Schaubroeck T, Henriksson PJG, et al. (2016) Environmental impact of non-certified versus certified (ASC) intensive pangasius aquaculture in Vietnam: a comparison based on a statistically supported LCA. Environ Pollut 219:156–165. doi: 10.1016/j.envpol.2016.10.006.

Österblom H, Jouffray J, Folke C, Rockström J (2017) Emergence of a global science – business initiative for ocean stewardship. PNAS 1–6. doi: 10.1073/pnas.1704453114.

Paprocki K, Cons J (2014) Life in a shrimp zone : aqua- and other cultures of Bangladesh's coastal landscape. J Peasant Stud 0:1–22. doi: 10.1080/03066150.2014.937709.

Pelletier N, Audsley E, Brodt S, et al. (2011) Energy intensity of agriculture and food systems. Annu Rev Environ Resour 36:223–246. doi: 10.1146/annurev-environ-081710-161014.

Potts J, Wilkings A, Lynch M, MacFatridge S (2016) State of Sustainability Initiatives Review: Standards and the Blue Economy. IISD, Winnipeg, Manitoba.

Poynton S (2015) Beyond Certification. D Sustainability, Oxford.

Ruben R, Fort R (2011) The impact of fair trade certification for coffee farmers in Peru. World Dev 40:570–582. doi: 10.1016/j.worlddev.2011.07.030.

Samerwong P, Bush SR, Oosterveer P (2018) Implications of multiple national certification standards for Thai shrimp aquaculture. Aquaculture 493:319–327. doi: 10.1016/j.aquaculture.2018.01.019.

Sampson BGS, Sanchirico JN, Roheim CA, *et al.* (2015) Secure sustainable seafood from developing countries. Science (80-) 348:504–506. doi: 10.1126/science. aaa4639.

Silver JJ, Hawkins R (2014) 'I'm not trying to save fish, I'm trying to save dinner': media, celebrity and sustainable seafood as a solution to environmental limits. Geoforum. doi: 10.1016/j.geoforum.2014.09.005.

Soto D, Aguilar-Manjarrez J, Hishamunda N (2008) Building an Ecosystem Approach to Aquaculture. FAO, Rome.

Steering Committee of the State-of-Knowledge Assessment of Standards and Certification (2012) Toward Sustainability: The Roles and Limitations of Certification.

Sumaila UR, Cheung W, Dyck A, *et al.* (2012) Benefits of rebuilding global marine fisheries outweigh costs. PLoS One 7:e40542. doi: 10.1371/journal.pone.0040542.

The Fish Site (2017) China's demand for Atlantic salmon set to grow by 25 percent per year. In: https://thefishsite.com/articles/consumption-predictions-for-atlantic-salmon.

Thilsted HS, Thorne-Lyman A, Webb P, *et al.* (2016) Sustaining healthy diets : the role of capture fisheries and aquaculture for improving nutrition in the post-2015 era. Food Policy 61:126–131. doi: 10.1016/j.foodpol.2016.02.005.

Thorlakson T, Hainmueller J, Lambin EF (2018) Improving environmental practices in agricultural supply chains: the role of company-led standards. Glob Environ Chang 48:32–42. doi: 10.1016/j.gloenvcha.2017.10.006.

Tilman D, Clark M (2014) Global diets link environmental sustainability and human health. Nature. doi: 10.1038/nature13959.

Tlusty MF (2012) Environmental improvement of seafood through certification and ecolabelling: theory and analysis. Fish Fish 13:1–13. doi: 10.1111/j.1467-2979. 2011.00404.x.

Tlusty MF, Tausig H (2014) Reviewing GAA-BAP shrimp farm data to determine whether certification lessens environmental impacts. Rev Aquac 1–10. doi: 10.1111/raq.12056.

Tlusty MF, Thorsen Ø (2016) Claiming seafood is 'sustainable' risks limiting improvements. Fish Fish 1–7. doi: 10.1111/faf.12170.

Tlusty MF, Thompson M, Tausig H (2016) Statistical tools to assess the breadth and depth of shrimp aquaculture certification schemes. Fish Res 182:172–176. doi: 10.1016/j.fishres.2015.10.008.

Toufique KA, Belton B (2014) Is aquaculture pro-poor? Empirical evidence of impacts on fish consumption in Bangladesh. World Dev 64:609–620. doi: 10.1016/j.worlddev.2014.06.035.

Towers L (2016) Indian, Thai shrimp farms encouraged to get BAP certification. In: thefishsite.com/articles/indian-thai-shrimp-farms-encouraged-to-get-bap-certification.

Troell M, Naylor RL, Metian M, *et al.* (2014) Does aquaculture add resilience to the global food system? Proc Natl Acad Sci 111:13257–13263.

Troell M, Jonell M, Henriksson PJG (2017) Ocean space for seafood. Nat Ecol Evol 1:1224–1225. doi: 10.1038/s41559-017-0304-6.

Tyedmers P (2004) Fisheries and energy use. In: Cleveland C (ed.) Encyclopedia of Energy. Elsevier, Amsterdam, 683–694.

Uchida H, Roheim CA, Wakamatsu H, Anderson CM (2013) Do Japanese consumers care about sustainable fisheries? Evidence from an auction of ecolabelled seafood. Aust J Agric Resour Econ 57:1–18. doi: 10.1111/1467-8489.12036.

van der Ven H, Cashore B (2018) Forest certification: the challenge of measuring impacts. Curr Opin Environ Sustain 32:104–111. doi: 10.1016/j.cosust. 2018.06.001.

Vermeir I, Verbeke W (2006) Sustainable food consumption: exploring the consumer 'attitude – behavioral intention' gap. J Agric Environ Ethics 19:169–194. doi: 10.1007/s10806-005-5485-3.

Waite R, Beveridge M, Brummett R, et al. (2014) Improving Productivity and Environmental Performance of Aquaculture. World Resources Institute, Washington, DC.

Walters B, Rönnbäck P, Kovacs J, et al. (2008) Ethnobiology, socio-economics and management of mangrove forests: a review. Aquat Bot 89:220–236. doi: 10.1016/j. aquabot.2008.02.009.

Xu P, Zeng Y, Fong Q, et al. (2012) Chinese consumers' willingness to pay for green- and eco-labeled seafood. Food Control 28:74–82. doi: 10.1016/j.foodcont.2012.04.008.

8 Biofuel sustainability certifications in the EU

Democratically legitimate and socio-environmentally effective?

Thomas Vogelpohl and Daniela Perbandt

1 Introduction

Once hailed a silver bullet for simultaneously tackling energy insecurity, climate change and rural poverty, biofuels are a matter of heavy debate since coming under fierce criticism from the mid-2000s. As more research studies were undertaken, conclusions emerged that biofuels are at best irrelevant to combating climate change, do not necessarily contribute to energy security in the developed countries, and endanger food security in developing countries (Franco *et al.* 2010; Mitchell 2008; Searchinger *et al.* 2008). Nevertheless, biofuels remain one of the major pillars to achieving European transport sector targets in carbon emission reductions. As the biofuel market is politically instituted through government support schemes, accompanying measures to safeguard the environmental and social sustainability at a global level were called for (Mol 2010; Pilgrim and Harvey 2010).

Sustainability certification became the major regulatory strategy in Europe in this regard. The European Union's Renewable Energy Directive (EU RED), which was adopted in April 2009, set mandatory sustainability criteria that companies must comply with to have their production counted towards the 10 per cent target established in the same directive. Compliance with these criteria can be proven using a voluntary certification scheme (VCS) recognised by the European Commission (EC; European Commission 2017b).[1]

These schemes are part of a general increase in private certification initiatives within the field of environmental governance (Cashore 2002; Pattberg 2005). In the case of EU regulation of biofuel sustainability, the VCSs on biofuels are incorporated into state regulation. The EU as a governmental organisation is relying on these VCSs and is actively integrating them into their regulatory frameworks. Thus, what we have is not only a private governance system, but one that goes "beyond the public and private divide" (Pattberg and Stripple 2008), making it a specific case of a public–private governance arrangement (PPGA) that includes the EU and its Member States on the one hand and the recognised private VCSs on the other.

Several benefits have been attributed to this PPGA as it is supposed to maintain the advantages of private governance while tackling its downsides by linking it with governmental regulation. In a publication of the German state-owned Deutsche Gesellschaft für Internationale Zusammenarbeit (GIZ), this kind of co-regulation is hailed for combining

> The strengths of both private and public regulatory capacities. Strengths in public regulation include democratic legitimacy, applicability to all firms within the jurisdiction, and enforceability through state supervisory agencies.... On the other hand, private regulation is often flexible, quick and innovative in nature, while being international in terms of focus and applicability.
>
> (GIZ 2013: 5)

This chapter will primarily deal with the following considerations given this situation.

> Is recognition by state authorities sufficient to confer democratic legitimacy to private governance schemes?
>   Can this really be the problem-solving "connection between legitimate democratic processes ... and effective environmental policies" that these new modes of governance seem to promise?
>
> (Bäckstrand *et al.* 2010: 15–16)

After presenting the contemporary situation of European sustainability certification of biofuels (section 2), we seek to provide a balanced critique of the regulatory strategy of sustainability certification of biofuels in the EU regarding both its democratic legitimacy (section 3) and its environmental and social effectiveness (section 4).

2 Sustainability certification of biofuels in the EU: a public–private government arrangement

Since the end of the 1990s biofuels have been regarded as a promising alternative to gasoline and diesel in the transport sector. Appearing as a silver bullet, increasing the use of biofuels seemed to promise less dependency on crude oil imports, a reduction of carbon emissions and prospects for rural development. Consequently, in early 2008 the EC proposed a binding 10 per cent target to be met by all Member States in 2020 to step up efforts to increase the use of biofuels as part of the proposal for a RED. Out of a need to react to the arising problems and questions with respect to social and ecological issues of an increased biofuels usage mentioned above, the EC proposed tying the mandatory 10 per cent biofuels target to compliance of these biofuels with certain sustainability criteria.

Thus, the RED, which was finally adopted in late 2008 and came into force in 2009, determines four sustainability criteria to be fulfilled by the biofuel producers; these criteria only cover the environmental dimension of sustainability (European Union 2009: 36–37; see Table 8.1).

Table 8.1 Sustainability criteria for biofuels determined under the EU RED (2009)

1. Reduction of greenhouse gas emissions by at least 35 per cent
   - In effect immediately, but solely for biofuels produced in installations that were put into service after 23 January 2008 (for biofuels, which were produced in older plants, this criterion applies only from 1 April 2013)
   - At least 50 per cent GHC savings as of January 2017 (for all biofuels)
   - At least 60 per cent GHG savings as of January 2018 (only for biofuels produced in installations that were put into service after January 2017)

2. No raw material from land with biodiversity value
   - Forest undisturbed by significant human activity
   - Highly biodiverse grassland
   - Nature protection areas (unless compatible with nature protection)

3. No raw material from land with high carbon stocks
   - Wetlands
   - Continuously forested area
   - Undrained peatland

4. Cross compliance
   - Agricultural raw materials cultivated in the EU must meet EU agricultural "cross compliance" rules applied under the EU Common Agricultural Policy

The predominant option[2] for biofuel producers offering their products on European markets to demonstrate compliance with these criteria is certification by a VCS. Prior to this, recognition[3] of the VCS by the EC for a time span of five years is necessary. The EU recognition process is regulated in a Commission communication which "sets out how the Commission intends to carry out its responsibilities leading to such decisions" (European Commission 2010: 1). This communication states that applying schemes will be assessed against the sustainability criteria laid down in the RED as well as against the requirements regarding documentation management, independent auditing and a mass balance system, which are explained in the communication.

With the 2015 ILUC directive,[4] these requirements have been extended, now also comprising aspects of transparency, internal monitoring and conflict resolution (European Union 2015). Thus, assessment and recognition are restricted to the mandatory criteria of the RED (see Table 8.1) and some procedural aspects, while nonmandatory sustainability aspects like socio-economic issues are not assessed during this process (European Court of Auditors 2016).

Within in the EC, the recognition process itself is led by the Directorate-General for Energy (DG ENER), which passes on applications to a private contractor who supports the EC in assessing the applying VCSs. During the first and second turn of scheme assessment, the Dutch consulting firm Ecofys Investment B.V. mainly served as an external contractor. The private contractor prepares an assessment report on which a draft implementing decision by DG ENER is based. The following internal consultation of DG ENER and other Directorates General enters the "comitology process!",[5] after which the recommendation to adopt the Commission Decision is declared and the recognition decision is published. If granted, recognition is valid for a period of five years.

By the end of 2011 seven VCSs were recognised by the EC, one year later five new schemes joined and by 2016, a total of 19 voluntary schemes had been recognised by the EC. By December 2017, 17 schemes were recognised by EC. Seven of the 12 VCSs recognised in 2011 and 2012 have been newly recognised, with another two re-recognitions pending. Three of these 12 VCSs – Abengoa RED Bioenergy Sustainability Assurance (RBSA), Greenergy Brazilian Bioethanol verification programme (Greenergy) and Ensus Voluntary Scheme under RED for Ensus Bioethanol Production (Ensus) – will not apply for recognition again.

In addition, the 2015 ILUC directive established the possibility to recognise national voluntary certification systems on the European level. Austria was the first member state that registered the national standard as a voluntary scheme, which was recognised in 2016 as "Austrian Agricultural Certification Scheme (AACS)" by the EC (European Commission 2017b). Of the 17 schemes currently recognised by the EC, we will focus on only 16 (Table 8.2), since one scheme is merely a carbon emission calculation tool and not a full certification scheme.[6] The 16 schemes differ significantly as to (1) feedstock(s) covered, (2) extent of supply chain covered and (3) scope of certification. For feedstock, three groups of schemes can be determined: (a) wide range feedstock of which there are nine schemes, (b) crop groups like cereals, oil seeds or sugar beet of which there are four schemes, (c) special crops like sugarcane (Bonsucro), palm oil (RSPO) and soy (RTRS) of which there are three schemes. The extent of the supply chain mainly differs between full supply chain certification (ten schemes) and certification from the producer to a processor or delivery point respectively (six schemes). While the scope of most schemes are limited to the mandatory criteria (ten schemes), six schemes include additional social and ecological criteria.

3 Democratic legitimacy

There are different views of how democratic legitimacy can or should be conceptualised with regard to private governance arrangements (Bernstein and Cashore 2007; Dingwerth 2007). Drawing on Susanne Schaller's definition, we focus on a prescriptive-normative approach to legitimacy, which refers "to the conditions under which authority can be morally evaluated as legitimate" (Schaller 2007: 11; see also Zürn 2004: 260). In this context, we refer to a model that distinguishes between input, throughput and output legitimacy (Bäckstrand 2006; Dingwerth 2003: 74–76; Partzsch 2011; Zürn 1998: 233–236). While input and throughput legitimacy are dealt with in this section, we largely equate output legitimacy with the effectiveness of a governance arrangement, to be addressed in section 4.

Table 8.2 Overview of voluntary certification schemes recognised by the EC (by December 2017)

Voluntary Certification Scheme (VCS)	Date of EC-decision	Regional focus	Feedstock	Extent of supply chain covered	Scope of certification
REDcert GmbH	10.08.2017	Germany	wide range	full	mandatory
ISCC System GmbH	09.08.2016	Worldwide	wide range	full	extended
Bonsucro	21.03.2017	South America	sugar cane	full	extended
RSB	09.08.2016	Worldwide	wide range	full	extended
2BSvs	26.08.2016	France	wide range	full	mandatory
RSPO	23.11.2012★	South East Asia	palm oil	full	extended
HVO	09.01.2014	Finland	wide range	partly	mandatory
KZR IniG	03.06.2014	Poland	wide range	full	mandatory
SQC	09.06.2015	Great Britain	cereals and oilseeds	partly	mandatory
Gafta	03.06.2014	Great Britain	wide range	partly	mandatory
UFAS	17.09.2014	Great Britain	cereals, oilseeds and sugar beet	partly	mandatory
TASCC	17.09.2014	Great Britain	cereals, oilseeds and sugar beet	partly	mandatory
AACS	11.05.2016	Austria	wide range	full	mandatory
Better Biomass (NTA 8080)	31.07.2012★	Worldwide	wide range	full	extended
Red Tractor	13.12.2017	Great Britain	cereals, oilseeds and sugar beet	partly	mandatory
RTRS	19.11.2017	South America	soy	full	extended

Note
★ Recognition expired, applied for re-recognition, currently still pending.

3.1 Input legitimacy

Input legitimacy refers to the quantity and structure of actors participating in a private governance arrangement. Through broad involvement and participation of a sufficient number of affected stakeholder groups, authority is transferred directly to these affected stakeholders. It therefore creates a more legitimate system and introduces an element of democratic control (Bäckstrand 2006; Partzsch 2011).

Main criteria for input legitimacy in this context are a balanced membership structure of the recognised VCSs and the existence of governance structures that facilitate equal participation. *De jure*, VCSs don't have to fulfil any input legitimacy criteria to be recognised by the EC; however they could still do so. In this context, the schemes can be differentiated according to their ownership and membership structure. In general, schemes run by industry and industry-related stakeholders (11 of the 16 schemes[7]) do not provide for a balanced membership structure or equal participation of stakeholders. This is not, however, surprising considering their limited regional focus and the limited part of the supply chain they are covering.

The five remaining schemes qualify as multistakeholder initiatives (MSIs): Roundtable on Sustainable Palm Oil RED (RSPO), Roundtable on Sustainable Biomaterial (RSB), Roundtable of Sustainable Soy (RTRS), Bonsucro (formerly Better Sugarcane Initiative) and International Sustainability and Carbon Certification (ISCC). They include industry, traders, farmers as well as social and environmental NGOs. In many cases, companies and NGOs are members of several schemes. For example, the World-Wide Fund for Nature (WWF) has joined all multistakeholder schemes.

These MSIs go beyond the nonexisting EU requirements regarding input legitimacy. Usually, they are not only providing for a somewhat balanced membership structure, but also for the right to a say for different stakeholder groups in the decision-making procedures of the scheme. This is assured by setting up representational quotas for each stakeholder group regarding the main governing bodies and boards of the schemes. Furthermore, differentiated membership fees, financial aid for attending meetings for less wealthy stakeholder groups or the possibility for these to be represented by a proxy in meetings are supposed to provide for equal representation of the different stakeholders.

None of the VCSs recognised by the EC under the RED perfectly fulfils all criteria. Some of the remaining schemes are performing better than others regarding input legitimacy criteria. For example, the RSB classifies its members into five chambers that elect the Assembly of Delegates. This is the main governing body of the organisation, which appoints a Board of Directors, oversees the RSB Secretariat and is responsible for the day-to-day running of the organisation. Furthermore, membership fees are differentiated according to the financial resources of the individual member and meetings are often organised via Skype to keep to the financial burden of partaking in these meetings, making them affordable for less wealthy members. The RSPO is organised in a similar way, even though the organisation of RSPO chambers is more industry friendly than that of the RSB. The same is true for Bonsucro, RTRS and especially ISCC.[8]

Thus, even though they are far from perfect in this regard, these MSIs are enhancing their input legitimacy, even though they are not forced to do so by the EC requirements. The RSB in particular is often lauded in this context, because it – putatively – "provides an example of a 'multi-stakeholder' model of standards development that is assumed to confer greater legitimacy on the sustainability standards that are produced" (Fortin 2017: 1). This is, however, debatable even regarding the RSB (Fortin 2017; Fortin and Richardson 2013; Ponte 2014) and even more questionable regarding the other MSIs considered here – which altogether only represent one-third of the VCSs recognised by the EC. This shows that the theory of private governance schemes going beyond government requirements regarding input legitimacy criteria can only partly be supported.

While these examples demonstrate that MSI schemes do go beyond EU requirements in terms of input legitimacy, the majority do not. This shows that market and civil society pressure alone do not suffice to have ambitious input legitimacy criteria fulfilled by PPGAs. As long as input legitimacy is not provided for in a structural way by the EU, the viability of private governance as a promise of effectiveness and legitimacy as a whole could be questioned (European Court of Auditors 2016: 27).

3.2 Throughput legitimacy

Throughput legitimacy refers to procedural level legitimacy. One dimension of throughput legitimacy can be described as the democratic quality of decision-making processes and its transparency. In this context, it is of crucial importance that adequate mechanisms are in place to guarantee equal participation of different stakeholders in a transparent and nondiscriminative way (Minderhoud 2010: 105; Müller 2007: 47). The second dimension of throughput legitimacy refers to the accountability of a governance system. A private governance system in theory establishes a legal framework that provides binding rules for every participant that should guarantee appropriateness as well as compliance; bias-free mechanisms of control and accountability are vital to curb political power (Dingwerth 2003; Meidinger 2007). Regarding the case of the EU biofuel sustainability certification, we analyse these two dimensions of throughput legitimacy with regard to what the EC requires from VCSs applying for recognition under the RED (*de jure* throughput legitimacy) and with regard to what the recognised VCSs do beyond these requirements (de facto throughput legitimacy).

Besides the ability to provide accurate data on RED sustainability criteria, the EU requires the VCSs to use a mass balance system and in addition an adequate standard of independent auditing (European Union 2009: 75). While the former of the two categories is rather technical, the latter touches on through-put legitimacy. With regard to transparency and accountability a VCS:

- must have an audible documentation management system for the evidence related to the claims they make or rely on and it must keep any evidence for at least five years;
- needs to accept responsibility for preparing any information related to the auditing of such evidence;
- must make sure that economic operators are audited before they are allowed to participate in the scheme;
- shall arrange for regular, at least yearly, retrospective, properly planned, conducted and reported on auditing of a sample of claims made under the scheme.

Regarding the auditor it must be assured that he or she:

- is independent of the activity being audited (third-party);
- is free from conflict of interest;
- has specific skills and relevant experience, namely regarding land-use criteria, the Chain of Custody system and GHG accounting.

For this reason, the auditor must be accredited by a national accreditation body or by the International Social and Environmental Accreditation and Labelling (ISEAL) Alliance or commit to comply with the ISO/IEC 17011 standard. Lastly, the audits shall be properly planned, conducted and reported on according to the ISO 19011 standard (European Commission 2010).

In addition to these criteria introduced in 2010, the EC extended the criteria as a part of the 2015 ILUC directive. VCSs applying for recognition since then also have to meet additional transparency criteria regarding the economic operators certified under the scheme, the latest version of scheme documents including the guidelines for audits; the certification bodies that are permitted to conduct audits; annual reports that include relevant information concerning the operation of the scheme[9] (European Union 2015).

As this shows, the EU recognition requirements consider some criteria of throughput legitimacy, especially the additional requirements stipulated in the 2015 ILUC directive have further enhanced transparency of the system. Thus, the EU has significantly strengthened the *de jure* throughput legitimacy of its biofuels sustainability certification system. There are, however, still some aspects of throughput legitimacy that are not adhered to. For example, the participation of local stakeholders is not required and neither are on-site audits or unannounced control visits (European Court of Auditors 2016: 29).

Examining the de facto throughput legitimacy, a mixed picture appears that is very much in line with the input legitimacy performance of the schemes. While industry-run schemes just fulfil the criteria set up by the European Commission, the MSIs (and Better Biomass) at least partially go beyond them and, for example, provide for a structured and institutionalised external or local stakeholder consultation. The RSB's stakeholder consultation procedures, for instance, are based on the FPIC (free, prior and informed consent) principle, also including gender-specific aspects. In case of conflicts, decisions with affected stakeholders are reached consensually. Furthermore, the RSB identifies affected stakeholders through a specific tool and includes an obligatory stakeholder analysis as part of the impact assessment process. Bonsucro organises its stakeholder consultation similarly, although with a less clear decision-making procedure on whom the stakeholders that are affected by the to-be-certified economic operation are. RTRS and ISCC, in contrast, have stakeholder involvement procedures installed that either "do little to ensure effective community relations" (ISCC) or do not go beyond "the community" in specifying who should be involved (RTRS; German and Schoneveld 2012: 774). A similar picture appears regarding grievance procedures, which the MSIs had installed already before the extended 2015 ILUC directive requirements. Again, RSB and Bonsucro have adopted extensive complaint and conflict resolution procedures, whereas for ISCC and RTRS "a grievance mechanism must exist but does not need to be considered legitimate by all involved parties" (German and Schoneveld 2012: 774).

Thus, there are some provisions in place regarding participation and transparency as well as control and accountability of the VCSs, be it *de jure* or de facto, even though they are far from satisfactory or even exhaustive. In practice however, these imperfect provisions can also turn out to be paper tigers, as described in section 4.2 below. In a nutshell one can conclude that the EC (still) requires too little in terms of throughput legitimacy from the VCSs and that this lack is insufficiently made up for by the recognised VCSs' actual certification procedures, especially when one considers the pitfalls of implementing adopted procedures in practice.

4 Output legitimacy: socio-environmental effectiveness

Effectiveness can be understood as a third dimension of legitimacy called output legitimacy, which "is normally related to 'effective' or 'efficient' problem-solving" (Steffek 2015: 266). Thus, output legitimacy is given if a policy is effective and efficient (Dingwerth 2003: 75) or, in other words if the implemented political standards lead to desired environmental and social outcomes (Bäckstrand 2006: 295), thereby lending a PPGA its legitimacy ex-post by its results. Hence, the development and use of biofuels should "help to improve qualities of life for all those affected or, at the very least, should not exacerbate or intensify existing social or environmental inequalities" (Blaber-Wegg *et al.* 2015: 181).

More concretely, effectiveness regarding social and environmental sustainability is not only a question of whether the schemes define broad social and environmental criteria (section 4.1), but also of how these criteria are enforced in practice and supervised by a superior authority. In section 4.2 we therefore concentrate on the de facto implementation of these standards through third-party certification and auditing by (independent) accredited certification bodies as requested by the EU RED. Finally, the effectiveness of such a system relying on voluntary certification very much depends on which of the recognised VCSs is used by economic operators and to what extent (section 4.3).

4.1 Adequate scope and specification of sustainability criteria

The discussion about the adequacy of sustainability criteria of the RED and the recognised VCSs is widespread within both the scientific community and society (European Court of Auditors 2016; Ponte and Daugbjerg 2015; Selbmann and Pforte 2016; WWF Germany 2013). Besides the ecological criteria of the RED (see Table 8.1), environmental criteria recommended in addition are related to aspects of biodiversity and nature conservation, such as endangered and protected species, invasive species or use of GMOs, water issues (use and efficiency, protection of surface and groundwater), soil aspects (erosion prevention, crop rotation or topography), air quality (dust exposure and other pollutants), the use of agrochemicals and fertilisers (integrated pest management) as well as waste documentation and management (FAO 2013; NRDC 2014; WWF Germany 2013). As social criteria are not mandated by the RED, reports consistently refer to them as vital for the sustainability of biofuel production. Essential social criteria are labour conditions such as forced or child labour; working conditions and health protection; discrimination; and equal distribution of incomes; as well as aspects of surrounding communities such as social welfare; land availability and rights; food security; and participation (Blaber-Wegg *et al.* 2015; NRDC 2014; WWF Germany 2013).

These studies congruently conclude that the mandatory criteria of the RED alone do not ensure sustainability in an appropriate way, since ecological and social aspects are not balanced. Rather than mandating it, reaching social sustainability is tried in a more informal way, via monitoring and reporting instead of via strict and compulsory specifications.[10] Consequently, a closer look at the VCSs reveals that – just like regarding the aspects of input and throughput legitimacy (see above) – only a few of the recognised VCSs go beyond the mandatory criteria and that these VCSs are almost entirely MSIs (see also Table 8.2).

In addition to the inadequacy of the scope of the mandatory sustainability criteria defined by the RED, the implementation of the mandatory criteria differs among the schemes. This is mainly caused by the RED itself, which lacks guidance or provides room for interpretation of several aspects. An example is the definition of highly diverse grassland. In 2016, the European Court of Auditors (ECA) stated that until late 2014, when a definition of highly biodiverse grassland was finally presented by the EC, this lack of guidance enabled certification of biofuels compliant with the RED without knowing whether the material was derived from these areas or not (European Court of Auditors 2016). Similarly, de Man and German (2017) point to the possibility of enhancing the GHG performance of biofuels up to 35 per cent by using different calculation tools without changing the production process, due to variable standard values and different methodologies for N_2O calculations that are not specified by the RED.

The adequate specification of sustainability criteria does not only refer to the interpretation of RED regulations but also to the appropriateness of the indicators and the rules of indicator fulfilment defined by the voluntary schemes. In their literature review, de Man and German (2017) highlight several instances of inadequate indicators, for example regarding the safeguarding of endangered species by RSPO (Ruysschaert and Salles 2014) or an ineffective indicator for water use defined by Bonsucro, whose fulfilment does not require any change of practice for certified firms (Sneyd 2014). Furthermore, the level of compliance with determined indicators varies among the schemes. ISCC, for example, differentiates between major and minor *musts*. While all major *musts* are to be fulfilled, the fulfilment of 60 per cent of the minor *musts* suffices for successful certification. Bonsucro works similar in that an overall fulfilment of indicators of 80 per cent must be reached, whereas only core indicators are to be met entirely. While 2BSvs recommends social and ecological criteria in addition to the mandatory RED criteria, these are not obligatory for a successful certification under the scheme (FAO 2013; de Man and German 2017). This practice of variable levels of compliance can turn sustainability certification into a chimaera without providing sustainable effects.

4.2 Practical implementation of sustainability certification

An assessment of biofuels sustainability standards effectiveness on the ground is not easy due to the lack of information provided by VCSs and certification bodies (Stupak *et al.* 2016). Furthermore, only little evidence can be traced in scientific literature (Blaber-Wegg *et al.* 2015). Nonetheless, several publications point to discrepancies between documented requirements for third-party auditing processes and reality (IEA Bioenergy 2013; IUCN NL 2014). The ECA stated: "In fact, our review of the work carried out by the certification bodies shows that the standards presented by the voluntary schemes as a basis for their recognition are not always applied in practice" (European Court of Auditors 2016: 28). Criticism usually is applied regarding:

- the audit process,
- the competences of auditors, and
- the financing of audits.

Audit rules have strong impact on the level of assurance of a certification system and its on-the-ground sustainability effects (NL Agency 2012). The requirements for the audit process seriously differ among VCSs (GIZ 2013; WWF Germany 2013) and, furthermore might not have been executed properly in several cases. Stupak *et al.* (2016) conducted a global stakeholder survey regarding the effectiveness of different sustainability standards. Their findings reveal inconsistencies in auditing practices due to the scope for interpretation the standard documents provide. For example, audits can be conducted on-site, respectively to assess the grade of compliance by inspection, documents' review and interviews, or via desk audit, which is a document review off-site. Furthermore, several VCSs offer self-declaration forms on their webpages for farmers (e.g. ISCC, REDcert) to declare the compliance of their farm or their cropping system with relevant criteria. Inspections by internal auditors are required but an independent verification of these self-declarations is usually not provided (IEA Bioenergy 2013). Relying on desk audits and self-declarations bears the risk of fraud regarding the compliance with scheme standards (WWF Germany 2013) and "non-compliances are possible as operators are not always obliged to reveal comprehensive documentation to the auditor" (Stupak *et al.* 2016).

In many cases, it is at the discretion of the auditor to handle the standards' audit guidelines in practice. The competences of auditors are therefore seen as an important factor for successful implementation of the biofuels sustainability standards (European Court of Auditors 2016). A report by the WWF Germany (2013) emphasises that almost all VCSs offer training courses for auditors. However, a lack of information regarding the quality of the training with respect to duration, contents and execution is also reported. Although several studies assess the competencies of auditors as good (IUCN NL 2014; Stupak *et al.* 2016), Stupak *et al.* also note little multidisciplinary knowledge and competences of new auditors which might influence the entire audit process. This might be a result not only of incompetency alone, but also of the applied indicators themselves, which can be complex and ambitious, requiring a higher level of knowledge and experience to make assessments under local conditions (Stupak *et al.* 2016).

Another important criterion is the financing of audits, and, closely related, the auditors' independency. Audit agencies, on the one hand, need to be accepted by the certification schemes and, hence, aim to fulfil their requirements regarding accreditation and cooperation. On the other hand, audit agencies are paid by the company or farm they assess. These interrelations entail manifold dependencies within the collaboration of VCSs, audit agencies and scheme users in practice. Regarding the collaboration of VCS and audit agency, for example, this might lead to a tendency for the auditing to focus on actors within the supply chain and a lesser preoccupation with other affected actors' interests (Blaber-Wegg *et al.* 2015; Fortin and Richardson 2013; de Man and German 2017; McDermott *et al.* 2013). Otherwise, the financial dependencies between audit agency and scheme user could cause the application of less stringent standards by the auditors because of their interest in retaining business (Lin 2011), particularly when cost intensive field audits are required by the scheme. Furthermore, the small number of audit agencies, the variability of scheme standards and the existing room of interpreting these standards provide scope for potential corruption (McDermott *et al.* 2013).

Finally, choosing a voluntary scheme is not least a cost-benefit calculation, since burdensome regulations of certification can provoke higher costs that might outweigh (economic) benefits. To increase attractiveness to users, schemes therefore apply several strategies. Beside cross-acceptance of other certificates and lower-priced certification alternatives such as desk audit or self-declaration, schemes handle noncompliances with standards differently. Indeed, noncompliance does normally not result in sanction or rejection of the respective user. In fact, voluntary withdrawal is the more common consequence. De Man and German (2017: 878) report 77 "withdrawn certificates" as of November 2016 by ISCC and 290 by 2BSvs, but only very few suspensions. Hence, poor performers choose to withdraw from certification schemes and save face rather than to comply. Furthermore, due to a lack of information exchange between audit agencies, it is possible for biofuel or biomass producers to choose a new certification body in order to obtain a certificate without implementing improvements that have been required by a first certification body (European Court of Auditors 2016).

4.3 Market share of recognised VCSs

The previous sections showed differences in scheme standards as well as problems related with the standards' implementation. However, to assess the effectiveness of certification standards appropriately, a close look at the numbers of issued certificates by the individual VCSs is needed, since they perform very unequally regarding compliance with criteria of sustainability, effectiveness and legitimacy (see above). When examining these numbers (Table 8.3), it should be borne in mind that they are not necessarily comparable, because the information given by the various VCSs is not consistent. For example, we do not know whether the certificates issued have been issued for biofuels in the EU.

Certain patterns can be discovered, and it becomes clear that the share of the VCSs in the EU biofuels certification market is very uneven. While ISCC and REDcert have already issued more than 1,000 currently valid certificates, both more than 10,000 in total, most of the schemes have issued less than a 100 thereof. 2BSvs and KZR IniG are in third and fourth place regarding currently valid certificates, both also well above 100. While these numbers have to be taken with a pinch of salt as mentioned above, they are quite in line with other studies on the market penetration of the VCSs recognised under the RED (IEA Bioenergy 2013; Ponte 2014).

A couple of explanatory approaches can be provided for this. First, one has to bear in mind that the feedstock for biofuels used in the EU mostly comes from EU countries (European Commission 2017a). For example, since a lot of this feedstock comes from Germany, the biggest biofuel-producing country

Table 8.3 Certificates issued by VCSs recognised under the RED in total as disclosed by the schemes' webpages (as of November 2017)

Voluntary Certification Scheme	Number of issued certificates	
	in total	currently valid
REDcert GmbH	12,343	1,934
ISCC System GmbH	16,200	3,050
Bonsucro	92★	90★
RSB	33	19
2BS Association	1,070	588
RSPO-RED	4	1
HVO	–	6°
KZR IniG	1,165	392
SQC	information not available	
Gafta	–	12°
UFAS	information not available	
TASCC	67	64
Austrian Agricultural Certification Scheme	–	122°
Better Biomass – RED	29	27
Red Tractor	information not available	
RTRS	22^	16^

Notes
★ from Bonsucro Outcome Report 2017, data from 2016 comprising certified mills and chain of custody certificates.
° only valid certificates are listed.
^ Producer and Chain of Custody certification holder.

in Europe (BLE 2016), the share of REDcert, which is the certification scheme of the German agricultural industry, is very high. The same can be said for 2BSvs, which is REDcert's counterpart from France, also a country with a lot of agricultural production.

On the other hand, with the notable exception of ISCC,[11] the share of MSI-run VCSs in the EU biofuels certification market is marginal. This means that the VCSs with the most stringent standards in terms of substantial environmental and social criteria, strong involvement of stakeholders and high requirements for the audit processes are also the least widespread.

These results are somewhat sobering as they seem to confirm the so-called "race-to-the-bottom" theory, which suggests that the cheapest supplier of a good, in this case: sustainability certificates for biofuels – which often implies the least ambitious one in terms of social, environmental and democratic standards – "wins" at the market-place and more ambitious schemes "lose" (Schleifer 2013). This "clear trade-off between standard quality and market share" (de Man and German 2017: 879), however, harbours the danger of privileging economic actors and undermining sustainable rural development. As Ponte (2014) shows, this seems to be already happening in the EU, which is very much in line with the results presented here, and the RSB has already reacted to this by restructuring its organisation accordingly (Fortin and

Richardson 2013). Regarding the effectiveness of the EU biofuels certification system, therefore, "the actual impact of certification on sustainability outcomes is", as de Man and German note, "at best limited and contingent, if not unknown" (2017: 880).

5 Conclusions

In this chapter, we have conceptualised and analysed the EU system of biofuels sustainability certification under the EU Renewable Energy Directive (EU RED) as a public–private governance arrangement (PPGA), in which the responsibility for safeguarding the sustainability of biofuels used in the EU is to a large extent given to private voluntary certification schemes (VCSs). The promise associated with PPGAs such as this one is that they are presumably able to combine the advantages of both private and public regulation, that is being flexible, fast and effective on the one hand, and legitimate, accountable and transparent on the other. Besides describing it, the aim of this chapter was to challenge the promise of PPGAs in terms of the combination of legitimacy and effectiveness regarding this PPGA.

While the system of biofuels certification under the RED seems to be working, see section 2, at least from a regulatory point of view (Schleifer 2013), we can see that the EU does not provide for the fulfilment of many of the criteria of democratic legitimacy. While criteria regarding input legitimacy such as stakeholder participation and respective intrascheme governance regulations are totally left out, only a few throughput legitimacy criteria concerning aspects such as transparency or accountability are addressed. In other words: the EU leaves it to the recognised schemes, to the market so to say, to take care of legitimacy issues. In section 3, however, we showed that most of the VCSs recognised by the EC do not go beyond the (marginal) mandatory EU requirements in this respect. In fact, only the multistakeholder schemes (MSIs) among them do so to a certain extent, while the other two-thirds of the recognised schemes do not do so at all.

A similar conclusion can be drawn regarding the socio-environmental effectiveness of the system. First, the sustainability criteria defined in the RED, which are limited to a few environmental criteria, are not sufficient to ensure the socio-environmental sustainability of the biofuels used in the EU. Even if these criteria were perfectly implemented by the recognised VCSs, their effectiveness would still be severely limited. It is further compromised by weaknesses in auditing guidelines as well as the specification of these criteria and room for interpretation regarding their implementation, which consequently differs among the schemes. Besides these issues regarding implementation, it is again almost only the MSIs among the recognised VCSs that go beyond the mandatory sustainability criteria under the RED, and include social and (additional) environmental criteria such as land rights, food security or water and soil protection, while the majority of the EC-recognised VCSs do not.

In addition to these already somewhat sobering results, a review of the success of the recognised VCSs at the European biofuels market shows that a "race-to-the-bottom" – or rather a "stuck-at-the-bottom" – is actually taking place in terms of a competition for the easiest and cheapest way of offering certification in the biofuels market (Ponte 2014). Thus, the VCSs that go beyond the mandatory EU requirements regarding sustainability and legitimacy – and therewith make certification more burdensome and expensive for economic operations along the biofuels supply chain – are not rewarded for this at the marketplace for biofuels sustainability certification, but rather punished for it. This can hardly be a surprise.

The aim of this analysis was therefore not to evaluate the schemes regarding their performance and to blame the ones performing poorly or the economic operations for not choosing the right schemes. Rather, the aim was to critically evaluate this PPGA against the promise of legitimacy and effectiveness that lies in this seemingly attractive governance model. Therefore, the main conclusion to be drawn from this case of a PPGA is that this kind of a governance arrangement does not necessarily fulfil this promise. In this case especially, sustainability certification seemed to be the silver bullet for keeping the biofuels strategy alive and at the same time tackling the heavily discussed sustainability problems. In fact, we can conclude that the EU biofuels sustainability certification PPGA, the way it is set up now, neither safeguards sustainability effectively nor does it conform to ideals of democratic legitimacy. Thus, it takes more to build up a PPGA that lives up to its promise of legitimacy and effectiveness than just recognising schemes that fulfil technical criteria.

Nonetheless, one should not be too harsh on the EC or the VCSs involved in this biofuels sustainability certification PPGA. It can be considered a form of field trial both for mandating sustainability criteria for agricultural products in general and for incorporating private certification schemes into the regulatory frameworks of the EU, or the state in general. Thus, even though it doesn't work perfectly at all, this trial should not be abandoned but allowed to continue and improve according to the aspects of effectiveness and legitimacy mentioned in this chapter. Eventually, this trial may then even become a role model useful for extending sustainability certification to all biomass-based products.

Notes

1 The European Union (EU) is a European supranational organisation with currently 28 Member States. The European Commission (EC) is the main administrative institution of the EU and its executive arm. Besides managing the day-to-day business of the EU, the EC acts as a cabinet government for the EU that is responsible for proposing legislation, adopting administrative acts and implementing decisions. EU legislation, which is binding for all Member States and often supersedes national legislation, is proposed by the EC and then adopted jointly by the EC, the European Parliament, which is elected by all EU citizens,

and the Council of the EU, in which the governments of the Member States are represented.

2 The other two options are the direct presentation of the information on the sustainability criteria by the biofuel producers and bi- or multilateral agreements for sustainability proofs. Because the former option is associated with immense time and effort for every single biomass producer and bi- or multilateral agreements were identified as tedious and inflexible, certification via EC-recognised VCSs quickly became the predominant pathway to proof compliance with the EU sustainability criteria (de Man and German 2017).

3 EC reference to approval.

4 ILUC stands for indirect land-use change.

5 The comitology process is a specific EU legislation procedure. Where the detailed interpretation of an EU directive is supposed to be exactly the same across all Member States, the Commission prepares a draft implementing decision, which is subsequently presented to an issue-specific committee of representatives of the Member States. They can give opinions on the matter of debate the Commission must take account of. The Commission retains the power to follow or neglect the committee opinion and can take the final decision.

6 The Biograce scheme is designed as a virtual calculation tool to determine greenhouse gas emissions released by a biomass-based product. Hence, users of this scheme have to get a further certification from another scheme that covers the remaining mandatory criteria, if they want to offer their biofuel on the European market. Due to its virtual character and limited applicability, we do not include this special scheme in our further discussion.

7 REDcert, 2BSvs, SQC, Gafta, TASCC, UFAS, AACS and Red Tractor are owned and run by (agricultural) industry associations, HVO (Nesté Oil) and KZR IniG are owned and run by private companies, and Better Biomass (NTA 8080) is a scheme owned and run by the Netherlands Standardization Institute NEN.

8 Especially ISCC, for example, can barely be called a "real" MSI. First, it didn't start out as a multistakeholder initiative, but goes back to a German state-initiated project, out of which the ISCC developed as a private initiative. However, essentials of the scheme were developed already back then without much multistakeholder participation, which has therefore been described as "shallow and cosmetic" (Ponte 2014: 268). Second, even though every natural or legal person can become a member of the ISCC Association, the main governing body of the scheme is dominated by industry actors. As of 22 November 2017, only three of the 92 ISCC members are civil society groups, while more than 80 are from industry. This is reflected in the ISCC Board, whose six members consist of two representatives of science, four representatives of industry and none of civil society.

9 These annual reports shall also include information on some aspects of throughput legitimacy like transparency and stakeholder involvement, especially regarding the consultation of indigenous and local communities. However, recognised VCSs only have to report on these issues, they don't have to meet any related criteria.

10 The reason for this is commonly seen in concerns within the European Commission that social standards would not be compatible with WTO covenants (Ackrill and Kay 2011).

11 The success of the ISCC at least seems to show, that a multistakeholder approach, extensive sustainability standards that go beyond the mandatory criteria defined in the RED, and market success can be combined. However, while the ISCC's approach might be successful, there are some specific reasons for the scheme's success that cast a cloud over it. Apart from the reasonable doubts whether the ISCC can be considered a "real" MSI (see section 3.1), there are weaknesses in ISCC's approach to stakeholder participation and grievance procedures (see

section 3.2), to social sustainability in terms of safeguarding land and resource rights, food security and local livelihood impacts which are only "minor musts" (see section 4.1), as well as questionable auditing and sanctioning noncompliance practices (see section 4.2) alongside a "lack of transparency in audit reports [that] also undoubtedly contribute to the standard's popularity" de Man and German 2017: 880). Thus, the success of the ISCC can hardly be considered a reliable counterexample to the "race-to-the-bottom" theory in voluntary sustainability certification.

References

Ackrill, R; Kay, A (2011) "EU biofuels sustainability standards and certification systems: How to seek WTO-compatibility", *Journal of Agricultural Economics* 62 (3), pp. 551–564.

Bäckstrand, K (2006) "Multi-stakeholder partnerships for sustainable development: Rethinking legitimacy, accountability and effectiveness", *European Environment* 16 (5), pp. 290–306.

Bäckstrand, K; Khan, J; Kronsell, A; Lövbrand, E (2010) "The promise of new modes of new modes of environmental governance", in Bäckstrand, K; Khan, J; Kronsell, A; Lövbrand, E (eds.), *Environmental Politics and Deliberative Governance: Examining the Promise of New Modes of Governance*, Cheltenham, Edward Elgar, pp. 3–27.

Bernstein, S; Cashore, B (2007) "Can non-state global governance be legitimate? An analytical framework", *Regulation and Governance* 1 (4), pp. 347–371.

Blaber-Wegg, T; Hodbod, J; Tomei, J (2015) "Incorporating equity into sustainability assessments of biofuels", *Current Opinion in Environmental Sustainability* 14, pp. 180–186.

BLE (2016) *Evaluations- und Erfahrungsbericht für das Jahr 2015: Biomassestrom-Nachhaltigkeitsverordnung, Biokraftstoff-Nachhaltigkeitsverordnung*, Bonn, Bundesanstalt für Landwirtschaft und Ernährung.

Cashore, B (2002) "Legitimacy and the privatization of environmental governance: How non-state market-driven (NSMD) governance systems gain rule-making authority", *Governance* 15 (4), pp. 503–529.

de Man, R; German, L (2017) "Certifying the sustainability of biofuels: Promise and reality", *Energy Policy* 109, pp. 871–883.

Dingwerth, K (2003) "Globale Politiknetzwerke und ihre demokratische Legitimation. Eine Analyse der Weltstaudammkommission", *ZIB Zeitschrift für Internationale Beziehungen* 10 (1), pp. 69–109.

Dingwerth, K (2007) *The New Transnationalism: Transnational Governance and Democratic Legitimacy*, Basingstoke, Palgrave Macmillan.

European Commission (2010) "Communication from the Commission on voluntary schemes and default values in the EU biofuels and bioliquids sustainability scheme", *OJ C* 160, pp. 1–7.

European Commission (2017a) *Renewable Energy Progress Report*, COM(2017) 57 final, Brussels.

European Commission (2017b) *Voluntary Schemes – Energy – European Commission*. URL: https://ec.europa.eu/energy/sites/ener/files/documents/voluntary_schemes_overview_dec17.pdf.

European Court of Auditors (2016) *The EU System for the Certification of Sustainable Biofuels*. Special Report No. 18, Luxembourg, Publications Office of the European Union.

European Union (2009) "Directive 2009/28/EC on the promotion of the use of energy from renewable sources", *OJ L* 140, pp. 16–62.

European Union (2015) "Directive (EU) 2015/1513 amending Directive 98/70/EC relating to the quality of petrol and diesel fuels and amending Directive 2009/28/EC on the promotion of the use of energy from renewable sources", *OJ L* 239, pp. 1–29.

FAO (2013) *Biofuels and the Sustainability Challenge: A Global Assessment of Sustainability Issues, Trends and Policies for Biofuels and Related Feedstocks*, Rome, Food and Agricultural Organization of the United Nations.

Fortin, E (2017) "Repoliticising multi-stakeholder standards processes: The Roundtable on Sustainable Biomaterials' standards and certification scheme", *Journal of Peasant Studies* 14 (5), pp. 1–20.

Fortin, E; Richardson, B (2013) "Certification schemes and the governance of land: Enforcing standards or enabling scrutiny?", *Globalizations* 10 (1), pp. 141–159.

Franco, J; Levidow, L; Fig, D; Goldfarb, L; Hönicke, M; Mendonça, ML (2010) "Assumptions in the European Union biofuels policy: Frictions with experiences in Germany, Brazil and Mozambique", *Journal of Peasant Studies* 37 (4), pp. 661–698.

German, L; Schoneveld, G (2012) "A review of social sustainability considerations among EU-approved voluntary schemes for biofuels, with implications for rural livelihoods", *Energy Policy* 51, pp. 765–778.

GIZ (2013) *Recognition of Private Certification Schemes for Public Regulation: Lessons Learned from the Renewable Energy Directive*, Bonn/Berlin, Gesellschaft für internationale Zusammenarbeit.

IEA Bioenergy (2013) *Task 1: Examining Sustainability Certification of Bioenergy*, Strategic Inter-Task Study (Tasks 40/43/38): Monitoring Sustainability Certification of Bioenergy, Paris, International Energy Agency.

IUCN NL (2014) *Betting on Best Quality. A Comparison of the Quality and Level of Assurance of Sustainability Standards for Biomass, Soy and Palmoil*, Amsterdam, International Union for Conservation of Nature – National Committee of The Netherlands.

Lin, J (2011) "Governing biofuels: A principal–agent analysis of the European Union biofuels certification regime and the clean development mechanism", *Journal of Environmental Law* 24 (1), pp. 43–73.

McDermott, M; Mahanty, S; Schreckenberg, K (2013) "Examining equity: A multidimensional framework for assessing equity in payments for ecosystem services", *Environmental Science & Policy* 33, pp. 416–427.

Meidinger, E (2007) "Beyond Westphalia: Competitive legalization in emerging transnational regulatory systems", in Brütsch, C; Lehmkuhl, D (eds.), *Law and Legalization in Transnational Relations*, London, Routledge, pp. 121–143.

Minderhoud, K (2010) *Round Table for Responsible Soy Association: Breaking Ground for Responsible Soy. An Institutional Response to Agricultural Expansion and Intensification in Argentina*, Master Thesis, Utrecht, Utrecht University.

Mitchell, D (2008) *A Note on Rising Food Prices*, Policy Research Working Paper 4682, Washington, D.C., The World Bank.

Mol, APJ (2010) "Environmental authorities and biofuel controversies", *Environmental Politics* 19 (1), pp. 61–79.

Müller, M (2007) "Überlegungen zur Legitimität von Umwelt- und Sozialstandards – best and worst practice für Biofuels", in econsense (ed.), *Klimafaktor Biokraftstoff. Experten zur Nachhaltigkeits-Zertifizierung*, Schriftenreihe zu Nachhaltigkeit und CSR – Band 1, Berlin, econsense, pp. 41–49.

NL Agency (2012) *Sustainability Certification for Biomass: Shaping the Biomass Market*, Utrecht, NL Agency (Ministry of Economic Affairs) – Netherlands Programmes for Sustainable Biomass.

NRDC (2014) *Biofuel Sustainability Performance Guidelines*, Washington, DC, National Resources Defense Council.

Partzsch, L (2011) "The legitimacy of biofuel certification", *Agriculture and Human Values* 28 (3), pp. 413–425.

Pattberg, P (2005) "The institutionalization of private governance: How business and nonprofit organizations agree on transnational rules", *Governance: An International Journal of Policy, Administration, and Institutions* 18 (4), pp. 589–610.

Pattberg, P; Stripple, J (2008) "Beyond the public and private divide: Remapping transnational climate governance in the 21st century", *International Environmental Agreements: Politics, Law and Economics* 8 (4), pp. 367–388.

Pilgrim, S; Harvey, M (2010) "Battles over biofuels in Europe: NGOs and the politics of markets", *Sociological Research Online* 15 (3), Article 4.

Ponte, S (2014) "'Roundtabling' sustainability: Lessons from the biofuel industry", *Geoforum* 54, pp. 261–271.

Ponte, S; Daugbjerg, C (2015) "Biofuel sustainability and the formation of transnational hybrid governance", *Environmental Politics* 24 (1), pp. 96–114.

Ruysschaert, D; Salles, D (2014) "Towards global voluntary standards: Questioning the effectiveness in attaining conservation goals. The case of the Roundtable on Sustainable Palm Oil (RSPO)", *Ecological Economics* 107 (Supplement C), pp. 438–446.

Schaller, S (2007) *The Democratic Legitimacy of Private Governance: An Analysis of the Ethical Trading Initiative*, INEF-Report 91/2007, Duisburg, Institute for Development and Peace, University of Duisburg Essen.

Schleifer, P (2013) "Orchestrating sustainability: The case of European Union biofuel governance", *Regulation and Governance* 7 (4), pp. 533–546.

Searchinger, T; Heimlich, R; Houghton, RA; Dong, F; Elobeid, A; Fabiosa, J; Tokgoz, S; Hayes, D; Yu, TH (2008) "Use of U.S. croplands for biofuels increases greenhouse gases through emissions from land-use change", *Science* 319 (5867), pp. 1238–1240.

Selbmann, K; Pforte, L (2016) "Evaluation of ecological criteria of biofuel certification in Germany", *Sustainability* 8 (9), p. 936.

Sneyd, A (2014) "When governance gets going: Certifying 'better cotton' and 'better sugarcane'", *Development and Change* 45 (2), pp. 231–256.

Steffek, J (2015) "The output legitimacy of international organizations and the global public interest", *International Theory* 7 (2), pp. 263–293.

Stupak, I; Joudrey, J; Smith, CT; Pelkmans, L; Chum, H; Cowie, A; Englund, O; Goh, CS; Junginger, M (2016) "A global survey of stakeholder views and experiences for systems needed to effectively and efficiently govern sustainability of bioenergy", *Wiley Interdisciplinary Reviews: Energy and Environment* 5 (1), pp. 89–118.

WWF Germany (2013) *Searching for Sustainability: Comparative Analysis of Certification Schemes for Biomass Used for the Production of Biofuels*, Berlin, World Wildlife Fund Germany.

Zürn, M (1998) *Regieren jenseits des Nationalstaates: Globalisierung und Denationalisierung als Chance*, Frankfurt am Main, Suhrkamp.

Zürn, M (2004) "Global governance and legitimacy problems", *Government and Opposition* 39 (2), pp. 260–287.

9 The path to credibility for the Marine Stewardship Council

Scott McIlveen, Riley Schnurr, Graeme Auld,
Shannon Arnold, Keith Flett, and Megan Bailey

Introduction

Globalized production and trade, brought into life in the last several decades through neoliberal reforms to multilateral and domestic institutions, have stretched and complicated the paths goods and services travel from sites of production to sites of consumption. Consumers are far removed from production activities, and governments are often unable to establish policies that offer adequate oversight of these complex production relations (Vermeulen and Seuring, 2009). These challenges have not gone unnoticed. Activists, non-governmental organizations, and corporations, alone and in partnership, have advanced diverse new governance arrangements across sectors of the global economy (forestry, garments, farming, seafood, energy) that seek to introduce ethical and environmental considerations via market-centered and market-friendly initiatives, such as eco-labels. As one particular type of label, eco-labels exist to provide assurance to a consumer on so-called credence qualities about a product, for example its origin or production method, and often highlight sustainability-related information that a consumer could be seeking.

The sustainable seafood movement was born out of such a label. Dolphin-safe or dolphin-friendly eco-labels emerged in the 1980s and quickly dominated the canned tuna market. Since then, a plethora of seafood eco-labels and buying guides have emerged, including Friend of the Sea, Monterey Bay Aquarium's Seafood Watch, the Marine Stewardship Council (MSC), Ocean-wise, Aquaculture Stewardship Council (ASC), Naturland, and Fair Trade USA, among others. But not all eco-labels are created equal. The gold standard in labeling conveys information that a fishery or a seafood product has been assessed by a third party against, and met, a certain standard. In these cases, the sustainability-related information indicated by the label meets a specific standard and is thus seen as credible and trustworthy (Vermeulen and Seuring, 2009). The problem therein is that products carrying an eco-label promoting sustainable production are assumed to be sustainable just by the presence of the logo.[1] But does credibility vary from eco-label to eco-label? The answer is almost indisputably yes (Thrane *et al.*, 2009; Van der Ven,

2015). Even the MSC, considered a leading program in seafood labelling (e.g. by its recognition and membership in the ISEAL Alliance and through its adherence to the Food and Agricultural Organization's Guidelines for Ecola-belling of Fish and Fish Products), has had its credibility questioned since the program's inception, with questions raised about whether labeled fisheries are truly sustainable and whether the standard is consistently applied across fisher-ies (see Bailey *et al.*, 2018 for a summary of some of these issues).

Credibility of eco-labels and third-party standards is important, as they are forms of private governance, and more specifically of nonstate market-driven governance (Cashore, 2002), and must gain (and maintain) authority to govern. Private authority is derived in part from credibility, or the extent to which a standard is seen as trustworthy. Credibility, for its part, is built through several key practices, such as scientific rigor, inclusiveness, transpar-ency, independence, and impact (see Miller and Bush, 2015) (Figure 9.1). In this chapter, we focus on the first four of these practices, ignoring for the time being impact that certification has on sustainability of the stocks them-selves. Rather we focus on the practices of the MSC, including scientific rigor and independence that goes into the assessment process, inclusiveness of the governance system, and value chain transparency through the Chain of Custody standard and ask: What can be done to improve the credibility of the "gold standard" for sustainable seafood products?

Our attention to the assessment process and governance system offers a summary of some key points raised by existing work examining the MSC. We offer greater depth of analysis to the final category, given this last issue has been less examined. We also provide the Forest Stewardship Council,

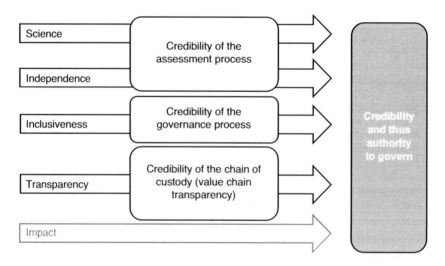

Figure 9.1 In this chapter we focus on four key practices for credibility: scientific rigor, independence, inclusiveness, and transparency. The fifth practice, impact, is not addressed here.

FSC, as an informal comparative certification throughout. While the MSC was developed and modeled after the FSC, things are done differently in the two certification processes. About one-third of the world's forests and one-fifth of the world's wild-capture fish are certified with some type of eco-label (Auld, 2014).

This analysis raises important and specific questions about how these trans-national and voluntary "governance" structures have allowed themselves (and have been allowed) to be authorities on such issues as multifaceted globalized production systems. We call to question presumptions about the practices of these "authorities" themselves, and discuss how and whether such organizations have the capacity to transparently act as authorities between consumers and producers. Furthermore, we highlight specific issues related to the supply chain itself, drawing awareness about methodological shortcomings that many eco-labels maintain and fail to address even after a "certification" has been given to a product.

Rise of the MSC

Amidst concerns of accelerating forest degradation around the globe, the FSC was established in 1993. Founded by a coalition of stakeholders consisting of timber industry, traders, and environmental and social non-governmental organizations, including the World Wide Fund for Nature (WWF), the FSC promotes timber use that not only helps protect the environment, but may be socially and economically beneficial to countries, communities, and people around the world. The FSC had humble beginnings, but it quickly consolidated many local initiatives to become a global standard and certification program in 1996 (Auld, 2014). Since the mid-1990s, the FSC has rapidly continued to grow in the global market: from approximately 200 chain of custody certificates in 1998, to over 33,000 in 2017. Today the FSC is seen as a leader in forest sustainability eco-certification, with certificates in 84 countries covering an area of almost 200 million hectares.

The FSC was created at a time when the sustainability of fisheries was being called into question, prompted by one of the world's most iconic fisheries collapses. In 1992, a moratorium was placed on cod fishing in the Northwest Atlantic, having devastating and lasting socioeconomic consequences for fishing communities up and down the coast of Canada. The world started taking notice of the impending fisheries crisis, and calls for sustainable fishing rang out. In answer to these calls, the MSC was founded in 1996 in a collaborative effort between WWF and global conglomerate Unilever. The goal was simple: to use their eco-label to reward sustainable fishing practices, and to influence the consumer to make sustainable choices when buying seafood. The MSC immediately had its eyes on global markets, taking only four years for its product to hit the shelves after its certification of Western Australian Rock Lobster and Thames Herring, making it the fastest eco-label to go global in its time (Auld, 2014). Despite some difficult beginnings, the MSC has since seen substantial growth; from 100 certified products in 2002 to 24,768 products in 2017. They now have certified fisheries in 34 countries and they account for roughly 15 per cent of global marine catch worldwide (MSC, 2017). The other largest global seafood eco-label, Friend of the Sea, has a wild-capture certified volume of almost ten million tonnes, or roughly 8.5 per cent of production, made up of about 2,000 product forms (Friend of the Sea, 2016).

Scientific rigor, independence, and the assessment process

In third-party certification programs, like the MSC, an independent body must assess the fishery against the standard. These bodies are called Conformity Assessment Bodies (CABs), and are accredited by ASI – Accreditation Services International. Independence of third-party certifications has been conceptualized in different ways, with Hatanaka and Busch (2008) differentiating between organizational and operational independence. We argue here that issues of opaqueness around interpretations and financial conflicts lead to questions about the operational independence of the MSC, i.e., the practices employed during the decision-making process.

In assessing against the standard, CABs are required to interpret the standard, doing so based on their own experiences, as well as, in the case of MSC, interpretation guidance. There are two sets of documents, the first being the MSC Certification Requirements document, which is an extensive guidance document that ensures CABs are interpreting the standard properly. These guidance notes are paired with each performance indicator (PI), are public, and are consulted on. This first set of guidance gives the impression of transparency in assessing the science and the fishery. But there is a second set of documents: private interpretations that CABs use, which are not public and not consulted on. These interpretations are a whole other set of documents that influence decisions but are not even known to exist by stakeholders. Interpretations are given at the request of CABs when they encounter a new case that Certification Requirements documents do not adequately address.

The main issue here becomes that the information that goes into the decision-making process (deciding whether a fishery should pass an assessment or not) is not forthcoming. This limits credibility of the process by altering the extent to which one can judge the scientific rigor of the assessment. It also sets out issues with the objections process. If any stakeholder wishes to object to an assessment, they must spend a painstaking amount of time going through every element of the standard, noting where they assume that the CABs interpretations of the standard are not adequate. But this must be done without knowing what guidance on interpretations the CAB had to begin with (WWF, 2016). For an example, the requirement to have harvest control rules (HCRs) for fish that are shared and managed under regional fisheries management organizations (RFMOs) led WWF to object to certified tuna in the Indian Ocean (IO) (WWF, 2016). Specifically, WWF noted "The facile conclusion is that the complete absence of HCRs means that no IO tuna fisheries should meet the MSC Fisheries Standard" (WWF, 2016). Yet CABs were interpreting that HCRs need not be present, but only committed to by the RFMO, but this interpretation was not communicated to stakeholders until late in the objections process.

Indeed, despite many formal objections to MSC fisheries certifications, where interested parties have reason to believe that certification should not be awarded, seldom are objections upheld (WWF, 2016; Christian *et al.*, 2013; Jacquet *et al.*, 2010). In most instances, when pushed to change, the MSC has responded with procedural shifts to its process, not substantive responses, such as redoing an assessment on the basis of a stakeholders' concerns (Gulbrandsen and Auld, 2016). That is to say, it has focused on procedural shifts to the process through which its norms are operationalized, but not necessary shifts to the norms themselves, norms that may associate credibility with effectiveness. Additionally, the recent withdrawal of NGOs from the objections process of "Echebastar tuna", because of what they assert are actions by an independent adjudicator that are in direct contravention of the MSC's own transparency principles (Ramsden, 2018), speaks to the combined complexity and intersections of scientific rigor, independence, the objections process, and credibility.

If CABs were seen as independent from the outcome of the assessment process, this may be an annoyance but one that stakeholders could live with. However, the lack of independence and impartiality of CABs has been called into question several times by scholars (Jacquet *et al.*, 2010; Christian *et al.*, 2013), stakeholders, and practitioners (WWF, 2016, 2018; Ramsden, 2018). A particular note of concern is that a fishery undergoing MSC assessment can select its own CAB. There is therefore reason to believe the fishery would choose a CAB that has a history of favorably assessing past fisheries, meaning that for a CAB to guarantee work in the future, it is incentivized to be generous in its assessment, likely leading to lenient interpretations of the standard (Jacquet *et al.*, 2010). Recent work suggests this may have been occurring early in the MSC's operations, when Moody (later to become Intertek), SCS, and SGS were the main CABs. For these early audits, Moody's average scores were higher than its main competitors. However, the picture is more complicated after 2007. In this period, the scores of these three CABs become more aligned, and an important new entrant – Food Certification/Acoura Marine – had even lower average scores, suggesting that competition is not the only factor driving the leniency/stringency of CABs' interpretations (see Auld and Renckens, 2018).

It is important to note that it is essential but difficult to balance the ability for CABs to use expert judgment, i.e., to be given room for interpretation, with the need to make decisions in the absence of peer-reviewed and comprehensive information (Leadbitter and Ward, 2007). As a point of comparison, the FSC publically lists all of its interpretations documents (FSC, 2017), a laudable approach. The FSC objections procedure, however, remains only as an option to object to the practices of an already certified product or company, compared to the ability to object to an initial passing assessment against the MSC standard.

Inclusiveness and the governance process

Governance provides structure to an organization, establishing rules for membership, decision-making, certification standards, and more (Auld, 2014). Good governance is essential in the corporate and NGO world and can ensure accountability, which is essential for the credibility of a third-party standard setter. Yet various authors have criticized the legitimacy of governance structures within eco-label organizations (Christian *et al.*, 2013; Miller and Bush, 2015). On the governance section of their website, the MSC notes that independence, transparency, impartiality, and multistakeholder consultation are central to upholding MSCs values.[2] We argue that the governance structure, while perhaps being more credible than other eco-labels in the fisheries sector (Miller and Bush, 2015), has been designed with less attention to inclusiveness in part because of the instrumental way it treats participation as a source of feedback and information rather than an end in and of itself (Auld and Gulbrandsen, 2010).

The MSC features a top-down governance model that consists of the Board of Trustees, the Technical Advisory Board (TAB), and the Stakeholder Council (SC). The Board of Trustees holds all decision-making power, meets four times a year, and consists of up to 15 members, each nominated for knowledge, and expertise – usually recognized by existing members of the Board. Their main role is to strategically direct MSC and make sure that it is meeting its charitable aims. The TAB works to advise the Board on MSC standards, develop methodologies pertaining to certification and accreditation, and review the progress of existing fisheries certifications. The SC works to ensure that the interests of the MSC's many stakeholders are represented in decision-making. The SC comprises up to 17 members from various backgrounds that are appointed by the Board of Trustees. The TAB is represented by one Board of Trustees member (TAB Chair), while the SC is represented by two Co-Chairs who receive a place on the Board of Trustees. The vertical governance structure of the MSC has been a source of contention over the years, particularly due to the concentration of decision-making power in such a small group of individuals (Rafols and Brander, 2005). As noted by Miller and Bush, transparency is a key feature of self-governing eco-labeling programs as it demonstrates their capacity to put into practice the standards and ideals that they embody. As compared to many other initiatives, the MSC does disclose a great deal of detailed information about the audit process fisheries undergo and requires stakeholder consultations during this process (Auld and Gulbrandsen, 2014).

Funding creates challenges: It raises the questions about independence and the ultimate source of decision-making power, thus influencing notions of credibility, and it is a problem that faces both public and private regulatory efforts in fisheries and beyond. The current discourse on MSC governance and credibility is linked to where the MSC derives the majority of its revenues. In the past, the MSC was floated by substantial philanthropic contributions. While this form of funding comes with its own set of issues, as these donations have subsided, revenue must come from increased logo licensing fees, meaning that the perverse incentives for positive assessments, discussed under lack of independence of the CABs, may not end with the CABs themselves. Logo license fees for the MSC amounted to about $20 million in 2017 (Maritime Executive, 2018). The MSC itself has now set its sights on 30 per cent of global fisheries certified or in assessment against its standard by 2030,[3] i.e., double the current proportion. This aggressive pursuit of global scale growth has been posited as evidence of a lack of independence from the outcome of assessments (Webster, 2016), and not just for MSC, but for third-party certification programs in general, due to the programs becoming pursuits of business (Hatanaka and Busch, 2008). Increased participation and inclusiveness by stakeholders in the governance process of the MSC is one way that independence and thus credibility may be strengthened.

The FSC has always been held up as a counterpoint to the MSC since the very first governance reviews of the organization (Auld, 2014). Unlike the MSC, governance in the FSC is bottom-up and consists of three decision-making bodies: the General Assembly (GA), the Board of Directors, and the Director General. The FSC is principally governed by the GA, a global collective body of stakeholders. Those seeking membership to the GA may either join as an organization member (forestry companies, environmental groups, retailers) or as an individual member (activists, students, academics). Members are broken into a tripartite of decision-making representing business, social, and environmental interests, respectively. Each of these chambers gets a third of the vote, and are further broken into northern and southern hemispheres with half of the vote, respectively, and with organizational members receiving greater weight than individual members. The GA meets once every three years and motions are passed when they receive majority support balancing across the chambers and their northern and southern members; in the interim decisions are made by e-mail. The Board of Directors' role is primarily to ensure that decisions made by the GA are implemented into FSC policy and standards. They are voted in for three-year terms, and are representative of the tripartite decision-making seen in the GA with four board members representing each sector (environmental, social, economic). Lastly, the Director General supervises all activity of the FSC and is appointed by the Board of Directors.

The horizontal power structure of the FSC has promoted wider stakeholder engagement in the program's decision-making and strategic decisions. Participation has also meant debates over the direction of the program have been open to many more stakeholders and this information has been more broadly disseminated. Still, membership does not capture all relevant stakeholders in the forest sector, and questions about the appropriate balance between economic, social, and environmental interests have been longstanding within the program. Nevertheless, the FSC model leads to questions about the narrow conception of inclusiveness that the MSC has adopted for its governance decisions, which has had ongoing implications for it credibility with particular stakeholders.

Output transparency: chain of custody

As mentioned in the introduction, issues of MSC assessment and governance have been well studied. This is not true in the case of seafood traceability, or so-called chain of custody (CoC). CoC is documentation showing the "transfer of ownership of seafood product every time the product changes ownership and/or is altered or repacked" (Future of Fish, 2015). Documenting CoC should include the list of all organizations that take ownership or control of a product during production, processing, shipping, and retail, and is intended to protect and monitor the integrity of claims, and improve transparency in the supply chain (ISEAL Alliance, 2016). In this way, the CoC can act as a data source for supply chains and a form of verification that the product carrying a label indeed originates from a certified source. Yet to do so, CoC, and seafood traceability more generally, needs to increase transparency in the supply chain (Bailey and Egels-Zanden, 2016). This has not been the case to date, with much of the information remaining proprietary and retained for audits, but not outwardly communicated. Nor is there a process by which actors within CoC certification can be publically scrutinized or objected to. We discuss the CoC certification below, and speculate on ways in which transparency could help improve credibility within the standard.

Within the context of globalized production systems, supply chains themselves are complicated, transnational, and diverse, with upstream actors (producers, processors, etc.) hidden from downstream ones (i.e., the consumer). The seafood supply chain is uniquely complicated, because fish is one of the only protein sources still wild-caught, and the perishability of seafood adds uncertainty and vulnerability dimensions to the product and its movement along the supply chain (Bailey *et al.*, 2016; Future of Fish, 2015). In a seminal literature review of supply chain management literature, Seuring and Müller (2008) note that the challenges most associated with "sustainable" supply chains are costs and complexity for all stakeholders involved, but that pressure to produce sustainable supply chains remains. CoC offers one way forward for helping to operationalize and realize sustainable supply chains.

There are essentially four approaches to a CoC certification: identity preservation, segregation, mass balance, and certificate trading (ISEAL Alliance, 2016). In identity preservation, certified and noncertified products are always kept separate, with certified products being traceable back to a single point of origin. Segregation, which is the MSC CoC model, ensures that the certified product is kept separate, but permits mixing of certified products from different lots, batches, or consignments. Mass balance models are those that the FSC subscribes to, which allow for blending of certified and noncertified products, so long as the percentages of each are labeled. Finally, in certificate trading, certified material is completely decoupled from sustainability data.

In a segregation model, the certified product must remain completely separate from the noncertified product and, often in spite of the increased costs and effort needed for a segregated approach, producers and consumers benefit from a heightened guarantee of sustainability (Howe, 2005). The MSC, maintaining its position as the leader in certifiably sustainable seafood, introduced its first CoC Standard in August of 2000. Since then, it has undergone two revisions in 2005 and 2011, and most recently a major overhaul in 2015 (MSC, 2015). There are five principles to the MSC CoC scheme:

1   purchasing from a certified supplier;
2   certified products are identifiable;
3   certified products are segregated;
4   certified products are traceable and volumes are recorded;
5   and the organization has a management system.

Yet despite these principles, or in fact because of them, significant issues with supply chain practices have been raised by a recent campaign called "Off the Hook".[4] This campaign focused specifically on purse seine skipjack tuna as the source of its issues, but the practice of "compartmentalization", which we describe below, exists in other MSC fisheries. Here we review issues forwarded by On the Hook as a means of providing evidence for how shortcomings in the transparency of the MSC CoC is misleading consumers.

The Western and Central Pacific Ocean (WCPO) skipjack tuna fishery is one of the world's biggest, with much of the tuna caught there carrying the MSC label. The purse seine fishery in the WCPO covers the waters of eight island nations, including Micronesia, the Marshall Islands, Papua New Guinea, and the Solomon Islands. Under the Nauru Agreement, these nations, usually referred to as the Parties to the Nauru Agreement (PNA),[5] collectively control access to about one-quarter of the world's tuna supply. Fishermen use nets to catch free-swimming adult tuna and earn MSC certification for their catch. But these same fishermen can also use fish aggregating devices (FADs) – instruments that attract all kinds of marine life, including adult tuna, juvenile tuna, and hundreds of species of sharks, turtles, and other fish – to net their catch. Fishing on FADs is faster and less costly, but these devices are associated with high levels of bycatch, one of the main sustainability concerns in many fisheries, and something that should be dealt with under the MSC's Principle 2. Fishing on FADs does not currently earn MSC certification in the WCPO, but under normal operations, fishermen use both methods.

The result is that the same boats fishing "sustainable" MSC tuna may also use unsustainable methods to catch fish from the same stock of tuna on the same day. So while the segregation CoC model means that sustainable and unsustainable fish are kept separate, which is a good thing, certifying only one part of a company's practices while essentially ignoring their other part is antithetical to the "best environmental choice" in seafood. The On the Hook coalition, which was formed in August 2017, has argued that the CoC makes it possible to essentially reward fishermen for their sustainable catch, while allowing them to fish unsustainably, duping consumers into supporting companies that take part in bad behavior. Essentially lack of transparency in the CoC, which has a good method of separation, essentially obscures this "mixing" of fishing practices for the consumers.

This is possible due to "compartmentalization", which allows one portion of a fishing operation to be certified against the standard, as long as it is separated on board the vessel from the other portion of the operation, which would not be considered sustainable under the MSC standard. This is supposed to provide assurance to consumers that they are making a sustainable choice. Yet the negative environmental impacts connected to FAD fishing operations should surely also be considered in an MSC assessment. Currently, this does not happen. As such, a fleet using both methods can be part of a higher value premium market and earn financial security from the higher volume, yet unsustainable, fishery. If purse-seining tuna vessels need to subsidize their sustainable fishing with unsustainable practices, then MSC certification has not provided the incentive it set out to.

In January 2018, the MSC approved a modification of its standard, requiring that *all* fishing activities on a target stock in a single trip must be MSC certified in order to carry the MSC logo on the final product. The result was that any certified unit of assessment in the future would have to consider all forms of fishing, the good, the bad, and the ugly. A three-year transition phase was agreed to, providing a potential opportunity for increased output transparency through CoC improvements. However, in August 2018, the MSC reversed that decision, citing that industry and NGO groups felt that the changes were untenable or did not resolve the larger sustainability issues (Mereghetti, 2018). While the opportunity to improve CoC transparency is thus still open, it is unclear at present what changes, if any, will surface.

An additional potential issue with the MSC CoC is related to the fact that a supply chain actor is "eligible" for an MSC CoC certificate if the actor already handles certified products. That is to say, that if you have already been CoC certified for product x, you are automatically certified for product y. Issues associated with exports and re-imports of the same fish (although in transformed product) cause a headache for the MSC CoC. For example, a product that is MSC certified upon being caught, but is exported to China for processing and re-imported for the Canadian consumer market either retains its MSC certification, or upon re-import is labeled neither Canadian nor certified (assuming the Chinese processor is not CoC certified) (Govender *et al.*, 2016). So while certification can improve market value or open different markets, there is no guarantee for the producer that his/her product will end up with the MSC label at the downstream end. The fishery certification and CoC certifications are two separate processes, and most often, the fishery client is not the same as the processor or CoC client. Fishers and fleets can still claim the MSC logo to negotiate higher selling prices, but they have no power over the CoC process and what labeling ends up on the final product.

As a comparison, we turn to FSC, noting the FSC employs a very different CoC form, with its own set of challenges. The CoC standards for FSC immediately and directly impact the final certification. For instance, should certified and noncertified materials mix, an appropriate FSC logo indicates as such to the consumer, so a product does not lose its label, its label reflects the likely contribution of sustainable and nonsustainable inputs in the final product. In the FSC system, a consumer is provided information that highlights a distinct CoC reality, but can continue to make a more transparent and accurate consumer choice based on more detailed information. In the case of MSC, a consumer is shown a label that rightly suggests the product is sustainable, but in reality production of that product may have significant sustainability failures associated with the boat and businesses that caught the fish (as in the On the Hook campaign).

A lack of seafood supply chain transparency has been posited as a fisheries sustainability issue (Iles, 2007; Bailey and Egels-Zanden, 2016), and is something that CoC and seafood traceability could remedy (Future of Fish, 2015; Bailey *et al.*, 2016). And yet, a SeaChoice report on Canadian seafood supply chains highlights transparency recommendations for improving seafood sustainability, addressing these recommendations towards government inaction and policy shortfalls, rather than standard holders themselves (Govender *et al.*, 2016). We do not mean to argue that the FSC CoC system is perfect. There are still many issues with actually tracking, or proving, that product being moved throughout the chain is in fact the certified product it claims to be, or otherwise that certified product in fact met all its sustainability requirements (Poynton, 2013). That is, validation and verification are always a challenge. Interestingly, MSC is testing new supply chain traceability programs that will allow for FSC-style mass balance type CoC to be layered onto their current CoC model, and which prioritizes transparency for risk mitigation (MSC, n.d.).

There also remain issues of certification label fraud, where unauthorized parties use labels without having achieved the accreditation or misuse its application or relevance, intentionally or not (IISD, 2013). Indeed, both fish and forest resource production chains are complex, convoluted, and diverse in supply chain actor interactions. What becomes critical for certification schemes that attempt to tackle these issues under the intent of "sustainability" for consumers is the quality and accountability of information for consumers. This information is where the basis for decisions between sustainable or unsustainable are made, and why supply chain transparency remains important for credibility.

Conclusion

Credibility remains a moving target for the MSC, but is essential to be maintained if the eco-label hopes to keep its authority to govern seafood sustainability. Credibility can be gained and maintained through several key practices, four of which we summarize in this chapter: scientific rigor, independence, inclusiveness, and transparency. We suggest that if MSC is to improve its credibility, a much greater attention to these key practices is required. Specifically, improvements to the assessment process linked with public disclosure of interpretations and objections documents can help illustrate independence, attention to inclusiveness and stakeholder engagement in governance can improve the credibility of decision-making, and increased value chain transparency through the CoC Standard can better link consumers with producing companies, and enable consumers to make more informed choices. Additionally, alternative models to get around the incentives for payment for positive assessments, which further put into question the independence of the CABs in the first place, is also something that could be considered. A lack of independence in the MSC itself, insofar as positive assessments lead to more certified products, which lead to higher MSC revenues, as well as a highly vertical decision-making governance structure, leads to limitations in the extent to which credibility can be maintained. With the earlier-mentioned MSC goal of certifying 30 per cent of capture fisheries production by 2030, ensuring credibility is of paramount importance. Otherwise, the credibility of the sustainable seafood movement itself could be at risk, if it isn't already.

Notes

1 An Alaskan fishermen once made the astute observation to Bailey that with the MSC, the signifier has come to replace the thing being signified. That is to say, *a là* Saussure, that the MSC label itself has come to not just be the signifier of sustainability, but to be sustainability itself.
2 www.msc.org/about-the-msc/our-governance.
3 http://20-years-deep-dives.msc.org/.
4 A larger exposition can be read in The Conversation: https://theconversation.com/heres-why-your-sustainable-tuna-is-also-unsustainable-83560.
5 Currently, MSC skipjack tuna are caught under the brand Pacifical, and there is recent evidence to suggest that Papua New Guinea may be leaving the company (Mereghetti and Seaman, 2018).

References

Auld, G. 2014. *Constructing Private Governance: The Rise and Evolution of Forest, Coffee, and Fisheries Certification.* New Haven, CT: Yale University Press.

Auld, G., and Gulbrandsen, L.H. 2010. Transparency in nonstate certification: consequences for accountability and legitimacy. *Global Environmental Politics* 10(3): 97–119.

Auld, G., and Gulbrandsen, L.H. 2014. Learning through disclosure: the evolving importance of transparency for nonstate certification. In A. Gupta and M. Mason (eds) *Transparency in Global Environmental Governance: Critical Perspectives*, pp. 271–296. Cambridge, MA: MIT Press.

Auld, G., and Renckens, S. 2018. Micro-level interactions in the compliance processes of transnational private governance. W. UBC Community and Partner Publications. June 30. doi:http://dx.doi.org/10.14288/1.0368847.

Bailey, M., and Egels-Zanden, N. 2016. Transparency and traceability for just seafood systems. *Solutions* 7(4): 66–73.

Bailey, M., Bush, S.R., Miller, A., and Kochen, M. 2016. The role of traceability in transforming seafood governance in the global South. *Current Opinion in Environmental Sustainability* 18: 25–32.

Bailey, M., Packer, H., Schiller, L., Tlusty, M., and Swartz, W. 2018. The role of Corporate Social Responsibility in creating a seussian world of seafood sustainability. *Fish and Fisheries*. doi.org/10.1111/faf.12289.

Cashore, B. 2002. Legitimacy and the privatization of environmental governance: how non-state market-driven (NSMD) governance systems gain rule-making authority. *Governance* 15(4): 503–529. https://doi.org/10.1111/1468-0491.00199.

Christian, C., Ainley, D., Bailey, M., Dayton, P., Hocevar, J., LeVine, M., … Jacquet, J. 2013. A review of formal objections to Marine Stewardship Council fisheries certifications. *Biological Conservation* 161: 10–17.

Forest Stewardship Council. 2017. *Interpretations of the Normative Framework*. Forest Stewardship Council, Bonn, Germany.

Friend of the Sea. 2016. *Annual Report*. www.friendofthesea.org/public/page/fosfoe_annual_report_2016_web.pdf.

Future of Fish. 2015. *Making Sense of Wild Seafood Supply Chains*. The Nature Conservancy.

Govender, R., Hayne, K., Fuller, S.D., and Wallace, S. 2016. *Taking Stock: Sustainable Seafood in Canadian Markets*. Vancouver/Halifax: SeaChoice.

Gulbrandsen, L.H., and Auld, G. 2016. Contested accountability logics in evolving nonstate certification for fisheries sustainability. *Global Environmental Politics* 16(2): 42–60.

Hatanaka, M., and Busch, L. 2008. Third-party certification in the global agrifood system: an objective or socially mediated governance mechanism? *Sociologia Ruralis* 48: 73–91. doi:10.1111/j.1467-9523.2008.00453.x.

Howe, J. (Ed.). (2005, May 20). Chain-of-custody certification: what is it, why do it, and how? Dovetail Partners Inc.

Iles, A. 2007. Making the seafood industry more sustainable: creating production chain transparency and accountability. *Journal of Cleaner Production* 15(6): 577–589.

International Institute for Sustainable Development [IISD]. 2013. Challenges to eco-labeling. www.iisd.org/business/markets/Eco_label_challenges.aspx.

ISEAL Alliance. 2016. *Chain of Custody Models and Definitions*. ISEAL Alliance.

Jacquet, J., Pauly, D., Ainley, D., Holt, S., Dayton, P., and Jackson, J. 2010. Seafood stewardship in crisis. *Nature* 467: 28–29.

Leadbitter, D. and Ward, T.J. 2007. An evaluation of systems for the integrated assessment of capture fisheries. *Marine Policy* 31(4): 458–469. doi.org/10.1016/j.marpol.2006.12.008.

Maritime Executive. 2018. WWF: sustainable seafood label MSC needs reform. Marine Executive. www.maritime-executive.com/article/wwf-top-sustainable-seafood-label-needs-reform.

Marine Stewardship Council. 2015. *MSC Chain of Custody Standard: Default Version* (Version 4.0). Marine Stewardship Council, London.

Marine Stewardship Council. 2017. *Sustainable Seafood: The First 20 Years.* Retrieved December 8 from http://20-years.msc.org/.

Marine Stewardship Council. (n.d.). The MSC's response to On the Hook campaign announcement. Marine Stewardship Council.

Mereghetti, M. 2018. MSC to come up with new proposal, after U-turn on "unit of assessment" review. Undercurrent News. www.undercurrentnews.com/2018/08/28/msc-to-come-up-with-new-proposal-after-u-turn-on-unit-of-assessment-review/.

Mereghetti, M., and Seaman, T. 2018. Trouble in MSC tuna "paradise" as PNG seeks to break from Pacifical. Undercurrent News. www.undercurrentnews.com/2018/09/14/trouble-in-msc-tuna-paradise-as-png-seeks-to-break-from-pacifical/.

Miller, A.M.M., and Bush, S.R. 2015. Authority without credibility? Competition and conflict between ecolabels in tuna fisheries. *Journal of Cleaner Production* 107(Suppl. C): 137–145. https://doi.org/10.1016/j.jclepro.2014.02.047.

On the Hook. (n.d.). *On the Hook.* https://onthehook.org.uk.

Poynton, S. (2013, July 10). Chain of custody nonsense from FSC and PEFC: protecting income streams rather than the world's forests. *Mongabay.*

Rafols, X.P., and Brander, L. 2005. The stewardship council model: a comparison of the FSC and MSC. *ILSA Journal of International and Comparative Law* 11(3): 637–848.

Ramsden, N. 2018. Pole-and-line foundation, Shark Project pull out of Echebastar MSC process, will file complaint. Undercurrent News. www.undercurrentnews.com/2018/09/11/pole-and-line-foundation-shark-project-pull-out-of-echebastar-msc-process-will-file-complaint/.

Seuring, S., and Müller, M. 2008. From a literature review to a conceptual framework for sustainable supply chain management. *Journal of Cleaner Production* 16(15): 1699–1710. https://doi.org/10.1016/j.jclepro.2008.04.020.

Thrane, M., Ziegler, F., and Sonesson, U. 2009. Eco-labelling of wild-caught seafood products. *Journal of Cleaner Production* 17(3): 416–423.

Van der Ven, H. 2015. Correlates of rigorous and credible transnational governance: a cross-sectoral analysis of best practice compliance in eco-labeling. *Regulation and Governance,* 9(3): 276–293.

Vermeulen, W.J.V. and Seuring, S. 2009. Sustainability through the market: the impacts of sustainable supply chain management: introduction. *Sustainable Development* 17: 269–273.

Webster, B. 2016. Fishing's blue tick benchmark tainted by "conflict of interest". *The Times.* www.thetimes.co.uk/article/fishings-blue-tick-benchmark-tainted-by-conflict-of-interest-3qrsr5w0k.

WWF. 2016. *WWF Retrospective on Indian Ocean Tuna Harvest Control Rules.* WWF Indian Ocean Tuna Report.

WWF. 2018. WWF Statement on MSC certification of Spanish Purse Seine "Echebastar" Fishery in the Indian Ocean. http://wwf.panda.org/wwf_news/press_releases/?337217/WWF-Statement-on-MSC-certification-of-Spanish-Purse-Seine-Echebastar-Fishery-in-the-Indian-Ocean.

Part V

Industry and country specific primary research, evaluation and recommendations

10 Interoperability of mineral sustainability initiatives

A case study of the Responsible Jewellery Council (RJC) and the Alliance for Responsible Mining (ARM)

Renzo Mori Junior, Kathryn Sturman and Jean-Pierre Imbrogiano

Introduction

Since the Global Mining Initiative launched in 1998, the agenda for environmental and social responsibility in mining has grown rapidly in line with the movement for more sustainable business practices worldwide. In this context, sustainability initiatives such as certification schemes, frameworks and standards have grown in scope and specificity to verify compliance with these more sustainable business practices. As such initiatives have proliferated, stakeholders have raised concerns about duplication of efforts and voiced the need for combined effectiveness.

The success of an initiative is enhanced if it is able to engage, recognise and collaborate with other standards, certification schemes, guidelines, frameworks and legal provisions. Interoperability of sustainability initiatives has the potential to reduce costs and can amplify the reach and outcomes achieved by individual initiatives, as they exchange knowledge and best practices.

This case study addresses how to achieve better application of mining and metals sustainability initiatives through fostering interoperability between the Responsible Jewellery Council (RJC), which works mainly with organisations throughout the jewellery supply chain for diamonds, gold and platinum group metals, and the Alliance for Responsible Mining (ARM) standard: Fairmined, which works mainly with gold Artisanal Small-scale Mining (ASM). Aligning the requirements of the initiatives can lower the compliance costs of participation, particularly in developing countries. Identifying the similarities and differences between these initiatives may also facilitate comparison by procurers of metals and consumers of goods such as jewellery, electronic devices and automobiles. Interoperability may provide greater efficiency across all of these initiatives, leveraging more positive effects from each.

What is interoperability?

In simple terms, interoperability is the degree to which diverse systems, organisations and individuals are able to work together to achieve a common goal (Ide and Pustejovsky, 2010). Interoperability is considered an important business strategy that can bring benefits in terms of knowledge sharing, collaboration and integration. In addition, it is important for organisations to maintain business in a globalised and networked market, through which they need to use approaches and techniques to perform better and faster in a highly competitive environment (Dassisti *et al.*, 2013). Enterprise interoperability is considered a high-impact productivity factor affecting the quality, yield time, costs of transactions within the private and public sectors (Jardim-Goncalves *et al.*, 2012). In the sustainability initiatives arena, interoperability has the potential to reduce costs, increase performance, amplify outcomes, minimise overlaps and unproductive information flow, and exchange knowledge and practices (Barry *et al.* 2012; Brockmyer and Fox, 2015; ISEAL Alliance, 2013; Main *et al.*, 2014; Stark and Levin, 2011; WWF, 2013).

According to Vlassenroot (Vlassenroot and Van Bockstael, 2008), interoperability maximises synergies, reduces costs and bureaucracy, and increases legitimacy and reach. Furthermore, in avoiding duplication and overlapping among initiatives, interoperability can improve stakeholders' understanding on the credibility of such initiatives in the market place and their influence. Interoperability has been analysed across different areas such as information systems, communication, technology, Corporate Social Responsibility and business. Each area has analysed the concept of interoperability and its practical significance using different approaches. As a result, in practice it is a multifaceted concept reflecting different points of view (Dassisti *et al.*, 2013; Day, 2004; Kasunic, 2001; Mori Junior *et al.*, 2016; Yahia *et al.*, 2012).

Chen *et al.* (2008) argue that the concept of interoperability itself is still confusing and has different definitions in different sectors and domains. In the same vein, Ford *et al.* (2007) have identified 34 distinct definitions of interoperability used in research papers, standards and government documents. Chen and Doumeingts (2003) argued that interoperability implies support of communication and transactions between different organisations that must be based on shared business references. Similarly, Vernadat (2007) states that interoperability refers to the ability of a system or process to use information and/or functionality of another system or process by adhering to common standards. INSPIRE (2011) regards interoperability as the ability for people to interact with each other, between organisations and across domains of influence and geographical boundaries, to achieve a goal or objective, within accepted limits of performance.

We applied a broad definition of the interoperability concept when assessing sustainability initiatives in mining (Mori Junior *et al.*, 2016). This study highlighted that interoperability is not only the capacity of initiatives to recognise or reference other initiatives, it is also their capacity to interact with governments, industry sectors and civil society organisations to further their reach and outcomes. In this case study our analyses have not fully addressed the effects of interoperability in improving the capacity of initiatives to interact with governments, industry sectors and civil society organisations. Rather, it points out that interoperability processes can encourage and improve the capacity of initiatives to interact with governments, industry sectors and civil society organisations.

A working concept of interoperability for the purposes of this analysis is drawn from Dassisti *et al*. (2013). These authors think of interoperability as being on a continuum between the concepts of integration and compatibility. Integration is more than interoperability. It involves a degree of functional dependence between two systems and less flexibility between them. Compatibility is less than interoperability, where systems do not interfere with each other's functioning, but are able to work side by side (for example, by managing different parts of a supply chain). Within the range between compatibility and integration, we would place, 'collaboration', 'harmonisation', 'cross-recognition', 'complementarity' and 'shared process'. 'Collaboration' describes the activity of stakeholders from different sustainability initiatives working together towards common goals. 'Harmonisation' refers to the alignment of texts to adopt similar language across different sustainability initiatives, eliminating major differences and creating common minimum requirements. 'Cross-referencing' is when a sustainability initiative refers to and accepts provisions of another initiative as its own. 'Complementarity' refers to the extent to which activities of initiatives interacting fit with each other in prescribed ways (Tracey, 1994). 'Shared process' is the mechanism by which sustainability initiatives are able to operate jointly, for example, by joint auditing and other assurance processes.

Case study RJC and ARM collaborative project

This case study investigates whether there are substantial reasons for sustainability initiatives to invest in interoperability projects. This is with the idea that they might deliver positive outcomes, not only for the initiatives involved but also to their main stakeholders, and ultimately for more responsible mining practices. It focuses on a collaborative project between the RJC and the ARM standard: Fairmined. This project aims not only to enhance relationships between ASM, where ARM has an important presence, and large-scale mining, where RJC has an important presence, but also reducing overlap situations where both initiatives address the same part of the supply chain. For example, gold refiners, traders, manufactures and retailers. There are overlapping situations where organisations are certified by both initiatives at the same time.

The RJC and ARM signed a first Memorandum of Understanding (MoU) in November 2011. This first MoU aimed to: (1) explore collaboration opportunities to advance their shared objectives of improving social, environmental and labour practices, good governance and the implementation of ecosystem restoration practices in ASM; (2) enhance relationships between large-scale and ASM; and (3) increase market access for jewellery raw materials produced by ASM communities. This MoU was revised in February 2016, as a result 'facilitating the participation of the jewellery industry in both certification systems' was included as an additional shared objective.

Method

This case study draws on 12 semistructured interviews conducted in 2016. The interviews targeted RJC and Fairmined representatives, RJC and Fairmined accredited auditors and RJC and Fairmined members involved in this interoperability project. In addition, secondary data complemented this primary data to put the case study in context and refine the analysis. Participants were encouraged to provide their perceptions and opinions on the drivers for, benefits and challenges of, and lessons learnt from the Fairmined and RJC collaborative project.

Findings

Drivers for collaboration

Three main drivers for collaboration were observed: similarity between systems and goals, increased reach and reduced audit overlapping (subsequently reduced audit fatigue and costs). With similarity identified as the key driver for this project. The RJC and ARM share similar goals, operate within the same sector, have common members, and most of their stakeholders are the same. According to some of the participants, because of these similarities, a collaboration project was considered a natural step towards a more efficient approach to fostering responsible practices in the sector. For instance, one of the participants stated:

> We have the same goals, we are operating in the same sector, we have the same clients and many of our stakeholders are the same. Most of the processes we have are similar. So why not work together?
>
> (Participant 3, a certification scheme representative)

Increased reach was also one of the drivers for the RJC and ARM–Fairmined interoperability project. Some of the participants commented that both Fairmined and the RJC could be seen as complementary systems, and combining efforts could help them to increase reach throughout the supply chain. Working together, RJC and Fairmined can combine efforts and expertise in different parts of the supply chain to better support claims for responsibly sourced jewellery materials produced, processed and traded. In this context, ARM can use its expertise and focus on its core business, which is ASM, while the RJC can use its expertise and focus on the downstream industries.

Recognising each other's expertise and focus permits ARM and the RJC to be more effective. Also, such an approach combined with a set of requirements, enables verification of the eligibility and traceability of materials from mine to retail. On this topic three participants commented:

> We are complementary systems, and working together we can improve our reach.
>
> (Participant 1, a certification scheme representative)

> If there is another scheme doing a good job in another part of the supply chain, why not try to work together and improve outcomes?
>
> (Participant 4, a certification scheme representative)

> This project is recognition that Fairmined addresses a certain sector of the supply chain that is difficult for us to reach on our own.
>
> (Participant 7, a certification scheme representative)

Reduced audit overlapping was also an important driver for collaboration. According to some of the participants, there is general annoyance from different stakeholders – especially certified and authorised companies – that audit overlapping causes audit fatigue and results in unnecessary audit costs. The lack of harmonisation of the assurance processes used by different initiatives results in duplication of efforts and high costs of compliance, particularly when there are different schemes with similar standards addressing the same topics in the same part of the supply chain. For example, several participants highlighted:

> We are hearing so much pushback on this audit fatigue. We get so many complaints from our clients that they are just tired of having to have an audit body in there, day-in day-out. And there is very little synergy between all these audits. They say auditors come and ask the same questions and we have to pay twice.
>
> (Participant 8, an auditor)

> We recognise this burden of overlapping and we know that companies are also complaining about it.
>
> (Participant 7, a certification scheme representative)

> There is pressure from the industry to reduce overlapping. The market wants more collaboration.
>
> (Participant 3, a certification scheme representative)

Benefits

Leadership, access to market, cost reduction and internal processes and systems improvement were considered the key benefits of this interoperability project.

Leadership

In a scenario where the number of sustainability initiatives to address responsible practices is increasing, overlap situations among different initiatives are growing, and stakeholders are pressuring for more collaboration and interoperability. RJC and ARM are pioneers in addressing these topics which can easily establish them as leadership organisations. This RJC–ARM–Fairmined interoperability project could be used as a benchmark for initiatives that are facing the same challenges and are receiving the same pressure from their stakeholders to improve collaboration and to reduce overlap. Regarding this matter, one participant mentioned:

> Actually, politically it [the RJC and Fairmined collaboration project] is a huge benefit. It helps to place us as a leadership organisation.
> (Participant 7, a certification scheme representative)

Access to market

Access to market was another benefit mentioned by participants. Some of the participants pointed out that the RJC–ARM–Fairmined interoperability project could improve market access for certified gold. Such a situation is particularly beneficial for Fairmined, which can benefit from the vast membership of RJC. Upstream members are potential buyers of Fairmined gold. Regardless of their decision to engage at the moment with Fairmined gold or other certified gold initiatives, these RJC members can see that within the RJC–ARM–Fairmined interoperability project, certified gold and ASM could play an important role in their responsible sourcing strategies. This project can therefore be a great tool to spread the message of best practice in responsible sourcing, which can include Fairmined gold.

Cost reduction

Cost reduction was another important benefit mentioned by participants. The divergent assurance requirements of different initiatives operating in the same context increase the costs of compliance. Companies seeking certifications or keeping their certifications valid have to periodically contract third-party auditors to attest their compliance against certification schemes' requirements.

It is important to highlight that audit processes incur direct costs (audit fees and audit travel expenses) and indirect costs, such as the employees' time allocated to provide information for the audit teams. In such a situation, although there are similarities between both standards, and the RJC recognises the Fairmined standard as equivalent to its Code of Practices, companies have had to contract two different audit teams to attest compliance with the RJC Chain of Custody (CoC) and Fairmined standards. Regarding this matter, one of the participants stated:

> As a company it is not good when you have to allocate people to provide information for auditors and then another audit process starts asking most of the same things again and you have to allocate people's time to respond again.
>
> (Participant 5, a certified company representative)

To solve this problem of duplicity and reduce audit costs, the RJC and ARM launched the pilot 'Fairmined and RJC audit project'. This project aims to reduce the audit burden without compromising the quality and rigour of the audit process. To do so, three main activities were carried out: (1) RJC and Fairmined auditors' accreditation processes were aligned in order to increase the number of audit service providers accredited to conduct both assurance processes; (2) the RJC's and Fairmined audit workbooks and audit procedures were aligned to enhance usability and streamline assessment processes; and (3) the RJC's CoC and Fairmined standards were reviewed in order to identify similarities and to inform auditors about where and what these similarities are.

According to some of the participants interviewed, this pilot combined audit project presented important positive outcomes. The combined audit approach reduces the audit burden in terms of time and costs. In one participant's words:

> The cost savings with a combined audit are significant. Additional time on-site means we have to charge more, because we have to pay the auditor to be there; when combining two audits the overall time needed is less, so the price of the audit itself is less. There is also the travel costs – some of the facilities are in unusual locations, which means we have to bring auditors to that specific location. So if we need to come at two different times the site will need to pay for that travel cost twice. The travel costs can be substantial.
>
> (Participant 8, an audit company representative)

When asked to estimate the cost reduction, this participant pointed out:

> I would estimate a reduction of something between 20 per cent and 50 per cent of the audit time when combining audits. On top of that you have the travel costs reduced by half.
>
> (Participant 8, an audit company representative)

Internal processes and systems improvement

Improvement of internal processes and systems was also considered an important benefit by some of the participants. It was stated that the interoperability project between the RJC and ARM results in internal controls and systems improvement through a learning process facilitated by exchange of information and practices. Such a relationship helps both organisations improve their systems and practices as they can learn from each other's experiences. In this regard Participant 1, Participant 3 and Participant 7 added:

> We have learned from them and I am sure they have learned from us too.
>
> (Participant 1, a certification scheme representative)

> Learning and innovation are very important. When you work together you can see how things have been done in other organisations and you learn. You can see innovation opportunities and you can improve your processes.
>
> (Participant 3, a certification scheme representative)

> Such a relationship helps inform and strengthen our own organisation and systems. We are better aware of the issues they are facing and are grappling with. We have an intimate knowledge of the other certification scheme and we exchange information. All of this helps us as an organisation to be in a stronger position.
>
> (Participant 7, a certification scheme representative)

Participants were asked to provide examples of internal controls and systems improvements obtained through this learning process. ARM representatives mentioned improvements in its audit and accreditation processes. Participant 1 and Participant 3 highlighted that the RJC has comprehensive audit procedures and a very good accreditation process which were used as a model to improve Fairmined audit procedures and accreditation process. In these participants' words:

> For example, the RJC has a good accreditation process and audit strategy. So we basically used their experience to develop and improve our audit procedures and our accreditation process.
>
> (Participant 1, a certification scheme representative)

> For example, the audit processes. This is where we were not very strong and now we are improving. In the past we had only two audit companies accredited, and our guidelines to do it weren't so good. In this aspect the RJC has a good process, so we are using the RJC's knowledge to

improve our audit process. They are very open to sharing their knowledge. It was a jump in improvement. If we had to develop ourselves, we would take a long time to do it.

(Participant 3, a certification scheme representative)

As well as an improvement in their procedures, it was also important to recognise an interesting example of interoperability. ARM and the RJC now have in place an accreditation process that is used by both initiatives. Regarding this specific example, Participant 4 mentioned:

For example, their accreditation process is really good. So we got the RJC's process, we accepted its accreditation process and we recognised the RJC's work on it. So, the accreditation process is only one for both of us. The RJC's accreditation is the one in use – we just adapted and included our standards in this process.

(Participant 4, a certification scheme representative)

Additional themes

Traceability as an innovation opportunity

RJC representatives also provided examples of improvements in their systems and innovation opportunities. The traceability mechanism was one of the cases mentioned. ARM has a traceability system in place that automatically tracks Fairmined gold from the mining site to the final consumer through the whole supply chain. The RJC is working with ARM at the moment to explore opportunities to also use the Fairmined traceability system. One participant commented:

One of the challenges we have at the moment is traceability. We want to have data on how much certified gold has been traded through our supply chain, for example. This is an area where we need ARM to help us. They already have software in place helping to do that.

(Participant 6, a certification scheme representative)

Improved appropriateness in allocation of time and resources

Another important aspect mentioned addressed general aspects of project management. Participants highlighted the importance of having time and resources properly allocated to develop such a project. Financial and technical support to have professionals allocated to develop and implement the project, as well as firm commitment and support from management to conduct such a project, were considered important key success factors. Capacity constraints might be a risk for any collaboration or interoperability project.

Engagement and consent from members and other key stakeholders was also considered a relevant topic. Key stakeholders must understand and see the benefits of the project; without the support of these important stakeholders the success of any type of collaboration or interoperability project could be affected. This engagement can improve the legitimacy of the project and the level of participation. Also, engaging with these stakeholders can provide important insights and valuable improvement recommendations. When stakeholders or members do not feel involved it is likely that they will not support the project.

Premium price as a variable incentive

Premium price was another key theme mentioned during interviews. This is one of the differences of the RJC and Fairmined systems – the RJC does not have a premium price component on its system, but Fairmined does. Certified Fairmined miners will receive a Fairmined premium for community and business development.

The Fairmined premium is up to US$4,000 per kilogram of gold. For Ecological Gold (gold that has been extracted without the use of chemicals and with strict ecological restoration requirements), a premium – at US$6,000 per kilogram of gold – must be paid. This ecological premium price is a market incentive to cover costs of certification and to invest in mining operations, social development and environmental protection. However, according to some of the participants, the premium price has been criticised by some industries because it has a direct impact on costs and margins. Regarding this topic, Participant 6 stated:

> I hear from the industry that the premium price is an issue. The payment is an issue because it does limit the market. Some organisations are not willing to pay the premium price. It is a barrier to mainstreaming your standards. The deal is, for some companies, sustainability should not come at a premium price, it should be business as usual.
>
> (Participant 6, a certification scheme representative)

In the same vein, Participant 5 argued that some of the companies do not want to pay a premium price. In this participant's words:

> The RJC does not have a premium price and Fairmined has. Some of the clients complain about the Fairmined premium price. Consumers want certified gold but they don't want to pay the premium price. That is the truth.
>
> (Participant 5, a company representative)

Although there were some comments criticising the premium price, it is also important to highlight that the premium price is a crucial incentive to bring artisanal miners to certification. Without a direct economic incentive – in this case, the premium price – artisanal miners would not be interested in investing time and resources into improving their practices and obtaining the certification. Equally important, Fairmined introduced the possibility of negotiating the premium price based on the quantity of gold purchased: the premium price is reduced if a brand accommodates large purchase commitments.

Competition between initiatives as a challenge to interoperability

Competition among initiatives was considered a challenge to improving interoperability. Participants mentioned that some of the initiatives are competing to increase market share, gain business and increase funding. Interoperability or any type of collaboration could be seen as a barrier to improving collaboration for initiatives competing for the same funding opportunities and market share. Participant 3 provided an interesting comment on this issue. This participant stated that competition can affect interoperability, but lack of interoperability and the existence of overlap are not good for the beneficiaries. In this participant's words:

> There is a lot of competition, and sometimes it is not easy to improve collaboration when you are competing for funding. The problem is: lack of collaboration and overlapping is not good for the beneficiaries.
>
> (Participant 3, a certification scheme representative)

ASM and incentivising different stakeholders

Another interesting topic mentioned by participants was around the role initiatives should play in relation to artisanal and small-scale mining (ASM). ASM is widespread mainly in developing countries, and it represents an important livelihood for poverty-affected communities. ASM is also generally associated with social and environmental concerns, such as child labour, gender inequality, armed conflicts, poor health and safety conditions, and environmental impacts.

In this context, different participants stated the importance of incentivising different stakeholders, including consumers, governments and industries, to support ASM to move towards more positive practices rather than to disengage and disincentivise. Sustainability certification schemes, standards, frameworks and other initiatives can be fundamental tools for development in ASM communities, as such initiatives have the capacity to foster good governance and progressively transform and formalise informal mining and trading (Franken *et al.*, 2012). Participants stated that initiatives should play an important role in providing information on responsible supply chains to different stakeholders, and also in fostering the inclusion of ASM as part of responsible sourcing policies and strategies of upstream businesses.

Demand for ASM-certified gold is growing, but it is still so tiny. There are very few leading the pack, but the huge majority don't do anything, and the few that are doing something are still in the early stages of writing their responsible sourcing policies. We have to include ASM in these policies because this sector is marginalised. We have to inform companies that there is responsible gold from ASM! Unfortunately, with the complexity of the sector, some companies believe it is easier to source from different gold producers. This is a challenge but also an opportunity.

(Participant 3, a certification scheme representative)

Similarly, Participant 4 said:

We believe it is more responsible to try to engage and help ASM than to say that you will not work with artisanal miners and will ignore ASM. Why ignore when you can make the difference and collaborate to enhance local development in undeveloped countries.

(Participant 4, a certification scheme representative)

The RJC–ARM–Fairmined interoperability project provides an interesting and relevant example of how upstream companies and ASM can work together. This project demonstrates that different certification schemes can work together to improve responsible ASM practices and increase the awareness of different stakeholders about responsible sourcing policies and responsible supply chains. In this regard, Participant 6 concluded:

I think one of the key areas is how to include more ASM, responsible ASM, in the supply chain. This is something Fairmined is doing, the RJC is doing, a lot of people are doing, but we need to think of how to address this issue together.

(Participant 6, a certification scheme representative)

Summary of findings

Participants provided similar comments on the drivers for collaboration, challenges and key topics to get right in order to ensure a successful interoperability project. Similarity between systems and goals, increased reach and reduced audit overlapping were the topics most often mentioned by participants as the drivers for the RJC and ARM–Fairmined interoperability project.

In relation to the benefits, participants mentioned leadership, access to market, internal processes and systems improvement and cost reduction as the main benefits of such a project. It is important to highlight here the important work conducted to develop and implement the combined Fairmined and RJC CoC audit project. This combined audit project, the pilot of which was undertaken in November 2016, presented important positive outcomes, such as a reduction in audit costs and audit fatigue. According to the results presented, the combined audit process can significantly reduce the audit costs – participants estimated a 20–50 per cent reduction in audit fees, and a 50 per cent decrease in travel costs. Notably, this combined audit approach also has a positive impact on audit fatigue, as the time required of auditees to attend to auditors was reduced, as was the quantity of repeated audit questions and tests. Combining services and sharing information was considered a key topic for any interoperability project.

The combined audit project implemented by the RJC and ARM– Fairmined is an important example of interoperability, in which only one audit process can attest compliance against both certifications at once.

Key conditions for successful collaboration included

(1) Having common goals. (2) A credible and strong certification system was considered equally important. Participants stated that having a strong system and a robust governance structure in place, as well as a good reputation, are crucial conditions to develop collaboration and interoperability projects with other initiatives. Initiatives do not want to be associated with unreliable initiatives (reputational risk). (3) General aspects of project management and stakeholder engagement were also considered important issues. According to participants, resources and time should be properly allocated to the interoperability project in order to avoid capacity constraints, and members and other key stakeholders should understand and see the benefits of the interoperability project to guarantee legitimacy and participation.

Challenges to interoperability included

(1) Competition among initiatives. (2) The premium price: the premium price has been criticised by some industry representatives because it has a direct impact on their costs and margins. However, without an economic incentive it is hard to convince artisanal miners to invest in certification and improve their practices.

Future considerations

Responsible supply chains and responsible sourcing programmes are two examples of how initiatives can play an important role in helping companies and other important stakeholders to better understand the challenges and risks, but also the opportunities of engaging with ASM. Participants discussed the role initiatives should play in incentivising stakeholders to engage with ASM and to explore opportunities to foster more responsible ASM practices.

228   *Renzo Mori Junior* et al.

Conclusion

Sustainability initiatives are part of the global governance landscape that is always changing to accommodate competing interests, shifting alliances and multiple points of view. Setting norms in any sector is never a neat, systematic process as the political exercise of consensus-building does not often result in the policy that technically makes the most sense. The UN SDGs demonstrate that, at the highest level, there are common values and goals for sustainable development. The mining industry and metals supply chains are grappling with many universal ethical choices for responsible conduct, as well as issues that are specific to certain commodities and scales of mining. It is inevitable that the more attention that is paid to these issues, the more duplication and confusion may arise. The responsibility of all actors involved in these initiatives is, however, to put aside vested interests, and commitment to greater collaboration and harmonisation of efforts is necessary. In conclusion, recognising and valuing the importance of this RJC–ARM–Fairmined interoperability project as an example of best practice among what exists is important. This case study demonstrates that it is possible to have upstream companies and ASM working together towards a more responsible mining approach.

Acknowledgements

This case study is part of a research project conducted by the Centre for Social Responsibility in Mining at the University of Queensland and supported by the Deutsche Gesellschaft für Internationale Zusammenarbeit (GIZ) GmbH, Sector Project Extractives and Development, on behalf of the German Federal Ministry for Economic Cooperation and Development (BMZ). The contents of this publication do not represent the official position of either BMZ or GIZ. We also thank Prof Saleem Ali for his advisory role in the research project, participants for their valuable time, and RJC and Fairmined representatives for their support and valuable comments and insights.

Mori Junior, R., Sturman, K. and Imbrogiano, J. (2017). 'Leveraging greater impact of mineral sustainability initiatives: An assessment of interoperability'. Centre for Social Responsibility in Mining, Sustainable Mining Institute, University of Queensland. Brisbane.

References

Barry, M., Cashore, B., Clay, J., Fernandez, M., Lebel, L., Lyon, T., … Kennedy, T. (2012). Toward Sustainability: The Roles and Limitations of Certification. Washington, DC: RESOLVE, Inc.

Brockmyer, B., and Fox, J. (2015). Assessing the Evidence: The Effectiveness and Impact of Public Governance-Oriented Multi-Stakeholder Initiatives. London: The Transparency and Accountability Initiative.

Chen, D., and Doumeingts, G. (2003). European initiatives to develop interoperability of enterprise applications: basic concepts, framework and roadmap. Annual Reviews in Control, 27(2), 153–162.

Chen, D., Vallespir, B., and Daclin, N. (2008). An approach for enterprise interoperability measurement. Paper presented at the MoDISE-EUS.

Dassisti, M., Jardim-Goncalves, R., Molina, A., Noran, O., Panetto, H., and Zdravković, M. M. (2013). Sustainability and interoperability: two facets of the same gold medal. Paper presented at the On the Move to Meaningful Internet Systems: OTM 2013 Workshops.

Day, M. (2004). Preservation metadata initiatives: practicality, sustainability, and interoperability. In F. M. Bischoff, H. Hofman, and S. Ross (eds) Metadata in Preservation: Selected Papers from an ERPANET Seminar at the Archives School Marburg, 3–5 September 2003. Marburg, Germany: Archivschule Marburg, 91–117.

Ford, T. C., Colombi, J. M., Graham, S. R., and Jacques, D. R. (2007). Survey on Interoperability Measurement. DTIC Document.

Franken, G., Vasters, J., Dorner, U., Melcher, F., Sitnikova, M., and Goldmann, S. (2012). Certified trading chains in mineral production: a way to improve responsibility in mining. In L. Sinding-Larsen and F.-W. Wellmer (eds) Non-Renewable Resource Issues. Dordrecht: Springer, 213–227.

Ide, N., and Pustejovsky, J. (2010). What does interoperability mean, anyway? Toward an operational definition of interoperability for language technology. Paper presented at the Proceedings of the Second International Conference on Global Interoperability for Language Resources, Hong Kong.

INSPIRE. (2011). What is interoperability? (and how do we measure it?). Paper presented at the INSPIRE Conference 2011, Edinburgh.

ISEAL Alliance. (2013). Principles for Credible and Effective Sustainability Standards Systems: ISEAL Credibility Principles. London.

Jardim-Goncalves, R., Popplewell, K., and Grilo, A. (2012). Sustainable interoperability: the future of Internet based industrial enterprises. Computers in Industry, 63(8), 731–738.

Kasunic, M. (2001). Measuring Systems Interoperability: Challenges and Opportunities. DTIC Document.

Main, D., Mullan, S., Atkinson, C., Cooper, M., Wrathall, J., and Blokhuis, H. (2014). Best practice framework for animal welfare certification schemes. Trends in Food Science and Technology, 37(2), 127–136.

Mori Junior, R., Franks, D., and Ali, S. (2016). Sustainability certification schemes: evaluating their effectiveness and adaptability. Corporate Governance: The International Journal of Business in Society, 16(3), 579–592.

Stark, A., and Levin, E. (2011). Benchmark Study of Environmental and Social Standards in Industrialised Precious Metals Mining. Solidaridad.

Tracey, T. J. (1994). An examination of the complementarity of interpersonal behavior. Journal of Personality and Social Psychology, 67(5), 864–878.

Vernadat, F. B. (2007). Interoperable enterprise systems: principles, concepts, and methods. Annual Reviews in Control, 31(1), 137–145.

Vlassenroot, K., and Van Bockstael, S. (2008). Artisanal Diamond Mining: Perspectives and Challenges. Ghent: Academia Press.

WWF. (2013). Searching for Sustainability: Comparative Analysis of Certification Schemes for Biomass Used for the Production of Biofuels. Berlin.

Yahia, E., Aubry, A., and Panetto, H. (2012). Formal measures for semantic interoperability assessment in cooperative enterprise information systems. Computers in Industry, 63(5), 443–457.

11 Juggling sustainability certifications in the Costa Rican coffee industry

Melissa Vogt

Introduction

Approximately 25 million coffee farmers and families produce 70 per cent of the world's coffee on small farm holdings. Ninety-eight per cent of all coffee is traded by 44 International Coffee Organization (ICO) member countries (ICO, 2007). Of these, 19 members were least-developed countries. The impact of coffee on biodiversity is recognised as disproportional to land area dedicated to farming (Donald, 2004). Sustainability and poverty reduction efforts are therefore appropriate and required. Direct trade and sustainability certifications commenced in the 1980s and they have been considered a benefit for reducing poverty through trade, and as a market-based approach for sustainable development (Shaw and Black 2010). Since coffee not only represents the highest proportion of total global agricultural area certified (Lernoud *et al.* 2018), it is also one of the longest certified agricultural commodities. The history and expanded reach of certification across coffee farming landscapes provides advanced considerations of experience and effectiveness over time.

While macro-level study might accumulate comparable studies from certified coffee farming landscapes around the world, this chapter will instead provide specific example of trends in certified coffee markets and associated economic, environmental and societal outcomes in one country, Costa Rica. It is not a significant global coffee producer by quantity; however, rate of production by hectare is globally significant (Winson, 1989; Vogt, 2011). Costa Rica is well versed in the volatility and variability of the coffee industry. Between 2011 and 2012 it represented the highest share of certified coffee production, 32 per cent (Potts *et al.*, 2014), and nearly three decades of experience with sustainability certifications.

Perspectives and perceptions toward certifications from producers and cooperative managers collected through fieldwork in 2009 is considered alongside follow-up fieldwork in 2014 and literature review to date, providing an opportunity to understand how recommendations and findings from 2009 fared over time. The experience with sustainability certifications in Costa Rica provides foundation to explore and consider an overview of certification efforts, from original intentions, to a cumulative effect of

multiple certifications within the coffee industry. The need to juggle certifications, while not the absolute influencer of outcomes, becomes the meta-
phor for the chapter. The various contextual situations and certifications
introduce the shape, size and condition of the 'objects' that must be juggled.

Method

Fieldwork

In 2009, interviews and observations were carried out across 12 coffee
farming communities (Figure 11.1) with ten coffee cooperatives, and associ-

Figure 11.1 Coffee farming communities visited in 2009.

Source: Esri, USGS | Esri, HERE, Garmin, FAO, NOAA, USGS | Esri, HERE, Garmin,
FAO, NOAA, USGS.

Notes

Maps throughout this chapter were created using ArcGIS® software by Esri. ArcGIS® and
ArcMap™ are the intellectual property of Esri and are used herein under license. Copyright ©
Esri. All rights reserved. For more information about Esri® software, please visit www.esri.com.

ated communities, nine of which were members of the Fairtrade certified umbrella cooperative Coocafe R.L. Separate interviews were held with a Rainforest Alliance (RA) certified coffee plantation, with local RA representatives and with the leadership of Coocafe R.L., Hijos del campo and Cafe-Forestal. Communities visited represent a distinct experience by proximity to urban areas, history of coffee farming, international reputation for coffee quality, and direct experiences with international markets and varying 'sustainability' efforts, and experience of studies that explore certification or sustainability practices. The original research question sought to understand the distinction between RA and Fairtrade, and identify changes in practices attributable to either or both of the certifications. Fieldwork was written into a dissertation by 2011 (Vogt, 2011).

During follow-up fieldwork in 2014 I visited just two of the originally visited communities. The intention of the visit was distinct from the previous visits. The selected communities demonstrated a dynamic of agricultural practices and trade reliant on certifications and other 'sustainability' efforts. The follow-up visit allowed consideration of how these situations had changed over time. Quotes from the dissertation and follow-up fieldwork are used. The method for research was intended, despite scope for subjectivity. Where appearing overly critical or resentment presented, the international trade context and recognised power dynamics are considered as being equally influential. These more extreme quotes may not be indicative of an experience with certifications only, but do demonstrate certain inabilities of a certification effort. New efforts and processes may not yet be mature to a point of addressing the subtler dynamics of trade and sustainable development efforts between the developing and developed world, and within the developing world.

The timing of fieldwork and subsequent quotes, discussion and situation descriptions may appear outdated. It is, however, expected, as Costa Rica is one of the more advanced countries in terms of experience with certifications, that the trends during this time, particularly where compared with the current situation for certifications in Costa Rica, could become an example or study for other country experiences.

Literature

Discussion related to the 2014–2018 context is informed by a combination of fieldwork and literature. Literature furthers discussion related to findings in 2014, and to the current Costa Rican coffee industry and certified markets. Studies related to the specific topic from more recent times are from varying perspectives, most business disciplines (Diaz, 2015; Gyllensten, 2017; Babin 2015). Comparative studies, between certifications, between certifications and government programmes, and across countries and industries include Barham *et al.* (2011); Hanson *et al.* (2012); Macdonald (2007) and Ruben and Zuniga (2010). Other historic works are included in the bibliography as significant contributions to advancing understandings of coffee sustainability certifications in the initial stages of understanding and operation (Raynolds *et al.*, 2003, 2007; Wollni and Zeller, 2006; Adams and Ghaly, 2006; De Neve *et al.*, 2008; Luetchford, 2008; Bacon *et al.*, 2008; Jaffe and Bacon, 2008; Jaffe, 2012; Smith, 2008).

Lens for presenting and understanding assessment of information

Development as freedom (Sen, 1999) provides a lens through which information from 2009 was collected and organised, and a way for changes between 2009 and 2014 to be understood. By removing an obligation to provide a specific type of 'aid',[1] attention transfers to an ability to select preferred functionings through the development of capabilities. There can be a time where the 'aid' is no longer relevant or necessary. The 'aid' might be provisioning one element of many required to improve a situation, and it may maintain relevance only in this area for a longer period of time, or lose relevance more rapidly. Alternatively, the aid may have completed its intention, or there may be progress in offerings relevant for the temporal context. External developments may also assist to provide alternatives lacking at the time that an 'aid' was introduced. A receivers' own development leading to self-determination and empowerment to 'aid' oneself might have occurred independently, with assistance from or due to receiving 'aid'.

How ideas of obligation to an 'aid' that is no longer required or needed are understood within specific contexts is of interest. Where certifications are considered an 'aid', there is no obligation to stay committed where it inappropriately addresses concerns, or where it is no longer needed. Where 'aid' is no longer needed, with outcomes achieved, or where the 'receiver' has found an appropriate alternative, and where no damage has occurred, a success could be recognised. It is not often that an 'aid' will be considered an absolute success, particularly where offering something novel and not yet tried. Contextual understandings of appropriateness of an 'aid' are necessary. The idea of certifications as an 'aid' perhaps highlights the most significant contention with certification efforts which operate intramarket but represent themselves as non-governmental organisations (NGO). Discussion in this chapter will be based on appropriate benefit to producers over time within community specific contexts. It is recommended that detailed distinctions between situations be considered, and that the country context be firmly integrated in any assessment intended for different countries.

The coffee industry and Costa Rica

Since 1933, the Instituto de Café (ICafe) has governed the Costa Rican coffee industry. The Coffee Defence Institute became the Coffee Office which handled the management of coffee credit and encouraged the creation of cooperatives (Rovira, 2000). The signing of the International Coffee

Agreement (ICA) and the freeze on America's import price for coffee in the 1950s stimulated a global movement toward intense cultivation of high-yield arabica hybrid varieties within already settled coffee lands (Naranjo, 1997; Samper, 2000). As this was the beginning of the green revolution, from 1950 to 1970, there was a 170 per cent increase in average yield per hectare as the government subsidised transition to hybrid trees, and fertiliser and herbicide purchase necessary for maintenance (Mitchell and Pentzer, 2008).

By 1970, Costa Rica was the third most productive coffee exporter in the world and the most productive in Latin America (Winson, 1989), a significant statistic considering the size of the country. A Costa Rican agronomist observed:

> Coffee production in Costa Rica is in a state of complete exploitation. There is no technology. The agriculturalists are not concerned with conservation. They cultivate coffee like a mine, taking out and never returning anything to the land.
>
> (Winson, 1989)

In 1999, 100,000 hectares were dedicated to coffee farming, more than any other crop. Global oversupply of coffee resulted in the 2001 'coffee crisis', dramatically reducing the market price for coffee. Continuing to farm coffee, particularly for holdings of five hectares or so became a significant challenge (Vogt, 2011). Despite these difficulties, in 2007 coffee was the most valuable commodity per unit exported (Vogt, 2011) and in 2010, Costa Rica was the second most productive country in Latin America in terms of kilogrammes per hectare (Vogt, 2011). More recently, 92 per cent of all coffee producers manage landholdings less than five hectares, and represent 44 per cent of total coffee farming area. Six per cent of coffee producers manage between five and 20 hectares, and represent 20 per cent of total area, and 2 per cent of producers manage plantations larger than 20 hectares, representing 35 per cent of total area (ICafe, 2018).

Coffee certifications in Costa Rica

The first fair trade contract and agreement was introduced in Costa Rica in the same year as the 1989 collapse of the ICA. It was the second 'sustainable' trade effort, the first was Organic certification in 1982.[2] Established in 1988, Coocafe, a national umbrella cooperative for nine coffee cooperatives, accepted Fair trading partners of two-member cooperatives. The initial foci of 'Fair trade' arrangements in 1989 were a stable price, direct trade arrangements and forms of sustainable agriculture. In 1997 Fairtrade formalised efforts through a label and certification process. It was not, however, until 2008 that the Fairtrade Labelling Organisation (FLO) commenced work toward more detailed standards, and rigorous audit and regulatory procedures. Coocafe membership grew to 2,000 small producers, and involvement in certifications increased between these years. RA was established in 1986 with the intention of preventing rapid deforestation. The first office, a conservation media centre, was set up in San José, Costa Rica in 1989. The first certification programme, SmartWood, was initiated to improve forest management. RA then introduced a standard through the Sustainable Agriculture Network (SAN) to cover numerous agricultural crops grown around the world.

In 1997, the Costa Rican National Association of Organic Agriculture founded Eco-LOGICA, the first certification to be registered under the Costa Rican Ministry of Agriculture (Ministerio de Agricultura y Ganaderia, MAG). It now provides consultation services for other certifications available including international and national organic standards and certifications, and certifications that fit within the category of Good Agricultural Practices (Certificación de Buenas Practices Agrícolas, BPA) including GLOBALG.A.P., C.A.F.E. Practices, Utz Kapeh and Bird Friendly. They also administer Women Care Certified® (WCC) currently applied within the coffee industry. In addition to those administered by Eco-LOGICA, RA, Fairtrade and more recently a range of smaller certifications are used in Costa Rica. It is not necessary to work through Eco-LOGICA to be certified, nor is it required to be certified to trade and export coffee. Eco-LOGICA offers a service provision rather than required involvement.

Fieldwork 2009: the producer[3] perspective

The following section encourages understanding of how Fairtrade and RA were perceived and understood in Costa Rica. It can be read with confidence of the situation in Costa Rica in 2009, across a representative sample of communities and Fairtrade-certified coffee cooperatives. The comments should be understood as an expression of in-country opinions.

Increasing demand for multiple certifications – 2009

From 2008 to 2012, RA and Fairtrade-certified coffee sales grew at a rate equal or slightly higher than the increase in certified hectares (SSI Review, 2014, 167). As more certifications came to market, and as sales increased cooperatives and plantations were becoming certified due to the demand of existing clients. Additional certification can improve sales, business interaction or compliance with import country regulations. However, for producer groups it often represented additional investment and resource allocations, with unconfirmed benefit or increased legitimacy.

While not an explicitly 'forced to be certified' situation, existing power dynamics within trade arrangements, and the value of direct market access for producers, indicate an inevitable power of buyers. In 2009, several managers and administrators mentioned that multinational corporations (MNCs) develop quotas or percentages for certifications based on general market preferences, and their own administrative interests.[4] 'Ahora tenemos clientes que vienen y demandan café basado en la certificación' [We now have clients who come, and demand coffee based on certification].[5] If a cooperative is not certified as required by the market, it must either pay and work toward compliance to maintain the trade relationship or risk losing the business. Where considered alongside perceived advantages and disadvantages of Fairtrade and RA, an understanding of how an increasing demand for multiple certifications as both positive and negative develops.

Conditioned access to international markets based on compliance to any given and/or multiple certifications could appear positive. In theory, all sales would be tied to sustainable agricultural and fair business practices. The positive outcomes do, however, rely on appropriateness and quality of standards aligned with effective sustainable agricultural practices and fair, socially just business practice and effective implementation. Allowing the market to determine a preference for certification can be a slippery slope, particularly so if a valued benefit of certified markets for producer groups is market access, and more so where other outcomes are variably positive, and occasionally perceived as negative.

The importance of market access for producers – 2009

Fairtrade certification facilitated access to international certified markets, stability through long-term contracts and international networks, and a variable price benefit. RA-certified plantations noticed market access and a superior price. 'Las certificaciones son necesarias para acceder a los mercados especializados' [The certifications are necessary to access speciality markets].[6] The opinion was confirmed in other interviews, 'Básicamente las certificaciones son para acceso al Mercado' [Basically, the certifications are for market access].[7]

Negotiating contracts for long-term arrangements was an identified difficulty for Fairtrade-certified cooperatives, particularly with larger corporate buyers such as Starbucks. These difficulties were normally related to price, fairly consistently due to the cost of production in Costa Rica compared to neighbouring countries. Costa Rican producers were subject to comparative negotiating techniques to lower the agreed price, and only Fairtrade provided guidance to negotiate such situations to varying effect.

How certifications were perceived as distinct by producer groups – 2009

In 2003, RA certified the first coffee farm in Costa Rica, and the first coffee cooperative in 2007.[8] By 2009, no cooperatives were selling through RA-certified markets[9] and the SAN standard for small producer groups was under revision. A difference in appropriateness of the two certifications, dependent on the size of farm holding and the organisation type at that time, could subsequently be understood.

Farmers of smaller landholdings represent 90 per cent of all producers in Costa Rica, indicative of certification reach by producer but not to all people, as larger landholdings are likely to contract a significant number of labourers during harvest. Nor is it indicative of standard reach by hectares and therefore sustainable agricultural practices. Thirty-five per cent of total land dedicated to coffee is composed of farms larger than 20 hectares. Fairtrade and RA certification according to farm size does not therefore necessarily associate with scope of benefit, or according to environmental and societal outcome. It is, however, expected to vary the outcome.

The premise of each certification is also distinct, as recognised by producers, directing the prioritised approach of each:

> Fairtrade realmente trata de unir a las comunidades, a través de sus criterios tenemos una mejor visión de la producción, la industria y de la comercialización. La red de iniciativas, de países y organizaciones de Comercio Justo a través del mundo es más fuerte que Rainforest [Alliance]. [Fairtrade really tries to unite the communities and through their criteria we have a better vision of production, the industry and of commercialisation. The network of initiatives, of countries and organisations of Fairtrade through the world is stronger than Rainforest.][10]

> Fairtrade no solo certifica, sino que supervise, tiene premios y programas. Ayuda a tomar importantes decisiones económicas y políticas. [Fairtrade not only certifies but it supervises, it has premiums and programmes.[11] It assists in making important economic and political decisions.][12]

> Rainforest tiene un concepto que analizan, pero no organizan, aquí es donde veo la gran diferencia. [Rainforest has one concept that they analyse but they do not organise, this is where I see the big difference.][13]

> Las dos certificaciones tienen una diferencia, Fairtrade desde la base te protege un poco, desde lo alto son las mismas. [The two certifications have a difference, Fairtrade from the base it protects you a little, from the top they are the same.][14]

A representative of RA explained their approach,

> Somos una de las certificaciones que integran los tres pilares de la sostenibilidad a través de la red. No buscamos un premio de precio fijo. Es más holístico, y no da prioridad a un pilar sobre otro. [We are one of the only certifications that integrate the three pillars of sustainability through the network. We do not look for a fixed price premium. It is more holistic, and it does not prioritise one pillar over another.][15]

While standards and auditing methods of both certifications were observed as becoming more similar, RA standards were observed as inappropriate for some local contexts:

Cuando los inspectores de la RA vinieron a auditor nuestras fincas sentimos que sus preguntas estaban un poco fuera del contexto histórico, cultural y social para el granjero, por ejemplo, en una pequeña comunidad,
el inspector fue a finca y le preguntó: ¿proviene de un sistema público, de
la comunidad? Si no, es una falta del estándar. El campesino dice, 'Bueno
primero tengo que dar la gracia por tener agua, si no tengo un sistema
público el sistema no ha existido o en los últimos anos en esta área no ha
sido necesario'. Aquí en esta área hasta ahora, hay una fuente de agua en
cada finca, por lo que este requisito que determinaría el cumplimiento de
las normas RA y por tanto la certificación no parece relevante para
nuestra comunidad. [When the RA inspectors came to audit our farms
we felt that their questions were a little out of historic, cultural and social
context for the farmer, for example, in a small community, the inspector
went to a farm and asked 'The water that you consume, does it come
from a public system, from the community? If not, it is a breach of our
standard'. The farmer says, 'well I first have to give thanks that I have
water, if I do not have a public system it is not because I do not want to,
it is because the system has not existed or in the last years in this area it
has not been necessary'. Here in this area until now, there is a source of
water in every farm, so this requirement which would determine complying with RA standards and therefore achieving certification does not
seem relevant to our community.][16]

At the time, Fairtrade was also changing the way it set standards and monitored implementation:

Antes de Fairtrade era como una asistencia social, oh usted es pobre,
necesita ayuda, pero ahora Fairtrade es más como una certificación,
mirando a la salud, el medio ambiente. Es más similar a otras certificaciones ahora y este año se centran mucho en los estándares ambientales.
[Before, Fairtrade was like a social assistance, oh you are poor, you need
help, but now Fairtrade is more like a certification, looking at health,
environment. It is more similar to other certifications now, and this year
they are very much focused on environmental standards.][17]

The difference between RA and FLO by farm size certified, standard intentions and appropriateness and sustainability premise was therefore not only
recognised by certification representatives but also by producers and in
different ways.

Juggling multiple certifications in 2009

With variable perceived benefit of certifications, the juggling of paperwork
and resources to become compliant with numerous certifications raised the
question of whether there could be a better way.

The financial manager and assistant director of one cooperative explained in more detail certifying due to benefits provided, but also due to demand from buyers:

> Nos certificamos con Fairtrade porque en ese momento, el precio era bajo en café … y algunos compradores de café estaban buscando un café Tarrazu que fuera certificado Fairtrade y no existía así que decidimos certificarnos para ofrecer esta combinación al mercado. Entramos en C.A.F.E. Practices de Starbucks porque teníamos clientes demandando que cumpliéramos y luego teníamos otros clientes demandando café certificado RA, así que también trabajamos para ser certificados bajo el programa de RA. [We became certified with Fairtrade because at that time, the price was low in coffee … and some buyers of coffee were looking for a Tarrazu coffee that was Fairtrade certified and it did not exist, so we decided to become certified to offer this combination to the market. We entered into C.A.F.E Practices of Starbucks because we had clients demanding that we comply and then we had other clients demanding RA-certified coffee, so we also worked to become certified under the RA programme.][18]

He explained how his cooperative was managing three certifications:

> Hemos empezado a fusionar los diversos estándares en un estándar para la cooperativa. Si no hacemos esto los diferentes estándares son demasiado segregados para nuestros miembros y para nosotros y nos ahorramos tiempo.… Parece la forma más inteligente para gestionar toda esta información y el trabajo de papel. [We have started amalgamating the various standards into one standard for the cooperative. If we do not do this the different standards are too segregated for our members and for us and we save ourselves time … It seems the smartest way for managing all of this information and paper work.][19]

The required financial and nonfinancial investment versus benefit of implementing standards and becoming compliant to one and/or multiple certifications provides contextual understanding of a need to juggle certifications.

Investment versus benefit to implement standards – 2009

While ensuring certification is complemented with effective implementation is an assumed positive outcome – the operational investment to implement versus the benefit contributes to the discussion of advantages and disadvantages of certifications. The contribution of Fairtrade in Costa Rica during 2009 provides an example, and a comparison with RA further demonstrates how this situation can differ between certification requirements and approach. The Fairtrade price premium allocated to specific areas of technological upgrades for production, or to the community, and provision of a 'fair secure minimum price', stability through long-term trading contracts and relationships, organisational capacity building and participation of producers in the Fairtrade system were all benefits identified by participants. During the 2001 coffee crisis, coffee farming decreased as entire farms were abandoned. Survival at that time was attributed to the Fairtrade minimum price, with the exception of one cooperative. In 2009, that benefit was no longer identified; in fact, the opposite was true, as cooperatives claimed to be losing money.

> Este ano Fairtrade hizo que el productor perdiera el dinero a través del mercado Fairtrade. El mercado convencional este ano es $2.57 y Fairtrade $1.87, causo una perdida. [This year Fairtrade made the producer lose money through the Fairtrade market. The conventional market this year is $2.57 and Fairtrade $1.87, it caused a loss.][20]

This was confirmed by other interviewees:

> Los clientes que tenemos hacen tener la certificación Fairtrade vale la pena, pero el premio y el precio no vale la pena. Si vendemos café a $1.87 no es atractivo para mí, no cubre los costos. Costa Rica es diferente a otros países, el costo de producción es más alto, el transporte y la mano de obra es casi el doble que el de otros países. [The clients that we have make having the Fairtrade certification worth it but the premium and price is not worth it. If I sell coffee at $1.87 it is not attractive for me, it does not cover the costs. Costa Rica is different to other countries, the cost of production is higher, transport and labour is nearly double that of other countries.][21]

> Para tener estas certificaciones es un poco caro para nosotros, hemos estimado que, para cumplir con todos estos criterios de las certificaciones, la inversión es de aproximadamente 27 centavos por quintal de café, es una inversión, por lo que cubre muchas cosechas, pero si es una producción de 100 quintales por 3 hectáreas, hay que hacer mucho para hacerse confirme. Tienen que reconocer el trabajo que tenemos que hacer para lograr estos cambios. Cualquier certificación porque incluso si es una responsabilidad de hacer las cosas bien, si vendemos café al precio Fairtrade, no es sostenible. Hay personas que pueden vivir con estos precios, pero bajo qué condiciones, pueden comer, pero no pueden pagar la escuela. Fairtrade garantiza un tipo de vida, pero no vendemos un 40% a través de Fairtrade. Cuando del precio del café es bajo vendiendo 25% comercio justo y 75% al mercado por $1.11 es insuficiente. Fairtrade exige que invirtamos en salud, medio ambiente, etc. pero cuanto café estamos vendiendo a través de su mercado? [To have these certifications is a bit expensive for us, we have estimated that to comply with all these criteria of the certifications, the investment is approximately 27 cents a

quintal of coffee, it is an investment, so that covers many harvests, but if it is a production of 100 quintales[22] for three hectares, you have to do a lot to become compliant. They have to recognise the work that we have to do to make these changes, any certification, because even if it is a responsibility to do things well, if we sell coffee at the Fairtrade price, it is not sustainable. There are people who can live with these prices, but under what conditions, they can eat but they cannot afford school – Fairtrade guarantees a type of life – but we do not sell all our coffee, we sell 40% through Fairtrade but when the conventional coffee price is low, 25% Fairtrade, market $1.11 at 75% and this is insufficient. Fairtrade demands that we invest in health, environment etc., but how much coffee are we selling through their market.][23]

Ese es el problema que tenemos estoy haciendo un estudio comparativo de costos en Centroamérica, para demonstrar el problema que tenemos con los altos costos que el precio mínimo no cubre. Tenemos costos de producción más bajos en Costa Rica y tal vez en Centroamérica debido a la eficiencia, pero en la producción en la agricultura, no podemos manejar, trabajamos a mano, tenemos que pagar la seguridad social, etc. no podemos manejar esto. [That is the problem that we have, I am doing a comparative study of costs in Central America, to demonstrate the problem we have with high costs that the minimum price does not cover. We have lower production costs in Costa Rica and maybe in Central America because of efficiency, but in production in farming, we cannot manage, we work by hand, we have to pay social security etc. ... we cannot manage this.][24]

The eventual cost of Fairtrade certification alongside an inadequate minimum price prompted additional questions of sustainability and poverty reduction intentions. 'Es difícil justificar el pago de una certificación cuando no hay garantía o certeza de que se pagara un mejor precio'. [It is difficult to justify paying for a certification when there is no assurance or certainty that a better price will be paid.][25]

In 2009, cooperative leaders required support from government departments and international funding bodies to implement standards, with additional investment required to administer the certifications within the office. The financial and nonfinancial expense of compliance to numerous certifications reveals an additional and not so easily sustainable layer. The RA price is determined by clients and is not fixed. RA-certified markets offered 41–48 cents per pound above the standard price for plantations which was sufficient to cover the cost of compliance. For RA-certified small farmer cooperatives, the situation was different. 'RA desde el fondo no protege a usted y los tostadores que compran RA comprar a través de los precios del gobierno a la tasa de Mercado abierto de $1.73 y recibimos 97 centavos'. [RA does not protect you from the bottom, and the roasters that buy RA buy through government prices at the open market rate [of] $1.73 and we receive 97 cents].[26] The payment ahead of harvest, as pre-finance for farming activities, was a benefit of being certified by any international certification body in Costa Rica.

The benefit of accessing certified markets was considered valuable despite financial disadvantages in 2009. Conditional access based on being certified by multiple certifications did present an additional question of investment versus benefit, particularly as requirements for existing standards increased. 'Nuestro cliente solicito que seamos certificados con RA. Fairtrade está en un proceso de cambio en el momento de ser más completo y detallado en la implementación'. [Our client requested that we become certified with RA. Fairtrade is in a process of change at the moment to be more thorough and detailed in implementation.][27]

Working toward compliance for a number of small farms managed by different people, versus compliance of a large plantation managed by one or a few people is a significant difference to consider. Investment versus benefit outcome can therefore be understood within a context of appropriate standards and certification process according to farm-holding size and organisation.

Audit process

The audit process is not only an important consideration in terms of verification, it also represents a financial and nonfinancial investment. An extensive audit process was not identified for either of the certifications, with variability in thoroughness and legitimacy. In some communities, alternative systems demonstrated superior practice, yet certified producers paid for the certification audit process.

> En Fairtrade tenemos que invertir en un auditor, con [el sistema alternativo] que nos dan asesoramiento técnico de forma gratuita. Con los precios no son tan justos, por el momento Fairtrade no cubra el costo de producción para la cooperativa o las granjas. Tenemos un mercado fuera de Fairtrade que es $2.08, esto es más que Fairtrade. [In Fairtrade we have to invest in an auditor, with [the alternative system] the prices are not so fair, at the moment Fairtrade is not covering the cost of production for the cooperative or the farms. We have a market outside of Fairtrade which is $2.08, this is more than Fairtrade.][28]

> Tenemos que pagar dinero por la inspección, por la membresía, y por cada exportación que hacemos. Lo mismo sucede con Rainforest, con todas las certificaciones. Por ejemplo, con productos orgánicos, si usted tiene Maya-cert para venir e inspeccionar, usted paga por el transporte desde Guatemala. [We have to pay money for the inspection, for membership and for every export that we do, the same thing happens with Rainforest, with all certifications. For example, with organic, if you have Maya-cert to come and inspect, you pay for transport from Guatemala.][29]

The cost of monitoring and studies to confirm the existence and growth of specific trees required is identified by RA as a barrier to more farmers benefiting and being part of the market. RA's idea was to combine auditing that verifies compliance to stringent criteria with measuring carbon sequestered by trees planted to earn carbon credits. The monitoring costs would decrease and 'credibility of the results would be high'.[30] One RA-certified farm owner, a plantation, mentioned involvement in this programme.[31]

A thorough audit process provides opportunity for improved compliance, and potentially education for producers, a significant point for consideration regarding investment versus benefit for multiple certifications, and therefore potentially multiple audits.

The contribution of certified standards for sustainable agricultural practice – 2009

Attributing change in practices to a certification was difficult for many participants. There were, however, some common observations made such as economic limitation, farmer preference, legal requirements, and other programmes and/or efforts which also promoted changes. The benefits of reduced chemical use, particularly as a health outcome, were identified by farmers throughout Costa Rica in 2009. There were further environmentally sustainable practices observed.

> La salud de la familia, esto es muy especial al menos para mí. He visto que solo necesito aplicar productos químicos una vez al año no 8–9 veces. El ambiente es completamente diferente porque el café estaba completamente al sol, ahora hay sombra. [The health of the family, this is very special at least for me. I have seen that I only need to apply chemicals once a year not 8–9 times. The environment is completely different because the coffee was entirely in the sun, now there is shade.][32]

> En la mayoría, no usamos productos químicos por dinero, no por una conciencia ambiental. [In the majority, we do not use chemicals because of money, not because of an environmental conscience.][33]

> Tuvimos que dejar de usar productos químicos, Ya no nos lo podíamos permitir pagar. [We had to stop using chemicals; we could no longer afford it.][34]

> La certificación Fairtrade no ha influido en la industria cafetalera en Costa Rica. [Fairtrade certification has not influenced the coffee industry in Costa Rica.][35]

> Están certificando lo que ya está allí, el Mercado pide café de sombre, así que obtenemos certificaciones RA, pero tengo que certificar lo que ya

tengo. [They are certifying what is already there, the market asks for shade grown coffee, so we get RA certification, but I have to certify what I already have.][36]

A cooperative manager explained his understanding of the situation:

Los cambios en el uso de los productos químicos no son debido a una certificación es debido a nuestra propia conciencia. Costa Rica está muy informada por el gobierno y la ley – es obligatorio que productos químicos no se pueden usar … agua y desperdicio de agua, pero lo cierto es que no hay fondos para hacer estos cambios. [The changes in use of chemicals are not because of a certification it is because of our own consciousness. Costa Rica is very informed by the government and the law – it is obligatory what chemicals you cannot use … water and waste of water but the thing is there are no funds to make these changes.][37]

The most distinct benefit of certifications compared to other efforts identified by farmers in Costa Rica was reduced and more careful chemical use, particularly as a health outcome, and with subsequent environmental outcomes. Other identified benefits of certifications were improved agricultural and farm-based practices beyond legal requirements,[38] for example recycling practices and handling of chemicals, and more realistic labour standards for migrant workers, compared to the law.

Where chronologically a certification is ahead of the law, the gaps were filled, for example an RA employee confirmed in May 2009, they were recycling as required by SAN standards and that, 'la ley no cubre el reciclado aun en Costa Rica' [the law does not cover recycling yet in Costa Rica].[39]

It was not until May 2010 that the Law for an Integrated Management of Residues (La ley para la gestion integral de residuos: Ley 8839/2010) (Costa Rica, 2010) was passed by unanimous vote, with plans for implementation and regulation forthcoming by 2020. Whether certifications standards influenced such legal progress is not, however, evident. In addition, in 2009, the use of uniforms when handling chemicals, child care for labourers to prevent child labour, standards for housing and facilities provided for workers were all required in SAN standards but not in state law.

Variability in perceived and actual contribution of certification standard, were influenced by existing legal requirements,[40] and producer practices by contextual necessity and preference. In theory, compliance to certification standards is required before accessing certified markets, relying on an effective audit process which was also observed as variable in 2009. In this situation perceived benefits rely on sufficient understanding of standards and effective implementation from producers. RA-certified plantations have on-hand understanding of implementation, contributions and requirements of SAN standards. Fairtrade-certified cooperatives have limited control and visitation of all member farms, and will therefore often have thorough understanding of standard requirements and implementation at an administrative level, but second-hand understanding of implementation for the majority of individual farms.

The beneficio, *and water and waste management*

Wet processing of coffee is a significant source of water pollution in coffee growing regions (ICO, 2018). Regulation is provided by government law, ley 2762 (Costa Rica, 1961), and ICafe to promote sustainable processes and control pollution and contamination (ICafe, 2015). Where standards applicable to the *beneficio*[41] are not used, cultural practices of throwing waste directly into rivers (Danse and Wolters, 2003) could easily continue.

In 2009, Fairtrade-certified cooperatives used closed-circuit systems for waste management, attributed to ISO14001; ISO9001. There were reasonably strict waste water procedures, including two treatment lakes, some of which used trout to eat the expelled coffee pulp solutions, reducing acidity and assisting with water treatment. Some were upgrading equipment to recycle water used to clean and process berries to hulled beans and reduce water use. Contrary to other findings (Grabs *et al.*, 2016), consistent understanding of the number of litres used and estimates of how it might be further reduced were communicated. Pulp waste was reduced consistently through collection and conversion to organic fertilisers used on member farms. There was, however, one example of a new micro-mill located next to a river with little knowledge of cautious practices, leaving potential for cultural practices to develop.[42]

2009 fieldwork summarised

In 2009, different certifications were identifiable if not obvious to producer groups, while standards were identified as becoming more similar. RA was demonstrating most appropriate and effective for larger landholdings by affordability and standard appropriateness. Fairtrade demonstrated benefit for small farm holdings, provisioning organisational development, market access and involvement in international networks, with variable conditions. The provision, despite variable conditions, was beneficial due to limited alternative options. These benefits did, however, vary over time, as auditing and standard requirements became stricter, at the financial and nonfinancial expense of the producer.

As demand for certification appeared generated by market and consumer preference rather than, for example, in-country appropriate standards and processes, a comprehensive value of certifications was questioned. Demanding compliance to multiple certification criteria was generating a requirement for administrative juggling by producer organisations. The cause appeared to stem from market demand for certifications, suggesting a trend attributable to the intramarket location of certifications. Benefit could be obtained where complying with multiple certifications was affordable. Affordability relates not only to profitability but also harmony of the business. Appropriateness or inappropriateness of standards required is an example, as is how sourcing businesses negotiate and manage trade relations and contracts.

2009–2018

At the end of 2017, Utz Kapeh merged with RA, to 'rejuvenate agricultural landscapes, conserve forests, foster sustainable livelihoods and build climate resilience across vulnerable regions; transform business practices, drive source chain innovation, and engage consumers in positive change' (Rainforest Alliance, 2018). Such amalgamation is considered as positive progress from the certification effort to minimise the required juggling experienced by certified producers. Fairtrade has changed its marketing approach to focus on 'stable prices, decent working conditions and empowerment of farmers and workers around the world'. The standards still encompass social, economic and environmental standards (FLO, 2018). Fairtrade increased the minimum price for certified coffee by an average of five cents, rising to US$1.24 per pound for unwashed, and US$1.28 per pound for arabica coffee (FLO, 2018). The new minimum price intended to cover sustainable production costs for coffee-producing organisations. It was again increased in 2011 to US$1.35 per pound for unwashed and US$1.40 per pound for washed arabica. The increase in price did not, however, seem to improve the overall experience with FLO certification, influenced also by additional factors. By 2014 certification fatigue,[43] and reduced coffee production lowered certified coffee production in Costa Rica, also observed in 2016 (Grabs *et al.*, 2016). Information regarding follow-up fieldwork in 2014 provides more detailed information for two communities.

Micro-mills and direct trade through noncertified markets

The expansion of direct trade markets provided options beyond a conditioned 'access to different certified markets' trade dynamic, and therefore an alternative to certifications and cooperative membership. The increased emergence of micro-mills across the country, estimated at 150 (Gyllensten, 2017), complements ability to sell to this market. The Asociación de Productores Agropecuarios de las Comunidades de Acosta y Aserrí (ASOPROAAA), a democratically run association with 217 coffee growers known for quality of coffee exports and promotion of micro-mills, observed that micro-mill trade was 'giving producers a greater sense of pride and ownership for their work'.

While micro-mills and direct trade have provided consistent price premiums for sale of small farm holder produce (Vogt, 2011; Gyllensten, 2017; Vogt, 2019), and already certified and compliant produce, they do not independently assure sustainable farming and processing approaches. There is therefore a balance to be found between premium price of noncertified direct coffee trade, and effective environmental and social outcomes resulting from the farming and processing of coffee. This is particularly the case where intensive conventional coffee farming dominates, and regulation for pollution, leaching and contamination is poor.

While Costa Rica is a highly regulated industry on paper (Grabs *et al.*, 2016), in practice, it is not always the case. The location of a new micro-mill and limited intention for treatment and containment of waste water observed in 2009 evidenced a potential area for attention in the future. The closed-circuit waste treatment and management systems used by many Fairtrade-certified cooperatives in 2009 required significant investment. For 150 micro-mills financial and technical assistance is likely necessary. MAG and ICafe regulate against several environmental laws associated with wet processing of coffee at the *beneficio*. MAG was also involved in renewing or establishing micro-mills around the country. The Nationally Appropriate Mitigation Actions (NAMA) for Costa Rican coffee worked with 16 new coffee mills and 34 established *beneficios* in 2017, to encourage understanding of carbon and water footprint, and to develop strategies for reducing both. Reducing chemical fertilisers by using pulp waste for fertilisers, and reducing water used are included. The NAMA example, as an extramarket effort, demonstrates efficacy. Transparency and legitimacy, including 'sustainable' farming and processing practices remain necessary for direct, specialty and conventional markets.

Follow-up fieldwork 2014

Agua Buena

In 2009 the community cooperative Coopepueblos was Fairtrade certified, and representatives of an agroecological network were working with Coopepueblos to provide a different and less expensive approach to improving farming practices. They sold roasted coffee online providing a significantly higher price for coffee compared to Fairtrade. The agroecological network was considered superior by the community. Students in the community were interacting with farmers at an external expense, bringing income to the community through local accommodations They were organising direct sale of roasted coffee at a high price, which was looked upon favourably but was yet to achieve significant sales rates. In comparison:

> In Fairtrade we have to invest in an auditor, with CAN they give us technical advice for free. With Fairtrade, the prices are not so fair, at the moment Fairtrade is not covering the cost of production for the cooperative or the farms. We have a market outside of Fairtrade which is $2.08, this is more than Fairtrade. We sell 75% to the Fairtrade market.[44]

By 2014 Coopepueblos had closed, and the number of coffee farms had decreased. Coffee farming was not proving to be economically viable for local

Figure 11.2 Follow-up fieldwork locations 2014.

Source: Esri, USGS | Esri, HERE, Garmin, FAO, NOAA, USGS | Esri, HERE, Garmin, FAO, NOAA, USGS.

farmers, despite Fairtrade certification. There was one coffee farm still using agroecological techniques introduced around 2009, roasting on-farm and selling locally and exporting through the family business.[45] The agroecological network was, however, no longer in this community.[46] It is noted that Agua Buena is a more isolated community with low employment rates and proportional subsistence to trade economy. Bartering remained an active approach to trade as proportional to paid purchases. It is located next to Estación Biológica Las Cruces and near Wilson Botanic Gardens, which is a favourite location for bird watching, so can receive tourism flows.

Monteverde/Santa Elena

In 2009, the cooperative Santa Elena was a recognised presence within the community. It was one of the first cooperatives to sell via 'Fair trade' market channels in the country as a direct trade arrangement with a roaster in the USA. The investment to comply with Fairtrade standards over time was recognised as something of a sacrifice but not beyond benefit. The Fairtrade price was not consistently or exceptionally above the standard market price, with the exception of the original direct trade arrangement. The cooperative had established a café and was offering a coffee tour to take advantage of the significant local tourist market. The Fairtrade label also provided something recognised by tourists, increasing familiarity and perhaps then preference for associated products.

In 2014, direct trade arrangements, including in-country roasting and selling at local markets were favoured, with cooperative involvement considered increasingly complicated.[47] What is now, in 2018 an association, includes the same café, coffee tours and a sustainable agriculture programme. Certifications include Friends of Earth and Costa Rican programmes, Bandera Azul and NAMA. Original fair trade arrangements are maintained where the farmer and buyer decide. Monteverde is a popular travel destination of the country. As such the opportunities and situation in the community are distinct from other communities.

The two examples provided here do not represent a negative or irrelevant contribution of certification efforts. The effort to implement Fairtrade standards was made in both communities as necessary, arguably to the benefit of good environmental and health and safety practices. Where compliance was not prioritised, benefit may not be evident. In Santa Elena, the change in popularity and eventually involvement with Fairtrade could be understood as a natural progression. In Agua Buena, the reason for ceased involvement with Fairtrade was due to the closure of Coopepueblos. The varying 'difficulties' with the coffee industry and/or with the certification process had, within these communities, overshadowed the benefits of Fairtrade certification.

Certifications as a market movement: the elusive measure of consumer influence

The significant strength of influence of client demands through the source chain on coffee producers follows a demand for, or estimation of, certifications in 'consumer' countries.

The distance between consumers and producers can facilitate poor understanding of how certifications improve 'sustainable' trade and sourcing practices. Marketing efforts claim certifications 'make a difference' to sell labelled products. They can over-exaggerate or misrepresent the benefit of certifications, perhaps as necessary to promote sales. More than 50 per cent of coffee cooperative managers or employees interviewed in 2009 held the idea that certifications had become, 'simplemente un capricho del Mercado y del consumidor' [simply a whim of the market and consumer].[48] An imbalance between labelling and standards in perception and perhaps reality could be understood. Where consumer demand folds back to generate demand for multiple certifications with subsequent requirements for producers, this order

of influence becomes almost illogical. Producers' variable awareness of certifications also highlights distinction between labelling, standards and compliance: 'este es un miembro de Coope Agri y él no sabe que él es un
'campesino Fairtrade'. [This is a member of Coope Agri and he does not
know that he is a 'Fairtrade farmer'.][49]

The intramarket location of certifications provides more opportunity for
producer involvement in international markets, and therefore in power-
reliant processes of international markets. While producers rely on certifications for market access and perhaps increased price, market demand and
preference continue to provide significant influence on standards followed.
Where standard quality is high, sustainable agricultural practices can benefit;
where inappropriate, effort can be made with little sustainability outcome.
Where multiple standards are required, significant investment for implementation and crossreferencing to prove compliance will likely be necessary.
While increased investment and inappropriate standards may appear insignifi-
cant amongst other benefits, it requires more of producer groups with ideas
of sustainable development. Within an industry that exists across a well-
established geographic divide of developing and developed countries this can
become a situation not only of inappropriate standards and limited benefits,
but also of inappropriate approach.

This does not go unnoticed in producer countries. José Figueres Ferrer[50]
(in Martz, 1959, 243) explained, 'we resent the presence of speculators who
assert that their motive in investing money abroad is to foster the development of our countries'. One interview participant summarised certification
efforts within a broader context:

> Las certificaciones son solo un negocio, un negocio multimillonario que
> sigue tomando dinero del productor. En la mayoría, el productor siempre
> ha sido ambiental. ¿Quién no está consciente del medio ambiente? La
> gente del mundo desarrollado, nos dieron toda la basura, los agroquími-
> cos de la revolución verde y nos fuimos con ella. Nos hicieron envenenar
> nuestra tierra para no protegerla. Así que hoy necesitamos invertirlo, ellos
> piden estas certificaciones porque lo piden en Europa y Estados Unidos y
> ahora quieren que seamos los limpiadores del mundo. Eso está bien, pero
> como hemos tenido que pagar, tienen que pagar; Oxigeno vale mucho
> dinero, al igual que el agua. [The certifications are just a business, a
> multi-million-dollar business that keeps taking money from the producer.
> In the majority, the producer has always been environmental. Who is not
> environmentally conscious? The people of the developed world, they
> gave us all the rubbish, the agro-chemicals from the green revolution and
> we went with it. They made us poison our land not protect it. So today
> we need to reverse it, they ask for these certifications because they ask
> for it in Europe and the US and now they want us to be the cleaners of
> the world. That is fine, but as we have had to pay, they have to pay;
> oxygen is worth a lot of money, as is water.][51]

It is difficult to ensure that such situations cease from continuing. Increased exposure and experience with certifications may improve this dynamic. The intramarket location of certifications, while recognised as necessary and a valuable contribution to prompting change, could make this more difficult, but not impossible. An understanding of distinction between labels, standards and effective implementation is required.

If an understanding of market access benefit leads incentive to demand certified produce and subsequently to be certified, complying with standards becomes a necessary activity to achieve market access. Where becoming certified is understood within this idea, and producers have a limited interest in being 'sustainable', certification can still prompt improved 'sustainable' practices compared to a counterfactual. Evidence from fieldwork suggests this is not the case, as changes in practices occur for multiple reasons, including certifications. The distance between required standards and effective implementation is also a factor. The implications of such source chain dynamics encourage improved consideration of the role certifications play, not only intramarket but also within producing countries, toward improved outcomes, aligned with intentions. Studies with attention on how consumers influence certification demand, how they are influenced by ideas of 'sustainable' practices, and how sourcing businesses are influenced by and influence consumers may assist.

Summary

Certified markets for Costa Rican coffee

Costa Rica was one of the first countries to adopt certification for coffee. By 2014 certification fatigue,[52] and reduced coffee production lowered certified production, also observed in 2016 (Grabs *et al.*, 2016). Certification fatigue can be better understood by considering perspectives toward certifications in 2009. With a variable perceived value, allowing market preference to guide demand for certifications appears a symptom of industry trade dynamics. This may have overestimated positive producer perception of certification efforts, and in this situation certification fatigue is more likely to occur.

While conditioned purchases based on certification decentralises options for producers, it also allows a 'top-down' approach, irrespective of who initiates the certification process. Limited alternatives for secured market access can increase susceptibility to these demand dynamics. Benefit to organisational sustainability and sustainable practices ultimately depends on standard quality and implementation. Where investment compared to benefit is positive, compliance to multiple standards could improve sustainable agricultural practices and satisfy varying preferences for improved market access. If certifications were encouraging any form of diversified crop activity, this may be more so the case.

On the other hand, without investment capability, compliance to one certification standard can be difficult. Requiring compliance to multiple standards may not be the most effective way to increase reach of sustainable standards and practices. It could in fact be considered an inappropriate approach, as explained in the summary of 2014 fieldwork. Where larger corporations increasingly use certifications to guide sustainable sourcing, the financial ability to compensate requirements may facilitate producer compliance. This ultimately relies on transparency and legitimate and fair contractual negotiations for long-term agreements between producer groups and larger traders. Where certifications seek to maintain relevance with small producers, in-country producers and organisation requirements, and original 'sustainability' intentions must be well considered.

Noncertified direct trade markets

The variable experience with certifications informs preferred markets, and the downfalls potentially evidence the young nature of sustainability efforts. The promising alternative of noncertified direct trade seems a natural progression in preference. To seek out and move toward alternatives demonstrates a level of self-determination and empowerment to ensure continued functionings. A reciprocal relationship between income and a person's capability is described as a 'connection going from capability improvement to greater earning power and not only the other way around' (Comin, 2001, 90; Sen, 1999). As direct trade markets increased in accessibility, access to national and international markets increased, and the need for certifications and cooperatives reduced, with functionings continuing. In this situation the 'aid' of certifications becomes less relevant in the perception of the producing communities. Substitute activities to coffee farming in Agua Buena condition this situation at a community level. Improved opportunities with direct markets and micromills are therefore considered a reason for reduced certified coffee in Costa Rica. Consistent price premiums and improved simplicity, autonomy and independence,[53] compared to more complicated cooperative membership and politics, and what had become something of a certification saga were preferred. Direct trade markets do not, however, require improved or maintained sustainable agricultural and processing practices, or socially just trade conditions.

Improved attention to quality standards and verification is important across certified and noncertified markets. Legal requirements can contribute to required practices but are extremely reliant on country contexts. Certification standards also proved to be more advanced than legal requirements in 2009, suggesting a possible benefit of having intramarket standards and legal requirements only then limited or enabled by available resources for effective implementation. The additional layer to this observation is that within the undoubtedly influential consumer and market perception, standards remain associated to labels, and labels indicate little about standard quality and verified outcomes. While direct trade provides a more fluid and less strict approach, and improvement in price compared to certified markets, the difference is conditioned by the certification. Given different farm sizes use different certifications in Costa Rica, direct trade benefits compared to certifications will also be influenced by farm type. There is therefore little evidence to suggest that either approach, certified or noncertified direct trade markets will consistently or comprehensively improve practices and outcomes without internal improvement and additional influencing factors.

Notes

1 For the purposes of this chapter 'aid' can be referred to as an external intervention with intention to improve a community situation.
2 Cooperative manager (personal communication, 13 April 2009).
3 There are varying categories of coffee farmer ('producer') within certification discussions: one who is a small holding farmer, living on or off the farm; and then small holding farmers who are involved in community leadership, in a cooperative or regional government. There are also farmers or farm managers of larger landholdings. In 2009, a farmer of approximately five hectares who was also involved in leadership of a cooperative or other type of producer organisation, or of larger landholdings, was most likely directly involved in a certification process. Other farmers will be indirectly involved through the implementation of new processes and practices, generally without awareness that a change is occurring due to a certification. Business administrators quoted in this text are also referred to within the producer term, as many, particularly those involved in cooperatives, are also coffee farmers.
4 Administrator of certification programmes (Personal communication, 25 February 2009); Farm administrator (Personal communication, 17 February 2009); International marketing manager (Personal communication, 11 May 2009).
5 Financial manager and assistant director, 13 February 2009; Administrator of certification programmes, 25 February 2009; Farm administrator, 17 February 2009; International marketing manager, 11 May 2009.
6 Regional director of Pérez Zeledón (Personal communication, 11 May 2009).
7 Technical engineer and administrator of certification programmes (Personal communication, 2 February 2009).
8 Standards and policy technical coordinator (Personal communication, 6 May 2009).
9 Cooperative manager (Personal communication, 13 February 2009); Cooperative manager (Personal communication, 20 March 2009).
10 International marketing manager (Personal communication, 11 May 2009).
11 Premiums are allocated to technological advances or community development projects by cooperative member choice.
12 Director of Hijos del Campo and Café Forestal (Personal communication, 20 February 2009).
13 International marketing manager, Cooperative (Personal communication, 11 April 2009).
14 Cooperative manager (Personal communication, 20 February 2009).
15 Standards and policy technical coordinator (Personal communication, 6 May 2009).
16 Previous cooperative manager, coffee farmers and cooperative manager (Personal communication, 12 January 2009).
17 Cooperative manager (Personal communication, 11 March 2009).
18 Financial manager and assistant director (Personal communication, 13 February 2009).

19 Financial manager and assistant director (Personal communication, 13 February 2009).
20 Cooperative manager (Personal communication, 13 April 2009).
21 Cooperative manager (Personal communication, 11 March 2009).
22 60 quintal = fanega = 46 kg = 1 lb = 10 cajuelas.
23 Financial manager and assistant director of cooperative (Personal communication, 13 February 2009).
24 International marketing manager, RA-certified plantation (Personal communication, 11 May 2009).
25 Former cooperative manager, coffee farmer and cooperative member (Personal communication, 12 January 2009).
26 Cooperative manager (Personal communication, 20 February 2009).
27 Administrator of certification programmes (Personal communication, 25 February 2009); Farm administrator (Personal communication, 17 February 2009).
28 Cooperative manager (Personal communication, 25 February 2009).
29 International marketing manager (Personal communication, 11 May 2009).
30 Standards and policy technical coordinator (Personal communication, 6 May 2009).
31 Administrator of certification programmes (Personal communication, 25 February 2009).
32 'Roman' coffee farmer (Personal communication, 27 March 2009).
33 'Walter' coffee farmer (Personal communication, 27 March 2009).
34 Cooperative manager (Personal communication, 31 March 2009).
35 Director of Café Forestal and Hijos del Campo (Personal communication, 20 February 2009).
36 Cooperative manager (Personal communication, 20 February 2009).
37 Director of Café Forestal and Hijos del Campo (Personal communication, 20 February 2009).
38 The 1988 decree 18135 prohibited introducing Robusta varieties to Costa Rica. In 1989 decree 19302 eliminated any existing Robusta varieties across Costa Rica (MAG, 1988, 1989). While with potential to encourage shaded systems as required by most arabica, hybrid arabica varieties introduced during the green revolution do not require shade. In 1996, law N575 (Buckingham and Hanson, 2010) introduced land title with financial subsidies for reforestation efforts.
39 Standards and policy technical coordinator (Personal communication, 5 May 2009).
40 The opinions provided here are therefore based on pre-2009 standard content, and compliance expectations.
41 Coffee processing plant/mill.
42 Vogt, M. (Personal observation, 11 June 2009).
43 Farm owner (Personal communication, August, 2014).
44 Cooperative manager (Personal communication, 25 February 2009), translation.
45 A recommendation from 2009 fieldwork included an increase in source chain vertical integration. This involved roasting in-country and exporting coffee roasted directly to consumers with significant price premium. For broader industry application, this presented an issue related to cupping quality, due to time between roasting and grinding, most relevant for café-served coffee. It remains, however, a recommendation.
46 A point for exploration here is where a programme such as CAN, which demonstrated efficacy beyond Fairtrade, is no longer operating. Fairtrade would have capability to maintain operation where compliance is demonstrated, and the cooperative remained open. This is not a certain outcome for CAN. Efficacy by standard and approach of a sustainable effort is therefore useful where combined with an ability to sustain efforts.
47 Farm owner (Personal communication, August 2014).

48 Cooperative manager (Personal communication, 11 May 2009).
49 Regional director, ICafe (Personal communication, 11 May 2009).
50 President of Costa Rica 1948–1949; 1953–1958; 1970–1974.
51 Cooperative manager (Personal communication, 20 February 2009).
52 Farm owner (Personal communication, August, 2014).
53 Farm owner (Personal communication, August, 2014).

References

Personal interviews

Administrator of certification programmes. (2009, 25 February). Personal interview.
Cooperative manager. (2009, 4 February). Personal interview.
Cooperative manager. (2009, 13 February). Personal interview.
Cooperative manager. (2009, 20 February). Personal interview.
Cooperative manager. (2009, 11 March). Personal interview.
Cooperative manager. (2009, 17 March). Personal interview.
Cooperative manager. (2009, 20 March). Personal interview.
Cooperative manager. (2009, 31 March). Personal interview.
Cooperative manager. (2009, 13 April). Personal interview.
Cooperative manager. (2009, 11 May). Personal interview.
Director of Café Forestal and Hijos del Campo. (2009, 20 February). Personal interview.
Farm administrator. (2009, 17 February). Personal interview.
Farm owner. (2014, August). Personal interview/discussion.
Financial and assistant director. (2009, 13 February). Personal interview.
Financial manager and assistant director of cooperative. (2009, 13 February). Personal interview.
Former cooperative manager, coffee farmers and cooperative manager. (2009, 12 January). Personal interview.
International marketing manager, cooperative. (2009, 11 April). Personal interview.
International marketing manager, RA-certified plantation. (2009, 11 May). Personal interview.
Regional director, ICafe. (2009, 11 May). Personal interview.
'Roman' coffee farmer. (2009, 27 March). Personal communication.
Standards and policy technical coordinator, Rainforest Alliance. (2009, 6 May). Personal interview.
Technical engineer and administrator of certification programmes. (2009, 2 February). Personal interview.
Vogt, M. (2009, 11 June). Personal observation.
'Walter' coffee farmer. (2009, 27 March). Personal interview.

References

Adams MA. Ghaly AE. 2006. Determining barriers to sustainability within the Costa Rican coffee industry. Sustainable Development 15(4): 229–241.
Babin N. 2015. Coffee crisis, fair trade, and agroecological transformation: impacts on land-use change in Costa Rica. Agroecology and Sustainable Food Systems 29(1): 99–129.

Bacon C. Mendez E. Gliessman S. Goodman D. Fox J. (eds.) 2008. Confronting the Coffee Crisis: Fair Trade, Sustainable Livelihoods, and Ecosystems in Mexico and Central America. MIT Press.

Barham BL. Callenes M. Gitter S. Lewis J. Weber J. 2011. Fair trade/organic coffee, rural livelihoods, and the 'agrarian question': southern Mexican coffee families in transition. World Development 39(1): 134–145.

Buckingham K. and Hanson C. 2010. The Restoration Diagnostic, Case Example: Costa Rica. World Resources Institute. wri.org.

Comin F. 2001. Operationalising Sen's capability approach. Conference Justice and Poverty: Examining Sen's Capability Approach. Cambridge, 5–7 June. www.st-edmunds.cam.ac.uk/vhi/.

Costa Rica 1961. Ley 2762 del 21/06/1961: Ley sobre régimen de relaciones entre productores, beneficiadores y exportadores de café. Costa Rica, Asamblea Legislativa de la Republica de Costa Rica.

Costa Rica 2010. Ley 8839 del 8/12/2010. Decreta: Ley para la gestión integral de residuos. Asamblea Legislativa de la Republica de Costa Rica. La Gaceta 135. www.ucr.ac.cr/medios/documentos/2015/LEY-8839.pdf.

Danse M. Wolters T. 2003. Sustainable coffee in the mainstream: the case of the SUSCOF Consortium in Costa Rica. GMI 43: 37–51.

De Neve G. Luetchford P. Pratt J. Wood DC. (eds.) 2008. Hidden Hands in the Market: Ethnographies of Fair Trade, Ethical Consumption and Corporate Social Responsibility. Emerald.

Diaz D. 2015. Costa Rica: How quality pays for coffee farmers. responAbility Investments Ag. Zurich.

Donald P. 2004. Biodiversity impacts of some agricultural commodity production systems. Conservation Biology 18(1): 17–37.

Esri 2018. Terrain with Labels (local language) [basemap]. Scale not given. World Terrain Base. August 2018. www.arcgis.com/home/webmap/viewer.html?webma p=5f68957c846942f19d2ac5cb191842c8.

FLANZ and Oxfam Australia 2010. Tackling Poverty through Trade: How Australians Buying Fairtrade Benefits Producers in Developing Countries. www.oxfam. org.au/wp-content/uploads/site-media/pdf/oaus-tackingpovertyfairtrade-0409.pdf.

FLO 2018. www.fairtrade.net/.

Grabs J., Kilian B., Calderón Hernández D., Dietz T. 2016. Understanding coffee certification dynamics: a spatial analysis of voluntary sustainability standard proliferation. International Food and Agribusiness Management Review 19(3): 31–56.

Gyllensten B. 2017. Micro Mills, Specialty Coffee and Relationships: Following the Supply Chain from Costa Rica to Norway. Thesis. Reprosentralen, University of Oslo.

Hanson L. Terstappen V. Bacon CM. Leung J. Ganem-Cuenca A. Flores SRD. Rojas MAM. 2012. Gender, health, and Fairtrade: insights from a research-action programme in Nicaragua. Development in Practice 22(2): 164–179. http://dx.doi.org /10.1080/09614524.2012.640981.

ICA 2007. International Coffee Agreement 2007. www.ico.org/ica2007.asp.

ICafe 2015. El café sostenible de Costa Rica. www.icafe.cr/nuestro-cafe/proceso-de-liquidacion/.

ICafe 2018. Estructura del sector. www.icafe.cr/nuestro-cafe/estructura-del-sector/.

ICO 2007. International Coffee Agreement 2007. www.ico.org/documents/ ica2007e.pdf.

ICO 2018. Developing a Sustainable Coffee Economy. www.ico.org/sustaindev_e.asp.

Jaffe D. 2012. Weak coffee: certification and co-optation in the fair trade movement. Social Problems 59(1): 94–116.

Jaffe R. Bacon C. 2008. From differentiated coffee markets toward alternative trade and knowledge networks. In Bacon C. Mendez E. Gliessman S. Goodman D. Fox J. (eds.) Confronting the Coffee Crisis: Fair Trade, Sustainable Livelihoods and ecosystems in Mexico and Central America. The MIT Press.

Lernoud J. Potts J. Sampson G. Schlatter B. Huppe G. Voora V. Willer H. Wozniak J. Dang D. 2018. The State of Sustainable Markets: Statistics and Emerging Trends 2018. ITC, Geneva.

Luetchford P. 2008. Fair Trade and a Global Commodity: Coffee in Costa Rica. Pluto Press.

Macdonald K. 2007. Globalising justice within coffee supply chains? Fair trade, Starbucks and the transformation of supply chain governance. Third World Quarterly 28(4): 793–812.

MAG 1988. Decreto 18135 MAG: Prohibición para sembrar la variedad de café denominado Coffea Canephora Robusta. La Gaceta 106(25), 3 June.

MAG 1989. Decreto 19302 MAG: Autoriza al Instituto del Café de Costa Rica y al Ministerio de Agricultura y Ganaderia para eliminar las siembras existentes de la especie denominada Coffea Canephora 'Robusta'. La Gaceta 229(6–7), 4 December.

Martz JD. 1959. Central America: The Crisis and Challenge. University of North Carolina Press.

Mitchell MT. Pentzer S. 2008. Costa Rica: A Global Studies Handbook. ABC-CLIO.

Naranjo C. 1997. La modernización de la caficultura costarricense 1890–1950. Tesis de Maestría en Historia. Universidad de Costa Rica, 94–104.

Potts J. Lynch M. Wilkings A. Huppe G. Cunningham M. Voora V. 2014. The State of Sustainability Initiatives Review. International Institute for Sustainable Development, Winnipeg. www.iisd.org/pdf/2014/ssi_2014.pdf.

Rainforest Alliance 2018. www.rainforest-alliance.org/approach.

Raynolds L. Murray D. Taylor P. 2003. One Cup at a Time: Fair Trade and Poverty Alleviation in Latin America. Fair Trade Research Group, Colorado.

Raynolds L. Murray D. Wilkinson J. 2007. Fair Trade: The Challenges of Transforming Globalisation. Routledge.

Rovira Mas J. 2000. Estado y política económica en Costa Rica 1948–1970. Editorial de la Universidad de Costa Rica.

Ruben R. Zuniga G. 2010. How standards compete: comparative impact of coffee certification schemes in northern Nicaragua. International Journal of Supply Chain Management 16(2): 98–109.

Samper M. 2000. Derivaciones de la modernización e intensificación cafetalera. In Samper M., Naranjo C. Sfez P. (eds.) Entre la tradición y el cambio: Evolución tecnológica de la caficultura costarricense. SEE S.A.

Sen A. 1999. Development as Freedom. Anchor Books. www.mag.go.cr/legislacion/1989/de-19302.pdf.

Shaw D. and Black I. 2010. Market based political action: a path to sustainable development? Sustainable Development 18(6): 385–397.

Smith J. 2008. The search for sustainable markets: the promise and failure of fair trade. Culture and Agriculture 29(2): 88–99.

SSI Review 2014. Coffee Market. Chapter 8. www.iisd.org/pdf/2014/ssi_2014_chapter_8.pdf.

Vogt M. 2011. Tico Time: The Influence of Coffee Certifications on Sustainable Development and Poverty Reduction in Costa Rica: A Discussion with Coffee Farmers and Cooperative Managers. PhD. Flinders University, Faculty of Social and Behavioural Sciences.

Vogt M. 2019. Variance in Approach toward a 'Sustainable' Coffee Industry in Costa Rica: Perspectives from Within; Lessons and Insights. Ubiquity Press (UNDER REVIEW).

Winson A. 1989. Coffee and Democracy in Costa Rica. Springer, Political Science.

Wollni M. Zeller M. 2006. Do farmers benefit from participating in specialty markets and cooperatives? The case of coffee marketing in Costa Rica. Contributed paper prepared for presentation at the International Association of Agricultural Economics Conference, Gold Coast, Australia, 12–18 August.

12 To certify or not to certify

Flower production practices in Ecuador

Jeroen Vos, Pippi van Ommen, and
Patricio Mena-Vásconez

Introduction

Private certification of agricultural products has become an important govern-ance mechanism in global supply chains. It pertains to the wider activities of Corporate Social Responsibility (CSR). Companies have three basic reasons to engage in private certification (Hughes, 2001): First, retailers need to guar-antee constant supplies of products of sufficient quality to supermarkets. Sus-tainable standards prevent resource depletion and degradation that could jeopardise the supply. Second, supermarkets are very vulnerable to reputation damage. Low-quality products, health risks, and environmental disasters could easily harm the image of a big company. Third, for an increasing number of companies, fair trade and environmentally friendly products are a niche market that is growing in many countries.

Most private certification schemes have four main characteristics: a *publicly available document* detailing the standards; an *audit* usually performed by private third parties; either a *seal on the product* to notify the consumer or a *label* used only by the retailers; and a *certification organisation* that establishes and com-municates the standards, trains producers and inspectors, and authorises audit-ing agents (Mutersbaugh *et al.*, 2005).

Doubts have arisen regarding the effectiveness of private certification of social and environmental practices of companies (Bacon, 2010; Jaffee, 2012; Langen and Adenaeuer, 2013; Raynolds, 2014). Vos and Boelens (2014) identified six general critiques about private social and environmental certification:

1 Technocratic and uniform definition of standards (not adapted to local circumstances and valorisations),
2 Low levels of transparency and democracy in setting the standards,
3 Exclusion of smallholders (fees too high, standards not adapted to their conditions),
4 Negligible environmental benefits (relatively 'good' producers already had good practices before their certification, and companies with 'bad' practices do not opt for certification),

5   Risk of coopting and less stringent criteria, and
6   Difficulties in auditing and susceptibility to poor auditing and fraud.

To examine the effect of private certification and the relative contribution of certifications to the environmental and social change in a supply chain we take the example of flower production in Ecuador, which started in the northern Andean region in the early 1980s. Since 2010 Ecuador became the third largest exporter of flowers worldwide (UN Comtrade, 2018). Flower, mostly rose, production has enormous impact on the economy of the Cayambe-Tabacundo region, north of the capital Quito. The flower sector has been employing many people from the Indigenous communities, providing a livelihood, but inflicting deep cultural changes. Many concerns have been raised regarding work conditions, including health effects caused by pesticide use, and general environmental effects (Tenenbaum, 2002; Sawers, 2005; Breilh, 2007; Breilh et al., 2009). Although many interviewees stated that pesticide use has been reduced (see also Soper, 2013), Victor van Dijk, Area Manager South America with the Dutch flower trader FleuraMetz, stated in 2017: '[W]e strive for 90% sustainably-produced flowers. But in Ecuador we still have a long way to go' (Bloemisterij, 2017, own translation).

As irrigation water is increasingly scarce in the Ecuadorian Andes, a conflict arose over the use of a shared irrigation canal between smallholder subsistence producers and large flower companies (Mena-Vásconez et al., 2017). Smallholders gained control over the irrigation system and gained access to more irrigation water but still most water goes to the big companies. Those companies increasingly use water from groundwater wells and have built rainwater storage reservoirs.

Interestingly, and different from export flower production in other low and middle-income countries like Colombia and Kenya, since around 2005 many smallholders in the Cayambe-Tabacundo region have established their own small greenhouses and sell their flowers to traders or large flower producers. In this region, over 600 small flower producers sell flowers for export to international traders (Mena-Vásconez et al., 2016). This has led to the central question for this chapter: What is the relative contribution of the private certification on the environmental and social changes in this export flower production region of Ecuador?

Method

The data for this research were collected during field studies executed from 2013 to 2018. In 2013 a questionnaire was held with 53 representatives of big and small flower producers, including questions on certification. In 2017 and 2018 semistructured interviews were held with 23 representatives of small and medium-sized flower companies. During the whole period about 40 extended open interviews were conducted with several owners or managers of small and big companies and representatives of local municipal governments,

NGOs, water users' associations, flower traders, producer associations, certifiers, and breeders. The data was complemented with literature research. Interviewing owners/managers of big companies proved difficult, which might have created a biased view.

Places, forms and spaces of power

In our analysis, environmental and social standards are not treated as objective rules that are applied by objective organisations for the general benefit of all. We will look at specific interests of the stakeholders and use power analysis to examine the making and application of environmental and social regulations in the flower production in Ecuador. In addition, we look at the dominant discourses that legitimise the structure of representation and the accepted norms and values in the environmental governance of the flower industry.

We concur with Lemke (2007, 58) in that to understand social change we should study 'practices instead of object, strategies instead of function, and technologies instead of institution'. Therefore, we will structure this chapter along the strategies, practices, and technologies of five key agents in the flower business in Ecuador: (a) certifiers and audit companies, (b) big flower producers, (c) small flower producers, organised in communities and water users' associations, (d) governmental organisations at different levels, and (e) NGOs.

A practical conceptual framework to investigate the possibilities of social change by agents is Gaventa's (2006) power-cube. The power-cube is three-dimensional: *spaces* for participation, *levels and places* for engagement, and *forms of power*. Within the dimension of spaces, Gaventa defines three types: closed, invited, and claimed spaces. Closed spaces refer to processes of decision making where policy makers, bureaucrats, or experts take decisions without participation of stakeholders. In invited spaces, decision makers invite representatives of stakeholders to be involved in decision making. The degree of say of these representatives can vary from just being informed to a real voice in decision making. However, in invited spaces the topics of discussion and the rules of decision making are set by the organisers. Claimed spaces are created when organised civil society groups succeed in obtaining real influence and can shape or determine the agenda and the rules of decision making themselves.

The dimension of places for engagement refers to the scale of governance from global to household. Institutions and regulations are increasingly defined at global levels. Rooted, bottom-up strategies are applied by local organisations to defend themselves against top-down universalising rules.

The dimension of the forms of power refers to the type of power in a given place and space. Visible forms of power are, for example, the official political structures, the formal rules and procedures of decision making. Hidden power is a form of power that is in principle visible, but actively concealed by powerful people and organisations. This power works by excluding others from setting the agenda. Invisible power functions through the shaping of meaning and truth, and what is acceptable, desirable, and normal. This is what Foucault called disciplinary governmentality: the internalisation of what is desired, normal, and true (Foucault, 1991).

Examining the practices of flower certification through the lenses of the three dimensions of power will help to scrutinise how, where, and why environmental and social regulations are designed and applied.

Flower production in Ecuador and its challenges

Flower production in Ecuador started in the early 1980s. Mainly foreign entrepreneurs were attracted by the favourable climate, constant daylight hours, cold nights, and high altitude,[1] relatively cheap labour, permissive environmental regulation, low taxation, and proximity to Quito's international airport (Soper, 2013; Mena-Vásconez et al., 2017). The quality and big size of the Ecuadorian roses are world famous. Flower exports have increased from US$195 million in the year 2000 to US$881 million in the year 2017 (UN Comtrade, 2018).

Most flower production occurs in the municipalities of Cayambe (capital Cayambe) and Pedro Moncayo (capital Tabacundo), a one-hour drive north of Quito. In this rural region large estates (*haciendas*) remain from colonial times, alongside Indigenous communities. The flower sector employs over 116,000 workers (USDA, 2009), the majority Indigenous, 60 per cent of them being women (Korovkin, 2003). Irrigation water is scarce, and Acequia Tabacundo, the main irrigation system supplying water to both big flower companies and peasant communities, has been at the core of fierce battles. In 2006 the irrigation system was taken over by the water users' association CODEMIA, which is controlled by peasant communities (Mena-Vásconez et al., 2017).

The flower industry in Ecuador can be divided in two groups: 'big businesses' and 'small enterprises'. There are around 300 big companies (>2 ha) and about 700 small (<2 ha) family-run flower companies[2] (Mena-Vásconez et al., 2017). Most big flower companies were established on former *haciendas*. They started in the 1980s and developed rapidly. Most are now Ecuadorian companies, but also French-, Dutch-, German- and Colombian–owned companies can be found. Export is mainly to the US, Russia, and Europe.

Big and small businesses consist of one or multiple greenhouses. The plastic-covered structure is built with steel or local eucalyptus poles. The flowers are grown in rows and are all drip-irrigated. Drip-irrigation technologies vary from rudimentary rubber tubes with holes in them running over ground, to the most advanced computerised underground systems. Usually, the smaller the business, the simpler the irrigation system. Some of the used agrochemicals are dissolved in the irrigation water. Larger farms include post-harvest (stockpiling, processing, cold-room) facilities while smaller ones usually sell directly to flower traders. Similarly, larger farms possess their own specialised transportation while smaller ones must hire trucks.

Since 2005, hundreds of peasant farmers have started small flower production enterprises, fomented by several factors: credit, experience and knowledge gained in the big flower businesses, desire for financial means,[3]
flexibility in working hours, and the appeal of becoming an entrepreneur
(Mena-Vásconez et al., 2016). Smaller businesses are typically family-run but
might employ one or more permanent workers. The research of Mena-
Vásconez et al. (2016) found that in 2002 there were no under-one-hectare
greenhouses in the Cayambe-Tabacundo study area, but in 2013 there were
over 300, and in 2016 an estimated 600. The effects this boom of small
greenhouse farms has had on the community, social relations, the environment, and the economic situation of the region have not been studied yet.

Smaller businesses build their greenhouses on small pieces of land, either
where they used to have cows or traditional crops, or which they bought from
someone in their community. Starting a small flower farm was done with the
help of the state-owned BanEcuador,[4] which provides credit to smallholders
against relatively low interest rates, or private institutions. Credit to build greenhouses is not easily granted to smaller farms. Thus, some families must rely on
savings to start up, or get support from a big flower company. Some companies
supported small ones by providing training, building materials for the greenhouses, irrigation installations, or pesticides. Working with these small companies is a way for big companies to spread their risk. Family-run farms may
thus not be independent, relying on a large company to which they sell their
flowers. The company in turn exports the flowers branded as their own, thus
reducing the large company's per-unit costs and financial and production risks.

Floriculture in Ecuador has had severe environmental and socioeconomic
impacts. One of the main problems reported has been the pesticides used
(Korovkin, 2003; Breilh, 2007; Soper, 2013). Flowers have been typically
grown with the help of large amounts of chemical fertilisers and pesticides
(Korovkin, 2005), often with products that have been banned in Europe and
North America. Reported symptoms of pesticide intoxication include head-
aches, dizziness, rashes, nausea, asthma, blurred vision and even stillbirths and
cancer (Korovkin, 2003; Breilh, 2007; Franze and Ciroth, 2011). It has not
helped that safety gear has reportedly been lacking (Soper, 2013). Because of
these characteristics and others, like denial of health services, less-than-
minimum wages and forced overtime, the cut flower industry has often been
described as harsh and exploitative (Tenenbaum, 2002; Sawers, 2005). It is
not only workers that have been affected through contamination from the use
of chemicals, but the entire community, as well as soil and water around the
greenhouses (IEDECA, 1999; Breilh, 2007; Breilh et al., 2009).

Additionally, floriculture can have negative socioeconomic effects because
it requires a lot of water for irrigation. Conflicts have arisen in communities
with flower farms over access to water resources (Mena-Vásconez et al., 2016,
2017; Hidalgo et al., 2017). During the last decade many large flower companies started to use groundwater and most have constructed reservoirs that
collect rainwater from the greenhouses' roofs.

Working conditions have been regarded as harsh: working days were reported to be long (72–84 hours/week), child labour to be common, overtime often not paid, and workers frequently not getting a contract (Franze and Ciroth, 2011). Floriculture is also said to have negative impacts on the social relations in local communities. According to Korovkin's research (2003) where she describes the 'erosion of communal organization' in flower-growing areas, community organisations were falling apart, even though on a national level Ecuador witnessed the rise of a powerful Indigenous and peasant movement. Korovkin blames the individualistic process of production and profit-oriented agribusiness that clashes with Indigenous community norms of collective responsibility and respect for nature (see also Mena-Vásconez et al., 2016; Hidalgo et al., 2017). A book published by the Indigenous group 'Cayambis' (GADIP, 2015, 71, own translation) states:

> Not only the floriculture in itself has teared up the Cayambis, but also the lack of a fair market has impeded the communal undertakings of the population. The hegemony of an unjust trade favours big producers and not the small ones.

In addition, gender relations changed because of the high number of women working in the flower industry. This situation made them more economically independent, which changed also cultural gender norms (Korovkin, 2003; Ferm, 2008).

In recent years the working conditions and environmental impact of flower production have improved (Soper, 2013). Several factors have contributed, such as the rise of a more conscious market in the West, which has spurred the growth of standard-setting organisations like Fairtrade International and Rainforest Alliance. These organisations have taken interest in the flower industry and started working together with some flower companies, assuring the consumer that the working conditions on plantations comply with the standards. However, as we will show below, many other factors have contributed to improve the flower production process: (1) the increased minimum wage set by the national government; (2) competition over workers among big and small flower producers; (3) the struggle of peasant communities and irrigation water users' associations over the re-allocation of irrigation water; (4) the pressure of local environmental NGOs like Agronomes et Vétérinaires Sans Frontières (AVSF) and CEAS; and (5) national, provincial, and municipal environmental regulations.

Flower certification

Recent years have seen the rise of a commitment in the flower sector to combat the problems outlined above. Several governmental regulations have been promulgated to monitor the flower sector. Besides these government regulations several private standards have been created by international organisations to reduce the negative social and environmental impact of flower production. Some companies, however, also wanted to give their flowers a better position in the niche market for sustainable and fair trade flowers. This section gives an overview of different standards in floriculture. Furthermore, the audit process of the certification is described and analysed.

These standards are set in a top–down manner at a global scale in a 'closed space' as defined in the power-cube analysis presented in the conceptual framework section. Private certification practices normalise the idea of regulation through competition in the global market. This empowers the companies that set the standards through the 'invisible power' (or 'governmentality') of the neoliberal discourse. The big flower companies are empowered because they gain market access (without much monitoring of their practices), legitimise the use of water for irrigation (because they are 'efficient'), and set the norms about production. Thus, certification strengthens the universalisation of, for example, the 'efficiency' norms of water use. This is a form of hidden power, as the certification bodies predetermine the agenda for the discussion on impacts of the flower industry. It becomes an 'invisible' form of power (a 'governmentality') because the norms are accepted and internalised by the farmers that start to regard their own water-use practices as 'inefficient'. Small farmers consequently accept the large share of the scarce irrigation water taken by the big flower companies.

Below we describe the five most used private standards: (1) Flower Label Program (although this programme ended in 2016 it is interesting because it was the first programme and stands out because it was set up by NGOs together with flower companies), (2) FlorEcuador, (3) Veriflora, (4) Rainforest Alliance, and (5) Fairtrade. Most big flower companies interviewed exported flowers certified by one or more certifying companies, although some reported to not engage in, or not need, certification. The Flower Label Program (FLP) was the only programme where standards were developed with the involvement of local worker unions of flower workers, environmental organisations, farmers' organisations, local or national governments or consumer organisations. In the other cases the standards were set by the standard-setting company with some consultation of sector stakeholders. An example of stakeholder involvement in standard setting is the 'Revision and Stakeholder Review Process' executed by SCS Global Services for the Veriflora standard (SCS Global Services, 2013). However, as indicated by Bacon (2010) regarding the participation process in the setting of the Fairtrade standard, the decision-making power of affected stakeholders is limited.

Certification is especially relevant for companies exporting to countries in the north of Europe and the US. Other countries, like Russia, China, and Spain, do not require certification. A flower company owner said:

In Russia and China, they do not care about our working conditions, they do not need any certifications or labels to prove anything. In the

United States they care just a little bit, but it's more the people in Europe who are more conscious and demand sustainability or things like that.

(personal communication, 11 May 2017)

A former broker responds to the question on sustainability and the market's demand: 'No, no, we do absolutely nothing with sustainability. It really does not matter in our business, it's not a subject … Organic flower farms? No that is impossible, nor is it very interesting' (Marcelo Vallejo, personal communication, 13 May 2017). Flower businesses have a choice which market they want to focus on. Many sell to Russia, a country not interested in certifications. However, some farmers are anxious because the recent crisis left many businesses bankrupt. They spread their risk by selling to the United States, where certified flowers are a growing niche market. About one out of three flower traders in the US requires a label (manager of a 20-ha flower company, personal communication, 10 April 2013). A former inspector of the FLP, Orlando Felicita, noticed that many of the big flower company managers wanted to get a certification because of peer-pressure: he paraphrased this idea as follows: 'if the neighbour has a certification label, we also want one' (personal communication, 2 April 2018).

Flower companies constantly strategise between market opportunities, with different certification requirements and costs for certification. As many traders who sell to Russia, Southern Europe, and China do not require certification of flowers, the producers do not really need to have their flowers certified. This can leave flower producers quite critical toward standards-setting companies. The standard-setting companies are dependent on the flower producers, and thus have an incentive to reduce the strictness of the criteria. This causes a 'race to the bottom' regarding the strictness of the standards between the companies that compete in the market for standards (Balas *et al.*, 2008). This is a form of invisible power, where the acceptance of the economic discourse (or neoliberal governmentality) gives power to the big companies that gain market access and legitimise water use, without much strict monitoring.

Flower Label Program

The Flower Label Program (FLP) was established in 1999 in Germany by NGOs and flower businesses. It was a round table certification initiative set up by Brot für die Welt, FIAN, and Terre des Hommes. It worked in several flower exporting countries like Ecuador, Colombia, and Kenya. In Ecuador they worked together with the NGO CEAS. In 2006, there were 56 Ecuadorian flower companies certified with FLP (SIPAE, 2016). It stopped in 2016 because the certification scheme did not involve third-party auditing.

CEAS was quite successful in putting the health effects of pesticide use in the flower business on the political agenda. They put pressure on the big flower businesses to reduce pesticide use and introduce measures to protect flower workers from being exposed to pesticides during their work in the greenhouses. They also put pressure on the government to regulate the use of toxic pesticides (Breilh, 2007; Breilh *et al.*, 2009).

FlorEcuador

With their head offices in Quito, Expoflores is an association of big companies that started in 2007. They report to cover 80 per cent of all flowers exported from Ecuador. All their companies are bigger than 15 ha. Expoflores only recognise the existence of around 100 large flower companies, of which they represent about 30. Members pay a monthly fee depending on the area of greenhouses. Every three months they come together in an assembly to discuss recent and future developments. The association is not in charge of export, all members having their own clients and post-harvest facilities. According to the local representative of the organisation in Cayambe, 'the advantage of working as an association is that you can get more done, share information, and you can also make better deals with, for example, the government' (personal communication, 10 May 2017).

Expoflores developed their own standard, FlorEcuador, in 2007. Nowadays, to be part of Expoflores the FlorEcuador certification is required. The standard of FlorEcuador has nine obligatory criteria and 121 criteria of which 80 per cent must be met (Expoflores, 2016a). From the obligatory criteria two stand out: one that forbids child labour under 15 years, and one that requires the flower company to have an environmental licence (see below). The other 121 criteria are mainly general requirements relatively easy to satisfy (Expoflores, 2016b). An exception is the criterion on quality of effluent water, which is strict. However, the four criteria for 'rational water management' require only a water quality test if the water is used for human consumption, a licence for the use of pumped irrigation water, and a registration of irrigation water use. As a certification can be obtained by meeting only 80 per cent of the criteria, the strict criteria can be circumnavigated. Auditing is done by Bureau Veritas Ecuador.

Veriflora, SCS Global Services

Veriflora is a programme developed by Scientific Certification Systems Global Services (SCS Global Services) from the US. Their vision is: 'providing cut flower and potted plant producers from all over the world with a detailed roadmap to satisfy the emerging market for sustainable products' (Jennifer Watters, SCS, personal communication, 20 March 2017). The audits are done by SCS Global Services. In 2012 in Ecuador 15 flower companies had the Veriflora label (SCS, 2012a).

The Veriflora standard, Version 3–1 (SCS 2012b), has nine 'elements' with a total of 152 criteria grouped in two 'Tiers'. Flower companies should comply with all prerequisites (Section 6 about planning and registration) and the 50 'critical requirements'. Furthermore, of Tier 1 criteria, 90 per cent should be met. From Tier 2 criteria 80 per cent should be met. The obligatory criteria require compliance with local legislation, such as pesticide use, record keeping on resource, and input use and planning. Most of the criteria are formulated in a nonquantitative and multi-interpretable way. For example, criterion 9.0 (Element 3), Tier 1 reads:

> Water conservation is an important component of sustainability. The Producer is required to conserve water through the use of effective water delivery systems, conservation and monitoring methods and technologies, and the institution of water quality management practices to protect the quality of these resources.

A more strictly formulated criterion is 9.1.2.6. (Tier 2) on irrigation: 'The Producer shall install irrigation systems that minimise water consumption through direct application to the root zone'. However, while all big flower producers comply to this criterion as they all have drip irrigation, this does not guarantee the absence of negative effects of over-extraction of local water resources or competition with local water users.

Criteria for water use refer to 'increased use efficiency', 'water conservation', and 'water saving'. This appears sustainable; however, the production of flowers or any other crop requires a certain volume of water per unit of product. Most of the time, keeping other inputs constant, reduction of application of this volume of water will reduce the production and thus will not change the amount of water used per unit of product (see Van Halsema and Vincent, 2012, for further explanation). If beforehand more water was applied than needed by the crop, this water would runoff or drain to surface water or aquifer and be available for use by other users. Thus, the reduction of applied water will only lead to so-called 'dry water savings' (Seckler, 1996), implying that this 'water saving' is not a 'real' one. At the same time, the dominant discourse of 'water use efficiency' is a powerful discourse that provides legitimacy to certification and the flower companies that are certified, and at the same time disempower the small flower producers that do not use advanced irrigation technology. This is a 'hidden' form of power in Gaventa's terminology.

The Veriflora criteria for labour conditions and rights are stricter than the environmental criteria. In conclusion, although the criteria on pesticide use forbid the most toxic chemicals to be used, the environmental criteria are permissive and will not prevent negative impacts on the environment.

Rainforest Alliance

Since 1992 Rainforest Alliance (RA) certifies banana plantation agriculture and since 1993 forests. In 1995 RA certified the first coffee farms, and in 1998 RA launched the Sustainable Agriculture Network (SAN), dedicated to providing standards for sustainable agriculture. In 2001 RA started certifying flower producers.

The RA Sustainable Agriculture Standard (RAS, Version 1.2, July 2017) has five principles and includes two categories: (1) 37 Critical Criteria, and (2) 82 Continuous Improvement Criteria (Rainforest Alliance, 2018a). RAS has seven Critical Criteria regarding environmental protection: criteria 3.1 to 3.7. They concern Integrated Pest Control plans, disposal of waste water, and use of sewage water. They prohibit the use of genetically modified organisms (GMOs) and certain pesticides and spraying agrochemicals from airplanes when plantation workers are in the field.

Regarding the Continuous Improvement Criteria, to remain certified farms must demonstrate an increasing degree of compliance with them over time. The system evaluates farms according to their level of implementation of good sustainability practices, from 'Good' (Level C) with 65 per cent after one year, to 'Better' (Level B), with 50 per cent after three years, and to 'Best' (Level A), 50 per cent after six years. Examples of Continuous Improvement include: Water-related criterion 3.16: 'Any new irrigation system is designed to optimise crop or pasture productivity while minimising water waste, erosion and salinization' (Performance Level C) and criterion 3.19: 'Based on record-keeping, the farm demonstrates reductions in water used for irrigation, processing, or cattle production per unit of product produced or processed' (Performance Level A). These criteria relate to 'water savings' and 'efficiency' lead to 'dry water savings', like the criteria of the standards described above.

In 2018 a total of 45 large flower producers in Ecuador had an RA Sustainable Agricultural Standard certificate (Rainforest Alliance, 2018b). The audit company in all cases was the Ecuadorian company CyD Certified.

Fair trade

Fair trade certification started in the 1980s by nonprofit organisations in Europe to help producer organisations of smallholder farmers in the Global South. The advantages for the smallholder farmers were, first, to have long-term contracts to sell to an international market, and second, a minimum price in case the world market price would plunge, advance payments, and an additional premium payment to the producers' association to spend on collective assets. In 1997 the Fairtrade Labelling Organization (FLO) was started, named Fairtrade International (FI) since 2009. FI now certifies over 300 products in 66 producer countries and sells in 120 consumer countries (Lyall, 2014). Apart from FI other fair trade organisations exist like Fair Trade USA, the World Fair Trade Organization (WFTO), and the European Fair Trade Association (EFTA). FLOCERT, ECOCERT and SCS Global Services are their auditing companies.

Since 1994, certain products produced on plantations can be Fairtrade certified. This is an important break with the original idea. Here, labourers should be assured certain labour rights, and the association of plantation labourers will receive the Fairtrade premium. First tea and bananas from plantations were certified, and from 2001 flowers. Both Fairtrade tea and flowers are only sourced from plantations. Also, specific environmental criteria apply.

The standards are set in consultation rounds with representatives of the producers' associations and retailers. Bacon (2010), however, showed that smallholder coffee producers have little say in the important price-setting phase. The first flowers from Ecuador were Fairtrade-certified in 2002. In 2016 a total of 12 flower companies had Fairtrade certification according to Valeria Bedón of the Ecuadorian Fairtrade promotion association CJEC (personal communication, 11 May 2016). Similar numbers are also reported for earlier years by Lyall (2014) and TransFair (2010).

There are mixed results from Fairtrade certification in Ecuador. Raynolds (2014) found that overall workers of flower companies in Ecuador were satisfied with the working conditions and that labour relations were more stable in Fairtrade-certified flower companies. However, she also found that labourers were not allowed to join worker unions. Grosse (2016) showed that Fairtrade certification in flower companies in Ecuador did not give sufficient attention to the needs of female labourers with children:

> Women described generally good working conditions, but highlighted their job's long hours, low pay, and inadequate childcare. Their job necessitated that they organised private 'gendered economic strategies' … for securing childcare – strategies which allowed them to provide financial support for their children, but which strained their ability to fulfil gendered expectations about care. Despite its benefits … fair trade provides insufficient support for care in its standards and production structures. In this case, it falls short of facilitating care arrangements that would further development.
>
> (Grosse, 2016, 30)

Furthermore, most consumers of Fairtrade flowers expect to be helping smallholders:[5] 'Sales are being driven by consumer's belief that organics are healthier, more nutritious, better tasting, better for the environment and better for *smallholder* producers' (Tamaki, 2013, 183, emphasis added). However, contrary to what most consumers expect, the 12 Fairtrade-certified flower companies in Ecuador are big companies, and the many small flower producers in Ecuador do not have, and cannot obtain, a Fairtrade certification. Small flower producers cannot obtain a certificate because no specific Fairtrade standard for small flower producers exists. Small flower producers mostly employ one or two permanent workers. That disqualifies them as 'small producers' as defined by Fairtrade regulations (see Standard for Social Producer Organisations on www.fairtrade.net).

In Cayambe-Tabacundo some 170 small flower producers organised themselves in a producer association named AsoAgriPedro, which will be described in more detail below. According to the spirit of fair trade, one would expect them to be able to get a certificate. However, this is not possible: small flower producers cannot get Fairtrade certificated as big companies do, which disempowers the former. Simultaneously this shows the hidden power of the certification as fair trade flower consumers think they buy from small producer associations but can only buy Fairtrade flowers from big companies.

Other standards

Besides the abovementioned standards, other standards exist. For example, the Dutch MPS offers a variety of standards (MPS-ABC, MPS-SQ, MPS-GAP) with a varying degree of strictness. To our knowledge, only one producer, the large flower company Princess Roses, a Dutch company exporting to the Netherlands, had the MPS-QS and MPS-GAP labels in 2018. Another standard is the Business Alliance for Secure Commerce (BASC) standard that guarantees against trafficking of drugs (BASC, 2018). Many large companies have this label, but it does not include social or environmental criteria.

Practices of auditing

Inspections are done by private auditing companies. In Ecuador several national and international private auditing companies provide such services: CyD Certified, ECOCERT, FLOCERT, SCS Global Service, Bureau Veritas, Control Union, Ceres Certified, and Kiwa BCS ÖKO-GARANTIE. The inspection costs are paid by the flower companies. Auditing of the flower companies usually takes place once a year. Normally the audits are announced beforehand. During the audit experts will visit the producing premises. If any findings result from the audit the flower companies have the opportunity to improve their practices. The audit company usually gives four to 12 weeks to show proof of such changes to comply with the standard (manager of a 20-ha flower company, personal communication, 10 April 2013).

The competition between audit companies results in audit companies becoming more permissive. A company that applies the environmental and social regulations strictly will soon face a declining number of companies that contract them for audits. This is a second 'race to the bottom' besides the setting of the standards themselves (explained above). Auld *et al.* (2008) reported that in the case of corrective action required in forest management for FSC certification, most requested improvements related to documentation and reporting practices, not to actual changes required on the ground.

Several reports (Auld *et al.*, 2008; Albersmeier *et al.*, 2009; Gulbrandsen, 2009; Klooster, 2010; Jaffee, 2012) suggest that field audits by private audit companies face many problems, such as multiple interpretations of criteria and susceptibility to fraud, thus making auditing much less effective than claimed. Auditing is also vulnerable to pressure from the audited companies as they are paying for the audits and could switch to a competitor.

Flower certification is buyer-driven: the flower companies, unlike most organic producers, are only interested in fulfilling the standards to gain access to the market. As only a relative small part of the market requires labels, only those producers with relatively good practices bother to get a certification, while the other companies sell to less demanding markets like Russia. This implies that for the flower sector in Ecuador overall, certification does not improve practices. This effect has been described for forest management by Auld *et al.* (2008) and Klooster (2010), and for the fishing sector by Gulbrandsen (2009). This was also experienced while doing the field research in Cayambe-Tabacundo: we visited BellaRosa, a seemingly perfect flower farm one would like to work at, with air-sucking devices to kill insects and all workers in protective clothing, but it was only one of the very few farms willing to be interviewed. Two other big companies were visited; their greenhouses were very different from BellaRosa's: green and purple substances were dripping, and the air was stingy. For individual companies it is hard to tell if practices improved because of compliance to standards, or that other factors like internal motivation of the owner or managers, competition over labour force with small flower producers, or if pressure from government agencies, farmer communities, or NGOs induced the improvements.

Another limitation of the inspections is that the auditors only inspect the company itself and disregard the social embeddedness and environmental surroundings of the flower company. An employee of the NGO AVSF in Ecuador explained (Sylvian Bleuze, personal communication, 21 March 2017):

> Certification schemes often just look at one company and how they, for example, manage their water. They don't study what kind of impact the company and its water managing practices have on a bigger scale, the community or the entire water shed. They barely look at the bigger picture.

What inspectors also disregard is that part of the exported flowers is produced by the many uncertified smallholders and sold to the certified big companies.

As big flower companies do not depend on private third-party certification to sell flowers they have quite some power over the auditing companies. The system of third-party auditing by competing private companies is set globally in a 'closed space'. This norm is a form of invisible power, empowering the big flower companies.

Government regulation in the flower sector

The Ecuadorian government has four types of government regulations with potential to reduce the negative effects of flower production: environmental licences, municipal spatial planning, national environmental and social standards, and Agrocalidad.

Environmental licence

The first regulation is the environmental licence. This is obtained by presenting a detailed Environmental Impact Assessment (EIA) to the regional environmental authority (Autoridad Ambiental de Aplicación Responsable, AAAr), this being most of the time the provincial government. These EIA reports are conducted by specialised companies. An example is the case of the EIA of Fiorentina Flowers (MoyaGest, 2016). The EIA report is lengthy (300 pages) but provides hardly any critical information on environmental or social impacts of the flower company. This monitoring instrument seems to be mainly a 'paper exercise'. Thus, the EIA studies of the big flower companies are a form of 'hidden power': they are presented and accepted as an instrument to regulate the flower sector, but detailed study of the reports reveal that potential environmental impacts and risks, like water contamination or competition with smallholders over water, are not addressed.

Municipal spatial planning

The second type is municipal spatial planning. The municipality grants permission for the building of a flower greenhouse. It checks against the local regulations and land use planning policies. An example of such regulation is that in Pedro Moncayo greenhouses should not be built within 50 metres of houses. However, regulations differ per municipality and monitoring is permissive in most municipalities. For example, in Pedro Moncayo many greenhouses have been built very close to houses.

Environmental and social national standards

Third, the national government has several standards that prohibit the use of certain pesticides, standards for water quality, work conditions, and minimum wage. The constitutionally ordered annual rise in the minimum wage over the last decade has been a significant advance in government regulation of the flower sector. In 2007, when President Rafael Correa came to power, it was US$170 a month. Ten years later it has risen to US$375, one of the highest in Latin America and covering all basic basket goods. Since the wages paid in other flower exporting countries are lower, competition has become tougher for the Ecuadorian flower producers. However, it has meant an improved socioeconomic situation for the flower workers in the highlands who all get paid at least the minimum wage.

In terms of regulating for compliance, prohibition of toxic pesticides seems effective (Breilh, 2007), the salaries paid have kept pace with the rise of the official minimum wage, and work conditions have improved (Soper, 2013).

Agrocalidad

The fourth is the monitoring system maintained by a special government agency called Agrocalidad. Respondents from flower companies report that Agrocalidad is the only government agency that carries out inspection for compliance. They very actively monitor the quality of export products and big flower businesses all reported to be controlled by Agrocalidad. They mainly control the number of aphids and thrips on flowers. As all imports of flowers into a country from Ecuador might be blocked completely if aphids are encountered in a cargo, it is in the interest of all flower exporters to be very meticulous in control. The national government has taken upon itself to do this monitoring. Agrocalidad inspects big farms weekly; when there is a problem with the flowers, they come twice a week. Smaller farms are also checked, around once a month, but there are more small farms than Agrocalidad has registered and thus not all are checked. They also keep an eye on the use of forbidden chemicals in the farms. A former inspector for the FLP said that although the most toxic agrochemicals are prohibited, some workers of the big flower companies used the 'strong' chemicals to attain higher quality roses, demanded by the export market, even without their managers knowing. The sale of agrochemicals is not well monitored by the government (Orlando Felicita, personal communication, 2 April 2018). Thus, Agrocalidad sets the agenda by only monitoring pests, and not environmental or social problems: this is a form of 'agenda setting' or 'hidden power' exercised by the national government.

Local struggles for improvements

From the perspective of certification programmes, it seemed the reduction in toxic pesticide use and improvement in labour conditions were the result of the certification programmes. From the perspective of the government it looked like it had firm control over big flower companies and enforced the improvements.

Studying the reality of the changes in Cayambe-Tabacundo we have learned that local struggles for improvements have also been crucial. Three such local struggles are described in this section: (1) the fight over the Tabacundo irrigation system; (2) the fight over labourers and labour conditions between the big and small flower producers; and (3) the launch of AsoAgriPedro, the small flower producers' organisation.

Fight over irrigation water control

Water for the big flower companies in the area is mainly provided by the Tabacundo irrigation system. It was built some hundred years ago and managed by the municipality until 2006. The approximately 90 big companies with 1,045 ha share the irrigation canal with some 2,500 smallholders, with a total of 2,400 ha. The allocation of water has been very unequal: annually big flower companies receive eight million cubic metres, while the many smallholders only receive two million cubic metres (Mena-Vásconez *et al.*, 2017).

In February 2006 the smallholders organised a protest march and took control of the canal. From that time onwards, the water users' association of the smallholders, CODEMIA, managed the irrigation system. They still allocate water to the big flower companies, because many family members of the smallholders work in those companies, but slowly the water has been reallocated to the smallholder sector. The big flower companies have built rainwater storage reservoirs and drilled deep wells. More strict control over water distribution has resulted in improved water availability for the small-scale food producers in the tail end sector of the canal (Mena-Vásconez *et al.*, 2017). The increased access to irrigation water resulting from the struggle of the smallholders over the control of the irrigation system helped many smallholders to start their own small flower greenhouse. However, in two out of five irrigation sectors the Water Users' Association's (WUA) board forbids the establishment of flower greenhouses (see also Mena-Vásconez *et al.*, 2017). These local struggles are forms of 'claimed spaces' in water governance. The local water users' organisation applied visible power when they marched to take over the control of the canal.

Competitive labour market

Small flower producers compete with big flower companies over labourers. This forces big flower companies to treat their labourers better than before, for example spray less insecticides in the presence of the workers and pay higher wages. The head engineer at the company BellaRosa (53 ha) spoke of his view on the smaller businesses:

> The competition with smaller flower producers is quite tough. It is quite unfair because there are a lot of illegal small flower farms which do not pay royalties or do not comply with working condition standards. These small farms should work together to reach the standards and comply with all the rules. If they do, you won't be hearing me, because then it will be fair competition.
>
> (personal communication, 20 March 2017)

The advancement of small flower producers empowers the labourers as they have a better position to negotiate labour conditions (thus claiming a space for decision making according to the power–cube conceptual framework). Many workers prefer to start their own small greenhouse because it allows for flexibility in working hours and might reward entrepreneurship. Others prefer the stable income from working with a large company, with the tighter labour market giving them a better negotiating position.

The launch of AsoAgriPedro

Since early 2017, after two years of preparation, an organisation of small flower cultivators, AsoAgriPedro, has been established, with 169 proprietors, altogether owning 300 ha. Head administrator Isabel Sánchez talked about the process so far. She had a relatively big farm of 2.5 ha and she was independently selling to clients. Some neighbours asked if she could help them do this too, and thus she started the initiative with ten other small (flower) producers. The municipality of Pedro Moncayo supported them and gave them land where they located their headquarters and post-harvest facilities. Since April 2017, the governmental body of the Pichincha province showed their interest and offered to help increase their technical capabilities.

Once per month all members come to the assembly. Absences are paid with a five-dollar fine. During the meeting they discuss problems and design strategies for the future. They share a post-harvest facility and manage the export of flowers together. There is an appointed sales commission. It contacts clients and designs commercial strategies. Furthermore, there is a board of 27 members, an administration unit of seven, and 30 post-harvest workers.

There are no requirements to be a member of the association, only to be registered by Agrocalidad and have all the legal papers. There is no member fee, but per sold flower, a couple of cents are paid to the association. A lot of the farmers spoken to had never heard of the association before nor were interested. According to one man 'You are better off alone than in an association with one bad partner' (Raúl Moreno, personal communication, 10 May 2017). Others, who had also never heard of the association, wished they knew of one, because they did see advantages. Marcos Gualavisí, a small greenhouse owner: 'There is no help, but there is a will. We need help' (personal communication, 8 May 2017). Ana Farinango with her farm, 'where work is 24/7': 'I don't have the time to associate with other small businesses' (personal communication, 4 March 2017). For her, her flowers are 'like her children' and thus she is also afraid to 'share' her flowers with others in an association. Nevertheless, she did claim to be interested in an association (see below).

On the question where change must come from, she answers:

> Change needs to come up from below. We need to realise we are not 'pequeños productores' (small producers). Thinking that is a big mistake. As an association we are the biggest flower business of Ecuador, which makes it even more important for us that we focus on the social side of things and we take care with, for example, the chemicals we use.

Isabel Sánchez did admit that working conditions might not have been as depicted by law, as, for example, children did help their parents in the greenhouses. Certifying these farms might be difficult, but the association was not looking for that: 'Big companies need to keep their glamour, that is why certifications like Fairtrade may appeal to them, but for us that is not important right now'.

This associativity might be becoming a trend, but it is too early to say. Ana Farinango (personal communication, 10 March 2018), having just surmounted her initial fears of associating, is now leading a group of six floriculturist women in her community. Her goal is to eventually establish a formal association yet for now she is happy with all of them contributing, in typical *minga* fashion, to build their own post-harvest facility; she is investing there the small surplus she managed to accumulate after a relatively successful Valentine's season as she is not able to get more official credit from the national bank. There she will have cold storage facilities to collect and process her roses and those of the rest of the group and beyond. Besides forging ahead, she wants her neighbours to avoid the high risks and hassle of depending on flower traders that she has been suffering for years.

AsoAgriPedro and other, smaller, flower producer associations could be understood as claimed space opening room for manoeuvre and financial gain for smallholders, albeit being disempowered because they cannot get Fairtrade certificated. If they can export directly, without big flower companies or traders, the smallholders gain economically. However, the precarious success of the small flower producers could also be analysed as contributing to the invisible power (or governmentality) of economic discourses that value money over food sovereignty, and private entrepreneurship over identity as collective food producers. This discourse empowers big and small flower entrepreneurs over the small food-producing farmers who need access to irrigation water for their food crops.

Discussion and conclusion

Many drivers exist for changes in social and environmental impacts of export production. CSR policies adopted by private companies often include environmental and social standards that should guarantee a certain limit to negative social and health impacts for the workers involved in the production process and minimal environmental impact for the production locations. However, the actual contribution of those standards to improvements in social and environmental impacts seems limited. Many other dynamics influence the social and environmental impacts of export agriculture.

The case study of large-scale export flower production in the north of Ecuador shows that five factors, besides private certification, have contributed to the improvement of the practices of the flower industry in Ecuador: (1) the increased minimum wage set by the national government, (2) the competition between the big and small flower producers, (3) the struggle of the peasant communities and irrigation water users' associations over the reallocation of irrigation water, (4) the pressure of local environmental NGOs, and (5) environmental regulations of the national, provincial, and municipal governments.

Examining the practices of flower certification with help of Gaventa's power-cube provided insight into the ways the practices of flower production evolved, influenced by different stakeholders. Private standards like Veriflora, Flower Label Program, Rainforest Alliance, FlorEcuador, and Fairtrade had relatively little effect on the practices of the flower industry, because the standards and their auditing systems show signs of a 'race to the bottom' induced by competition between the standards and the auditing companies, leading to permissive standards and auditing practices. The demand for certified flowers is limited to Northern Europe and certain buyers in the US, while a large proportion of the flowers is exported to other regions, like Russia, that do not demand certification. The standards, however, do empower the certified companies as they gain market access and legitimate water use by large-scale flower producers. The private-regulation discourse behind the standards is a form of invisible power: a neoliberal governmentality. The standards, and the EIA regulations of the national government, represent closed spaces within our power-cube analysis, where norms are set without participation of the producers and affected stakeholders. The internalised norms (like 'efficiency is good') act like invisible forms of power, empowering the big flower companies that have licences and certificates.

A large contradiction was encountered regarding the Fairtrade certified flower businesses. In Ecuador about ten large companies are Fairtrade certified. Contrary to the expectations of Fairtrade consumers, small producers cannot be Fairtrade certified. In this way Fairtrade certification leads to hidden power of the big Fairtrade-certified companies and traders. Since April 2017, a small flower producer association, AsoAgriPedro, has been established with some 170 members. Although they operated in the spirit of fair trade, the Fairtrade standard did not allow them to be certified. This association trend might still be solidifying, and it may, in the future, be able to benefit from certification, but this would most likely require changes in the required standards.

Notes

1 Although the climate is favourable for rose production, all roses are produced in greenhouses to regulate night temperature and protect from rain.
2 This divide is somewhat artificial as some family-run flower enterprises have grown larger than two hectares.
3 Increased need for financial means must be seen in relation with increasing privatisation of public services like health and education in Ecuador. See also Mena-Vásconez et al. (2017).
4 BanEcuador is a public bank that provides credit to small entrepreneurs and farmers. It was created in 2016 as a successor of the Banco Nacional de Fomento, which had the same function.
5 In a research about fair trade coffee in France, De Ferran and Grunert (2007) found that 25 out of 44 respondents mentioned 'small producers organisations' as a reason to buy fair trade coffee.

References

Albersmeier, F., Schulze, H., Jahn, G. and Spiller, A. (2009) 'The reliability of third-party certification in the food chain: from checklists to risk-oriented auditing', *Food Control*, vol 20, no 10, pp. 927–935.

Auld, G., Gulbrandsen, L. H. and McDermott, C. L. (2008) 'Certification schemes and the impacts on forests and forestry', *Annual Review of Environment and Resources*, vol 33, pp. 187–211.

Bacon, C. M. (2010) 'Who decides what is fair in fair trade? The agri-environmental governance of standards, access, and price', *Journal of Peasant Studies*, vol 37, no 1, pp. 111–147.

Balas, J., Vessel, S. and Fassler, M. (2008) 'Eco-social certification in international floriculture: a war of labels?', Proceedings of the first IS on Horticulture in Europe, Vienna, *Acta Horticulturae*, vol 817, pp. 195–200.

BASC (2018) 'Business Alliance for Secure Commerce'. www.wbasco.org/en.

Bloemisterij (2017) 'Ecuador heeft nog een lange weg te gaan in duurzaamheid' (Ecuador has a long way to go to sustainability), 6 November 2017. www. hortipoint.nl/vakbladvoordebloemisterij/ecuador-heeft-nog-een-lange-weg-te-gaan-in-duurzaamheid/.

Breilh, J. (2007) 'Nuevo modelo de acumulación y agroindustria: las implicaciones ecológicas y epidemiológicas de la floricultura en Ecuador', *Ciênc. Saúde Coletiva*, vol 12, no 1, pp. 91–104.

Breilh, J., Campaña, M., Felicita, O., Hidalgo, F., Lourdes Larrea, M., Sánchez, D., Straka, N. and Yassi A. (2009) 'Consolidación del estudio sobre la relación entre impactos ambientales de la floricultura, patrones de exposición y consecuencias en comunidades de la cuenca del Granobles (Sierra Norte, Ecuador) Informe técnico final', Centro de Estudios y Asesoría en Salud – CEAS, Quito, Ecuador.

De Ferran, F. and Grunert, K. G. (2007) French fair trade coffee buyers' purchasing motives: an exploratory study using means-end chains analysis', *Food Quality and Preference*, vol 18, no 2, pp. 218–229.

Expoflores (2016a) Certificación FlorEcuador, Reglamento General para empresas de producción, exportación y comercialización de flores, Versión 2.2, June 2016. http://expoflores.com/wp-content/uploads/2016/12/reglamento_general_FlorEcuador.pdf.

Expoflores (2016b). Certificación FlorEcuador, Lista de Chequeo [Check list]. http://expoflores.com/wp-content/uploads/2016/12/lista_chequeo_FlorEcuador_Certified_julio16.pdf.

Ferm, N. (2008) 'Non-traditional agricultural export industries: conditions for women workers in Colombia and Peru', *Gender and Development*, vol 16, no 1, pp. 13–26.

Foucault, M. (1991) 'Governmentality', in Burchell, G., Gordon, C. and Miller, P. (Eds.), *The Foucault Effect: Studies in Governmentality* (pp. 87–104). The University of Chicago Press, Chicago, IL.

Franze, J. and Ciroth, A. (2011) 'A comparison of cut roses from Ecuador and the Netherlands', *International Journal of Life Cycle Assessment*, vol 16, pp. 366–379.

GADIP (Gobierno Autónomo Descentralizado Intercultural y Plurinacional del Municipio de Cayambe) (2015) 'Somos Cayambe', Cayambe, Ecuador.

Gaventa, J. (2006) 'Finding the spaces for change: a power analysis', *IDS Bulletin*, vol 37, no 6, pp. 23–33.

Grosse, C. E. (2016) 'Fair care? How Ecuadorian women negotiate childcare in fair trade flower production', *Women's Studies International Forum*, vol 57, pp. 30–37.

Gulbrandsen, L. H. (2009) 'The emergence and effectiveness of the Marine Stewardship Council', *Marine Policy*, vol 33, no 4, pp. 654–660.

Hidalgo, J. P., Boelens, R. and Vos, J. (2017) 'De-colonizing water: dispossession, water insecurity, and Indigenous claims for resources, authority, and territory', *Water History*, vol 9, no 1, pp. 67–85.

Hughes, A. (2001) 'Global commodity networks, ethical trade and governmentality: organizing business responsibility in the Kenyan cut flower industry', *Transactions of the Institute of British Geographers*, vol 26, no 4, pp. 390–406.

Instituto de Ecología y Desarollo de las Comunidades Andinas, IEDECA (1999) 'Impacto de la floricultura en los campesions de Cayambe', IEDECA, Quito.

Jaffee, D. (2012) 'Weak coffee: certification and co-optation in the fair trade movement', *Social Problems*, vol 59, no 1, pp. 94–116.

Klooster, D. (2010) 'Standardizing sustainable development? The Forest Stewardship Council's plantation policy review process as neoliberal environmental governance', *Geoforum*, vol 41, no 1, pp. 117–129.

Korovkin, T. (2003) 'Cut-flower exports, female labor, and community participation in highland Ecuador', *Latin American Perspectives*, vol 30, no 4, pp. 18–42.

Korovkin T. (2005). 'Creating a social wasteland? Non-traditional agricultural exports and rural poverty in Ecuador', *European Latin American and Caribbean Studies*, vol 79, pp. 47–68.

Langen, N. and Adenaeuer, L. (2013) 'Where does the fair trade price premium go? Confronting consumers' request with reality', *Social Enterprise Journal*, vol 9, no 3, pp. 293–314.

Lemke, T. (2007) 'An indigestible meal? Foucault, governmentality and state theory', *Distinktion: Journal of Social Theory*, vol 8, no 2, pp. 43–64.

Lyall, A. (2014) 'Assessing the impacts of fairtrade on worker-defined forms of empowerment on Ecuadorian flower plantations', Final report commissioned by Fairtrade International and Max Havelaar-Foundation.

Mena-Vásconez, P., Boelens, R. and Vos, J. (2016) 'Food or flowers? Contested transformations of community food security and water use priorities under new legal and market regimes in Ecuador's highlands', *Journal of Rural Studies*, vol 44, pp. 226–238.

Mena-Vásconez, P., Vincent, L., Vos, J. and Boelens, R. (2017) 'Fighting over water values: diverse framings of flower and food production with communal irrigation in the Ecuadorian Andes', *Water International*, vol 42, no 4, pp. 443–461.

MoyaGest (2016) 'Estudio de impacto ambiental ex post y plan de manejo ambiental finca florícola "Fiorentina Flowers S.A"'. http://fiorentinaflowers.com/wp-content/uploads/2017/05/Fiorentina-Flowers-Environmental-Plan-EsIA-Ex-Post-FIORENTINA-2016-002.pdf.

Mutersbaugh, T., Klooster, D., Renard, M. C. and Taylor, P. (2005) 'Certifying rural spaces: quality-certified products and rural governance', *Journal of Rural Studies*, vol 21, no 4, 381–388.

Rainforest Alliance (2018a) 'Cultivating earth-friendly flowers'. www.rainforest-alliance.org/articles/rainforest-alliance-certified-ferns-flowers.

Rainforest Alliance (2018b) Rainforest Alliance Sustainable Agriculture Standard, 2017, Version 2.1. www.rainforest-alliance.org/business/sas/wp-content/uploads/2017/11/03_rainforest-alliance-sustainable-agriculture-standard_en.pdf.

Raynolds, L. T. (2014) 'Fairtrade, certification, and labor: global and local tensions in improving conditions for agricultural workers', *Agriculture and Human Values*, vol 31, no 3, pp. 499–511.

Sawers, L. (2005) 'Sustainable floriculture in Ecuador'. *International Journal of Economic, Social, and Environmental Sustainability*, vol 1, pp. 3–9.

SCS Global Services (2012a) 'Veriflora certified producers, handlers and approved input materials manufacturers'.

SCS Global Services (2012b) Veriflora. Certification of Sustainably Grown Cut Flowers and Potted Plants: Requirements for Growers and Handlers, Version 3-1. www.scsglobalservices.com/files/standards/SCS_STN_Veriflora_V3-1_100912. pdf.

SCS Global Services (2013) Revision and Stakeholder Review Process and Guidance on Key Changes, Version 1.1 www.scsglobalservices.com/files/program_documents/ vfv4_revision_stakeholder_review_process_110416.pdf.

Seckler, D. (1996) 'The new era of water resources management: from "dry" to "wet" water savings'. IIMI Research Report 1. Colombo, Sri Lanka: International Irrigation Management Institute (IIMI).

SIPAE (2016) 'Impactos de la certificación FLP (Flower Label Program) en el sector florícola ecuatoriano', Quito, Ecuador.

Soper, R. (2013) 'Reclaiming development: Indigenous community organizations and the flower export industry in the Ecuadorian highlands', in Backer, M. (Ed.), *Indigenous and Afro-Ecuadorians Facing the Twenty-First Century* (pp. 128–149). Newcastle upon Tyne: Cambridge Scholars Publishing.

Tamaki, R. (2013) 'Consumers' perception of fair trade coffee in Australia and Japan' (Doctoral dissertation). Curtin University. School of Management Curtin Business School.

Tenenbaum, D. (2002) 'Would a rose not smell as sweet?', *Environmental Health Perspectives*, vol 110, no 5, pp. A240–A247.

TransFair (2010) 'Fair Trade Certified™ Flowers: 2009/2010 Impact Report', Transfair, USA.

UN Comtrade (2018) UN Comtrade database. http://atlas.media.mit.edu/en/profile/ hs92/0603/.

USDA Foreign Agricultural Service (2009) 'Ecuador fresh flower industry situation' (EC9006). Office of Global Analysis, Quito.

Van Halsema, G. E. and Vincent, L. (2012) 'Efficiency and productivity terms for water management: a matter of contextual relativism versus general absolutism', *Agricultural Water Management*, vol 108, pp. 9–15.

Vos, J. and Boelens, R. (2014) 'Sustainability standards and the water question', *Development and Change*, vol 45, no 2, pp. 205–230.

Part VI

Summarising outcomes for society and the environment

13 Collating correlations, conclusions, recommendations and ideas for future research, evaluation and practice

Melissa Vogt

Introduction

Understanding outcomes resulting from any voluntary sustainability certification effort relies on a range of variables. The intramarket introduction and implementation of standards and procedures, and the varying definitions of sustainability opens assessment and considerations of effectiveness to varying disciplines, methodologies and methods. It was therefore expected that multiple themes emerge when scholars and practitioners of varying disciplines were asked to consider the efficacy of sustainability certification efforts across agricultural and natural resource industries for societal and environmental outcomes. The included industries are representative of longstanding and certified, to newly certified, or newly developed industries with partial certification. The efficacy of various sustainability certifications as associated with environmental and societal outcomes is then considered within these different contexts.

Authors invited to contribute chapters for this book were not provided any guidance on preferred methodology or methods, or parameters beyond considering the outcomes for society and the environment of sustainability certifications within a specific industry, or according to specific certifications. The resulting chapters also therefore provide an example of the varying ways scholars choose to assess and understand outcomes, and of the maintained or newly emerging topical issues and achievements.

A summary of themes, disciplines, certifications considered, methods used, conceptual advances, outcomes and key findings according to each chapter is presented in Figure 13.1. The chapter proceeds to consider a comparative correlation between common outcomes and recommendations in an effort to present a summarising discussion of key findings and recommendations across all chapters. From this process, recommendations for future research are provided.

The outcomes, key findings and recommendations across chapters are comprehensive within their respective considerations, with the possibility to extrapolate to other sustainability certification efforts where the appropriateness of doing so is well considered.

Figure 13.1 A summary of chapter details

Chapter	Key themes	Disciplines	Certifications considered	Methods used	Conceptual advances	Key findings and outcomes
2 *Cultural implications*	Cultural flows from consumers to producers; cultural influence of and on stakeholders; culture of certifications as organisations and entities	Cultural studies	General	Narrative review		– Sustainability certifications contribute to a sustainability culture shift. – Embedding sustainability in the culture of each stakeholder can promote an aligned sustainability culture. – Sustainability certifications are conducive to embedding sustainability culture across several stakeholders. – Cultural implications result from sustainability standards and approaches to implementation and verification and are relevant for all certified stakeholders, and consumers. – Cultural appropriateness is also relevant to dynamics between stakeholders, and dynamics between stakeholders and the certification or third-party verifier. – Consumer influence, particularly at the population level, can have cultural implications that reach producers. – Appropriateness of outcomes will determine how positive and possibly long term the culture shift is. – Definitions of and intentions for sustainability significantly influence cultural shifts. – Misleading claims and cultural inappropriateness may cause a rift in positive cultural flows. Inappropriateness might be determined by how sustainability certifications reinforce existing trade power dynamics. – Thresholds for sustainability certification label claims might be introduced to manage and reduce misleading claims. – There is a need to find balance between cultural appropriateness and seeking compliance. A contextual rapport is likely required. – Participatory Guarantee Systems offer an opportunity for producer communities to maintain a cultural familiarity and control in required processes – Not all farmer or producer communities prefer PGS, and some might prefer autonomy in their community offered by international certifications. – Business-based versus individual consumer preferences for certifications may appear less subjective; however, business interest in preferred trade terms may lead to equal levels of subjectivity based on different preference terms. – Improving consistency across certification efforts is necessary with or without individual consumer preferences. – The value of allowing individual consumer preferences as a sustainability cultural shift appears unpredictable but could provide opportunity for balance against stakeholder bias.

Determining influencing factors for positive outcomes

– Appropriateness of:
  o Standard criteria, and approach to implementation and verification; corporate cooperation particularly regarding negotiating trade terms and encouraging contextual rapport.
  o Influence of consumer preference to label preferences and therefore required practices of stakeholders and producers; and how well informed consumer understanding of label outcomes is.
  o Negative implication of misleading claims, and contrary outcomes.
  o Effectiveness of PGS, and how it is used by certifications.

Areas for improvement

– Ensuring consistent cultural appropriateness.
– Finding balance between adequately shifting practices to be more sustainable, and cultural appropriateness of required changes and introduced processes.
– Reducing availability of 'non-ethical' products and therefore removing a need for what can be a subjective consumer preference.
– Further consideration of how PGS maintains cultural appropriateness within producer communities.

3	Biodiversity outcomes	Implying versus evaluating biodiversity outcomes associated with sustainability certifications; contextual considerations; bio-based economies; farm and landscape heterogeneity; confounders; future evaluations, research and practice	Environmental and energy science and studies; evaluation; landscape planning	Mention of 26 certification standards for agriculture and biofuels; and Fairmined; Organic; RA; RSPO	Narrative conceptually framed review	ESHR

– Biodiversity outcomes associated with any given sustainability certification are difficult to determine at a macro-level.
– Of the few advanced studies available, many indicate positive outcomes; further qualification is, however, required.
– Basic indicators that are easiest to observe, and compliance monitoring are currently the reliable data sources.
– Defining biodiversity is an essential element for evaluating biodiversity outcomes.
– Mixed methods are recommended for thorough evaluations.
– The industry, bioregion, and country and landscape contexts influence evaluations.
– Effective evaluations will consider baseline conditions; temporal range; contexts; counterfactual. They will also consider confounding variables such as different certificates held by one landholding; variation in standard implementation status; variation in landholding size and standard requirements; variation in certificate held by one or a group of producers.

continued

Figure 13.1 Continued

Chapter	Key themes	Disciplines	Certifications considered	Methods used	Conceptual advances	Key findings and outcomes
						– Temporal considerations are important. – Standard reach is different to effective implementation and influences actual outcomes. – Quantification of certificates by bioregion can assist to inform location for future evaluations. – Standard criteria for different certifications perform differently against a biodiversity benchmark standard. – Standard criteria and certifications could better encourage farm and landscape heterogeneity and conserve generationally diverse farms, offering an opportunity for improved biodiversity outcomes. – Certifying environmentally damaging industries such as mining is expected to contribute to improved biodiversity outcomes where compliance is maintained. **Determining and influential factors for positive outcomes** – Understanding biodiversity outcomes according to reliable evaluation techniques. – Ensuring effective intentions through stringent and comprehensive standard criteria for biodiversity performance. **Areas for improvement** Improved understanding of outcomes through: – Improved and consistent approaches to evaluations; – Intentions for biodiversity outcomes according to standard criteria consistency, inclusion and performance
4	FSC	Biodiversity outcomes as associated with FSC; evaluation techniques; bioregions by certificates and evaluations	Evaluation; landscape planning; forest management; conservation	FSC	Narrative literature review		– Evaluations are most reliable where combining methods and sources of information, and integrating rigourous in-field observations and findings. – 10% of all FSC certified forest is in tropical bioregions, yet most studies are carried out in the tropics – There is one scientific paper produced for *c.*0.7 Mha of tropical forest against one for *c.*26.7 Mha of temperate and one for *c.*33.3 Mha of boreal forest. – The definition of deforestation used, particularly process/cause, temporal and forest structure considerations can limit how biodiversity outcomes are evaluated. – FSC certification has the potential to help maintain ecological values by overcoming gaps in national forest governance. – Using certification as a strategy for the protection of the last remaining intact forests is limited by the fact that most forestry practices are in contradiction with the current definition of IFL. – Embedding the conservation of IFLs into certification could be achieved based on a local, context-specific definition of intactness that considers forest

- The size of most IFLs largely exceeds the area of influence of FSC, which is limited to the area of certified concessions. Effective protection of intact forests also therefore requires landscape-wide approaches and the consideration of other disturbances than those associated with the forestry sector.
- While biodiversity outcomes are recognised as influenced by and as influential to other environmental and societal outcomes, it is necessary to substantiate details of biodiversity outcomes and then consider how they influence or are possibly influenced by other environmental or societal factors.

Determining and influential factors for positive outcomes

Understanding biodiversity outcomes according to reliable evaluation techniques.

Areas for improvement

Improved understandings through:
- Improved and consistent approaches to evaluation;
- Representative evaluations;
- Increased number of evaluations.

Authors' opinion

FSC offers significant benefits for biodiversity outcomes in managed forest areas, and surrounding landscapes. FSC could further contribute to conserving intact forest. Evidence of outcomes is, however, variable and opportunity for improvement could be better informed.

5	*Biochar*	Science of biochar production and application	Physical geography; soil science; environment and planning	European Biochar Certificate

Literature review, and summaries of existing studies; quantitative and various statistical analyses

1. Biochar production certification is in progress; biochar application certification is, however, a concept in its infancy with development challenges listed below:
   a. Trade-offs between soil functions;
   b. A much longer time horizon than traditional soil amendments;
   c. Limited mechanistic understanding regarding the nature and extent of effects relevant to specific biochar and soil crop climate combinations.
2. Integrated strategies such as OBD for any specific application, biochar contaminant bioavailability criteria and effect-based approaches, alongside synergistic programmes, scientific guidance and training throughout production, commercialisation and consumption chains are a promising way forward.
3. Sustainability biochar production and sustainability environmental biochar application are two sides of the same coin.

Determining and influential factors for positive outcomes

Scientifically developed, tested and proven standards and verification techniques.

Areas for improvement

Continued research and use of the certification via integrated strategies.

continued

Figure 13.1 Continued

Chapter	Key themes	Disciplines	Certifications considered	Methods used	Conceptual advances	Key findings and outcomes
6 *Animal welfare*	Farm animal well-being; standard and monitoring approache; Welfare quality standard; precision livestock farming; possible contribution to existing certification standards	Animal welfare; human geography; ethology	Welfare quality standards; Freedom Foods; Cruelty free	Literature review, and summaries of previous studies and practical work outcomes of contributing authors		– Members of the European public believe that current animal farming practices in Europe deliver better animal welfare than in the rest of the world. Still they have higher expectations for the quality of life of farm animals than what is currently available. – Improving farm animal welfare is a key value for European society and the development of an effective tool such as the WQ protocols for measuring and assessing the welfare of farm animals is an important first step to promote better welfare. – Existing certification standards and verification procedures do not comprehensively encourage or ensure animal welfare, and label claims are not always substantiated. Outcomes are therefore difficult to determine. – Animal welfare is a multifaceted concept and encompasses more than any one of the many claims found on labels, such as free range. – The Welfare Quality Standard provides specific, consistent and reliable guidance for standards and verification procedures relevant for certification standards that include farm animal welfare. It has developed over many years and is scientifically grounded in terms of what animal welfare is and how it can be monitored. – Animal welfare outcomes resulting from sustainably certified practices are expected to improve where standards such as those introduced by the Animal Welfare Quality Standard are used to guide certification standards and approaches to verification. – Interest in using the Welfare Quality Standard is demonstrated by sustainability certifications. – Precision livestock farming can offer a complementary method for monitoring animal welfare compliance and in turn improve understanding of outcomes. **Areas for improvement and future research** – Develop more animal-based measures that address public concerns about animal emotions and natural behaviours. – Develop new techniques for collecting farm animal measures. **Authors' opinion** The Welfare Quality protocols are tools for measuring the welfare of farm animals on farm and at slaughterhouses; the current challenge is to make these tools more flexible and cost effective for a broader application by stakeholders.

| 7 | Aquaculture | Aquaculture certification programmes; prerequisites for certification to have more positive effect | Aquaculture certification programmes | Literature review; study methods from literature include: LCA; farm audits and improvements used for evaluation | Currently there is little evidence of positive environmental impacts from implementation of aquaculture certification and the few studies published have not used credible counterfactuals. Published work nonetheless shows slightly better performance for certified farms for emissions of greenhouse gases and nitrogen/phosphorus as well as land use.
For societal outcomes see Hatanaka (2010).
For certification to deliver significant positive environmental impacts five prerequisites are required:
1. Increased global coverage in terms of species and systems certified and markets targeted for certification
2. Inclusion of small-scale producers and less well performing producers with respect to environmental impacts
3. Mechanisms implemented to ensure a continuous improvement of certification standards
4. Additionality to conventional state-led regulation
5. Capacity to support production systems with strong sustainability.
There is limited evidence of environmental effects of certification based on published academic research. Several prerequisites for certification to (1) measure effects and (2) contribute to sector-wide improvements suggested.
Areas for improvement
There is a need for more research on environmental and societal outcomes of aquaculture certifications. Specifically, broader systemic insights on whether certification could increase consumer demand for inherently more environmentally impactful products and thereby have indirect negative effects should be prioritised. There is also a need to better understand ecosystem effects of certification, thus impacts beyond farm gate. Related to this, the potential to expand certification to encompass a landscape level rather than farm level merit scholarly attention.
In addition, to effects from implementation of traditional certification, there is also a need to better understand effects of related mechanisms such as aquaculture improvement projects and the linkages between state-led regulation and market-based mechanisms.
Authors' opinion
More research is needed to evaluate aquaculture certification. If certification is to have any substantial effect at scale, a larger span of producers and markets needs to be included and covered, this at the same time as the credibility of certification standards are maintained and improved. |

continued

Figure 13.1 Continued

Chapter	Key themes	Disciplines	Certifications considered	Methods used	Conceptual advances	Key findings and outcomes
8 *Biofuel*	EC recommended and endorsed biofuel sustainability standards; effective implementation and governance	Policy analysis; multi-level governance	REDcert GmbH; ISCC System GmbH; Bonsucro; RSB; 2BSvs; RSPO; HVO; KZR InG; SQC; Gafta; UFAS; TASCC; AACS; Better Biomass (NTA 8080); Red Tractor; RTRS	Conceptually framed narrative review	Input, throughput and, output legitimacy	The main conclusion to be drawn from this case is that this kind of a Public Private Governance Arrangement (PPGA) does not necessarily fulfil the promises of legitimacy and effectiveness that lies in this seemingly attractive governance model. In fact, we can conclude that the EU biofuels sustainability certification PPGA the way it is set up now neither safeguards sustainability effectively nor does it conform to ideals of democratic legitimacy. In contrast, the reviewed schemes raise the suspicion that a 'race-to-the-bottom' is actually taking place in terms of a competition for the easiest and cheapest way of offering certification in the biofuels market in Europe.

- EC endorsement of biofuel certifications does influence preference for the biofuel certifications used and demanded in source countries, and subsequently outcomes resulting from biofuel certification use.
- Limitations to input, throughput and output legitimacy of the EU PPGA means sustainability certifications are endorsed without adequate understanding of expected or positive environmental outcomes. Societal outcomes are generally not considered, and where considered it is only to a limited extent.
- The ecological criteria mandated in the RED are far too few and limited, leaving too much space for interpretation during their implementation for ensuring the environmental sustainability of the biofuels used in Europe.
- Social sustainability criteria are not mandated by the RED. Therefore, most recognised schemes do not consider social aspects such as labour conditions or land availability and rights, and those that do mostly do so in an incomprehensive manner. Thus, social sustainability of biofuel production will, at best, only marginally improve because of the RED sustainability provisions.
- PPGAs that adequately verify legitimacy of certification procedures prior to endorsement are equally if not more important and require as much attention and investment as recognising schemes that fulfil technical criteria.

Determining and influential factors for positive outcomes

Legitimacy of EC endorsed biofuel sustainability certifications that will be endorsed and required.

Areas for improvement

- Improved definitions and approaches to verifying legitimacy of the biofuel sustainability standard schemes endorsed by the EU through PPGA.
- We suggest practical improvements in the field of input, throughput and output legitimacy. Input legitimacy should be provided for in a structured way by the EU, aiming a balanced participation of all relevant stakeholder groups. Throughput legitimacy could be improved by procedures that allow equal participation of different stakeholders in a transparent and non-discriminate way within the recognition of VCSs and the management of these schemes. And last, output legitimacy should be improved by adequate and comprehensive environmental and social criteria with little room for interpretation, standards in data acquisition and independent audit processes specified by the EU in order to prevent the so-called 'race-to-the-bottom' in biofuels sustainability certifications.

Authors' opinion of outcomes

- PPGA increase use of certifications for biofuels; however, limited ability to verify legitimacy makes determining associated outcomes from certification use difficult.
- The actual PPGA for biofuel sustainability certification in the EU so far is rather disappointing in terms of legitimacy and in terms of effectiveness. However, it can be considered a form of field trial for mandating sustainability criteria for agricultural products in general and for incorporating private certification schemes into the regulatory frameworks of the EU, or the state in general. Even though it does not work perfectly at all, the trial should not be abandoned but allowed to continue and improve according to the aspects of effectiveness and legitimacy. This trial may then even become a role model useful for extending sustainability certification to all biomass-based products.

continued

Figure 13.1 Continued

Chapter	Key themes	Disciplines	Certifications considered	Methods used	Conceptual advances	Key findings and outcomes
9	MSC	The extent to which MSC could improve credibility; governance structure; chain of custody; stakeholder engagement.	Governance; sustainability fisheries	MSC; FSC	Conceptually framed literature review; comparative certification study.	Procedural and outcome transparency	– Loose and undefined interpretations in the MSC standard, a lack of stakeholder engagement in decision making and opaque supply chain interactions are worrying. – Transparency and therefore credibility for MSC could improve where governance structures, Chain of Custody (CoC) programmes and standard related procedures improve, in some cases lessons can be learnt from FSC. – Improvements to the assessment process linked with public disclosure of interpretations and objections documents, attention to inclusiveness and stakeholder engagement in governance and increased value chain transparency through CoC and more visible supply chain information could improve credibility of MSC. **Determining and influential factors for positive outcomes** Credibility through MSC procedures **Areas for improvement** Opportunity for MSC to learn from FSC transparency and CoC procedures to improve credibility. **Authors' opinion of outcomes overall** Positive but also dependent on future developments and improvements in credibility.
10	The Responsible Jewellery Council (RJC) and the Alliance for Responsible Mining (ARM)	Gold mining sustainability initiatives; perceptions from the ground	Corporate Social Responsibility and Sustainability	RJC; ARM; Fairmined	Conceptually framed original research case study; interview quotes used to explore topic	Interoperability	– It is possible to have upstream companies and ASM working together towards a more responsible mining approach. – This RJC–ARM–Fairmined interoperability project could be used for initiatives that want to maximise their sustainability impact. – Similarity between systems and goals, increased reach and reduced audit overlapping are some of the drivers of interoperability. – Leadership, access to market, internal processes and systems improvement and cost reduction are the main benefits of interoperability. **Determining and influential factors for positive outcomes** Coordinating sustainability-associated practices between upstream companies and ASM. **Areas for improvement** Improve opportunity for interoperability by: – Increasing opportunity for similarity between sustainability systems and goals. – Decreasing overlap between audit. **Authors' opinion of outcomes overall** Promising, particularly where interoperability is used.

11	*Coffee*	Certifying coffee; Costa Rica; difference between RA and FLO; managing multiple certifications	International development; management and marketing; sustainability	Fairtrade; Rainforest Alliance	Review and original research: one country: ten communities; interview quotes used to explore the topic	The role of and obligation to an aid	

- The intramarket role of certifications introduces an intricate context within which they work to bring a certified product to market, it moves beyond an aid or development role.
- Observed environmental and societal outcomes did differ between RA and FLO in 2009. They included:
  o Improved recycling: RA: yes; FLO: yes; Improved chemical handling: RA: yes; FLO: yes; Reduced chemical use: RA: yes; FLO: yes; Improved condition for labourers: RA: yes; FLO: undetermined through standard criteria and implementation, also influenced by small farm holder status; Improved price: RA: yes; FLO: no; Cultural appropriateness of standards: RA: not mentioned; FLO: not consistent; Environmental or societal standards more advanced than law at the time: RA: yes; FLO: yes; Contributions to community: RA: variable through standard criteria; FLO: yes, through premiums – however, cooperative discretion determined whether premium went to the community or to technological upgrade for coffee production.
  o The ability to balance power dynamics varied according to the certified producer business or cooperative, and the certification. This was influenced by the stable footing each producer business already has in the international market, by the procedures required by each certification, and the dynamics between certifications, business and producers.
- Improvement in effectiveness or ease for producer groups has not been assured, nor have consistent positive outcomes.
- The required resource and financial investment of certification standards, and particularly where multiple standards are requested or required of producer groups is resulting in imbalance compared to benefit.
- Without investment capability, compliance to one certification standard can be difficult. Requiring compliance to multiple standards in this situation is not the most effective way to increase reach of sustainable standards and practices and could be considered inappropriate by approach.
- Purchases conditioned by certification in producer countries can reinforce a top-down approach.
- Where investment compared to benefit is positive, compliance to multiple standards could improve sustainable agricultural practices and satisfy varying preferences for improved market access. If certifications were encouraging any form of diversified crop activity, this may be more so the case.
- Alternatives to certifications could better frame understanding as moving past a need for help, and as a market adaptation.
- Where producer groups are using certifications to enter certified international markets, or international markets for the first time there is opportunity for power imbalances.

Figure 13.1 Continued

Chapter	Key themes	Disciplines	Certifications considered	Methods used	Conceptual advances	Key findings and outcomes
						– Where larger corporations increasingly use certifications to guide sustainable sourcing, transparency and legitimate and fair contractual negotiations for long-term agreements between producer groups and larger traders are necessary for positive outcomes. – Considerations of the 'counterfactual' often result in an impression of limited to insignificant outcomes as independently associated to any sustainability certification according to in-country informal stakeholder assessment. – Direct trade arrangements are becoming a valid and for some small farmers a preferred alternative to certified markets. – Direct trade arrangements do not demonstrate consistency by intention or outcomes for environmental or societal outcomes. **Determining and influential factors for positive outcomes** – Maintaining relevance and actual benefit of sustainability certifications. – In-country perspectives. – Allowing alternatives to develop and being open to how alternatives can complement sustainability certifications to continue to improve outcomes. – Market access could be a significant determining factor for involvement with flow on outcomes recognised as beneficial. **Areas for improvement** – Reducing reliance on sustainability certifications where resulting in more harm than good. – Ensuring improvement for continuing producers including understanding of required investment versus benefit. – Reducing opportunity for misunderstanding and resentment from producing communities and countries. – Reducing misaligned outcomes to stated intentions. Example of 'fair price' is an example. – Clarifying benefit from producer country perspective. **Author's opinion of outcomes overall** Variable with significant negatives and positives.

| 12 | *Flowers* | Certifying flowers in Ecuador's Cayambe-Tabacundo region; water resource management | Flower Label Program (FLP); FlorEcuador; Veriflora; Rainforest Alliance; Fairtrade | Conceptually framed original research case study, one community; interview quotes used to explore the topic | Forms and spaces of power | Content (see below) |

- Compliance to any certification is out of reach for small flower producers (because of costs and regulations).
- In-community agricultural production associations develop to support small producers regardless of certifications.
- NGOs, community (water users) organisations and government organisations at different levels assert pressure on private flower companies to apply to government and private environmental and labour regulations, such as addressing water use and contamination issues. This leaves the actual contribution of certifications in improvements in Ecuadorian flower production in question.
- For these communities the value of becoming certified is questioned; however, certification provides access to specific market segments in the US and Europe.
- Only big flower producers were certified with a Fairtrade label, as small producers could not be certified.
- International trade power dynamics can be reinforced by sustainability certifications.

Determining and influential factors for positive outcomes
- Standards required and verification processes.
- Access to certified markets; and availability of alternatives such as local associations for producer support, to improve sustainability practices and international market access.
- Public regulation of water use, and conservation more effective.

Areas for improvement
- Increasing opportunity for access to certified markets.
- Increasing support to the alternative associations which support small producers where certification cannot.
- Ensuring benefit of public effort compared to certification is understood and reducing emphasis of benefit of certifications for environmental outcomes.

Authors' opinion of outcomes overall
Nonexistent to variable for smaller producers.

Methodology, methods and conceptual framings and advances

The range of methodologies and methods used through the chapters of this book, and the resulting reviews, evaluations and assessments demonstrate the many ways efficacy of certifications can be considered according to environmental and societal outcomes. The methods used include *literature review, conceptually framed or standard*, and *original research* and *combinations of these methods*. The conceptual frames and advances include *interoperability, legitimacy, transparency and credibility, forms and spaces of power*, and *the role of and obligation to an aid.*

Themes include comparing between certifications, comparing certifications with national or regional public regulations, standards and criteria, producer perspectives, alternatives to certifications, power dynamics, interoperability between certifications within the same industry, achieving stated aims and intended outcomes, advantages and disadvantages of multiple certifications within the same industry, requirements for implementing standards, improvement over time, culture, and approach to evaluation.

Disciplines

Chapter authors are from a range of disciplines including *environmental science; agriculture; ecology; physical geography; multilevel governance; field spectroscopy; policy analysis; evaluation; animal behaviour and management; ethology; landscape planning; ecosystem management; water resource management; botany; bio-based economies; soil science; and corporate social responsibility and sustainability.* Many have been considering sustainability certifications in varying ways for five or more years, some for more than ten years. They hold varying positions and have experience within certification organisations, corporations, standard development associations and academic institutions. They were therefore given autonomy in their approach to considering societal and environmental outcomes associated with sustainability certifications.

Considering outcomes across chapters

How existing evaluations consider wider-reaching topics of culture and biodiversity outcomes are considered in Chapters 2–4 to inform understandings of how some societal and environmental outcomes might result and how they are currently determined. They do not therefore provide definite outcomes, but rather encourage consideration of these topics. Cultural implications and influences on the sustainability certification process are considered according to different stakeholders and influential flows. Cultural shifts are relevant to any stakeholder, including the certification organisation, and influential flows can become contextual and influential to how successful a certification process is. The three chapters consider potential implications and how existing evaluations provide consistent and comprehensive understandings of biodiversity outcomes, rather than specific ideas of societal or environmental outcomes. At this time, evaluation availability is somewhat limited and as such, comprehensively summarising how sustainability certifications contribute to biodiversity outcomes even for one certification is difficult. Studies that do provide such information are mentioned.

Chapters 5–12 on the other hand include specific studies according to outcomes associated with certifications and industry, and some are specific according to industry and country.

An overlay of comparative outcome categories was developed and outcomes from Chapters 5–12 were determined—in consultation with authors— to be positive, negative or neutral. These are presented in Figure 13.2 in order to provide a summative idea of outcomes according to specific certifications and industries. The results are accumulated within Figure 13.3 to present commonly positive, negative or neutral outcomes across the industries and certifications considered.

As authors were allowed independence to develop their study, paying attention to the topics they currently specialise in or to the topics they find most of interest or in need of attention, Figures 13.2 and 13.3 should be understood as a comparison of outcomes specific to the chapters in this book. The collation of outcomes does not, however, represent how all certifications are expected to successfully achieve particular outcomes. It is merely to demonstrate some commonalities in outcomes, and how outcomes can differ across those considered in this book. Understanding the comparison as an indication of how certifications are performing within the industry and certification contexts allowed is possible.

To qualify the results presented in Figures 13.2 and 13.3 refer back to the relevant chapter for more detailed information about the outcome and why it was positive, negative or neutral.

The outcomes in Figure 13.2 are summarised and should be recognised as determined using varying methods and methodologies. The rate of indeterminable outcomes can be considered an indication of an opportunity for more effective evaluations, however not as a sign of weakness in the chapter approach. Authors were asked to fill in this chart after writing their chapter.

Figure 13.2 demonstrates consistency in positive, negative or neutral outcomes according to specific outcome categories, with further information available within each chapter. Outcomes most consistent as positive, negative and neutral by category are quantified and listed in Figure 13.3.

Referring back to the chapter will assist to substantiate the summary points provided in this figure.

Figure 13.2 Considering outcome categories across chapters according to common environmental and societal outcome categories

CHAPTERS

OUTCOMES	5 European Biochar Certification	6 Animal Welfare Quality Standard*	7 Aquaculture	8 EU Biofuel PPGA and legitimacy	9 MSC	10 RJC and ARM interoperability	11 Coffee	12 Flowers
ENVIRONMENT	+	+	+	+	+	+ +'	+	?
Improved biodiversity	+	+	+	?	?	?	+	?
Water system protection	+	+	?	?	?	+	+	?
Limiting deforestation	+			?			−	−
Limiting land degradation	+'			−			+	
Limiting damaging chemical use	?		+	−			+	+
Limiting damage to neighbouring or other ecosystems/ landscape patches	?			−			+	?
Improved recycling	+							
Improved animal welfare		+						
Negative or neutral emissions	+		+					
Farm and landscape heterogeneity – terrestrial or water based		+'		−			+	
Industry heterogeneity				+				−
SOCIETY**					?			
Increased or maintained income for producers.	+	+	+	?		+	+	?
Human health	+	+		?		+	+	?
Cultural appropriateness	+	+		?		+	+	?
Improved conditions for workers	+	+		?	?	+	+	
Improved chemical handling and storage	+	+		?	?	+	+	
Realistic expectations for producers	+			?				
Realistic expectations for stakeholders	−	?		+				
Complementary to legislated or policy-based requirements	+	+		+	+	+	+	
Advancing legislated or policy-based requirements	+				+	+ +		−
Observed contributions to producer community		?						
Producer satisfaction with standard requirements	−			?				
Realistic investment requirements			−	−				
Small producer inclusion						+	+	−
AS RELATED TO CERTIFICATION PROCEDURES								
Standard implementation verifiable	+	+		?	−	+	+	?

Outcome					
Required procedures affordable	+	+	+	−	?
Required procedures verifiable	+	+	−	−	?
Legitimate according to required procedures	+	+	−	−	?
Culturally appropriate	+	?'	+	−	−
Balancing power dynamics	+	−	+	−	−
Consistency in expectations, stringency, legitimacy and outcomes according to and across certifications****	+	?	+***		
Allowance for mergers between certifications to ease need to comply with multiple standard sets	+	?	?		
Allowance for contextual adaptations in standard and procedural requirements without compromise to and/or with improvement for intended outcomes	+	?	+	−	?
Allowance for interoperability and merges across stakeholders who comply with different standard sets and different certifications	+	?	+	?	
Satisfaction with certification process	?	+	−	?	
Public effort superior to certifications	?	+	−	?	
Public effort complementary to and demonstrated to support certification effort	?	+	+		

Please note: the outcomes in this figure are summarised and considered higher level generalisations. They should be recognised as determined using varying methods and methodologies. The rate of indeterminable outcomes can be considered an indication of an opportunity for more effective evaluations, and the variability in positive and negative outcomes indicative of how well understood associated outcomes are. Undetermined or variability in positive or negative outcomes is not, however, a sign of weakness in the chapter approach as all authors were asked to write their chapters according to their standard study approach rather than to address or consider all outcomes listed. The outcomes listed are a result of collating outcomes and key findings considered across chapters, and not the other way around.

Authors were asked to fill in this chart after writing their chapter.

+   Positive outcome found – see chapter for further details regarding associated certification and detail of outcome

+'   Possible indirect outcome

−   Negative outcome found – see chapter for further details regarding associated certification and detail of outcome. In some cases it is compared to offerings of other mechanisms

−'   Possible indirect outcome

?   Neutral, or indeterminable outcome. Where no entry is found the outcome was not considered

?'   Possible indirect indeterminable outcomes

*   Animal welfare standard responses are relevant to the Animal Welfare Quality Standard and not to animal welfare certifications and labels

**   Not all listed outcomes are intended by every certification, and not all listed outcomes were considered in each chapter. Where any outcomes were observed it is noted in this table.

***   Readers should go to the relevant chapter to determine how the outcome was associated to a certification

   At producer groups, or stakeholders' discretion and not formally by certifications. See Chapter 3 also for further consideration of how standards that encourage positive biodiversity outcomes differ between certifications

****   Merger between Rainforest Alliance and Utz Kapeh in 2018 is recognised here as a relevant development.

Figure 13.3 Accumulated positive, negative and neutral/indeterminable outcomes demonstrate an almost equal proportion of positive and neutral/indeterminable outcomes, and a smaller proportion of negative outcomes. The results support the idea of need for further research and for improvement in understanding the certification process and outcomes

OUTCOMES	Positive	Negative	Neutral/Indeterminable
FOR ENVIRONMENT★★			
Improved biodiversity	2	2	5
Water system protection	2	3	2
Limiting deforestation	1		3
Limiting land degradation	2	1	3
Limiting damaging chemical use	1	2	4
Limiting damage to neighbouring or other ecosystems/landscape patches	1	2	4
Improved recycling	2		2
Improved animal welfare	1		
Negative or neutral emissions	2		2
Farm and landscape heterogeneity – terrestrial or water based	2	2	2
Industry heterogeneity	1	3	2
TOTAL	17	15	29
FOR SOCIETY★★			
Increased or maintained income	3	2	3
Human health	4		3
Cultural appropriateness	3	3	3
Improved conditions for workers	4		3
Improved chemical handling and storage	4		1
Realistic expectations for producers	3	2	1
Realistic expectations for stakeholders	1	1	3
Complementary to legislated or policy-based requirements	5		1
Advancing legislated or policy-based requirements	5		1
Observed contributions to producer community	1		3
Producer satisfaction with standard requirement		3	1
Realistic expectations by investment required		1	1
Small producer inclusion	1	2	

AS RELATED TO CERTIFICATION PROCEDURES

Standard implementation verifiable	3	2	2
Required procedures affordable	2	3	1
Required procedures conducive to sustainable trade practices	3	1	3
Required procedures verifiable	3	2	1
Legitimate according to required procedures	2	1	2
Culturally appropriate	2	4	2
Balancing power dynamics	1	3	
Consistency in expectations, stringency, legitimacy and outcomes according to and across certifications	3	3	1
Allowance for merges between certifications to ease need to comply with multiple standard sets	2	1	3
Allowance for contextual adaptations in standard and procedural requirements without compromise to and/or with improvement for intended outcomes	1	1	4
Allowance for interoperability and merges across stakeholders who comply with different standard sets and different certifications	1		3
Satisfaction with certification process	2	2	3
Public effort superior to certifications	2	1	3
Public effort complementary to and demonstrated to support and improve certification	4		1
TOTAL	31	24	29
TOTAL: ENVIRONMENT AND SOCIETY OUTCOMES	82	53	82

Note

** Not all listed outcomes are intended by every certification, and not all listed outcomes were considered in each chapter. Where any outcomes were observed it is noted in this table. Readers should go to the relevant chapter to determine how the outcome was associated to a certification

Considering recommendations across all chapters

Recommendations for future research and use of certifications: operational

Recognising investment requirements to realistically ensure outcomes

Recognising, allocating and allowing for the necessary resource and financial investment to comply with standards and to adequately implement and fund verification and improvement processes is required and relevant for all stakeholders, and possibly of most concern to producing communities (Aizawa *et al.* 2018; Chapter 11; Chapter 12; Chapter 10). How it might influence preferences for certifications among larger corporate influencers and PPGA which seek to encourage, at minimum, use of a sustainability certification of sustainability standards through sourcing practices requires further consideration (Chapter 8). Imbalance in preferential influence toward sourcing business and corporate budgets results in lower quality standards and certification procedures being favoured, with unsubstantiated influence within producer countries.

Investment required to develop high-quality standards is an additional consideration with time requirements also extremely relevant (Chapter 5; Chapter 6). The contribution is, however, significant and benefit therefore must be considered alongside necessary investment.

Possible associated outcomes could range from less stringent requirements which may be favoured by producers; however, their understanding and opinion of sustainability standards and certifications might then lower according to observed differences in environmental and societal outcomes. Where required investment remains significant, this can result in slightly negative impressions where interest in responsibility to do 'the right thing' according to sustainable practices should be encouraged. Alternatively requiring more stringent standards will likely require increased investment, financial and non-financial, which may introduce different types of resentment, where support is not readily available. There is then the circumstance of requiring compliance to multiple certifications and standards to achieve sales through certified markets. While this might actually result in improved environmental and societal outcomes associated with more comprehensive standard criteria, the required investment for implementation and compliance must be considered. The funnelling of standard implementation within the same land areas can also limit geographic reach of this benefit. It is ultimately important to maintain detail in standard criteria and geographic reach of implemented standards for improved outcomes. The overlay to these considerations are the power dynamics of international trade and how the unique position of sustainability certifications is conducive rather than counterproductive to what can be understood as an imbalance toward the sourcing countries and companies.

Figure 13.4 Comparison of basic chapter recommendations and aggregated recommendations from 11 chapters

Recommendations

Chapter	Continue with use of certifications	Consider, possibly improve complementary public sector support for certifications	Decrease exclusion from certified markets	Consider alternatives	Improve standard quality	Improve verification procedure including audit	Improve approach to standard development, introduction and verification	Improve coordination and management of multiple certification requirements	Improve evaluations	Recognise and accommodate investment required
Cultural implications	×						×			
Biodiversity outcomes	×				×	×	×		×	
FSC evaluation	×								×	
Biochar	×	×			×	×	×	×	×	
Farm animal welfare	×		×	×	×	×				
Aquaculture	×			×	×		×	×	×	
Biofuels	×	×		×	×	×	×	×	×	
MSC FSC	×						×			
RJC and ARM	×				×	×	×	×		
Coffee		×		×	×	×	×	×	×	×
Flowers			×	×						×
AGGREGATED /11	9	3	2	5	7	6	8	5	6	2

Note
The authors were asked to fill in this chart post completion of their chapters. It is intended as a simple summary and details found in each chapter are necessary for comprehensive understanding.

Limiting rifts in positive cultural flows

Ensuring reduced incidence of marketing techniques which are contrary to outcomes in producing countries and misaligned with sustainability outcomes while allowing for nonlinear processes toward improvement is necessary. Where inaccuracies in marketing are proven, evidence of improvement should become an acceptable conditioning of how such inaccuracies are dealt with. Fair trade in the Costa Rican coffee industry and certifying flower production in Ecuador provide country-specific examples of a negative impression in-country. In some cases negative associations with ongoing trade and power imbalances between 'emerging and developed' economies (see Chapters 11 and 12), can lead to frustration expanding on existing negative associations with ongoing trade and power imbalances between 'developing and developed' economies and countries (see Chapters 11 and 12). Such situations also have negative cultural implications, and can be understood as culturally inappropriate within a context of international trade and historical legacy of power imbalances. Additional examples for other industries where sustainability certification certifies practices contrary to positive environmental or societal outcomes (Chapter 12; Chapter 6; Chapter 5; Chapter 7) leave significant potential for disillusion and frustration within producing countries, and in consumer countries also. Such situations contribute to rifts in positive sustainability cultural flows and also reinforce ideas of sustainability certifications as international mechanisms that serve international business, or perspective needs above producer country well-being.

Encouraging cultural appropriateness within several crosscultural contexts

Ensuring capacity and consciousness related to contextual rapport between stakeholders to ease standard introduction and compliance approach and reduce opportunity for cultural inappropriateness is more challenging within international trade contexts. Ensuring cultural appropriateness of standards and allowing adaptations which do not compromise stringency according to the sought and agreed upon necessary improvement in outcomes can assist.

Improved coordination between certifications

Improved coordination between different certifications to reduce required investment for implementation and improve outcomes becomes more necessary as the number of certifications and labels increases (Chapter 10; Chapter 11). Coordination is relevant to standard development, approach to introducing standards, approach to encouraging and actually implementing standards, approach to verification and to trade.

Considering opportunities to merge certifications and standards and/or to coordinate by industry, country, stakeholder or other measure, or simply across certifications is expected to become more necessary in the future.

Recognising the need for flexibility according to significant and more subtle contextual differences and therefore allowing adaptability while maintaining appropriateness and ambition for most positive outcomes is necessary.

Improving certification procedures across stakeholders to increase confidence

Limited or variable procedural consistency, according to transparency and verifiable implementation and outcomes, does limit confidence in the sustainability certification effort (Chapter 9). Where efforts are made for further improvement, by learning from other certification approaches, receiving varying types of support from public mechanisms, or relying on and integrating alternative approaches through the certification process, including interoperability (see Chapter 2; Chapter 10), or allowing and encouraging the certification process to complement, or be complemented by alternative mechanisms (Chapter 8; Chapter 11; Chapter 12), confidence can increase with several benefits.

Opportunities to adapt the certification process; separate standard development from introducing and verifying standards; and separate from involvement in and guidance provided for trade procedures

Strengthening stakeholder capacity to be sustainable and improving the culture of sustainability across stakeholders can allow a reduced range of roles certifications are expected to or seek to fulfil. Subsequently the opportunity to critique certifications across so many aspects can reduce as the more complicated and less beneficial elements of the certification process reduce, and the most influential and positive roles can receive more attention. For example, separating standard development from introducing and verifying standards is often an operational requirement for certification organisations. Evaluations can therefore follow this lead.

An additional consideration is whether sustainability certifications should mediate between corporate trade culture and producers to encourage a stable benefit to producers. Where no role is to be played yet the dynamic is unbalanced, determining which mechanisms might complement or assist to improve balance according to principles of sustainability and societal outcomes, including ideas of fair trade, is an important consideration.

Improving standard development and criteria

The importance and influence of standard criteria to adequately guide and encourage environmental and societal outcomes is significant (Chapter 3; Chapter 5; Chapter 6; Chapter 7). Larger organisations such as ISEAL have, over the years, taken organisational and technical measures that could be considered influential to improvements. Improvements are, however, limited to ISEAL members. Ensuring consistency in standard criteria quality and allowing for local adaptations to ensure quality remains contextually appropriate, is required. They will be influenced and supported by broader considerations of how positive outcomes are defined, and how they could continue to advance and improve according to scholarly and practical advances and findings.

Including and considering locally developed standards

Locally developed and verified standards (Chapter 2) may assist to ease imbalance in power dynamics and cultural flows, particularly where standards can come to a compromise between satisfying wide-reaching criteria requirements according to the multiple certifications and standards operating, and culturally appropriate practices. Consistent and culturally appropriate environmental and societal outcomes within producer countries could then become assured, reducing the opportunity to prefer less stringent or legitimate certifications (Chapter 8; Chapter 3).

Considering how effective locally developed and verified versus third-party verified standards are within an international trade context, and if they are preferred by individual producing communities and producers is necessary. Establishing more consistent and stringent sourcing procedures and practices through all certifications could then provide a complementary add-on, and reduce the opportunity to prefer not only certifications requiring less stringent standards, but ones that also represent lower overall levels of legitimacy. Within PPGAs, more selectively accepting certifications and perhaps working on developing capacity in those that demonstrate lower levels of legitimacy could be a positive way forward. A transfer between less to more legitimate certifications might also be possible and effective.

Improving how public–private guarantee arrangements (PPGA) select and verify endorsed sustainability certifications

PPGAs have substantial influence in certification preference, to the point of determining which are permitted. Ensuring PPGAs lend sufficient attention to the quality of the certification procedures and outcomes endorsed is therefore important. Distinguishing between PPGA endorsement for internationally versus locally sourced certified natural resources and products is also recommended for future studies, evaluations and practices. Using conceptual advances such as input, throughput and output legitimacy to better understand the varying verification stages can assist with improvement (Chapter 8).

Increasing equitable reach of sustainability standard criteria and implementation

Sustainability certification reach according to certified hectares has increased dependent on industry; however, limited access to officially certified markets

(Chapter 12) is observed. In addition, several evaluations indicate preference for certifying 'more biodiverse' or sustainable productive land patches above less sustainable productive land patches (Chapter 3; Chapter 7). It is therefore necessary to ensure extended and equitable standard reach, where standard criteria are proven as creating positive and improved outcomes, to address those land patches that are actually more in need of improvement and support to achieve such improvement. Reliance on sustainability certifications to achieve such extended, inclusive and equitable reach may not be realistic. Recognising and supporting alternative mechanisms that support inclusion and the necessary standard adjustments may become the most positive approach. It is expected that as inclusive and equitable sustainability standards are increasingly permitted and encouraged, continual adjustment in standard criteria will be required.

Increase amalgamation of standards and reduce funnelling of multiple standard criteria sets into the same landscape patches

While increasing the number of standard criteria set requirements could be positively associated with environmental and societal outcomes, increases often occur within the same land patches and within already certified farms and productive or extractive areas. At a procedural level this funnelling might be considered logical to reduce organisational adaptations, working with producer groups and businesses already familiar with the certification requirements. Working with the already 'converted' is commonly a preferred approach which can increase or reinforce existing positive influence for environmental and societal outcomes by standard criteria detail required. Introducing additional certifications to already certified producer groups and business can, however, limit certified hectare reach and associated standard implementation. The proportion of total farms and hectares of the certified producer groups and businesses that are already certified will also condition outcomes.

Maintaining perspective

Encouraging, learning from and not being threatened by alternative sustainable production, extraction and trade mechanisms for natural resources

To eventually come to recognise alternative mechanisms that are just as or perhaps more beneficial according to particular aspects of sustainable trade (Chapter 11; Chapter 12) provides significant opportunity for varying response. From a certification organisation perspective, it may bring about adaptations or perhaps ideas of competition. Maintaining a wide perspective of intentions for sustainable trade practices may better contextualise these developments, and recognise the contribution of sustainability certifications. Balancing between a need to sell certified produce and promoting the benefits of other mechanisms that may prove useful where producer groups are not allowed into certified markets is an example.

*Developing thresholds for performance between sustainability certifications and
other sustainability mechanisms*

Developing a threshold to determine where continued effort for improvement is worthy and where alternatives can be preferred, or where select elements of the certification process can proceed toward improvement is another
example. Investment versus benefit could inform such a threshold; and could
be better informed where options like interoperability, shared understandings
of effective processes between certification, effective approaches to managing
multiple standard requirements within producer groups and perhaps for other
stakeholders are understood, tried and tested, and outcomes associated with
sustainability certification versus alternatives are well understood.

Evaluating and understanding outcomes

Improving understanding of associated outcomes in producing countries and communities

Sustainability intentions within international trade are conditioned and influenced by several stakeholders, particularly for producing countries and communities. Imbalanced power dynamics, negative environmental outcomes and
societal inequalities resulting from previous approaches to local and international trade further condition and influence intended outcomes.

As consumer verification is influential, distanced verification for producer
country outcomes can dominate. As such, verification is ultimately influenced by
the reliable procedures of the sustainability certifications and independent evaluations and studies which may or may not easily or adequately demonstrate outcomes associated with any one product (see Chapters 3 and 4 for further detail).

Where public sector endorsement and verification can contribute to
improved understanding of associated outcomes in producing countries and
communities, verification can then rely on additional and possibly more independent sources.

Improving and increasing number of evaluations by detail, consistency and representation

Several evaluations of outcomes associated with standard criteria, and implementation of standards provide a preliminary understanding. There is, however,
need for improvement in evaluations, and an increased number of evaluations
by specificity, consistency and representation (see Chapters 3 and 4).

*Encouraging multidisciplinary, ranging methods, consistency in sustainability
definitions and specific sustainability pillar considerations that draw back to
inclusive, all-pillar evaluations, practice and research recommendations*

Multidisciplinary research is extremely necessary and an advantageous way
to truly encompass and encourage understanding of the relevance of sustainability certification efforts across industries, countries and landscapes.

Multidisciplinary considerations should not, however, compromise the rigour and detail required of one discipline and how specific disciplinary findings inform multidisciplinary considerations. The same consideration can be maintained for methods and methodologies used, and for the pillar of sustainability considered, and details within. There is a need to recognise and benefit from recognising how each discipline, method, methodology, pillar of sustainability and details within pillars interconnect as related to what sustainability certifications seek to and actually do achieve, to inform understanding and eventually facilitate improvement in sustainability certification research, evaluation and practice.

*Encouraging conceptual advances for understanding and assessing
sustainability certifications*

The conceptual advances and frames used to evaluate and assess how sustainability certifications influence societal and environmental outcomes for several of the chapters could serve useful for future practice, assessments, evaluations and considerations. They provide ideas for solutions and also for areas that require more detailed consideration, such as

- power dynamics across stakeholders and countries and within producing countries;
- expanded understanding of intentions such as legitimacy, transparency and credibility contributing to understanding of how to achieve intentions;
- interoperability to encourage coordination between different certifications within the same industry, particularly where certifications pay attention only to particular stakeholders within a sourcing chain;
- expanded understanding of evaluating biodiversity outcomes, and how definitions of biodiversity and interdependence with some societal outcomes can be considered;
- standard quality and approaches to standard development, implementation and verification;
- balancing cultural appropriateness across several crosscultural intricacies;
- managing balance between the societal, economic and environmental, such as cultural appropriateness with market demand, increasing opportunity for sustainability certifications to utilise diverse selling points or accommodate several verification requirements;
- actual outcomes for producing countries;
- considering how advanced or progressive standard criteria influences national law and policy advances.

Whether examples of countries moving past preference for using certifications should be thought of as a negative or positive outcome, given an understanding of original intentions within ideas of aid, and obligations of and to an aid, is an additional consideration. This additional consideration becomes particularly relevant where the offerings become contrary to intentions or irrelevant given other aligned and improved offerings available.

Recommendations for sustainability certification and standard development

Improving opportunity to recognise intact land patches, and landscapes within standard criteria

Where environmental and societal outcomes receive improved attention in terms of sustainability certification intentions, there is an opportunity to recognise and encourage the value of intact areas directly (Chapter 4). Currently conservation of these areas can have indirect results by ensuring reduced expansion of productive land use; occasionally specific efforts to ensure the conservation of such areas is maintained (Chapter 3; Chapter 4). Proactively certifying or developing criteria for intact landscapes expands the concept of the certification purpose; however, this would present an increased opportunity for assigning market value, and would complement in-country efforts to conserve these areas.

Facilitating farm, landscape and industry heterogeneity to better align with sustainability intentions

Reconsidering practices that sustainability certifications are willing to certify and becoming more selective according to actual sustainable practices in production and trade rather than certifying slight changes in conventional trade practices is possible.

How certifications encourage expansion of conventional industries versus how they might serve to encourage diversification of industries, with subsequent potential influence on farm and landscape heterogeneity; reduced need for supplying homogenous crop and natural resource offerings; and increased sourcing according to maintaining balanced ecosystems (see Chapter 3), is an example. The attention to shifting conventional trade practices will, however, remain necessary, and sustainability certification can serve an important role in this invention.

Clarify intentions, capabilities and role of sustainability certifications to address and better set expectations for how different aspects of sustainable trade are encouraged

As certifications occupy a unique position and opportunity for consistency in guidance for sustainable practice among several contrasting interests, and different stakeholders, expectations for outcomes can become extensive. It may be necessary and useful to more definitively communicate expectations, or understand and expect that some of the associated outcomes may be outside the reach of what sustainability certifications can achieve. Where this understanding is accepted, it could be that supporting or complementary mechanisms are identified and recognised as capable or in a better position to 'fill the gaps'. It should not necessarily therefore be considered a negative outcome where certifications are not preferred or used in producing countries, particularly where there is, and certainly where they are conditioned by, an availability of alternatives that prove more effective at generating positive environmental and societal outcomes.

Ideas, developments and possibilities for the future

Certification of operational procedures and standard criteria as 'product ranges'

As more certifications and labels, and continual improvements in original certification efforts across industries continue to emerge, understanding that a 'product range' of certification processes and standard criteria sets have emerged could facilitate how the sustainability certification 'movement' is understood, and subsequently how it is evaluated. Product ranges could be considered by certified crops, or by certification label and allowed market-based terminology and consideration. Within this idea, several 'micro-products' and procedural requirements with potential relevance to several certifications would be recognised. For example (1) micro-standard criteria sets relevant to several crops, industries and certifications; and (2) approach to standard development and verification procedures.

For the first example, more specific standard criteria sets are considered positive contributions for larger or macro-level standard criteria sets to improve consistency and performance against various benchmark measures. Biochar and farm animal welfare quality standard criteria may be used as part of a diversified agricultural or productive system. The corresponding chapters—Chapters 5 and 6—provide examples of how scientifically detailed, proven and tested standards can provide stable grounding for sustainability certification standards, which is far from simply introducing loose standard criteria to support a sustainability intention and premise with variable verification processes. The years of research, practice and expertise necessary to develop such standard criteria sets requires acknowledgement.

Specificity in standard criteria can assist to address and achieve sustainability intentions long-term. However, it must be combined with opportunity for contextual adaptations.

For the second example, emphasising standards and certification procedures across stakeholders, as well as the difference between standard criteria and procedural requirements according to industry and country is important. Some certifications and external supportive mechanisms have invested significant time and resources to provide detailed and sophisticated considerations within standard criteria and verification procedures. Third-party verification procedures, Participatory Guarantee Systems (PGS) and Public–Private Guarantee Arrangements (PPGA) are examples. Their performance against measures does, however, vary, and opportunity for improvement is identified (see

Chapter 3 for more detail). Allowing for contextual adaptation in standard criteria is already used by several certifications in practice, as is acceptance of various compliance levels. Consistency across certifications and across or within industries is not yet proven.

A PGS or other parallel in-community sustainability effort can further contribute to ensuring scientifically developed standards find some compromise and provide an opportunity to ensure local understanding, appropriateness and endorsement. Approach to evaluation will ultimately assist to determine where this might be necessary and an opportunity for improvement.

Detailed verification processes used to substantiate and/or endorse particular sustainability certifications and standard criteria sets are also required. Third-party verification or PGS-based verification offer distinct approaches. They can be preferred or appropriate as determined by community and individual producer preferences. PPGA or similar efforts then offer an additional layer of verification with significant endorsement and certification preference influence. For internationally sourced certified produce such verification is, however, distanced.

As such, leaving verification combinations open to contextual appropriateness rather than allowing the selected certification to determine approach is suggested as a future area for research and practice. It will, however, only be possible where capability for all verification approaches is established. Opportunity for further information exchange and reciprocal learning between industries and certifications; certifications; certifications and complementary efforts; scholarly, practitioner, evaluation expertise, and experience; and industry, certifications and complementary efforts, exists. Positive and effective elements of their efforts could proceed in a uniform way, such as guiding external standards and third-party verification. Other elements may be adapted or simply become irrelevant.

Developing past existing 'certification' formats

Within ten or so years, it may be that sustainability certifications as they have been used develop past the existing format, as is already occurring. Voluntary standards with compulsory verification are expected to be maintained, but whether they continue to be developed and introduced at an international level and via certifications could vary. A combination of internationally and locally developed, or only locally developed standards might be used, with an increased and balanced use of scientific input for standard criteria and assessment. Verification approaches might also adjust to accommodate coming change in existing sustainability certification formats. Learning from existing and parallel community-embedded sustainability efforts may also increase and will have most benefit where effective community-embedded efforts are not inappropriately shifted. An opportunity for individual producer autonomy within the community provided by international efforts could, however, result in the continued value and benefit of an internationally based certification format.

Sustainability certifications, complementary mechanisms and alternatives

Sustainability certifications are one of several mechanisms used to encourage improved sustainable trade and sourcing practices. Concern for sustainability, and environmental and societal outcomes and efficacy, and appropriateness of mechanisms for any given context should ultimately influence the preferred sustainability mechanisms.

Developing a threshold to determine whether to continue with sustainability certification versus alternative mechanisms could more easily resolve how sustainability certifications are an appropriate solution or complement within given contexts. Recognising that other mechanisms could very well be more effective in different contexts, reduced use of certifications could result, or less structured, and more encompassing and/or contextually appropriate certification 'products' could be preferred. Where the format of certifications is maintained they might, in some contexts, prove effective compared to and alongside emerging mechanisms and approaches. Approach to evaluation will determine how effectiveness is measured and understood. Evaluating how more detailed certification standards contribute to or influence national legal or policy advances and progress is one area that might justify continuing use of certifications. In other situations, opportunities for shifted certification format might improve their relevance and effectiveness as complementary to other mechanisms.

Summary

Intentions for, and actual improvements in sustainable extracting, producing, sourcing and trading practices has been inconsistent with several different angles or approaches used to understand the varying aspects.

The legacy of trade practice and subsequent influence on society and the environment allows promotion of even incrementally successful efforts that improve the situation. Sustainability certifications are a form of consistent mechanisms and approaches used for three or more decades.

As a complementary transnational and voluntary effort (Gulbrandsen 2010) for Corporate Social Accountability (CSA), sustainability certifications are an important precedent for the era of protecting the environment and society from conventional commercial interest and dominance through agricultural and natural resource industries and international trade. They have in some cases proven controversial and certainly unique according to the support they provide toward embedding sustainability culture. They improve understanding of what sustainable production, extraction and trade is, and influence activities and mentalities across stakeholders, from producing and extracting to consuming.

Market demand is a significantly influential premise for sustainability certifications, opening opportunity for understanding benefit within market terms. The premise does, however, also provide significant opportunity for misunderstanding, misrepresenting or over exaggerating in-producer country benefit. So while serving, and certainly continuing to serve as a pedagogical tool for industry and consumers, assisting to transform and better inform conventional commercial practice, improvement is necessary for truly positive contributions.

While positive outcomes are significantly influenced by the involved stakeholders and how they willingly comply and complement sustainability certifications in all practices and approaches to trade, there are currently several intricate disadvantages to the sustainability certification effort with oversights such as producer inclusion affecting equitable reach of standards, and several ineffective and misaligned outcomes compared to intentions. While advances are possible and in some cases underway, such oversight does leave opportunity for rifts in positive influence, and rationale for preferring alternative mechanisms. Positive outcomes are also significantly influenced by the involved stakeholders and how they willingly comply and complement sustainability certifications in all practices and approaches to trade.

As the years dedicated to sustainability in production, extraction and trade of natural resources continue to increase, expecting further and advancing ambition from all stakeholders is reasonable. Certifying stakeholders across a source chain may continue to develop and evolve by format and how they seek to complement versus compete with complementary mechanisms. Consideration of required investment and cultural shift might better inform such developments. Reducing availability of unethical products and increasing availability of and access to ethical produce and products as an overarching positive intention and outcome, and accepting nonlinear temporal and cross-sustainability pillars and cross-stakeholder advances is relevant. It is also valuable to understand how subjective preferences of consumers and business, and how supportive contributions of policy and legal mechanisms and structures that rely on stilted change allow progress.

For example, market based efforts can allow a fast-tracking of sustainability practices and change within conventional markets. Market mechanisms might more easily promote openness to industry and market diversification and transformation. Efforts in producing countries in terms of certifying hectares prior to market demand, or working with in-country processes to improve sustainability practices without the need for alternative market demand or incentive are, however, also important. Guidance and regulatory mechanisms which further facilitate transnational and cross-sector reach are vital. These may be subsequently supported by consumer, country, policy or legal mechanisms, then complemented by market-based incentive. The market-based effort does allow a fast-tracking of sustainability practices and change within conventional markets.

Opportunity for newly developed markets which can be extremely valuable for improved sustainability can also be provided. Outcomes must, however, be substantiated and an increase in number of evaluations, and improved and consistent approaches to evaluation of outcomes are required.

The considerations of evaluations and outcomes as associated to sustainability certifications provided in this book—see Chapters 3 and 4—are therefore useful. They can contribute to how we understand those outcomes, and assist in recognising where understandings are quite consistent and evident, and where limited existing understandings might be. They can also and subsequently assist to inform how efforts to consistently use, source and trade natural resources in a way that is positive for environmental and societal outcomes can continue to improve and move forward.

Beginning perfectly and accomplishing comprehensive positive outcomes along the significant learning curve that the novel contribution that sustainability certifications move is difficult. Fast-tracking misleading or misaligned practices, and subsequent negative cultural flows, impressions and outcomes with potentially long-term negative implications, however, must be kept to a minimum. Considering required and realistic investment, the ability to verify practices and outcomes, standard criteria quality and contextual appropriateness remain essential to minimise and resolve such effects and to improve outcomes. A combination of procedural mechanisms as complementary will also likely maintain relevance and optimise outcomes. While the contribution of certifications is recognised, verified alternatives and complementary mechanisms within particular contexts should be encouraged to ensure intentions similar to sustainability certifications are not limited to officially certified markets, and that response to negative outcomes is not limited to waiting for an improvement through the certified market channel. Continued improvement in certifications would eventually either remove a need for alternatives or maintain their role alongside, as complementary mechanisms. Alternatives and complementary mechanisms can also become the beginning of improvement for any or all aspects of the certification process.

Acknowledgements

Melissa Vogt wrote this chapter, developing all figures including the comparison of outcomes between all chapters, and identifying and explaining key findings and recommendations. The ideas, discussion, outcomes and findings from all chapters has eventually influenced material in this chapter and so thanks is also extended to all authors for contributing chapters which allowed development of such a conclusion and ideas for future consideration related to sustainability certifications.

An author from each chapter has had an opportunity to confirm how outcomes, key findings and recommendations from their chapter are summarised within Figures 13.2 and 13.4. Thanks is extended to them for taking the time to confirm or complete each figure, ensuring understandings from their chapters are accurately represented.

References

Aizawa M., dos Santos D.C., Seck S.L. (2018). Financing human rights due diligence in mining projects. In S.K. Lodhia (ed.). *Mining and Sustainable Development: Current Issues.* Routledge.

Cuéllar M.C., Ganuza-Fernandez E. (2018). We don't want to be officially certified! Reasons and implications of the participatory guarantee systems. Sustainability, MDPI, Open Access Journal 10(4): 1–15.

Gulbrandsen L. (2010). Transnational Environmental Governance: The Emergence and Effects of the Certification of Forests and Fisheries. Edward Elgar.

Home R., Nelson E. (2015). Feeding the People: Agroecology for Nourishing the World and Transforming the Agri-Food System. IFOAM. www.ifoam-eu.org/sites/default/files/ifoameu_policy_ffe_feedingthepeople.pdf.

Index

accountability 3, 8, 9, 13, 31, 185–7, 193, 204, 209, 315
additionality 116, 172, 178
agriculture 10, 13, 29, 39, 66, 73–5, 77–8, 104, 125, 234–5, 249, 268, 277, 287
Alliance for Responsible Mining 18, 218, 297; *see also* ARM
animal welfare 11, 17, 137–41, 143–50; science 142; assessment 137, 141–4, 148–9
aquaculture 12, 17, 159–61, 165–6, 168–75, 177–80, 294; Aquaculture Certification 178
Aquaculture Stewardship Council 13, 160, 202; *see also* ASC
ARM 18, 87, 218, 220–6, 229–31, 297, 303, 308
artisanal 12, 77, 215, 225–7
ASC 12, 160–3, 171–2, 174, 176, 179, 202
assessing and evaluating standard criteria: assessment 75–6, 314; definitions 76; evaluation 79, 310; influence on and study counfounders 78–9; measuring performance 76; study methods 73, 94
association: associations 11, 20, 33; brand 11, 47, 50–1; organisation 52, 143, 147, 195, 235, 246, 249, 261–2, 264, 267, 269–71, 275–9, 298, 306; research and evaluation 15, 47, 78

biochar 12, 16–17, 50, 76, 113–29; certification 114, 118, 130
biodiversity 17, 49; benchmark 66, 73–6, 291; biochar 116, 127–9; biofuels 181, 188; collating correlations, recommendations and conclusions 287–9, 299–300, 302, 305, 311;

evaluation 65–7, 69, 71, 78, 84; FSC and evaluation 93, 95–8, 101–5
bioenergy 66, 115–16, 126, 182, 189–91; feedstock 75
biofuel (s) 12, 18; biochar 114; biodiversity 68, 70, 81, 83; EU and VCS 179–96, 287, 292, 300, 305

certification schemes 12, 17–18, 41, 71–3, 293; FSC 102; aquaculture 158–60, 166, 171; biochar 119–21, 128–30; Biofuels 183, 190–1, 194; certified mining 215, 220, 225–6; flower production practices 259, 272; MSC 209
certification standard criteria; biochar 113, 115–16, 313; Fairmined standard 77; FlorEcuador 267; FSC 94, 97; RA 243, 269; VeriFlor 267; *see also* Biodiversity Benchmark
certified: certified markets 32, 36, 51, 235, 239, 244–5, 247, 249, 299–300, 308, 311, 313; certified products 11, 34, 36, 38, 100, 206–7, 210
Chain of Custody 186, 192, 200–1, 206, 221, 294; *see also* CoC
CoC 159, 206–10, 221, 226
codes of conduct 4, 9, 32
coffee 10, 18, 68–9, 72, 78–80, 230–7, 239–49, 251, 253–5, 295, 300, 305–6
collaboration 220
consumers 2, 17, 32, 34–5, 42–5, 47–53, 100, 125, 137–9, 142, 147, 150, 165, 170, 172, 199, 201, 207–9, 215, 224–6, 249, 251, 270–1, 286, 315–16; consumer influence 48, 249, 286
contextual rapport 38, 53, 289–90, 309
continuous improvement 169, 177, 294

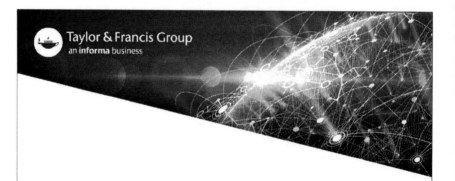